Wirtschaft und Politik

Reihe herausgegeben von
Gerhard Wegner, Erfurt, Deutschland
Guido Mehlkop, Erfurt, Deutschland
André Brodocz, Erfurt, Deutschland

Die Schriftenreihe „Wirtschaft und Politik" vereint empirisch wie theoretisch orientierte Forschungsarbeiten aus der Volkswirtschaftslehre, Politikwissenschaft und politischen Soziologie, die Fragen der Wirtschaftspolitik und Institutionenökonomie sowie der Konstitution und dem Wandel ökonomischer und politischer Ordnungen thematisieren. Darunter fällt insbesondere die Behandlung politischer Themen mittels ökonomischer Erklärungsansätze und umgekehrt die Auseinandersetzung mit ökonomischen Phänomenen aus Sicht der Politikwissenschaft oder der Soziologie.

The series "Economy and Politics" combines empirically and theoretically oriented research from the fields of economics, political science and political sociology, which analyzes issues of economic policy and institutional economics as well as the constitution and the change of economic and political orders. This includes, in particular, the treatment of political issues by means of economic approaches and, conversely, the examination of economic phenomena from the perspective of political science or sociology.

Weitere Bände in der Reihe http://www.springer.com/series/16152

Robert Fritzsch

Adaptive Efficiency During the Great Recession

An Analysis of the Institutional and Organizational Determinants of Crisis Resilience

Springer Gabler

Robert Fritzsch
Erfurt, Germany

Dissertation der Universität Erfurt, 2018

ISSN 2524-5945 ISSN 2524-5953 (electronic)
Wirtschaft und Politik
ISBN 978-3-658-27408-5 ISBN 978-3-658-27409-2 (eBook)
https://doi.org/10.1007/978-3-658-27409-2

Springer Gabler

This Springer Gabler imprint is published by the registered company Springer Fachmedien Wiesbaden GmbH part of Springer Nature.
The registered company address is: Abraham-Lincoln-Str. 46, 65189 Wiesbaden, Germany

Acknowledgements

This thesis was written as a dissertation project at the University of Erfurt during the years 2014 to 2018. Apart from the scientific references, which are cited in the main text, it builds on the influence of people who do not appear in the reference list.

Above all, I would like to thank my parents and grandparents for raising my awareness for political and societal problems while I was growing up. Without their influence, I would not have pursued the path that led to this thesis. Special thanks also goes to my main supervisor Professor Gerhard Wegner, from whose seminars I profited during my time as a student, who gave me the opportunity to write this thesis at his chair and who supported me on the way with valuable comments and advice. I also thank Hannah Vermaßen, not only for her helpful suggestions and comments during countless discussions about the thesis but also for moral support. I owe further gratitude to colleagues and faculty members at the University of Erfurt and to the participants of the annual doctoral colloquium of the Röpke Institute – in particular to my colleague Christoph Hindermann and to my second supervisor Professor Guido Mehlkop. Finally, I would like to thank all friends whose company cheered me up whenever writing on the thesis had given me a hard time.

Content

Abbreviations

Acc.	Account
Account.	Accountability
BRS	Bank Regulation and Supervision Database
Civ. Libert.	Civil Liberties
Com.	Commodity
Cor.	Corruption
Dep. Var.	Dependent Variable
Dev.	Developing
Dev. Econ.	Developed Economic
Econ-	Economic
EMU	European Monetary Union
EU	European Union
Exp.	Exports
FA + FL	Foreign Assets and Foreign Liabilities
FH	Freedom House
Fras.	Fraser Institute
FRDB	Fondazione Rololfo De Benedetti
Gov.	Government
Her.	Heritage Foundation
H-NWW	Hypothesis based on North, Wallis and Weingast's Account
H-O	Hypothesis based on Mancur Olson's account
H-S	Hypothesis based on structural stability arguments
GCI	Global Competitiveness Index
GDP	Gross Domestic Product
IMF	International Monetary Fund
Leg. Syst.	Legal System
Manuf.	Manufactured
Mio.	Million
NWW	Douglass North, John Wallis and Barry Weingast
OECD	Organisation for Economic Cooperation and Development
OLS	Ordinary Least Squares

Org.	Organizations
Pol.	Political
Priv. Cred.	Private Credit
Prop.	Property
RESET	Regression Equation Specification Error Test
SPSS	Statistic Program *IBM SPSS Statistics*
S.T. Ext.	Short Term External
UK	United Kingdom
US	United States
USD	US Dollar
WB	World Bank
WGI	Worldwide Governance Indicators

Figures

Tables

1. Introduction

This thesis investigates the question whether the properties of economic and political orders in different countries had an impact on these countries' crisis resilience during the years 2008 to 2012. As the so-called Great Recession is widely considered to be the most severe economic crisis since the Great Depression of the 1930s,[1] answers to this research question have strong implications for much wider issues, such as questions concerning the general merits and deficits of democracy or of the market economy.[2] Unfortunately, although there has been intense general debate about the impact of institutions on the severity of the recession, empirical research on a cross-country basis still remains rather scarce.[3] With this thesis I try to fill that gap by studying the effects of economic institutions, political institutions and interest group activity on crisis resilience during the years 2008 to 2012 in a systematic way.[4]

Already at first sight, the above-stated task is a complex one as it touches quite disparate scientific fields, such as business cycle theory, institutional theory or comparative politics. Furthermore, there exists a wide variety of potential methodological approaches to study the relationships of interest empirically. To keep the task still manageable and to remain on firm theoretical and methodological ground, I relate the theoretical and empirical analyses below to two established strands of literature.

First, the main reference points for the theoretical framework of this thesis are Mancur Olson's book *The Rise and Decline of Nations* (Olson, 1982) and the book *Violence and Social Orders* by Douglass North, John Wallis and Barry Weingast (subsequently NWW, 2009). Both books and the related literature, which is commonly summarized under the label *New Institutional Economics*, analyze the effects of institutions and interest group activity on economic performance. The main theoretical concept linking the explanatory variables of interest (economic institutions, political institutions and interest group activity) to the dependent variable (crisis resilience) in both accounts is *adaptive efficiency*. This concept of efficiency differs from the concept *allocative*

---

1 Authors who, amongst many others, share this evaluation regarding the severity of the crisis include Grusky et al. (2011, p. 3), Imbs (2010), IMF (2009, p. 14), Jenkins et al. (2013, p. 1) or Reinhart & Rogoff (2009, p. 20).

2 See, for example, Streeck (2011, p. 5), who argues that the financial crisis is an expression of "the normal condition of democratic capitalism".

3 Two exceptions are Giannone et al. (2011), who assess the potential effects of economic institutions (especially financial freedom) on the depth of the downturn during the years 2008 and 2009, and Essers (2012), who studies the relationship between democracy and crisis resilience.

4 The timing of the considered period needs a short explanations. Although first signs of a financial crisis became apparent already in 2007, the event that triggered recessions in different countries throughout the world was the bankruptcy of the investment bank Lehman Brothers on September 15th 2008. I, therefore, start the empirical assessment in that year. The final year of the considered time period 2012 is an arbitrary choice that completes a five year period. I discuss this issue in detail in section 4.1.

R. Fritzsch, *Adaptive Efficiency During the Great Recession*,
Wirtschaft und Politik, https://doi.org/10.1007/978-3-658-27409-2_1

efficiency, which is normally applied in neoclassical analysis. As I will illustrate in the theoretical discussion below, expanding on that particular perspective offers a variety of interesting insights and hypotheses regarding the properties of economic and political orders that are relevant for promoting crisis resilience. In a nutshell, both Olson (1982) and NWW (2009) agree for the most part on the necessary economic institutions, as they point out the positive effects of limited regulations and of impartially-enforced property rights and contract laws.[5] The authors, however, put forward different views on whether interest group activity promotes these economic institutions or whether it is harmful to them. While Olson (1982) emphasizes the detrimental effects of interest group activity on economic institutions and crisis resilience, NWW (2009) argue that competition amongst special interest groups, which typically operate within open political institutions, supports open economic institutions.

Second, the main reference point for the empirical part of this thesis builds on a recent strand of literature that analyzes the determinants of crisis incidence in terms of GDP decline during the Great Recession on a cross-country basis.[6] That literature focuses mainly on relating the depth of the crisis to macroeconomic vulnerabilities stemming from trade linkages or pre-crisis financial deepening. It, however, pays little regard to explanatory variables representing economic institutions, political institutions or interest group activity. I adopt the approach of that literature by running cross-country regressions which use similar dependent and control variables, but I adjust it to the purpose of this thesis by additionally including the explanatory variables of interest representing institutions and interest group activity. Furthermore, I extend the scope of the analysis by not only explaining crisis incidence during the downturn period 2008 to 2009 but also during the period of potential recovery 2010 to 2012.

By studying the relationships between economic and political institutions, interest group activity and crisis resilience, this thesis extends the existing scientific literature in a variety of ways. First, it augments the abovementioned empirical literature which investigates the determinants of crisis incidence during the Great Recession, as it includes additional explanatory variables. So far, only very few papers have explicitly investigated the effects of institutions on crisis resilience during the Great Recession on a cross-country basis (Giannone et al., 2011; Essers, 2012). These notable exceptions, however, have a much narrower scope than this thesis, as they focus on a

[5] As I will point out below, Olson (1982) focuses mainly on limited economic regulations, whereas NWW (2009) point out the importance of impartially-enforced property rights and contract laws. Both authors, furthermore, disagree regarding effects of large government sectors. While Olson puts forward a pessimistic account that emphasizes the detrimental effects of government activity, NWW take up a more optimistic stance.

[6] These papers include Berglöf et al. (2010), Berkman et al. (2012), Blanchard et al. (2010), Claessens et al. (2010), Frankel & Saravelos (2012), Giannone et al. (2010), Groot et al. (2011), Lane & Milesi-Ferretti (2010) as well as Rose & Spiegel (2010, 2011, 2012). I review them in more detail in sections 4.1 and 4.2.

few specific institutions and as they analyze only the downturn period 2008 to 2009. Second, this thesis applies institutional analysis to the problem of *crisis resilience*. So far, the majority of theoretical and empirical papers has focused on investigating the institutional prerequisites of *economic growth*.[7] Only a few notable exceptions have studied the determinants of crisis resilience and output volatility, typically by analyzing different crisis episodes at once across a larger time interval.[8] This thesis complements that literature by assessing the determinants of crisis resilience during the particularly severe Great Recession. Third, the empirical analysis provides an additional test of Olson's theory regarding the harmful effects of interest group activity on economic institutions and economic performance. So far, the empirical literature on Olson's arguments has focused almost entirely on economic growth as the main performance expression of the effects of interest group activity.[9] This is somewhat surprising as Olson (1982) dedicated an entire chapter to applying his theory to the analysis of crisis resilience. This thesis provides an unprecedented empirical test of that application. Finally, it tests empirically a central argument of NWW (2009) by assessing whether open access to economic and political competition indeed has a positive effect on crisis resilience.

The empirical results of this thesis suggest that institutions (and to some degree interest group activity) matter for explaining crisis resilience during the Great Recession. When considering the entire sample of countries, developed countries with secure rule of law, open goods markets, open financial markets, larger public sectors, high degrees of democracy and more interest group activity performed significantly worse than less developed countries with the opposite institutional features. However, when dividing the sample into developed and less developed countries, results differ considerably between the two sub-groups.[10] Amongst less developed countries, those countries showed better crisis resilience which were least developed, featuring small public sectors, strict financial regulations and absence of democracy. Within the sub-group of developed countries, on the other hand, those countries fared better which had more open economic institutions including impartially-enforced property rights and contract laws, open goods and labor markets and flexible exchange rates. Furthermore, within that sub-group, there exists some evidence that the

[7] For reviews of the vast literature regarding the institutional determinants of growth see, for example, Aron (2000), de Haan et al. (2006) and Ugur (2010). I review that literature in section 3.1.

[8] Important contributions are Rodrik (1999) and Acemoglu et al. (2003), who consider political and economic institutions. More recently, Bjornskov (2016) assesses the potential effects of different aspects of 'economic freedom'. I review their arguments and empirical findings in sections 4.3 and 4.4.1.

[9] For reviews of that literature see especially Bischoff (2007) and Heckelman (2007). The latter author mentions a few papers that assess sclerotic effects other than low growth rates. None of these papers, however, investigates the effects of interest group activity on crisis resilience.

[10] For details on the distinction between developed and less developed countries see section 3.2.

abovementioned resilience-enhancing economic institutions are associated with a high degree of democracy and with larger numbers of interest groups.

These empirical results are partly at odds with the predictions derived from Olson's and NWW's accounts, especially within the entire sample and the sub-sample of less developed countries. Therefore, they call for theoretical re-considerations. Within the sub-sample of developed countries, however, the empirical results correspond fairly well to the predictions derived from NWW's theoretical framework, therefore suggesting a qualification of their account to be applicable predominantly to developed countries. Concurrently, the same empirical regularities in developed countries contradict parts of Olson's theoretical predictions – especially regarding the detrimental effects of interest group activity.[11]

Given these findings, the main contribution of this thesis lies in providing a first systematic and comprehensive analysis of the relationship between economic institutions, political institutions, interest group activity and crisis resilience during the Great Recession according to an encompassing theoretical framework based on Olson's (1982) and NWW's (2009) accounts. Thereby, the analysis opens up a wide spectrum of future research paths regarding the institutional determinants of crisis resilience. These potential paths range from theoretical work (for example regarding the institutional determinants of crisis resilience in less developed countries) or the application of more advanced empirical methods (such as micro-level analyses of actual adaption processes or macro-level analyses with panel design looking at adaption over time) to the consideration of different dependent variables representing other aspects of crisis resilience besides output stabilization (such as avoidance of additional unemployment or avoidance of social hardship to the poorest people in a society).

Following this introductory chapter 1, chapter 2 discusses the main arguments of Olson (1982) and NWW (2009), incorporates them into a common analytical framework and derives hypotheses regarding the institutional determinants of crisis resilience. Then, chapter 3 discusses the methodological approach to testing these hypotheses, which is next set into practice in chapter 4. Chapter 5 concludes with a summary of the results and an outlook to potential future research paths.

[11] When it comes to testing Olson's theory, however, empirical results have to be treated with caution as the most widely-used measures for interest group activity are not very precise. For a discussion see section 4.4.2.

2. Theories of Adaptive Efficiency and the Determinants of Crisis Resilience

In this theoretical chapter, I reconstruct the theories of Olson and NWW and formulate hypotheses regarding the institutional and organizational determinants of crisis resilience. First, in section 2.1, I define the main concepts - *institutions, organizations, adaptive efficiency and crisis resilience* - and build a simple analytical framework for the analysis of adaptive efficiency. Next, in sections 2.2 and 2.3, I reconstruct Olson's and NWW's theories with reference to that analytical framework. In section 2.4, I highlight an aspect of adaptive efficiency that both Olson and NWW do not discuss in their accounts. Section 2.5 concludes the theoretical discussion by summarizing the aspects of adaptive efficiency that are relevant for the promotion of crisis resilience and by formulating hypotheses.

2.1 Definitions of the Main Concepts and Outline of the Analytical Framework

As this thesis builds on the theories of Olson, NWW and the related literature associated with New Institutional Economics, I adopt the definitions and concepts established within that literature. In this section, after (1) briefly defining the two main concepts *institutions* and *organizations*, I (2) turn to the concept of *adaptive efficiency* which is central for evaluating the way institutions and special interest groups affect economic performance in general and crisis resilience in particular. Next, in order to facilitate the reconstruction of Olson's and NWW's theories with regard to the determinants of adaptive efficiency and crisis resilience, I (3) outline a preliminary analytical framework of adaptive efficiency that differentiates between two levels of analysis. Finally, I (4) point out the limits of this framework and discuss the way it narrows down the scope of analysis in this thesis.

(1) According to North (1990, p. 3), "institutions are the rules of the game in a society or, more formally, are the humanly devised constraints that shape human interaction. In consequence they structure incentives in human exchange, whether political, social, or economic".[12] North (1990, p. 4) further distinguishes formal institutions, including all kinds of written-down rules and laws, from informal institutions, including conventions and codes of behavior. According to him, both types of rules constrain human interaction by defining what individuals or groups of individuals are forbidden and permitted to do under different kinds of circumstances. Usually, institutions are enforced by some type of formal (legal prosecution) or informal (ostracism) sanction mechanism.[13] Hence, by reducing the amount of feasible choices in different situations,

[12] This enumeration of political, social and economic exchange is somehow misleading, as it suggests a distinction amongst the three categories. More adequate appears to be the notion that economic and political exchange are both sub-categories of social exchange.

[13] This enforcement of rules through formal and informal sanction mechanisms and their obligatory character distinguishes institutions from mere social regularities such as weekly gatherings of merchants in market places or of students in the park near the university (Esser, 1993, pp. 5-6).

R. Fritzsch, *Adaptive Efficiency During the Great Recession*,
Wirtschaft und Politik, https://doi.org/10.1007/978-3-658-27409-2_2

they enable actors to build stable expectations about the activity of other actors, reduce uncertainty and provide order to human interaction (North, 1990, pp. 3-6).

This thesis considers formal *economic* and *political* institutions. First, *economic* institutions are the rules which structure economic activity, involving the production of goods and services or the transactions between economic actors.[14] Throughout this thesis, I consider three basic aspects of economic institutions: first, *property rights and contract laws*, second, *regulations of economic activity* and, third, the *size of the public sector*. This distinction is a pragmatic one and corresponds to the institutional features discussed by Olson and NWW.[15] The first aspect – *property rights and contract laws* - is a necessary prerequisite for the creation of private markets in the first place. The second aspect - *the extent of regulations of goods, labor and capital markets* - constrains the scope of permitted activities in these markets. Finally, the third aspect - *the size of the public sector* - indicates the portion of economic activity that actually takes place within private markets.

Next, *political* institutions are the rules of the political game that structure political activity. Political activity, in turn, is directed towards the creation and enforcement of general and collectively-binding decisions affecting groups and individuals within the relevant political entity (most importantly for this thesis - the state).[16] Examples of political institutions are constitutional rules defining the election processes of office holders (democratic elections; appointment by the king or a committee of the ruling party), rules defining the distribution of powers amongst different political bodies (relationship between president, government and parliament; specification of competences and veto rights etc.) or politically-relevant individual rights that regulate political competition and public debates (freedom of the press, freedom of assembly, free speech etc.). This distinction between rules structuring the economic realm and rules structuring the political realm is not exclusive as the same institutions, such as the right to form organizations, may affect economic and political competition at the same time. In fact, a proper distinction between the two types of institutions would require a detailed discussion of what constitutes the economic realm and what constitutes the political realm.[17] As this, however, would be a task going beyond the

---

[14] North (1990, p. 61), too, identifies transformation and transaction as the two main economic activities. According to him, "[i]nstitutions affect the performance of the economy by their effect on the costs of exchange and production" (North, 1990, p. 5).

[15] Other authors such as Rodrik & Subramanian (2003) distinguish according to *function* between market-creating, market-regulating, market-stabilizing and market-legitimizing institutions.

[16] This account of political activity mainly follows Patzelt (2003, p. 22), who defines politics to be "jenes menschliche Handeln, das auf die Herstellung und Durchsetzung allgemein verbindlicher Regelungen und Entscheidungen (d.h. von ‚allgemeiner Verbindlichkeit') in und zwischen Gruppen von Menschen abzielt".

[17] Luhmann for example identifies the economic system based on the distinction *payment – no payment* and the political system based on the distinction *power – no power*. Following his account, even the smallest objects of social analysis *communications* cannot be attributed exclusively to one societal system, as they can be observed according to different systemic distinctions or logics

capacity of this thesis, I distinguish both realms in a pragmatic way and attribute certain institutions predominantly to one of the two societal realms.

While institutions are the metaphorical rules of the game, organizations are the metaphorical teams of players.[18] According to NWW (2009, p. 15), "organizations consist of specific groups of individuals pursuing a mix of common and individual goals through partially coordinated behavior. Organizations coordinate their members' actions, so an organization's actions are more than the sum of the actions of the individuals". Although organizations - as institutions - rely on internal rules comprising their internal structure (including the definition of positions and processes), they feature additional characteristics which distinguish them from mere institutions. Most importantly, organizations pursue common organizational objectives and rely on formal membership (Esser, 1993, pp. 5-6). Examples of economic organizations are companies, trade unions or business associations; and examples of political organizations are parties, governments, bureaucratic agencies or different kinds of political interest groups (North, 1990, p. 5).[19] The type of organizations most relevant for this thesis are special interest groups.[20]

Together, institutions and organizations comprise two mutually interdependent aspects of a society's structure. In the one direction of influence, institutions affect the way organizations evolve by constraining their activity and the way they can be organized. In the other direction of influence, organizations can induce changes in the shape of institutions whenever existing institutions do not meet their demands (North, 1990, pp. 74-78, 80-82). This thesis builds on the premise that institutions and organizations affect the long-run performance of a society including various performance dimensions such as growth rates, the volatility of growth rates, the life expectancy or happiness of inhabitants, the literacy rate, the unemployment rate or the degree of equality. Specifically, I focus on the question how *economic institutions*, *political institutions* and *interest group activity* affect *crisis resilience in terms of output stabilization*. I thereby define crisis resilience as a country's ability to overcome an economic shock without severe losses in output. This includes, first, avoiding a sharp

(*payment – no payment*; *power – no power*) at the same time. In a similar way, certain institutions may be part of the program structures of different societal systems at the same time, thereby deciding which communications are conducive for generating payments *and* for obtaining political power. For an accessible exposition of that account see Luhmann (1990 [1986]).

18 See North (1990, pp. 4-5) and Pelikan (1986), who use the same metaphor.

19 Strictly speaking, however, there cannot be a sharp distinction between economic and political organizations because most organizations are engaged in both societal realms. A predominantly economic organization such as a joint-stock company, for example, may have a public relations or lobby department; and a political party may sell merchandise articles to generate funds for the next election.

20 See sections 2.2.2 and 2.3.2 for more details on what constitutes a special interest group according to Olson and NWW.

downturn in reaction to the shock and, second, recovering quickly and strongly following the initial downturn.[21]

(2) Discussing the question how institutions and special interest organizations affect crisis resilience based on the theories of Olson and NWW already directs the analysis towards a specific theoretical approach centering on the concept of *adaptive efficiency*. According to North (1990, p. 80), "[a]daptive efficiency is concerned with the kinds of rules that shape the way an economy evolves through time. It is also concerned with the willingness of a society to acquire knowledge and learning, to induce innovation, to undertake risk and creative activity of all sorts, as well as to resolve problems and bottlenecks of the society through time". Following this definition, the ability to overcome an economic shock ("to resolve problems and bottlenecks of society through time") as well as the ability to expand the factors of production which generate economic growth ("to acquire knowledge and learning, to induce innovation, to undertake risk and creative activity of all sorts") are the two performance dimensions of adaptive efficiency; and both dimensions, in turn, depend on economic institutions ("the rules that shape the way an economy evolves").[22] Adaption in this context refers to the adjustment of productive structures, including the internal structure of economic organizations as well as the channels of cooperation amongst different actors (individuals and/or organizations). Departing from neoclassical theories which analyze the allocative efficiency of prices and quantities within *given* organizational structures and *given* channels of cooperation, this approach analyses the *modification* of organizational structures and channels of cooperation in reaction to changing circumstances.[23] One of the best outlines of the problem provides Pelikan (1986, pp. 4-5), who states that "'[a]daptive efficiency' denotes the ability of an economy to self-organize – that is, to suitably modify its structure", and who adds, "[i]n order to be adaptively efficient, the economy must, in essence, allow new production organizations to form, induce existing organizations to keep adapting to economic and technological changes, and force the organizations which cannot adapt to dissolve".

The ability to change organizational structures and channels of cooperation, in turn, depends to a great extent on economic institutions. They affect the direction of structural economic change by constraining and incentivizing certain economic activities and, thus, pave the way for certain paths of development. Property rights, for example, define which activities offer reliable returns, thereby opening up or closing

---

21 For a detailed discussion of the way crisis resilience can be conceptualized and measured see section 4.1.

22 In a conceptual framework of *the flexible economy* which builds on North (1990), Killick (1995, pp. 12-17) makes a similar distinction between *responsive flexibility* and *innovative flexibility*.

23 See Pelikan (1986, pp. 2-4) who credits Schumpeter for being the first author to formulate this problem. Schumpeter (1996 [1943], p. 84) stated: "the problem that is usually being visualized is how capitalism administers existing structures, whereas the relevant problem is how it creates and destroys them".

down alternative directions for economic expansions; regulations of labor and capital affect the ability of companies to alter the combinations of input factors such as workers and capital assets, thereby defining the range of potential organizational set-ups of the production process; and contract laws influence the feasibility of long-term cooperation amongst economic actors, thereby affecting the scope of the societal division of labor.

Apart from economic institutions, there are also political determinants of adaptive efficiency which can influence the ability of economic actors to modify organizational structures and channels of cooperation. These effects may either be direct or indirect. Direct effects, on the one hand, may for example emanate from public investment programs, economic stimulus packages or from discretionary monetary policies. Indirect effects of political decision-making, on the other hand, depend on the choice of efficiency-enhancing or -inhibiting economic institutions. The two theories which are at the center of this thesis discuss direct *and* indirect effects. However, each theory focuses on different aspects of the political process leading to collectively binding decisions. While Olson (1982) provides a theory about the problems of collective action and the consequential power asymmetries amongst different interest groups, NWW (2009) focus on the role of political institutions for shaping the political decision-making process.[24]

(3) Following the short outline above, the structural determinants of adaptive efficiency can be conceptualized as in figure 1.[25]

On the horizontal axis, there are two performance dimensions of adaptive efficiency that correspond closely to North's (1990, p. 80) previously cited definition: first, the ability to overcome an economic shock ("to resolve problems and bottlenecks of society through time") and, second, the ability to stimulate long-term economic growth ("to acquire knowledge and learning, to induce innovation, to undertake risk and creative activity of all sorts"). As will become apparent in the more detailed discussion below, both performance dimensions rely on very similar institutions and adaption processes.

---

[24] These two determinants of political decisions studied by Olson and NWW refer to two different sources of political power. According to Acemoglu et al. (2005, pp. 390-391), the organizational strength of special interest groups (in addition to the distribution of wealth) is decisive for *de-facto* political power, whereas political institutions assign *de-jure* political power to different political actors. Olson's and NWW's accounts may be regarded as two variants of this distinction, Olson analyzing the emergence of de-facto political power by special interest groups and NWW emphasizing the importance of political institutions for assigning de-jure political power.

[25] This analytical framework is inspired by a framework of economic flexibility offered by Tony Killick (1995, p. 8), although it differs from the latter in some aspects. Killick, for examples, considers three levels of analysis by differentiating between individuals, organizations and institutions. I, however, prefer to combine the adaption of individuals and organizations to one level *adaption of actors*.

		Dimension of Adaptive Efficiency	
		a. Ability to overcome economic shocks	**b.** Ability to generate long-term economic growth
Level of Adaption	**I.** Adaption of economic actors (individuals and organizations)	*Structural Determinants:* ▪ Economic institutions ▪ Political institutions ▪ Strength of special interest organizations	
	II. Adaption of economic institutions	*Structural Determinants:* ▪ Political institutions ▪ Strength of special interest organizations	

Figure 1: An analytical framework of adaptive efficiency.

On the vertical axis of figure 1, there are two levels of analysis. On the first level, the analysis focuses on the structural determinants of the adaption of economic actors (individuals or economic organizations) in their functions as consumers, producers, employers, employees or entrepreneurs. These actors make their choices within the options and constraints defined by economic institutions such as property rights and contract laws or regulations of businesses, labor markets and capital markets. Furthermore, political decisions, which are influenced by political institutions and interest group activity, may have a direct impact on the direction of individual adaption.[26] Thus, the first level of analysis examines the way economic institutions and the two determinants of political decisions (political institutions and interest group activity) affect the adaption of economic actors and thereby economic outcomes.

The second level of analysis asks which factors determine the shape of economic institutions. As formal economic institutions depend on some type of legislation, the political process from which this legislation originates moves to the center of this level of analysis.[27] As on the first level of analysis, two determinants of political decisions are of interest: first, political institutions determining the exercise of de-jure power, and second, the strength of special interest organizations affecting the distribution of de-

[26] Besides affecting adaptive efficiency via influencing the political decision-making process, interest group activity may also affect adaptive efficiency through the formation of cartels. As I will argue below, however, even this activity needs to be backed up by political decision makers. Therefore, throughout this thesis, I mainly focus on interest group activity that tries to affect political decisions and disregard cartelistic behavior.

[27] Many authors stress that economic institutions depend on active choices of political power holders. See, for example, Acemoglu et al. (2005, p. 390). Others, such as Hayek (1980, pp. 34-35), provide a more evolutionary account of the way institutions emerge as increasingly-efficient outcomes of an institutional discovery procedure. Even North (1990, p. 7) only abandoned such an "efficiency view of institutions" in later works by pointing out the existence of both processes – *active creation* and *emergence* (North, 1990, p. 4). Following that account, economic institutions always need to be backed up by political power holders whose de-jure power depends on political institutions and whose de-facto power stems from the strength of their political organizations.

facto power. Hence, the second level of analysis examines the influence of political institutions and interest group activity on economic institutions.

The vertical distinction between the two levels of analysis bears resemblance to other theoretical accounts within the related literature. Brennan and Buchanan's (2000 [1985], pp. 8-10) differentiation between *choice within rules* and *choice of rules*, for example, resembles the distinction between economic actors adapting within the constraints set by economic institutions (level I) and these economic institutions being determined by political decision-making (level II). Furthermore, the distinction between the two levels of analysis is compatible with the common idea that there exists a hierarchy of rules running from political institutions and political decisions through economic institutions down to economic decisions and economic performance.[28] Of course, there are also feedback effects from the economic realm to political rules,[29] but as political institutions are often rigid constitutional laws that are difficult to alter, the non-consideration of reverse effects in the framework below seems to be a warrantable abstraction from the more complex reality.

(4) The above-depicted analytical framework shows those aspects of adaptive efficiency that I will substantiate throughout this thesis. I, thus, focus on certain aspects of adaption and disregard others. As indicated above, for example, the two performance dimensions (the ability to overcome economic shocks and the ability to generate long-term economic growth) both refer to economic output, thereby ignoring other important dimensions of performance such as unemployment rates, the severity of external effects or inequality. Furthermore, the framework concentrates on structural determinants of adaptive efficiency such as economic institutions, political institutions or the strength of special interest organizations, while it doesn't consider concrete individual decisions. Most importantly, I leave out the question how discretionary monetary and fiscal policies affect crisis resilience.

It is important to point out that this focus on output as the dependent variable and on its structural determinants does not mean that the left-out aspects are irrelevant. For example, it can hardly be disputed that discretionary political decisions about stimulus packages or monetary policies have an important impact on crisis resilience. However, focusing on output and its structural determinants is a necessary abstractions from a much more complex reality to keep the subsequent analysis manageable. A more complete analysis of adaptive efficiency would have to include non-structural explanatory variables such as individual capabilities and discretionary policies as well as non-output-oriented dependent variables such as unemployment rates or

[28] See, for example, Acemoglu et al. (2005, p. 390), North (1990, p. 48) or Borner et al. (2004, pp. 29-31).

[29] Acemoglu et al. (2005, p. 392), for example, mention effects from the distribution of economic resources, which provide de-facto political power, on political institutions; and NWW (2009, pp. 20 and 24-25) stress the existence of a double balance between the political system and the economic system, which runs both ways.

inequality. Keeping these limitations in mind, I next turn to the reconstruction of Olson's and NWW's accounts according to the analytical framework developed in this section. I begin with Olson and then turn to NWW.

2.2 Mancur Olson's Account of Adaptive Efficiency

2.2.1 Olson's General Account

In this section, I recapitulate Mancur Olson's account of interest group formation, institutional sclerosis and economic inflexibility with special focus on the research question posed above. The main reference points are his books *The Theory of Collective Action*, *The Rise and Decline of Nations* and *Power and Prosperity*.[30] In a nutshell, Olson argues that, as societies remain politically stable over an extended period of time, they accumulate an increasing number of special interest organizations whenever people with common interests manage to overcome the difficulties of collective action. When such special interest organizations become larger and more numerous, they use their organizational power to increasingly create economic rents at the expense of the rest of society. They do this either directly by exercising cartelistic power in markets or indirectly by exerting influence on political decision makers to redistribute resources, to fix prices or to limit access to economic activities via complex regulations. Thereby, they cause a gradual degeneration of economic institutions towards a competition-inhibiting economic order. Eventually, this so-called *institutional sclerosis* causes inferior economic performance in terms of lower growth rates and a diminished ability to overcome economic crises.[31] Following Gray & Lowery (1988) or Bischoff (2007), Olson's argument may be divided into three steps:

Step 1: The long-lasting stability of a society leads to the formation of an increasing number of more powerful special interest organizations.

Step 2: The political influence of an increasing number of more powerful special interest *(Level II)* organizations entails rent-creation and competition-inhibiting economic institutions (institutional sclerosis).

[30] While in *The Theory of Collective Action*, first published in 1965, Olson lays out the general foundation of his theory of group formation and collective action, in *The Rise and Decline of Nations* from 1982 he applies these theoretical ideas to the problem of rent-seeking by special interest organizations. Based on various empirical examples he tries to demonstrate the adverse effects of such organizations on economic institutions and economic performance. Most famous is his interpretation of the differential growth rates of developed democracies after World War II. Less well known but more relevant for the purpose of this thesis is his discussion of *Stagflation, Unemployment and Business Cycles* in the final chapter of *The Rise and Decline of Nations*. Olson's third book *Power and Prosperity*, published in 2000, deals with an application of his formerly developed arguments to autocracies. In that book he also makes some important qualifications about the role of political institutions for maintaining an open economic order. For a more detailed discussion of the evolution of Olson's ideas see Rosser (2007).

[31] The most compact exposition of this argument can be found in chapter 3 of *The Rise and Decline of Nations*. See Olson (1982, pp. 36-75). For secondary literature see, for example, Bischoff (2000).

Step 3: More rent-creation and competition-inhibiting economic institutions lead to inferior *(Level I)* economic performance in terms of lower growth rates and crisis resilience.

Steps 2 and 3 correspond to the two levels of analysis outlined in the analytical framework depicted in figure 1 as they deal with the determinants of economic institutions (step 2 and level II) and the determinants of crisis resilience (step 3 and level I). Below, I discuss these two steps in detail and disregard step 1.[32]

2.2.2 Olson's Account of the Determinants of Economic Institutions

Step 2 of Olson's argument, which accords to the second level of analysis depicted in figure 1, links the shape of economic institutions to interest group activity, as Olson argues that interest groups engage in rent-seeking activities and thereby cause an *institutional sclerosis*. To summarize this relationship between interest group activity, rent-seeking and institutional sclerosis, I first (1) briefly outline Olson's understanding of rent-seeking, then, (2) discuss the two main types of rent-seeking he considers throughout his books and, third, (3) summarize the potentially harmful effects of rent-seeking on economic institutions.

(1) Rent-seeking in the sense Olson (1982, pp. 41-47) understands it, refers to distributional struggles over bigger shares of output at the expense of the rest of society, as contrasted to productive activities that benefit everybody. The organizations for collective action that are at the center of his theory are "overwhelmingly oriented to struggles over the distribution of income and wealth rather than to the production of additional output – they are 'distributional coalitions' (or organizations that engage in [...] rent seeking)" (Olson, 1982, p. 44). Olson (1982, pp. 42-44, 47-49) argues that especially small groups tend to become such distributional coalitions, as they reap all the gains from furthering their special

[32] To summarize step 1 according to the first chapter of *The Logic of Collective Action* and in the second chapter of *The Rise and Decline of Nations*, having common interests does not necessarily induce self-interested individuals to pursue them collectively by forming a group or organization. Obstacles to affiliation arise because the outcomes of collective action (for example particularistic legislation as a result of lobbying, non-competitive prices following the formation of a sales cartel or higher wages due to union activity) resemble public or common goods for all potential contributors, thereby creating free rider problems (Olson, 1975 [1965], pp. 11, 14-16). Overcoming these obstacles to affiliation, which particularly concern large groups with latent interests, often requires favorable circumstances that allow the groups of collective actions to put selective incentives into place (Olson, 1975 [1965], p. 51; 1982, pp. 21-22). These selective incentives either punish non-contributors (picketing or ostracism towards strikebreakers) or reward contributors (granting preferential access to business relationships only to members of the respective trade association or lobbying organization). Hence, from this insight that the formation of special interest organizations takes time and from the additional insight that organizations tend to survive even if their original purpose no longer exists, Olson (1982, p. 41) derives the statement which makes up the first step of his argument that "[s]table societies with unchanged boundaries tend to accumulate more collusions and organizations for collective action over time".

interests but endure only a small proportion of the global loss their rent-seeking activity entails for the entire society. In general, however, his arguments regarding the adverse effects of interest group activity hold for small groups *and* for large groups (which he labels *encompassing organizations*).[33]

(2) Olson considers two main types of rents, which distributional coalitions may try to secure: first, *sales prices above competitive levels due to entry restrictions* and, second, *direct redistributions of wealth and income*.

Regarding the first type, firms or individuals may try to restrict the quantities they sell in order to charge higher sales prices for their goods and services. Thus, they act collectively in a similar way as one single monopolist. The two means by which distributional coalitions can achieve this is either by lobbying for favorable government legislation, which fixes prices or wages above competitive levels, or through the formation of cartels in which each member agrees to restrict quantities and raise prices (Olson, 1982, pp. 44-46). One necessary condition for the creation of rents through prices above competitive levels are barriers to market entry. If goods markets were contestable,[34] higher prices would quickly attract new competitors whose market entry would either drive prices back down to their competitive levels or, if prices are fixed, reduce the quantity each member of the coalition could sell (Olson, 1982, pp. 45-46, 66-69). Often such entry barriers rely on some type of government regulations which officially aim at the correction market failures (Olson, 1982, p. 63).[35] Although Olson acknowledges that regulations may also have legitimate purposes, he decides to "bypass the problems of environmental pollution and other externalities" because they "would be merely a distraction" for his theory (Olson, 2000, p. 220, footnote 12).

---

[33] Although Olson points out that encompassing organizations face certain incentives to make the societies in which they live more prosperous, he emphasizes that this does not mean that they actually act this way because there also exist forces that work in the opposite direction. He, for example, argues that larger groups have stronger bargaining power than smaller groups, that they often act according to the interests of their leaders instead of the interests of their rationally-ignorant constituents and that they represent less diversity of views, opinions and checks to potentially erroneous political ideas (Olson, 1982, pp. 49-50, 52-53). Therefore, "it would be a mistake [...] to suppose that any increase in the extent to which a special interest organization is encompassing is necessarily desirable" (Olson, 1982, p. 49).

[34] For the concept of contestable markets see, for example, the review article of Brock (1983).

[35] Olson, however, does not provide concrete examples of such government regulations which constitute entry barriers. Some obvious examples in goods markets are license requirements, complex quality standards or high bureaucratic hurdles, which constitute obstacles to market entrants who cannot as easily comply with them as established firms. Often, such entrance barriers for domestic competitors have to be accompanied by tariffs or other trade restrictions to keep foreign competitors at bay, as well. In labor markets, positions of established employees may be strengthened at the expense of outsiders by means of very strict hiring-and-firing regulations. Such regulations restrict the entry of new job applicants, protect existing jobs and allow established employees to demand higher wages than they could otherwise achieve under competitive conditions.

For his argument it only matters that interest group activity, ceteris paribus, increases the extent of economic regulations that fix prices and restrict market entry.

The second general type of rents Olson considers are direct redistributions. As examples he mentions subsidies and tax exemptions or bail-outs for failing firms (Olson, 2000, pp. 44, 63, 71). Similar to the qualification made above, Olson points out that not all redistributions are expressions of rent-seeking. At various instances he, for example, expresses a general consent with the view that redistributions to poor people are morally justified or resemble public goods (Olson, 1982, pp. 173-174; 2000, p. 190). He, however, takes the pessimistic view that only a small part of redistributions actually serves such purposes because "[i]n reality many, if not most, of the redistributions are inspired by entirely different motives, and most of them have arbitrary rather than egalitarian impacts on the distribution of income – more than a few redistribute income from lower to higher income people" (Olson, 1982, p. 174). Therefore, according to Olson, the majority of redistributions fall under the category of rent-seeking, as they provide benefits to small groups at the expense of the rest of society.

(3) Rent-seeking of the two kinds explained above affects economic institutions adversely because, in order to create such rents, distributional coalitions often need backup by the rules governing economic activity.[36] Changing these rules is, therefore, one essential part of rent-seeking activities. Being able to charge prices above competitive levels and creating entry barriers for potential competitors often requires some type of government regulation (e.g. license restrictions, complex quality standards, high bureaucratic obstacles and trade barriers for foreign competitors in goods markets; or excessive union privileges, hiring-and-firing regulations and wage floors in labor markets). In a similar way, the ability to obtain direct redistributions usually depends on specific government programs which benefit small groups of individuals or firms.

Additionally, according to Olson, distributional coalitions affect economic institutions by obtaining preferential treatment with respect to existing regulations and redistributive programs, thereby adding even further to the extent of regulations and the scope of government activity.[37] He summarizes: "Lobbying increases the

---

[36] According to Olson (1982, pp. 41, 59 and 69), there are two types of distributional coalitions: First, politically engaged lobby groups, and second cartels operating in markets. While lobbying aims directly at altering economic institutions, effects from the cartels could in principle also work without political assistance to change economic institutions. In reality, however, it is very hard to imagine how a sales cartel that charges extraordinarily high prices could permanently detain new competitors from entering their market without the legal backup by formal economic institutions. Even unions cannot easily use violent means against strikebreakers in states with well-enforced individual rights.

[37] Olson (1982, pp. 26-29, 69-70) explains that lobbying for loopholes is possible because normal citizens are rationally ignorant. Therefore, it does not pay off for them to spend much time on

complexity of regulation and the scope of government by creating special provisions and exceptions. A lobby that wins a tax reduction for income of a certain source or type makes the tax code longer and more complicated; a lobby that gets a tariff increase for the producers of a particular commodity makes trade regulation more complex than if there were a uniform tariff on all imports and much more complex than it would be with no tariff at all" (Olson, 1982, p. 69). Hence, following these arguments, more interest group activity should, ceteris paribus, be associated with more comprehensive regulations in goods and labor markets as well as larger government sectors.

Furthermore, according to an argument Olson puts forward in *Power and Prosperity*, interest group activity may also influence the enforcement of property rights. He argues that secure individual rights are the strongest obstacle to extensive redistributions because they limit political and administrative discretion to confiscate economic gains from successful market participants. "To the extent that individual rights keep the government from capturing the returns in exceptionally profitable enterprises, they also leave the government with fewer resources to dissipate on enterprises that are a drain to the society" (Olson, 2000, p. 192). From this argument it follows that, if the government wants to assist special interest groups to capture large parts of a society's wealth, undermining property rights is a necessary prerequisite. The weaker individual rights are and the more power governments have over their citizens' property, the more wealth they can redistribute.

In summary, Olson's abovementioned arguments entail the following three effects of interest group activity on economic institutions:

1) More interest group activity leads to more regulations in goods and labor markets. Goods market regulations restrict market entry of new competitors and raise sales prices above competitive levels. Labor market regulations constrain market entry of new job applicants, protect existing jobs and raise wages above competitive levels.
2) More interest group activity leads to larger government sectors to administer extensive regulations and redistributive programs.
3) More interest group activity leads to an erosion of the rule of law (including partial enforcement of property rights and contract laws) to increase the government's ability to redistribute wealth.

2.2.3 Olson's Account of the Determinants of Crisis Resilience

Step 3 of Olson's argument, which accords to the first level of analysis, explains mal-adaptions of economic actors and inferior economic performance (including worse crisis resilience) through rent-seeking by special interest groups and through the three sclerotic economic institutions outlined above. Below, I summarize that account by

monitoring political decisions, as their personal contributions have only a very small influence on the decision itself.

taking the following three steps. First, (1) I illustrate that Olson understands economic performance primarily in terms of adaptive efficiency instead of allocative efficiency. Second, (2) I contrast Olson's account of adaption in unconstrained markets to his account of adaption in sclerotic markets and, third, (3) I discuss how mal-adaptions in sclerotic markets have negative effects on crisis resilience.

(1) Olson distinguishes two main aspects of economic efficiency: static efficiency and dynamic efficiency,[38] the former corresponding closely to the concept of allocative efficiency and the latter corresponding to adaptive efficiency as outlined in chapter 2. Olson discusses static efficiency only briefly in the fourth implication of chapter 3 in *The Rise and Decline of Nations*. There, he explains how output restrictions and prices above competitive levels inhibit mutually-beneficial transactions and, therefore, reduce economic output *at one point in time*.[39] His primary concern, however, is the dynamic aspect of economic efficiency which refers to changes of output *through time*. This includes both the ability to generate economic growth (positive rates of output change through time)[40] and the ability to avoid severe recessions (negative rates of output change through time) following economic shocks.[41]

Throughout his discussion, he mentions two primary processes required for dynamic efficiency: first, the quick re-allocation of productive factors to their most productive uses and, second, the generation of innovations by entrepreneurs.

First, quick re-allocations of input factors to their most productive uses are necessary because, according to Olson (1982, p. 58), the environment of economic activity is constantly changing due to advances of scientific knowledge, altered consumer tastes, discoveries of new resources or even the weather. Hence, maintaining a (nearly) efficient allocation requires constant adaptions to these changed circumstances, including the implementation of newly-available production technologies, investment into new machinery, re-combinations of input factors or cooperation between different business partners. Especially in his discussion of the seventh implication in *The Rise and Decline of Nations*, Olson (1982, p. 63) highlights the "rate at which

---

38 Olson uses different labels for these two aspects of economic efficiency. Sometimes he distinguishes static efficiency from its "dynamic or growth-oriented counterpart" (Olson, 1982, p. 65). In other instances, he distinguishes "the efficiency of an economy" from "its rate of growth" (Olson, 1982, pp. 61-62).

39 Following that account, static efficiency requires markets to be in equilibrium, thereby securing an optimal allocation of input factors and of consumption goods within the boundaries set by the business environment at one point in time (including, for example, the available technologies, available factors of production or actual consumer tastes).

40 For the theoretical discussion see Olson (1982, pp. 61-65); for his application to explaining growth rates in developed countries see Olson (1982, pp. 75-117).

41 The main exposition of these arguments can be found in the final chapter of *The Rise and Decline of Nations* on *Stagflation, Unemployment and Business Cycles: An Evolutionary Approach to Macroeconomics* (Olson, 1982, pp. 181-238).

resources are reallocated from one activity of industry to another in response to new technologies or conditions" as an important aspect of dynamic efficiency.

Second, Olson also points out the importance of actually generating innovations by entrepreneurs, who constantly search for better applications of the existing factors of production. Echoing Hayek's (1981, pp. 100-110) account of markets as discovery procedure, he argues in *Power and Prosperity*: "Because uncertainties are so pervasive and unfathomable, the most dynamic and prosperous societies are those that try many, many different things. They are societies with countless thousands of entrepreneurs who have relatively good access to credit and venture capital. There is no way that a society can predict the future, but if it has a wide enough span of entrepreneurs able to make a broad enough array of mutually advantageous transactions, including those of credit and venture capital, it can cover a lot of the options – more than any single person or agency could ever think of" (Olson, 2000, p. 188).

These two processes required for the promotion of dynamic efficiency are closely related to Schumpeter's (1936 [1934]) account, who was an important reference point for Olson.[42] Schumpeter distinguished between *adaptions within the process of the circular flow* and *economic development*.[43] The process of the *circular flow* "describes economic life from the standpoint of the economic system's tendency towards an equilibrium position, which tendency gives us the means of determining prices and quantities of goods, and may be described as an adaption to data existing at any time" (Schumpeter, 1936 [1934], p. 62). The process of *development*, on the other hand, focuses on "changes in economic life as are not forced upon it from without but arise by its own initiative, from within" (Schumpeter, 1936 [1934], p. 63). In other words, *adaptions within the process of the circular flow* are permanent and small-step adaptions of prices and quantities in reaction to continuous changes outside of the economic systems,[44] which include re-allocations of input factors and changes of input prices, as discussed by Olson. The process of development, on the other hand, refers to the generation of often revolutionary, innovative changes within the economic system, which extend the boundaries of production possibilities through recombining innovative technologies with the available input factors (Schumpeter, 1936 [1934], p. 82). In reality, the two processes behind dynamic (or adaptive) efficiency – *the quick re-allocation of factor inputs to their newly most productive uses* and *the ability to generate innovations within the economic system* – often go together as carrying out innovations normally involves a re-allocation of productive factors to innovative

[42] Olson (1982, p. 36), for example, claims to build his dynamic analysis on "'Schumpeterian' insight[s] into innovation and entrepreneurship".

[43] As Schumpeter (1936 [1934], p. xi) pointed out in the preface to the English edition of *The Theory of Economic Development*, he first used the terms „statics" and „dynamics", as well, but abandoned them in later editions.

[44] As examples of such changes in data, Schumpeter (1936 [1934], p. 62) mentions natural conditions, war, policies or consumers' tastes.

activities (Schumpeter, 1936 [1934], pp. 68, 71). Therefore, the two aspects of adaption discussed above should not be regarded as two distinct processes but, rather, as two ideal-type processes which together constitute dynamic (or adaptive) efficiency.

(2) Olson contrasts adaption in *unconstrained markets* to mal-adaption in *sclerotic markets*. In *unconstrained markets*, according to his account, "there is normally no barrier to entry into any industry or line of economic activity and also no barrier to imitation of any profitable pattern of activity" (Olson, 1982, p. 59). In those markets, innovative activity and adaption to changed circumstances take place permanently, thereby generating a trial-and-error process of imitation and innovation. Olson (1982, p. 59; 2000, pp. 188-189) explains that, as the direction of social and economic development is unpredictable, economic actors cannot possibly know the most profitable investments, the best way to employ factors of production, the best products to meet future consumer demands or the most profitable production technologies. Those entrepreneurs who are quickest to choose the most suitable paths within the constantly changing circumstances, either because they possess outstanding entrepreneurial skills or simply because they are lucky, can achieve extraordinary profits. Such extraordinary profits, in turn, attract other businesses to take similar paths in order to make high profits, as well. As more entrepreneurs adapt and as more capital and labor flow into the newly-profitable activities, profits of the original innovators slowly deteriorate until they are no longer extraordinarily high (Olson, 1982, p. 59). According to Olson, allowing this process of trial and error and innovation and imitation to take place without serious constraints is key to economic prosperity in an ever-changing economic environment.

In *sclerotic markets* featuring rent-creation and sclerotic economic institutions, in contrast, "distributional coalitions [.] interfere with an economy's capacity to adapt to change and to generate new innovations" (Olson, 1982, p. 62). Throughout his three books, Olson provides four theoretical links between sclerotic economic institutions and mal-adaptions: first, restricted competition in over-regulated markets reduces the number of market participants engaged in innovation- and imitation processes; second, collective decision-making by distributional coalitions is much slower than unilateral decision-making by individual market participants in unconstrained markets; third, sclerotic markets bring about more inflexible market participants; and, fourth, the absence of secure and impartially-enforced property rights limits the scope of feasible transactions. All four impediments affect the two aspects of adaption in unconstrained markets outlined above – the *ability to create innovations* for solving a society's problems and the *ability to quickly reallocate resources to the most profitable activities*. Below, I explain all four theoretical links in turn.

The first cause of mal-adaption stems directly from the entry barriers associated with rent-seeking and sclerotic institutions. As explained in the previous section, in order to maintain high sales prices, cartels need to inhibit outside companies from competing in their markets. Similarly, in order to receive higher wages, workers associations need to hold off outside workers from entering their profession. Both impediments restrict innovative activity and the quick re-allocation of productive factors to the most profitable uses. Entry restrictions constrain innovative activity because they restrict the number of companies and workers engaged in trial-and-error processes.[45] Furthermore, they impede a quick re-allocation of productive factors by inhibiting outside companies from investing in protected markets and outside workers from finding employment in protected professions. This restricts the potential for expansion to already established market participants. Analogous to entry restrictions, distributional coalitions may also generate restrictions to exit, by lobbying for bail-outs in favor of failing firms or for subsidies and employment protection schemes in favor of workers in declining industries. Both types of exit restrictions restrain capital and labor from moving out of unproductive applications into more productive ones (Olson, 1982, pp. 63-64; 2000, pp. 189-190).

The second cause of mal-adaption in sclerotic markets, following Olson, is the slow decision-making within distributional coalitions. As all members of a coalition have to agree on a new course of action, he argues, they have to rely on consensual bargaining or on constitutional procedures to collectively arrive at decisions. Both, according to Olson, takes much more time than unilateral decision-making by single market participants. Furthermore, if the government is involved in fixing prices or regulating entrance to markets, re-negotiations of regulations cause even longer delays (Olson, 1982, pp. 53-56). This slow decision-making within distributional coalitions, in turn, entails delayed adoption of technological innovations because coalitions have to renegotiate the distribution of the gains and because innovations may change the distribution of power within the coalition. Out of these reasons, unions may oppose labor saving innovations, and cartels may block the introduction of new technologies by other cartel members. Especially when scientific advances and opportunities to innovate are small and numerous, there is a constant need for bargaining over every issue, which reduces the rate of innovative advancement even further (Olson, 1982, pp. 62-63).[46]

The third cause of mal-adaption is more subtle and follows from a short argument Olson brings forward regarding the effects of interest group activity on social evolution. He argues that economic actors (individuals and companies) develop those character traits which are rewarded by the incentives in their particular society. "If a society mainly rewards production or the capacity to satisfy those with whom one engages in free exchange, it stimulates the development of productive traits" (Olson, 1982, pp.

---

[45] Olson does not bring forward this argument explicitly, but it follows from his discussion about the importance of trial and error by a great number of entrepreneurs (Olson, 2000, pp. 188-189).

[46] Slow decision-making may also entail a slow reallocation of resources to the most profitable economic activities, as rigid prices cannot properly function as signals of scarcities (Hayek, 1945, 526-528).

72-73).[47] Turned around, this argument implies that if a society instead rewards rent-seeking and lobbying activities, it stimulates the development of alternative character traits that make actors successful under those circumstances. Companies, for example, might develop large and unproductive departments for legal issues and public relations, and individuals might become lethargic, form work-to-rule attitudes or spend more time for intra-company rent-seeking than for solving problems and generating profits. Such developments, as well, are likely to reduce the rate of innovations in a society and the speed of resource re-allocations to the most productive activities simply because actors are less competent to generate innovations or to recognize opportunities for profit-making.

The final cause of mal-adaption follows from an argument Olson makes in the final chapter of *Power and Prosperity*. There, he explains that impartially-enforced individual rights extent the range of feasible contracts and, hence, allow those transactions to take place which are most beneficial for economic progress and development. Olson (2000, pp. 174-180, 183-189) argues that irrepressible markets or informal sectors involving contracts with low transaction costs exist everywhere. What distinguishes rich from poor countries, however, is the existence of socially-contrived markets which provide legal enforcement for more complicated contracts with high transaction costs. Such contracts are necessary conditions for long-term investment projects, complicated insurance transactions or the cooperation of many companies over an extended period of time. They are particularly important, as they facilitate the division of labor[48] and capital-intensive production that allows producers to exploit economies of scale. If, however, secure individual rights are absent or undermined by rent-seeking activities, this impedes innovative activity and the quick re-allocation of resources to the most profitable activities. Then, innovative activity is restricted to activities which involve little inter-company cooperation and to labor-intensive production because "no one would normally engage in capital-intensive production if he or she did not have rights that kept the valuable capital from being taken [...]" (Olson, 2000, p. 186). Furthermore, the quick re-allocation of capital may require larger investments, which have to be protected by secure property rights or enabled by capital markets that pool the savings of many individuals into single projects.

(3) All four abovementioned theoretical links between sclerotic economic institutions and mal-adaption affect the dynamic (or adaptive) efficiency of an economy, which includes the two performance dimensions outlined in figure 1. The first and most obvious expression of mal-adaptions are low growth rates, as the rate of innovation and the accumulation of capital and labor (put to efficient uses) are important factors

---

[47] At another instance, Olson (1982, p. 59) argues that "[f]ree entry also entails that no firm has any shelter from a Darwinian struggle for survival, so none can remain lethargic or inefficient and survive".

[48] The recognition that the division of labor is a central cause for economic prosperity goes back as far as to Adam Smith (1960 [1776], pp. 9-17).

contributing to economic growth.[49] Accordingly, the most well-known application of Olson's theory is his analysis of differential growth rates in developed economies after World War II. The second expression of mal-adaptions, which is central for the research question of this thesis, is low crisis resilience. Olson himself undertakes such an analysis in the final chapter of *The Rise and Decline of Nations*, where he applies his theory to the recessions in many Western countries during the 1970s. In that chapter he focuses mainly on the demand-side effects of rent-seeking activity and sclerotic economic institutions. His general account laid out in the previous section, however, also entails arguments regarding supply-side effects – that is, effects on the output potential of an economy. I will first discuss the latter and then turn to the former.

To understand the effects of sclerotic economic institutions on the output potential, it is again useful to resort to Schumpeter. In the final chapter of *The Theory of Economic Development* he argues that overcoming a depression, which may either be the consequence of an external shock (Schumpeter, 1936 [1934], pp. 218-222) or the necessary consequence of a preceding boom (Schumpeter, 1936 [1934], pp. 223-236), requires a "process of resorption and liquidation" of superfluous activities (Schumpeter, 1936 [1934], p. 236).[50] Schumpeter (1936 [1934], pp. 238-239) emphasizes the difficulties for economic actors in such a situation: "The uncertainty and irregularity are quite comprehensible. The customary data are altered for every business. The extent and nature of the change, however, can only be learned from experience. There are new competitors; old customers and dealers fail to appear; the right attitude towards new economic facts has to be found, incalculable events – unsuspected refusals of credit – may occur at any moment". Hence, when old business plans, prices and employments of productive factors are no longer adequate for the suddenly altered situation, businesses have to struggle for adaption to find alternative employment for factors of production. They have to cut back on unprofitable activities and change their business plans if they want to survive (Schumpeter, 1936 [1934], p. 242). Specifically, this means that investors have to look for alternative investments, workers have to accept lower wages or find another job, and businesses have to search for innovative ideas or new business opportunities in different sectors of the economy. In other words, there need to be re-allocations of factors of production and re-orientations of innovative activity – the two aspects of dynamic (or adaptive) efficiency

[49] According to neoclassical theory, labor and capital are the two main ingredients of growth besides technological progress. See Solow (1956).

[50] In a nutshell, Schumpeter argues that the swarm-like appearance of new combinations of entrepreneurs alongside the established companies creates a disturbance to the economic system that constitutes a boom period (pp. 228-230). Once, however, this boom ends and a secondary boom caused by additional entrepreneurial demand and by high purchasing power (p. 226) also ceases, companies face high prices for factors of production, low sales prices for their products and lower general purchasing power due to deflationary tendencies throughout the economy (pp. 232-236). This causes losses and a situation of strain for most businesses, which can only be overcome by a resorption and liquidation of the superfluous activities the boom has created (p. 236).

in unconstrained markets outlined by Olson – to regenerate the output potential of an economy.

However, re-allocations of productive factors and innovative activities may be inhibited by sclerotic economic institutions. First, exit- and entry-restrictions in goods and labor markets prevent actors from abandoning crisis-ridden activities and from engaging in still profitable ones. Second, slow decision-making within distributional coalitions slows down the pace of innovation, investment and job creation in sectors with potential for expansion. Third, adverse incentives render economic actors less competent to innovate and to modify their business plans. Finally, badly-enforced property rights increase the uncertainties in the business environment and limit the range of feasible, potentially innovative activities. All four obstacles inhibit the quick return of growth rates to their potential levels by slowing down the elimination of bad plans in sectors with low growth potential and by constraining the expansion of profitable plans in sectors with still high growth potential. Thus, such mal-adaptions during a recession can be understood as a special case of Olson's general account of dynamic inefficiencies. While he himself mainly discusses an economy's ability to generate innovations in growing sectors and to reallocate resources to them, the same argument applies to an economy's ability to pull resources out of no-longer growing sectors into sectors which still generate innovations.

Following this argument, sclerotic institutions only prolong a crisis by inhibiting the adaption of economic actors to new circumstances following the original disturbance. According to Schumpeter (1936 [1934], p. 243), "losses occur or are imminent [...] as long as all businesses, and hence the system as a whole, are not in stable equilibrium". Furthermore, he adds, "[t]he progressive trustification of economic live facilitates the permanent continuance of maladjustments in the great combines themselves and hence outside of them, for practically there can only be complete equilibrium if there is free competition in all branches of production. [...] There is also the practice of outside support being extended to firms or whole industries in difficulties, for example government subsidies [...]. In times of depression there is also frequently an outcry for protective duties" (Schumpeter, 1936 [1934], p. 244).

Besides these supply-side effects, Olson puts forward a detailed argument about the demand-side effects of sclerotic economic institutions during a recession. In the final chapter of *The Rise and Decline of Nations*, he argues that sclerotic institutions depress aggregate demand because they create downward rigidities of wages and goods prices, which inhibit an even greater number of mutually-beneficial trades from taking place during a recession than under non-recessionary circumstances. This argument contains two steps: first, an explanation why interest group activity creates downward rigidities of wages and prices and, second, an account of how such downward rigidities create additional inefficiencies following adverse shocks, thereby depressing aggregate demand.

First, as explained in section 2.2.2, distributional coalitions, who act collectively in a similar way as a single monopolist, benefit from prices or wages above competitive levels.[51] This alone would not create downward rigidities if distributional coalitions could adjust prices or wages immediately in reaction to adverse shocks. A demand drop for a good that is controlled by a sales cartel, for example, would require the cartel to lower its monopolistic price to extract the optimal amount of rents. If it could make these adjustments immediately, no additional inefficiencies would arise. Allocative inefficiencies would remain at a similar level as before the shock, now reflecting the cartel's new price-setting power under the altered circumstances. Following Olson's account, however, distributional coalitions need a lot of time for arriving at collective decisions. "Thus it can be a slow process for a price or wage that is influenced or set by lobbies or cartels to be determined. Once the price or wage is determined, it is not likely to change quickly even if conditions change in such a way that a different price or wage would be optimal for the coalition. So special interest groups bring about sticky wages and prices" (Olson, 1982, p. 203). According to Olson, this argument only holds for downward rigidities. Upwardly, on the other hand, prices and wages are less rigid because they are not subject to collective decision-making, as individual firms or workers can raise them unilaterally without violating the interests of other coalition members (Olson, 1982, pp. 203-204).[52]

Second, Olson argues that such downward rigidities of prices and wages depress aggregate demand because they create additional inefficiencies during the time it takes until prices and wages adjust to the new circumstances. If, for example, an unexpected shock reduces the demand for certain labor services, the old wage floor is further above the new market-clearing level than it used to be above the old market-clearing level before the shock. Therefore, in the meantime until organized labor associations reduce wages to the new rent-maximizing level, an even larger than usual amount of mutually-beneficial labor contracts is inhibited by excessive wage levels. More people become unemployed, thereby creating negative effects on aggregate demand (Olson, 1982, pp. 205-206). Similarly, downwardly rigid goods prices increase intermediate inefficiencies following adverse shocks in goods markets because the old price floor is further above the new market clearing level than it used to be above the old one before the shock. In the meantime until business cartels adjust their prices, an even higher than usual amount of mutually-beneficial trades of goods and services cannot take place due to high price levels. Thus, an even larger amount of factors of production remains temporarily unemployed or diverted into unproductive uses. This additional underutilization of factors lowers factor incomes, reduces aggregate

[51] Similarly, distributional coalitions who act as a single monopsonist may benefit from prices or wages below competitive levels. Olson (1982, p. 204), however, argues that monopolists creating price floors are more common than monopsonists creating price ceilings. Therefore, the latter case is less relevant for the problem at hand.

[52] This argument is, of course, based on the premise that monopolists creating price floors are more common than monopsonists creating price ceilings.

demand and therefore aggravates the recession caused by the original economic shock (Olson, 1982, pp. 205-210). In Olson's own words: "because of slow decision-making, crowded agendas, and cluttered bargaining tables, it can take a considerable time in some societies for a vector of prices as good as the pre-deflation or pre-shock vector to emerge. The result is a reduction in the demand for goods and for labor and other productive factors throughout the economy: there is a recession or depression" (Olson, 1982, p. 209).

Following the previous discussion, supply-side and demand-side effects of sclerotic institutions reduce an economy's ability to overcome an economic crisis. Supply-side effects, on the one hand, arise due to the limited availability of still-profitable activities and due to the additional time it takes to reallocate factors of production from depressed sectors to healthy ones. Both obstacles inhibit the profitable employment of available factors of production and, therefore, the regeneration of the output potential. Demand-side effects, on the other hand, occur because downwardly rigid prices and wages generate intermediate inefficiencies, which add to already existing ones, thereby depressing aggregate demand more than necessary following an adverse shock. Therefore, based on Olson's arguments, an economy's ability to adapt to changing circumstances should find an expression in its ability to quickly restore pre-crisis growth rates after having suffered an adverse shock.

2.2.4 Summary and Limits of Olson's Account

Following the detailed discussion above, Olson's account of the determinants of crisis resilience can now be summarized according to the two levels of analysis outlined in section 2.1.

Level I links individual adaption of economic actors and therefore crisis resilience to rent-creation and specific economic institutions. Following Olson's account, an economy's ability to overcome an economic shock quickly and with little output losses is one expression of dynamic efficiency (the ability to generate long-term economic growth being the other expression). Dynamic efficiency has two aspects. It depends, first, on a country's ability to generate innovations and, second, on its ability to quickly reallocate productive resources to their most productive uses. These two aspects of dynamic efficiency, in turn, depend on interest group activity and on economic institutions which structure economic interactions. Most importantly, three types of economic institutions matter: limited regulations of goods and labor markets, small public sectors as well as secure property rights and contract laws. These three economic institutions foster the two aspects of dynamic efficiency that promote crisis resilience by increasing the number of companies who are engaged in discovering solutions for a society's problems, by promoting quick and decentralized decision making, by generating more flexible and innovative economic actors and by increasing the number of feasible transactions.

Level II links the abovementioned economic institutions to the number of special interest groups. Economic institutions depend on the rent-seeking activities of special interest groups, who lobby for redistributions of wealth and income or for prices and wages above competitive levels. If these groups manage to create rents, they cause a sclerosis of economic institutions including more extensive regulations of goods and labor markets, larger public sectors and less secure property rights. The ability to generate rents, which entails a sclerosis of economic institutions and dynamic inefficiencies, in turn, depends on the number and organizational strength of special interest groups.

This summary leads to the following hypotheses about the institutional prerequisites of crisis resilience, as depicted in figure 2.

<table>
<tr><th></th><th>Disaggregated Hypotheses</th><th>Aggregated Hypothesis</th></tr>
<tr><td>Level II</td><td>H-O 1: more special interest organizations -> more sclerotic economic institutions</td><td rowspan="2">H-O 3: more special interest organizations -> deeper and longer economic crisis</td></tr>
<tr><td>Level I</td><td>H-O 2: more sclerotic economic institutions -> deeper and longer economic crisis</td></tr>
</table>

Figure 2: Hypotheses regarding the determinants of crisis resilience following Olson's (1982, 2000) line of argument.

First, at each level of analysis, there is one disaggregated hypotheses:

H-O 1: Countries exhibiting a larger number of special interest organizations feature the following sclerotic economic institutions: more rigid regulations goods and labor markets; larger public sectors; insecure and badly-enforced property rights.

H-O 2: Countries featuring more sclerotic economic institutions (more rigid regulations of goods and labor markets; larger government sectors; insecure and badly-enforced property rights) show deeper and longer-lasting economic crises.

Second, these two hypotheses can be aggregated to one hypothesis linking interest groups-activity directly to crisis resilience:

H-O 3: Countries exhibiting a larger number of special interest organization show deeper and longer-lasting economic crisis.

Before turning to NWW, it is necessary to point out one important qualification of Olson's account. Following the discussion above, interest group activity has a direct impact on economic institutions and on economic performance. Olson himself, however, acknowledges at some instances that the strength of this effect may also depend on the shape of political institutions, which structure the relationship between interest groups and political decision makers. Referring to the adverse effects of interest group activity on allocative efficiency, he for example states that "the argument [.] has only a lesser applicability to any country in which constitutional and structural factors constrain the number and power of lobbying organizations" (Olson, 1982, p. 45). At another instance he adds in a similar vein that "the power of special interest groups cannot be defined solely in terms of their organizational strength but should, strictly speaking, be defined in terms of a ratio of their power to that of more encompassing structures such as presidents or political parties" (Olson, 1982, p. 52). Hence, although Olson shows awareness in *The Rise and Decline of Nations* that political institutions might shape interest group activity, he did not grant them a central role in his theory. Rather, he treated political institutions as a negligible distractions to his account of rent-creation and institutional sclerosis based on the logic of collective action. Rosser (2007, p. 12) points out that Olson only started to consider the possibility of democratic political institutions shaping interest group activity at the end of his career. In the final passage of his posthumously-published book *Power and Prosperity*, for example, Olson granted political institutions a more important role for affecting the actual extent of rent-creation. There, he argues that the two necessary conditions for economic prosperity - secure individual rights and absence of excessive rent-creation - are supported by democratic political institutions. Specifically, he states (italics added): "These two conditions are most likely to be satisfied [...] in secure, rights-respecting *democracies* where the *institutions are structured in ways that give authoritative decision making as much as possible to encompassing interests*. Though lasting democracies (like long-stable societies of any kind) have in the past ultimately come to suffer from narrow special interests, *it is by no means inevitable that this must always be true*" (Olson, 2000, p. 198). Overall, however, Olson's account remains ambiguous regarding the way political institutions shape interest group activity and, therefore, constitute a serious qualification of his theory of collective action. The following section, which is dedicated to NWW's (2009) approach, discusses this particular question in more detail.

2.3 North, Wallis & Weingast's Account of Adaptive Efficiency

2.3.1 NWW's General Account

The reconstruction in this section focuses on NWW's book *Violence and Social Orders* (2009) but also relies on complementary arguments, especially those provided in North's earlier book *Institutions, Institutional Change and Economic Performance* (1990). In *Violence and Social Orders*, NWW provide a conceptual framework for the analysis of different types of social orders throughout recorded human history. Their analysis focuses on three main questions: first, how do different types of social orders deal with violence and provide stability, second, why do different types of social orders show different patterns of economic performance and, third, how does the transition from one order to the other take place (NWW, 2009, pp. xvii-xix). For this thesis, especially the second question – why different types of social orders show different patterns of performance – is of interest.

At the center of NWW's framework is the distinction between *limited access orders* (also called natural states)[53] and *open access orders*, which are the two predominant types of social orders found in the present world, according to the three authors.[54]

Limited access orders feature the following common characteristics: first, elite privilege to forming political and economic organizations, second, control of violence through extensive rent-creation by elites, third, limited access to political competition and, finally, limited access to economic competition (NWW, 2009, pp. 32-41). Such societies restrain most of their citizens from forming new organizations and from competing with already established elite organizations in the political and economic realm. By, thus, restricting access to valuable activities, established elite organizations create rents for themselves, which in turn provide incentives for the dominant coalition of elites to stay together and to refrain from violent intra-elite conflicts (NWW, 2009, pp. 18-19, 37-38). Limited access to politics and limited access to markets thereby reinforce each other. According to NWW (2009, p. 20), there exists a double balance between political power and economic power. In one direction, elites can use their political power in terms of violence potential to secure economic rent. In the other direction, these economic rents provide the means for maintaining political power and the incentives for keeping the dominant coalition together. Therefore, the characteristics of limited access orders are usually interconnected. Autocracies, which limit access to political power, are also rentier economies, which restrict market entry and provide privileged access for elites to valuable economic activities.[55]

---

53 NWW use the term 'natural' because this kind of order was the predominant type of social order throughout the world in the past 10.000 years. Open access orders only emerged in the past 200 years (NWW, 2009, p. 31).

54 The third type of order, which is less relevant in the present world, they label "foraging order" (NWW, 2009, p. 2). Examples of limited access orders are almost all societies and empires in the previous 10.000 years as well as the majority of today's developing and emerging countries. The only examples of open access orders are the liberal and industrialized countries often referred to as *developed countries*, which started to emerge around 200 years ago (NWW, 2009, pp. xvii, 31, 41).

55 Within the group of natural states, NWW (2009, pp. 42-47) distinguish between *mature*, *basic* and *fragile* natural states depending on their ability to support the formation of organizations outside of the dominant coalition. First, fragile natural states hardly support the formation of private elite organizations because pervasive uncertainty and a regularly changing distribution of power weakens the commitments of elites to upholding stable arrangements amongst themselves. Second, in basic natural states, elites are able to consolidate the arrangements amongst themselves and manage to form long-lasting elite organizations closely tied to the state. They, however, strongly inhibit the formation of organizations outside of the state, as this would undermine rents and potentially threaten stability. In this last aspect basic natural states differ from mature natural states. The latter possess "the ability to support elite organizations outside the immediate framework of the state" (NWW, 2009, p. 47), without risking immediate instability. Most importantly, mature natural states feature a legal framework that provides legal personality to

Open access orders feature different common characteristics: first, impersonal rights for all citizens to form political and economic organizations, second, enforcement of those rights and control of violence by the state, third, limited opportunities for rent-creation and, finally, open access to political and economic competition (NWW, 2009, pp. 112-117). The distinctive feature of those societies, according to NWW, is impersonal legal support by the state for all citizens to form economic and political organizations, which may freely enter democratic political competition or economic competition. Furthermore, the state in open access orders restricts violent conflicts within the society by establishing a monopoly on the legitimate use of violence that is subject to constitutional constraints (NWW, 2009, p. 110). This arrangement is stable because open access to political and economic competition provides checks for those actors who try to seize the violence potential of the state for their own purposes. Democratic political competition, on the one hand, ensures that no political party can remain in office who tries to abuse its temporary political power to restrict political access for the purpose of power consolidation or to restrict economic access for the purpose of rent-creation. Economic competition in contestable markets, on the other hand, secures that no economic rents are permanent and, therefore, no extraordinarily powerful economic actor can emerge who could possibly capture the violence potential of the state (NWW, 2009, pp. 23-24). According to NWW (2009, p. 110), "open access to organizations in all systems sustains competition in all systems. Competition in all systems, in turn, helps to sustain open access". Hence, in open access orders there exists a double balance between open access to politics and open access to the economy (NWW, 2009, pp. 24-25). This means that the distinctive characteristics of open access orders are also interconnected. Liberal democracies, which have a monopoly on the legitimate use of violence and which provide all citizens with impersonal rights to form organizations and to enter political or economic competition, are also market economies with limited rent-creation.

Both types of orders exhibit different patterns of economic performance. NWW (2009, pp. 3-4) provide evidence that open access orders are richer than limited access orders, which however does not stem from their ability to grow faster. Rather, "[m]odern societies that made the transition to open access [...] became wealthier than any other society in human history [...] because they greatly reduced the episodes of negative growth" (NWW, 2009, p. 4). These less frequent episodes of negative growth in open access orders, in turn, are due to their superior ability to adapt to changing circumstances. NWW (2009, p. 12) argue: "The variations in the economic performance of limited and open access societies over time reflect the inherent ability of the two social orders to deal with change". Hence, the most important performance features that distinguish both orders are the frequency and severity of recessions due to

organizations, thereby enabling these organizations to become perpetually-lived. They, however, restrict the formation of those organizations which pose an immediate threat to the power of the dominant coalition.

different degrees of adaptive efficiency. "When they grow, poor countries grow faster than rich countries. They are poor because they experience more frequent episodes of shrinking income and more negative growth during the episodes" (NWW, 2009, p. 6).

This brief illustration already indicates that NWW's account is highly relevant for the research question of this thesis, as it offers additional insights into the potential relationships between political institutions, economic institutions, rent-creation, adaptive efficiency and economic performance in terms of crisis resilience. As Olson, NWW relate superior adaptive efficiency and crisis resilience to open economic institutions and to the absence of extensive rent-creation. They, however, depart from Olson's account by arguing that interest group activity in open access orders does not lead to a deterioration of economic institutions because it is constrained by open political institutions. Arguing specifically against Olson, NWW (2009, p. 141) state: „Competitive markets in open access orders survive, despite the continued growth in the number and size of large, well-organized interests. [...] Neither Olson nor the public-choice, rent-seeking scholars can explain the long-standing survival of open access markets and competition in the face of organized interests that comprise the civil society".

NWW's account provides the following two relations at the two levels of analysis:

Level II: More democratic political institutions and a larger number of special interest organizations lead to less rent-creation and to competition-enhancing economic institutions.

Level I: More democratic political institutions, a larger number of special interest organizations and competition-enhancing economic institutions entail superior economic performance.

In the subsequent sections 2.3.2 and 2.3.3, I discuss the determinants of economic institutions (level II) and the determinants of crisis resilience (level I) in more detail.

2.3.2 NWW's Account of the Determinants of Economic Institutions

This section, which accords to the second level of analysis, deals with NWW's account of the determinants of economic institutions. According to the three authors, the potentially negative effects of rent-seeking differ depending on the kind of social order in which special interest groups operate. Therefore, economic institutions are not primarily a function of the number and organizational power of interest groups, as in Olson's theory, but rather a function of the political institutions which shape interest group activity. Below, I first (1) present NWWs account of rents and rent-seeking. Then, I (2) illustrate why the ability of interest groups to create rents depends on political institutions and, therefore differs in the two social orders. Finally, I (3) discuss the concrete economic institutions that result from interest group activity within the different political institutions of the two social orders.

(1) As Olson, NWW consider two main types of rents: first, *sales prices above competitive levels due to entry restrictions to valuable activities* and, second, *direct redistributions of wealth and income*.[56] While the former type is central for their theoretical framework, the latter type they only consider in passing. First, entry restrictions to valuable activities generate rents because they allow established actors to charge higher prices without losing market shares to potential competitors (NWW, 2009, pp. 19, 30). The second source of rents, which the authors only mention at some instances, are direct redistributions of wealth and income. However, departing from Olson, who puts forward a pessimistic interpretation of redistributions, NWW (2009, pp. 142-144) do not consider the majority of redistributions in open access orders as instances of rent-creation, although they indicate that certain redistributions – especially in limited access orders – are indeed personal and in favor of small groups.[57]

(2) According to NWW, rent-*seeking* by interest groups exists in all societies; what differs is the extent to which groups actually manage to *create* rents. The extent of rent-creation, the authors argue, depends on the type of social order in which interest groups operate – especially on the shape of political institutions. While rent-creation is an integral part of the logic of limited access orders, open access orders manage to limit the degree of rent-creation despite the larger number or special interest organizations operating in those societies.

In limited access societies, on the one hand, political institutions, which endow the dominant coalition with discretionary power to inhibit competition, entail a smaller number of special interest organizations and more rent-creation. NWW explain that dominant coalitions in limited access societies secure their own positions and rents by using their political power to inhibit opposition groups from organizing and entering economic or political competition. These rents, in turn, provide incentives for the members of the dominant coalition to refrain from violent intra-elite conflict.[58] The political institutions which stabilize the power of the dominant coalition can take various forms. As examples of limited access societies, NWW mention monarchies that directly tie political positions to specific persons (NWW, 2009, p. 34), one-party dictatorships (NWW, 2009, p. 45, footnote 16), failed states featuring no stable political institutions at all (NWW, 2009, pp. 42-43) or even democracies that lack the necessary prerequisites to make political competition free and open (NWW, 2009, p. 41). All

[56] NWW, however, have a slightly different notion than Olson regarding the relationship between interest groups and political power holders. While, in Olson's theory, interest groups act as lobbies to influence power holders, in NWW's account, interest groups are *part* of the dominant coalition that holds political power.

[57] As examples they mention direct transfers to government employees and teachers, guarantees to labor (NWW, 2009, pp. 138, 143) or direct redistributions of land in medieval England (NWW, 2009, p. 79).

[58] According to NWW (2009, p. 30), "[l]imiting access to organizational forms is the key to the natural state because limiting access not only creates rents through exclusive privileges but it also directly enhances the value of the privileges by making elites more productive through their organizations".

these societies have in common that they in some way limit access to political competition by restricting the formation of political organizations and that they create extensive economic rents for the dominant coalition. Hence, in limited access societies, political institutions that restrict competition entail a small numbers of politically-engaged special interest organizations and, at the same time, extensive rent-creation.

In open access societies, on the other hand, democratic political institutions, which promote competition and constrain discretionary power of office holders, entail a larger number of special interest organizations and less rent-creation. Following NWW, these societies enforce the formation of political and economic organizations (freedom of association) in an impartial way. The resulting larger number of special interest organizations, however, does not entail excessive rent-creation because, although political parties and affiliated special interest organizations *seek* rents, open political competition reduces the prospects of those groups to actually *create* them.

The two central aspects of open political competition which inhibit rent-creation in open access societies are electoral incentives for parties and the exercise of countervailing power by opposing interest groups.[59] First, electoral incentives for parties ensure that rent-creation cannot be excessive and permanent because this would threaten the public approval for – and therefore the political power of - the incumbent party. "A party cannot hope to win general elections with extremist positions or policies that fail to command support from a range of different interests, constituencies, and voters. Because parties need to gain the support of many interests, they must temper the (rent-creating) demands of each, lest the associated extreme positions hinder the party's electoral prospects" (NWW, 2009, p. 126). Second, departing from Olson's argument that no country would attain a symmetrical organization of interest groups, NWW point out that there is always a tendency towards an equilibrium of power. Whenever one special interest organization becomes particularly influential and threatens to extract excessive rents at the expense of the rest of society, other groups become active and try to countervail the power of the

[59] Besides these two mechanisms, NWW provide additional explanations how open political orders prevent excessive rent-creation, which are less central to their framework. The authors, for example, argue that parties have an interest in maintaining political competition because having an outside competitor supports cohesion within their own party. Furthermore, they point out that incumbents have fiscal incentives to abstain from rent-creation because excessive rents would shrink the economy, reduce the tax base and therefore lower the revenues of the government (NWW, 2009, pp. 125-129). This latter argument, however, cannot alone explain the absence of rent-creation. Olson, for example, showed very convincingly that governments or interest groups have only very little incentives to make the society they live in more prosperous, as they receive only a small share of overall prosperity as compared to the full benefits stemming from personal rents. If governments could choose between tax revenues from overall prosperity and personal rents, he shows, they would always choose the latter as long as they exceed the losses from reductions in the tax base (Olson, 2000, pp. 8-9). Without additional incentives preventing office holders from massive rent-creation (such as the ones mentioned above), fiscal incentives cannot by themselves account for the absence of rent-creation in open access orders.

rent-seeking organization (NWW, 2009, pp. 128, 141-142).[60] Hence, in NWW's framework, the intensity of interest group activity is not exogenously determined by their ability to overcome the difficulties of collective action, as in Olson's theory, but rather depends endogenously on the rent-seeking efforts of other groups.[61, 62]

Upholding party and interest group competition, in turn, depends on specific democratic institutions, which go beyond periodic elections.[63] NWW summarize them in the following statement:

> *"Other institutions support rights, such as a free press, freedom of expression, freedom of religion and conscience, and the right to assemble. All open access orders have some form of division of powers and multiple veto points [...], sometimes explicit, as in the American Constitution's separation of powers system, and sometimes implicit, as in the coalition governments of Europe with separate ministries, a prime minister, a cabinet within which coalition members negotiate and approve legislation, and parliament necessary to pass legislation. All open access orders also have judicial and bureaucratic mechanism for enforcing citizen rights and contracts. And finally, they all have constitutions [...] that provide for the limit condition – limiting the stakes of power so that everything is not up for grabs in the next election [...]"* (NWW, 2009, p. 115).

---

60 NWW adopt this concept from Galbraith (1952), who distinguishes between countervailing power within markets (pp. 115-139) and countervailing power within the political realm through seeking assistance in terms of state regulations (pp. 141-157). For NWW's argument especially the latter type is relevant.

61 "Taking an endogenous pluralist approach to group influence suggests that groups in open access orders have incentives to moderate their demands most of the time. Failing to do so risks mobilizing outsiders to become active in ways detrimental to the original groups interest. The endogenous approach suggests that a few open access order markets might be cartelized or protected [...]. However these markets are the exception, not the general rule" (NWW, 2009, p. 128).

62 According to NWW (2009, pp. 129-131), open economic competition complements and reinforces the positive effects of open political competition. At least three mechanisms are important: First, flexible prices function as a kind of sensor for rent-creation. If, for example, one interest group manages to create rents in one sector of the economy, flexible prices in other sectors ensure that this rent-creation will be quickly perceived throughout the rest of the economy. This, in turn, facilitates the monitoring of government activities and allows countervailing interest groups to react quickly (provided they are permitted to form and operate freely). If prices, on the other hand, were inflexible throughout the entire economy due to politically-determined rents, rent-creation in one sector would barely affect rents in other sectors. Second, flexible prices also share the gains of sectoral growth because higher wages in one sector generate higher wages in other sectors (due to factor price equalization). It is therefore in the interest of everybody to secure growth in all sectors throughout the economy. Finally, open international competition sets limits to excessive rent-creation, as rent-creation reduces international competiveness and therefore threatens the international market positions of domestic companies.

63 NWW (2009, p. 137, footnote 18) refer to Dahl's concept of 'polyarchy'. According to Dahl (1971, p. 1-4), free and fair elections as well as various civil liberties are the institutional prerequisites for bringing about the two dimensions of a polyarchy: 'public contestation' and 'inclusiveness'.

Thus, additional to elections, open political competition requires impartially-enforced individual rights and constraints against the abuse of political power. Especially, impartially-enforced individual rights promote the development of a diverse civil society including a variety of special interest organizations. Departing explicitly from Olson, NWW (2009, p. 141) argue that these organizations even increase the effectiveness of democratic political competition, as they "are the lifeblood of both political and economic competition. They are the vehicles through which economic and political entrepreneurs implement their ideas and affect the dynamics of the economy and the polity".

According to these arguments, the same political institutions which enable the formation of a large number of interest groups in open access societies also ensure that an excessive creation of economic rents is not possible; and the same political institutions which restrict the formation of special interest groups in limited access societies inhibit political competition and facilitate rent-creation. If a small number of groups seeks rents in limited access orders, which are marked by limited political competition, they are very likely to be successful. If, however, a large number of special interest groups operates in a competitive political environment, excessive rent-creation is much more difficult and unlikely. Hence, following NWW's account, rent-creation is not primarily a function of the number and organizational strength of interest groups, as it is in Olson's theory, but rather a function of political institutions that structure interest group activity. In other words, the ability to create rents does not depend on the properties of political actors but rather on the rules of the political game.

(3) The extent of rent-creation, in turn, affects economic institutions. NWW mention three institutional differences between open access orders and limited access orders, of which especially the first two are central for their account. First, open access orders feature rule of law (including impartially-enforced property rights and contract laws), second, they have larger government sectors and, third, they feature less rent-creating regulations.

First, excessive rent-creation entails an erosion of the rule of law. In order to secure privileges for themselves, powerful elites in limited access orders have to exclude other groups from making use of the right to form organizations (including companies) or to enter lucrative markets. Elites may accomplish this either by creating partial laws or by enforcing universal laws in partial ways. NWW (2009, p. 138), for example mention that laws in limited access orders are less specific and that the legal systems in those orders are more corrupt than in open access orders.

Second, according to NWW, limited access orders have smaller and more centralized governments than open access orders, as they are unable to supply public goods such as mass education, infrastructure or social insurance in an impartial way. They only provide partial favors to affiliated groups, such as protected jobs with high wages for government employees, unions and teachers (NWW, 2009, p. 138). While NWW acknowledge that government spending in limited access orders is indeed an instance of rent-creation, government spending for public goods and social insurance programs in open access orders is not. Rather, public goods and insurance programs are "relatively low-cost ways of sharing the gains of the market without disrupting it" (NWW, 2009, p. 122), as they "complement the market rather than interfere within it" (NWW, 2009, p. 124). Furthermore, larger government sectors in open access orders are necessary collaterals of providing open access because upholding an impartial legal system and enforcing complex political institutions requires a substantial amount of public spending (NWW, 2009, p. 123). Hence, in contrast to Olson, NWW provide a more optimistic account of government spending in open access orders.

Besides these two abovementioned effects, NWW occasionally indicate in passing that rent-creation may also be associated with more complex regulations. The three authors, for example, mention that limited access orders regulate access to trade (NWW, 2009, p. 38), and they also provide some scarce hints about domestic regulations in open access orders functioning as barriers to market entry. In their discussion of Olson's approach, for example, they state that some organizations "succeed in gaining policies that provide them with government-run cartels, subsidies, and rents" (NWW, 2009, p. 141),[64] thereby acknowledging that the Olsen-type of complex regulations are potential objectives of rent-seeking efforts. Thus, although NWW do not discuss the role of regulations as entry barriers in detail, their general account of limited access to markets is compatible with Olson's much more specific arguments regarding complex regulations functioning as barriers to market entry.

Following the previous discussion, competition-inhibiting political institutions,[65] which enable a small number of powerful groups to create economic rents, entail the following effects on economic institutions:

1) Competition-inhibiting political institutions entail a deterioration of the rule of law, including badly-enforced property rights and contract laws.
2) Competition-inhibiting political institutions entail smaller government sectors with a higher proportion of rent-creating redistributions and government programs.
3) Competition-inhibiting political institutions entail more rent-creating regulations.

This list of competition-inhibiting economic institutions differs from Olson's institutional properties of sclerotic markets. Both accounts include badly-enforced property rights and contract laws as well as rent-creating regulations (NWW putting

64 In a similar vein, they mention that rent-creation is based on privileges or exclusion (NWW, 2009, p. 140).

65 As indicated above, NWW (2009, p. 115) mention the absence of institutions such as free elections, rights to form parties, freedom of speech, freedom of assembly and legal provision which set limits to the use of political power by establishing divisions of powers and veto points.

more weight on the former and Olson focusing on the latter). The authors, however, disagree regarding the role of government activity. While Olson puts forward a pessimistic account of government spending by interpreting redistributions and other government programs predominantly as instances of rent-creation, NWW are more optimistic by pointing out the public good characteristics of most government spending in open access orders. Both accounts however tend to agree that government spending in limited access orders are usually constitutes rent-creation.

2.3.3 NWW's Account of the Determinants of Crisis Resilience

This section deals with NWW's (2009) and North's (1990) account of the determinants of crisis resilience. It accords to the first level of analysis outlined in figure 1. Below, I first (1) present North's and NWW's account of adaptive efficiency involving political and economic adaption processes, then, (2) discuss the authors' arguments regarding the impact of economic institutions, political institutions and interest group activity on adaptive efficiency and, finally, (3) illustrate the application of these arguments to the specific problem of crisis resilience.

(1) NWW point out that their framework does not analyze performance in a static way based on the concept of *allocative* efficiency but rather in a dynamic way based on the concept of *adaptive* efficiency. They define adaptive efficiency as "the ability of the society to survive in the face of an ever-changing array of problems and difficulties" (NWW, 2009, p. 133). More specifically, they explicate:

> *"All societies are subject to random and unpredictable changes in the world around and within them. Changes in external factors like, climate, relative prices, and neighboring groups as well as changes in internal factors like the identity and character of leader, internal feuds and disputes, and relative prices all contribute to persistent alterations in the circumstances with which societies must cope. The variations in the economic performance of limited and open access societies over time reflect the inherent ability of the two social orders to deal with change" (NWW, 2009, p. 12).*

This quote illustrates that NWW's concept of adaptive efficiency is closely related to Olson's concept of dynamic efficiency, as it deals with societies' abilities to adapt to changing circumstances. Adaptive Efficiency according to NWW's framework is based on *political* and *economic* adaption processes. In *Violence and Social Orders* the authors almost entirely focus on adaptive efficiency in the *political* realm and disregard economic adaption processes. For arguments regarding adaptive efficiency in the *economic* realm I have to resort to North's (1990) *Institutions, Institutional Change and Economic Performance*. Below, I discuss political and economic adaption processes, in turn.

Adaptive efficiency in the political realm, according to NWW, relies on two distinct process: the provision of credible commitments and the experimentation with new solutions to a society's problems (NWW, 2009, pp. 133-136). First, NWW argue that broad consent to policy changes depends on credible commitments. As policies dealing with new problems (such as economic crises) usually affect the interests and power of potentially antagonistic groups (including workers and business owners, agriculture and industry companies or rich and poor people), all groups have reasons to oppose changes if they worsen their relative position. If governments are able to assure all conflicting parties that each will carry some part of the burden of adaptions and that no group will exploit its altered position to increase its political power, agreement will be more likely. Similar to property rights, which increase the scope of feasible contracts in markets, the ability to provide credible commitments to policy changes widens the scope of feasible policies. This, in turn, expands the range of potential political solutions for new problems, including overcoming economic crises (NWW, 2009, p. 135).

The second determinant of 'good' political decisions and therefore adaptive efficiency is the degree of experimentation with new ideas in the political realm. NWW (2009, p.133) argue that "Schumpeterian competition provides political and economic entrepreneurs with incentives to devise better and more attractive solutions to their society's problems". Although this quote includes both *political* and *economic* entrepreneurs, NWW focus primarily on the *political* version of Schumpeterian competition throughout their discussion.[66] Pointing out the merits of this process in open access orders, they argue: "in comparison with natural states, open access orders more readily generate a range of solutions to problems; they more readily experiment with solutions to problems; and they more readily discard ideas and leaders who fail to solve them. [...] If the incumbent party biases its reaction to benefit its constituents rather than solve the problem, it grants its opponents a competitive advantage in the next election" (NWW, 2009, p. 134). Hence, in order to generate 'good' political decisions, the political process should generate a political discovery procedure which involves a large number of political competitors and rewards good solutions for a society's problems while punishing 'bad' ones. Therefore, the same competitive forces which safeguard societies against the capture of political power and against excessive rent-creation by self-interested politicians also provide the means for generating good solutions to a society's most pressing problems.[67] NWW summarize the nature of this political trial-and-error process in the following statement:

---

[66] Schumpeter (1996 [1943], pp. 269-273) describes the democratic process as a competitive struggle for leadership by elites who try to organize support for themselves from a partially uninformed and irrational electorate. He defines the democratic method as an "institutional arrangement for arriving at political decisions in which individuals acquire the power to decide by means of competitive struggle for the people's vote" (Schumpeter, 1996 [1943], p. 269).

[67] For a more detailed illustration of the policy-making process and its potential intelligence despite of cognitively-limited and self-interested policy-makers see Lindblom & Woodhouse (1993). Especially their third chapter on "The Potential Intelligence of Democracy" (pp. 23-32) corresponds fairly well to NWW's account of adaptively-efficient democracies. In later chapters, however,

"Open access and the free flow of ideas generate a range of potential ways to understand and resolve new problems. The larger the problem faced by the society, the more extensive is both the debate about the nature of the problem and the set of potential solutions. Political parties, interest groups, and organizations all compete to solve major problems and address crises. Those in power seek solutions to help them remain in power. Opposition parties and their support groups have strong incentives to expose the weaknesses in the incumbent's proposals and to devise more attractive alternatives. The larger the problem, the more individuals and organizations are affected by it, and the more widespread public input and discussion. The free and open expression of ideas means that many ideas will be heard" (NWW, 2009, pp. 133-134).

This quote also illustrates that NWW regard *political* parties, groups and organizations as the main agents of adaption, and that they view *political* debate and experimentation as the main mechanisms behind adaptive efficiency. *Economic* entrepreneurs and *economic* experimentation as sources of adaptive efficiency, on the other hand, they only mention in passing. In their most substantial statement about economic experimentation in *Violence and Social Orders* they explain: "entrepreneurs in market economies seek to discover and exploit new niches. Some problems faced by natural states never become problems for open access orders because markets emerge to solve or mitigate them" (NWW, 2009, p. 135). Beyond this statement, however, NWW (2009) have not much to say about adaption in the economic realm.

A more substantial account of the economic processes behind adaptive efficiency can be derived from North's book *Institutions, Institutional Change and Economic Performance* in which he describes the trial-and-error process that is central to generating adaptive efficiency in the economy. Drawing on Hayek's (1981, pp. 100-110) idea of markets as a discovery procedure, he explains: "In a world of uncertainty, no one knows the correct answer to the problems we confront and no one therefore can, in effect, maximize profits. The society that permits the maximum generation of trials will be most likely to solve problems through time [...]. We must also learn from failures, so that change will consist of the generation of organizational trials and the elimination of organizational errors" (North, 1990, p. 81). Hence, as Olson, North (1990) discusses the ability to acquire knowledge and to generate innovations as a central aspect of the adaption process in an efficient economy.

References to the second aspect of adaptive efficiency mentioned by Olson – the ability to quickly reallocate resources to their most productive uses – however, do not appear in North (1990). Therefore, North (1990) and NWW (2009), at first sight, seem to employ a narrower account of the economic processes behind adaptive efficiency

---

Lindblom & Woodhouse additionally point out obstructions to good decision-making in democracies, which NWW do not consider in much detail. Therefore, NWW's account can be regarded as a rather idealized version of democracy. I discuss further arguments regarding potential shortcomings of democracy in section 4.4.1.

focusing on the creation of innovations within the economic system or what Schumpeter (1936 [1934], pp. 57-94) labeled the *process of development*. They pay less attention to the necessity of constantly reallocating resources to their most productive uses in reaction to changes in the economic environment - or what Schumpeter (1936 [1934], pp. 3-56) labeled adaptions within *the process of the circular flow*. In the statement cited above, however, NWW (2009, p. 12) refer to adaptive efficiency as the ability of societies to deal with "random and unpredictable changes in the world around and within them". As this necessarily requires adapting prices and quantities, North (1990) and NWW (2009) may be well aware of the necessity to reallocate resources to their most productive uses but do not elaborate on that process because they take it for granted.

(2) After illustrating the necessary political and economic processes behind adaptive efficiency, I now turn to the question how these processes are affected by political and economic institutions and by interest group activity. I begin with the political processes and then turn to the economic ones.

In the *political realm* the availability of credible commitments and political experimentation – the two procedural prerequisites for generating 'good' political solutions for a society's problems – rely on the same democratic institutions as those already indicated within the previous discussion of the determinants of economic institutions at the second level of analysis. Recalling the longer quote cited in the previous section,[68] these political institutions include democratic and competitive elections, enforceable individual rights (free press, freedom to assembly, free speech) as well as constraints against the abuse of power. Together, these institutions generate a political discovery procedure featuring a large number of political entrepreneurs who compete for political power by offering different solutions for a society's problems. Competitive forces thereby assure that 'good' solutions prevail and 'bad' ones are eliminated. In limited access orders, on the other hand, a much smaller number of political actors creates a much smaller amount of potential solutions to a society's problems. Without competitive elections, potentially incompetent politicians can stay in power for a very long time; without individual rights such as free speech, free press and freedom to assembly, there are limits to the free flow of ideas; and without constraints against the abuse of power, politicians may be unable to commit credibly to political agreements (NWW, 2009, pp. 134-135).

[68] "Other institutions support rights, such as a free press, freedom of expression, freedom of religion and conscience, and the right to assemble. All open access orders have some form of division of powers and multiple veto points [...], sometimes explicit, as in the American Constitution's separation of powers system, and sometimes implicit, as in the coalition governments of Europe with separate ministries, a prime minister, a cabinet within which coalition members negotiate and approve legislation, and parliament necessary to pass legislation. All open access orders also have judicial and bureaucratic mechanism for enforcing citizen rights and contracts. And finally, they all have constitutions [...] that provide for the limit condition – limiting the stakes of power so that everything is not up for grabs in the next election [...]" (NWW, 2009, p. 115).

While political institutions affect the political processes behind adaptive efficiency, economic institutions affect a society's ability to generate economic innovations – according to North (1990), the main process behind adaptive efficiency in the *economic realm*. As NWW (2009) provide just a very limited account of this economic adaption process, I again resort to North (1990). Throughout his book, he mentions three theoretical links between open economic institutions and the generation of innovations. All three of which correspond to theoretical links discussed by Olson (1982, 2000). First, property rights increase the amount of feasible transactions, second, competition-enhancing economic institutions bring about more flexible economic actors and, third, absence of entrance barriers increase the number of market participants who are engaged in innovation- and imitation processes.

First, economic institutions, especially the existence of secure property rights and contract laws, affect transactions costs, the number of feasible transactions, the division of labor within an economy and therefore its long-run economic development. North (1990) builds on Adam Smith's (1960 [1776], pp. 9-17) central argument that the cooperative division of labor is the main prerequisite for economic development. Furthermore, from Ronald Coase (1937) he adopts the insight that the cooperative division of labor is restricted by transaction costs, which derive from various uncertainties, especially regarding the behavior of contract partners in an uncertain business environment.[69] Economic institutions, especially well-defined property rights and contract laws, reduce these ex-ante uncertainties about the behavior of contract partners and therefore make complicated contracts involving long-term cooperation of a large number of unknown partners feasible. This drastically increases the scope of economic cooperation and thereby promotes the division of labor and capital-intensive production technologies (North, 1990, pp. 33-35, 64-65).

The second theoretical link between economic institutions and innovative activity involves the character traits of economic actors – most importantly economic organizations. In his discussion of the interaction between economic institutions and economic organizations, North argues that the type of knowledge organizations acquire depends on the incentives provided by the rules governing entrepreneurial activity. He states that "the institutional framework will shape the direction of the acquisition of knowledge and skill and [.] that direction will be the decisive factor for the long-run development of that society" (North, 1990, p. 78). Following this argument, those societies which reward innovation and investment tend to produce organizations that are well-equipped for generating economic growth; and those societies which offer high returns for lobbying and other types of rent-seeking tend to develop organizations that are well-equipped for winning political favors (North, 1990, pp. 74-78). North (1990, p. 81) adds: "different institutional rules will produce different

---

69 North (1990, pp. 27, 32-33) focuses on information and enforcement costs. Other types of transaction costs are bargaining costs. For more details on this distinction see North (1990, p. 27, footnote 1), Coase (1937, pp. 390-392) or Dahlman (1979, pp. 147-148).

incentives for tacit knowledge. That is, the particular institution will not only determine the kinds of economic activity that will be profitable and viable, but also shape the adaptive efficiency of the internal structure of firms and other organizations by, for example, regulating entry, governance structures, development and the flexibility of organizations".

The third theoretical link between economic institutions and adaptive efficiency in the economic realm follows implicitly from NWW's argument that those societies which permit the largest number of trials are most likely to find suitable solutions for a society's problems.[70] If the number of trials depends on the number of competent competitors and if entrance barriers to markets (based, for example, on legal obstacles to group formation or on complex regulations) reduce the number of competent competitors, it follows logically that markets with fewer entrance barriers generate a larger numbers of trials and more experimentation with new solutions for a society's problems.

(3) The ability to avoid and overcome economic downturns is the primary expression of adaptive efficiency in NWW (2009) and one aspect of adaptive efficiency in North (1990). Therefore, the arguments presented above are directly applicable to the analysis of crisis resilience.

In the *political* realm, the availability of credible commitments and experimentation with new solutions to a society's problems are particularly relevant following an economic shock when hitherto unknown problems require hitherto unknown political measures as well as the accommodation of antagonistic interest groups. Then, credible commitments increase the list of feasible political solutions without risking political disorder; and a higher intensity of political competition among a larger number of political actors entails more debates and experimentation regarding the best courses of action. Hence, the three political institutions that promote the availability of credible commitments and experimentation (free and open elections, individual rights and constraints against the abuse of power) in combination with intensive interest group activity should have positive effects on crisis resilience.

Regarding the adaption processes in the *economic* realm, NWW (2009) remain largely silent, and North (1990) focuses on the generation of growth (rather than crisis resilience) as the main performance expression of adaptive efficiency. Nevertheless, North's (1990) arguments are also applicable to the problem of crisis resilience. First, secure property rights and contract laws, which reduce transaction costs and broaden the range of feasible contracts, are particularly important during a crisis when insecurities about the future and therefore transaction costs are even higher than

[70] "The society that permits the maximum generation of trials will be most likely to solve problems through time [...]" (North, 1990, p. 81).

during normal times.[71] Second, the flexible character traits of economic actors, which are associated with open economic institutions (the ability to innovate and to acquire knowledge), also facilitate the adaption to unknown circumstances during an economic crisis. In those times, following Schumpeter (1936 [1934], p. 239), "[t]he 'mere businessman' faces problems which lie outside his routine, problems to which he is not accustomed and in the face of which he makes mistakes which then become an important secondary cause of further trouble". Finally, a larger number of entrepreneurs permitted to operate in open access markets should also increase the availability of innovative ideas which can be the foundation of a renewed expansion in still profitable sectors. These arguments mainly refer to a quick resumption of innovative activity following an adverse shock. Other than Olson (1982), however, NWW (2009) and North (1990) do not provide arguments regarding the importance of quick resource re-allocations to still profitable activities.

2.3.4 Summary and Limits of NWW's Account

Following NWW's (2009) and North's (1990) accounts, the arguments referring to the two levels of analysis outlined at the beginning of this section can be summarized as follows.

At Level II, efficiency-enhancing economic institutions depend on a large number of special interest organizations and on the openness of political institutions – two factors which usually go together. In limited access societies, marked by competition-inhibiting political institutions (including absence of free elections, individual rights and constraints against the abuse of power), a small number of interest groups that is closely tied to the dominant coalition manages to create high economic rents. This entails economic institutions such as limited rule of law including insecure property rights and contract laws, limited government activity focusing on rent-generating redistributions instead of public good provision as well as complex regulations constituting entrance barriers to markets. In open access societies, marked by open and competition-enhancing political institutions (including free election, individual rights, and constraints against the abuse of power), on the other hand, a large number of special interest groups cannot create excessive rents. This entails stable rule of law including secure property rights and contract laws, more extensive government programs focusing on public good provisions instead of rent-generating redistributions as well limited regulations that constitute entrance barriers to markets.

At Level I, crisis resilience depends on the openness of political institutions, on a large number of special interest organizations and on efficiency-enhancing economic

[71] I recall Schumpeter's (1936 [1934], pp. 238-239) statement about the pervasive uncertainties during a crisis: "The uncertainty and irregularity are quite comprehensible. The customary data are altered for every business. The extent and nature of the change, however, can only be learned from experience. There are new competitors; old customers and dealers fail to appear; the rights attitude towards new economic facts has to be found, incalculable events – unsuspected refusals of credit – may occur at any moment".

institutions – three factors which according to Level II usually go together. Especially open political institutions and a larger number of special interest organizations promote adaptive efficiency in the political realm by improving the quality of political solutions to a society's most pressing problems due to the availability of credible commitments and due to a higher intensity of political experimentation. Adaptively-efficient (and therefore resilience-enhancing) economic institutions include well-enforced property rights and contract laws, larger government sectors that focus on public good provisions instead of rent-generating redistributions as well as limited regulations that permit free entry to markets. These three types of economic institutions foster innovative economic activity and therefore adaptive efficiency through three main channels: first, by increasing the amount of feasible transactions, second, by bringing about more flexible and innovative economic actors and, third, by increasing the number of competitors engaged in the trial-and-error process that generates economic innovations.

This summary leads to the following hypotheses about the institutional prerequisites of crisis resilience, as depicted in figure 3.

	Disaggregated Hypotheses	**Aggregated Hypothesis**
Level II	*H-NWW 1:* Open political institutions and more special interest organizations -> open economic institutions	*H-NWW 3:* Open political institutions and more special interest organizations -> milder and shorter economic crisis
Level I	*H-NWW 2:* Open economic institutions -> milder and shorter economic crisis	

Figure 3: Hypotheses regarding the determinants of crisis resilience following NWW's (2009) and North's (1990) lines of argument

At Level II, NWW link competition-enhancing political institutions and a larger number of special interest groups to the extent of rent-creation and therefore to specific economic institutions.

H-NWW 1: Countries with open, competition-enhancing political institutions (including democratic elections, individual rights and constraints against the abuse of power) and a larger number of special interest organizations exhibit open, competition-enhancing economic institutions (including secure property rights and contract laws, larger government sectors focusing on public good provision instead of rent-creation and fewer regulations).

At Level I, crisis resilience depends on adaptive efficiency in the economic realm and, therefore, on open economic institutions.

H-NWW 2: Countries with open, competition-enhancing economic institutions (including secure property rights and contract laws, larger government sectors focusing on public good provision instead of rent-creation and fewer regulations) should suffer milder and shorter economic crises.

Furthermore, crisis resilience also depends on adaptive efficiency in the political realm. Political decisions thereby affect crisis resilience directly and indirectly (mediated through the choice of resilience-enhancing economic institutions).

H-NWW 3: Countries with open, competition-enhancing political institutions (including democratic elections, individual rights and constraints against the abuse of power) and a larger number of special interest organizations should suffer milder and shorter economic crisis.

The main shortcoming of NWW (2009) is the lack of elaboration on the economic processes behind adaptive efficiency and crisis resilience, as they provide no clear theoretical link between open economic institutions and a society's ability to overcome an economic crisis. Focusing solely on NWW (2009) without additionally consulting North (1990) would suggest that adaptive efficiency and crisis resilience depend almost entirely on adaption in the political realm in terms of discretionary political decisions. Whether these decision include the choice of resilience-enhancing economic institutions remains open. A comprehensive account that also includes adaption processes in the economic realm only emerges when additionally considering North (1990) as background theory. But even then, the account falls short of that provided by Olson, as North (1990) mainly discusses the way property rights affect a society's ability to innovate and to generate economic growth, whereas he play little regard to the way institutions affect the re-allocation of productive factors to their best uses. Finally, his arguments focus primarily on the effects of property rights, whereas he pays little regard to the effects regulations, although these institutions may just as well affect the re-allocation of productive factors and the generation of innovations. Therefore, North (1990) provides only an incomplete theoretical link between open economic institutions and crisis resilience.

Furthermore, NWW's (2009) and North's (1990) accounts have little to say about the differing adaptability of different open access orders. While the authors distinguish amongst three different types of natural states according to the ability of these countries to provide stability, to enforce property rights, to grant impartial benefits to their citizens and to adapt to changed circumstances, there exists no equivalent distinction amongst open access orders. However, these countries, too, show considerable variability in growth rates or prevalence of crises.[72]

Hence, while NWW (2009) and North (1990) lack a detailed account of the economic processes conducive for overcoming an economic crisis, the merit of their framework (as compared to Olson) consists in providing a comprehensive account of the political process behind crisis resilience. Thus, Olson's and NWW's theories may be regarded as

[72] See, for example, the crisis resilience scores reported in section 4.1.2.

complementary to one another – Olson focusing on adaptive efficiency in the economic realm and NWW on adaptive efficiency in the political realm.

2.4 The Missing Aspect of Adaptive Efficiency - The Costs of Adaption and the Importance of Structural Stability

In this section, I consider another potential shortcoming of both Olson's and NWW's accounts. As I show below, a variety of authors suggest a third aspect of adaptive efficiency in the economic realm besides the ability to create innovations and the ability to re-allocate factors of production to their most productive uses – the two aspects outlined by Olson (1982, 2000) and partly by NWW (2009) and North (1990). While the previously-discussed authors focus on an economy's ability to generate change by adapting organizations and channels of cooperation to altered circumstances, the third aspect of adaptive efficiency involves avoiding *unnecessary* and *costly* change by stabilizing organizations and channels of cooperation during temporary bottlenecks. It is therefore the literal flip side of the coin making up the concept of adaptive efficiency. Below, I first (1) shortly discuss potential costs of adaption, second, (2) try to illustrate how economic institutions may support resistance to unnecessary and costly adaptions and, finally, (3) formulate a hypothesis regarding the first level of analysis that is partly alternative to the hypotheses H-O 2 and H-NWW 2.

(1) Every adaption to changing circumstances involves frictional costs. In a volume called *The Flexible Economy,* edited by Tony Killick, for example, several authors point out these costs of adaption. Especially the frictional costs associated with shifting labor or capital from one use to another are particularly relevant. Chang (1994) and Killick (1994), for example, argue that many economic values of labor or capital assets are specific to their current uses. Hence, shifting workers from one job to another is associated with a loss of productivity, which can only be re-gained after some time; and capital assets may even be totally useless outside of their current applications. Killick (1994, p. 19) explains: "An irrigation system cannot be used in factories; a miner cannot instantly be converted into a hotel worker; even within agriculture, land in a given ecological zone may not be suitable for conversion from cultivation of one crop to another". Furthermore, even if re-allocations to other adequate uses are feasible, they take time and involve transaction costs.[73] Using less specific factors of production is only possible to a limited extent, as large-scale and capital-intensive production necessarily involves locking up capital in specific assets and employing a very specialized workforce (Chang, 1994, p. 204). Thus, following these arguments, every re-allocation of labor, capital and natural resources to alternative uses involves

[73] Workers searching for new employment and investors looking for new investment opportunities, for example, have to incur information, bargaining and enforcement costs when dealing with new contract partners.

frictional costs due to the specificity of applications and due to additional transaction costs.

Besides frictional costs stemming from factor specificity, structural change may also involve psychological costs for individuals. In an early paper published prior to *The Theory of Collective Action*, Olson (1963) argues that fast economic growth, which entails changes in absolute and relative incomes and which requires the re-location of workers from the countryside to big cities, may cause social discontent and unrest. In the worst case, he argues, very quick structural change, which overstrains the capacity of individual actors to adapt to new circumstances, may even become a destabilizing political force by driving alienated and discontented individuals towards radical political groups. Although Olson focuses on the destabilizing effects of fast economic *growth*, the same arguments also apply equally to times of economic *crisis* when the number of absolute losers is even greater.

The previous arguments that every re-allocation of labor and capital entails costs entail that only those re-allocations should take place which are necessary for adapting the production structures to *permanent* alterations in the economic environment. Short-term adaptions during *temporary* bottlenecks, on the other hand, such as immediate dismissals of temporarily unneeded workers, the closing down of fabrics operating at a temporary loss or the immediate cutback of consumption patterns, may entail higher costs than benefits.

Furthermore, these immediate reactions during temporary bottlenecks may generate negative feedback in other parts of the economy due to accelerator or multiplier effects, which could potentially destabilize the economy even further.[74] Taking these potential feedback effects into account, the ability to stabilize patterns of production, employment and consumption during a however-caused temporary downturn becomes a crucial aspect of avoiding a more severe depression.[75] In this respect, it is again worthwhile to resort to Schumpeter's account of business cycles. While, as indicated above, he emphasizes the beneficial effects of restructuring superfluous activities during what he calls "the 'normal' process of resorption and liquidation", he also points out the dysfunctional character of the "'abnormal' process of liquidations" caused by panics, breakdowns of the credit system or epidemics of bankruptcies (Schumpeter, 1936 [1934], p. 236). Competitive economic systems, he argues, "cannot do without the *ultima ratio* of the complete destructions of those existences which are irretrievably associated with the hopelessly unadapted. But the losses and destruction which accompany the abnormal course of events are *really* meaningless and

74 While multiplier effects refer to reactions of consumption demand to past income, accelerator effects refer to investment activity reacting to changes in consumption demand. For interaction between the two effects see Samuelson (1939).

75 Martin (2011), for example, labels this aspect *the ability to resist* as opposed to *the ability to restructure*, which corresponds to the other two aspects of adaptive efficiency in the economic realm.

functionless" (Schumpeter, 1936 [1934], p. 253). Hence, avoiding the inefficient adaptions associated with the "'abnormal' process of resorption and liquidations" becomes a crucial aspect of adaptive efficiency during a recession. Summing up the relevance of this structural stability aspect of adaptive efficiency, Schumpeter explains:

> *"Situations emerge in the process of creative destruction in which many firms may have to perish that nevertheless would be able to live on vigorously and usefully if they could weather a particular storm. Short of such general crisis or depressions, sectional situations arise in which the rapid change of data that is characteristic of that process so disorganizes an industry for the time being as to inflict functionless losses and to create avoidable unemployment. Finally, there is certainly no point in trying to conserve obsolescent industries indefinitely; but there is a point in trying to avoid their coming down with a crash and in attempting to turn a rout, which may become a center of cumulative depressive effects, into orderly retreat"* (Schumpeter, 1996 [1943], p. 90).

Following the arguments above, the ability to avoid unnecessary structural change (involving, first, frictional costs due to factor specificity, second, psychological costs due to limited individual capacity to adapt to change and, third, depression costs due to negative feedback effects on aggregate demand) may be regarded as a third important aspect of adaptive efficiency besides the ability to create innovations and the ability to re-allocate factors of production to their most productive uses.

(2) This leads to the question, how economic institutions can influence the ability of an economy to stabilize economic activity during temporary bottlenecks. On the one hand, a market-oriented perspective suggests that preparations for bad times should simply be left to the individual actors, who can save funds or insure themselves against potential losses. Hayek (2011 [1960], p. 426), for example, argues that the state should provide "only a uniform minimum wage for all who are unable to maintain themselves and [...] reduce cyclical unemployment as much as possible by an appropriate monetary policy, any further provision required for the maintenance of the accustomed standard should be left to competitive and voluntary efforts". Other authors suggest that governments should take a more active stance, pointing out the positive effects of automatic stabilizers stemming from progressive tax rates or transfer payments (Dolls et al., 2010), of anticyclical government spending[76] or of demand stabilization via employment protection (Tridico, 2013). Also important for economic stabilization may be regulations of the financial sector, which aim at inducing banks and other financial corporations to abstain from excessive risk-taking, thereby reducing the risk of banking crises and securing a stable provision of credit to investors

[76] Schumpeter for example expresses sympathy toward the idea of postponing governmental construction projects to periods of depression, viewing such measures as "effective means of alleviating the cyclical movement and the danger of crisis" (Schumpeter, 1936 [1934], p. 253).

(Stiglitz, 2009). Schumpeter even mentions the potentially stabilizing effects of entry restrictions and rigid prices. Regarding entry restrictions he argues that "'restraints of trade' of the cartel type as well as those which merely consist in tacit understandings about price competition may be effective remedies under conditions of depression. As far as they are, they may in the end produce not only steadier but also greater expansion of total output than could be secured by an entirely uncontrolled onward rush that cannot fail to be studded with catastrophes" (Schumpeter, 1996 [1943], p. 91). Referring to the potentially stabilizing effects of rigid prices he adds: "Total output and employment may well keep on a higher level with the restrictions incident to that policy than they would if depression were allowed to play havoc with the price structure. In other words, under the conditions created by capitalist evolution, perfect and universal flexibility of prices might in depression further destabilize the system" (Schumpeter, 1996 [1943], p. 95).

(3) From this short discussion it stands out that the economic institutions presumably fostering structural stability during an economic downturn (such as high levels of government spending or stricter regulations of business, labor or the financial sector) are partly opposite to those institutions outlined by Olson and NWW to promote crisis resilience. Therefore, the arguments put forward in this short section provide an alternative hypothesis to the hypotheses H-O 2 and H-NWW 2.

H-S: Countries with larger government sectors, generous unemployment benefits and stricter regulations of business, labor and finance should suffer milder and shorter economic crises.

Although the theoretical foundation of this hypothesis is less elaborated than the theoretical foundation of H-O 2 and H-NWW 2, in this section it was necessary to highlight that there exists considerable arguments pointing out the need of economic institutions to promote structural stability to improve crisis resilience. The short explication above should have made clear that this aspect needs to be included in a thorough discussion of the institutional causes of adaptive efficiency and crisis resilience.

2.5 Summary of the Previous Discussion - The Theoretical Concept of Adaptive Efficiency

The previous discussion of Olson's and NWW's arguments now allows substantiating the analytical framework outlined at the beginning of this chapter. All institutional and organizational determinants of adaptive efficiency and the required adaption processes in the political and economic realm are summarized in figure 4 according to the two levels of analysis. While the first level analyzes the structural determinants of individual adaption and economic performance, the second level investigates the structural factors influencing the shape of economic institutions.

<table>
<tr><td colspan="2" rowspan="2"></td><td colspan="2">Dimensions of Adaption</td></tr>
<tr><td>a. Ability to overcome economic shocks</td><td>b. Ability to generate long-term economic growth</td></tr>
<tr><td rowspan="2">Level of Adaption</td><td>I.
Adaption of economic actors (individuals and organizations)</td><td colspan="2">Structural Determinants:
▪ Economic institutions
o Property rights and contract laws
o Size of government
o Regulations of trade, labor, business and capital markets
▪ Political institutions (de jure power)
o Democratic elections
o Individual rights
o Constraints against the abuse of power
▪ Strength of special interest organizations (de facto power)
Required Processes for Adaption:
▪ Economic adaption
o Promotion of entrepreneurship, and innovation in expanding sectors
o Re-allocation of productive factors to from unprofitable to expanding sectors
o Avoidance of costs associated with quick economic and social change as well as immediate adjustments during temporary bottlenecks
▪ Political adaption
o Choice of suitable discretionary programs
o Availability of credible commitments</td></tr>
<tr><td>II.
Adaption of economic institutions</td><td colspan="2">Structural Determinants:
▪ Political institutions (determining de jure power)
o Democratic elections
o Individual rights
o Constraints against the abuse of power
▪ Strength of special interest organizations (de facto power)
Required Processes for Adaption:
▪ Political adaption
o Choice of adaptively-efficient economic institutions
o Availability of credible commitments</td></tr>
</table>

Figure 4: Overview of the determinants of adaptive efficiency and the required adaption processes.

Below, I first (1) summarize the *economic* processes behind adaptive efficiency and the economic institutions necessary for stimulating them. Then, (2) I turn to the *political* processes and to the institutional and organizational prerequisites for setting them in motion. While economic processes affect crisis resilience exclusively at the first level of analysis, political processes are relevant for both levels of analysis as they affect individual adaption and the choice of economic institutions.

(1) Following the theoretical framework developed so far, the adaption of individual economic actors, such as companies, employers, employees or entrepreneurs, takes place within the economic institutions of the respective society. These economic

institutions provide incentives for economic actors to take certain courses of action and to abstain from others. They affect aggregate economic outcomes by rendering some directions of economic evolution more likely and others more unlikely. For the concrete case of economic adaption in reaction to an adverse shock, three economic processes are particularly important.

First, following Olson and NWW, societies need to be able to generate innovations in at least some sectors of the economy in order to provide a destination for unemployed productive factors – especially labor and capital. Resources which are no longer needed in crisis-ridden sectors (such as the construction sector during the Great Recession) find employment in other sectors and generate renewed economic expansion, now into different directions than before the crisis.

Second, a quick resumption of growth-generating economic activity in innovative sectors requires a quick re-allocation of productive factors to those sectors. Most importantly, investors have to re-invest their capital and workers have to change their occupations. Especially Olson points out the importance of resource re-allocations, whereas NWW and North seem to take them implicitly for granted.

It is important to note that these first two processes - innovative activity and re-allocations of productive factors - reinforce each other. Without the availability of innovations in expanding sectors, there are no suitable destinations for flexible productive factors; and without flexible productive factors, innovative sectors lack the resources to actually generate economic growth. If, however, both processes run smoothly, they should generate positive supply-side and demand-side effects during an economic crisis. On the supply side, the availability of innovative activities and a quick re-allocation of productive factors to them facilitate the quick recovery of lost production possibilities that occurred in crisis-ridden sectors. On the demand side, the same processes ensure that labor and capital do not remain unemployed in depressed sectors much longer than it is necessary to re-allocate them to innovative activities, thereby curtailing the decline of investment and consumption demand.

While the first two processes involve alterations of organizations and channels of cooperation in reaction to permanent changes in the economic environment, the third process behind adaptive efficiency in the economic realm involves the resistance to avoidable adjustments during temporary bottlenecks. This includes, for example, the ability of individuals to maintain stable patterns of consumption despite wage reductions or temporary unemployment, the ability of companies to continue operating despite temporary losses or the maintenance of investments in temporarily unprofitable activities. This third process behind adaptive efficiency promotes stability during a crisis, as it reduces the risks of chain reactions, which could destroy actually healthy organizations and channels of cooperation amongst economic actors.

These three processes necessary for adaptive efficiency depend on economic institutions, which provide the incentive structure for economic actors to take certain courses of action and refrain from others. According to Olson and NWW, three types of economic institutions support adaptive efficiency in general and crisis resilience in particular: first, impartially-enforced property rights and contract laws, second, the absence of unnecessary regulations and, third, government sectors which provide public goods but abstain from rent-creating redistributions.[77] Together, these three institutional features create a realm of private economic activity including private decision- making, private coordination of individual plans and competition as the selection mechanism amongst promising and futile economic activities.

Throughout the books discussed above, Olson and NWW mention various theoretical links between the three types of economic institutions and the first two aspects of adaptive efficiency. Following their accounts, I highlighted four ways how competition-enhancing economic institutions facilitate innovative activity and the re-allocation of factors of production: First, decentralized decision-making in competitive markets is faster than centralized decision-making in highly regulated markets, which also involves political participation. Second, competitive markets enable the operation of a larger number of economic actors who experiment with innovative ideas and organize the allocation of productive factors to these activities. Third, competition-enhancing economic institutions foster the evolution of more flexible character traits of economic actors, which improves their ability to generate innovations and recognize the best investments and employment opportunities. Finally, secure property rights and contract laws increase the number of feasible transactions and, therefore, facilitate cooperation amongst economic actors. This broadens the scope of innovative activity and reduces the insecurities associated with resource re-allocations to new activities.

Furthermore, following the discussion in section 2.4, economic institutions may also affect the third aspect of adaptive efficiency - the ability to resist unnecessary adjustment during temporary bottlenecks. Examples of economic institutions which are potentially relevant for promoting this aspect of adaptive efficiency are generous unemployment benefit schemes that support stable patterns of consumption, employment protection regulations that prevent large fluctuations of employment and capital market regulations that guarantee a steady and secure provision of capital.

Hence, there are three distinct and partly alternative hypotheses regarding the relationship between economic institutions and crisis resilience at the first level of analysis:

[77] The authors thereby disagree whether the last institutional feature involves a large or a small government sector. Following Olson's more pessimistic perspective on government programs, adaptive efficiency requires small government sectors, whereas, following NWW's more optimistic perspective, adaptive efficiency is associated with larger public sectors (especially in developed countries).

H-O 2: Countries featuring less sclerotic economic institutions (secure property rights and contract laws, smaller government sectors and less rigid regulations) show milder and shorter economic crises.

H-NWW 2: Countries with open, competition-enhancing economic institutions (secure property rights and contract laws, larger and decentralized government sectors focusing on public goods provision instead of rent creation and less rigid regulations) should suffer milder and shorter economic crises.

H-S: Stability-enhancing economic institutions (government programs providing social insurance and stricter regulations) should reduce the costs associated with extensive structural change and lead to better crisis resilience.

While there is no disagreement amongst the three hypotheses regarding the positive effects of secure property rights and contract laws, the accounts take different positions regarding the question whether smaller government sectors[78] and strict regulations[79] are associated with better crisis resilience.

(2) Besides individual economic adaption being affected by *economic* institutions, Olson and NWW also link adaptive efficiency to *political* decisions and, therefore, to political institutions and interest group activity, which both affect the political decision-making process. Political decisions may either have direct effects on individual adaption of economic actors (for example via discretionary program), or their impact may be mediated by the political choice of efficiency-enhancing economic institutions. As the political processes leading directly to better crisis resilience (level I) and the political processes leading to efficiency-enhancing economic institutions (level II) are similar, I discuss them together.

While Olson and NWW agree for the most part on the economic institutions that promote adaptive efficiency, their accounts differ considerably regarding the structural determinants of efficiency-enhancing political decisions. Olson, on one hand, points out the detrimental effects of organized interest groups on dynamic efficiency, as interest groups cause a sclerosis of economic institutions and impede individual adaption to changing circumstances. Based on the argument that interests are not symmetrically organized, he argues that interest group activity leads to sclerotic economic institutions, including badly-enforced property rights and contract laws, large government sectors with rent-creating redistributions as well as complex regulations. Olson, however, pays little regard to the potentially mediating influence

[78] As illustrated above, Olson points out the general rent-creating nature of government activity, NWW emphasize the public good character of government spending in open access societies, and authors following the structural-stability approach point out the stabilizing effects of government activity.

[79] As illustrated above, authors who put forward structural-stability arguments are more favorable towards strict regulations than Olson and NWW.

of political institutions on the economic effects of interest group activity, although he occasionally mentions that democratic political institutions might reduce the negative impact of interest group activity on economic institutions and economic performance.

NWW, on the other hand, explicitly depart from Olson by putting political institutions at the center of their analysis. They argue that more interest group activity does not entail worse economic institutions and performance because a larger number of interest groups can only emerge in open access orders, which are marked by open political institutions (including democratic elections, politically-relevant civil liberties and constraints against the abuse of power). Particularly, NWW highlight two requirements of the political process for the generation of efficiency-enhancing political decisions: First, the political process needs to resemble a discovery procedure which experiments with the best possible solutions to a society's most pressing problems. Second, the political system needs to support the provision of credible commitments, which increase the acceptability of new policies for antagonistic interest groups and widen the scope of politically-feasible solutions. According to NWW, interest groups are complements to open political institutions as they fulfil important functions such as monitoring the incumbent party, proposing political solutions to a society's problems and organizing or withdrawing support from power holders depending on the quality of their political decisions.

Hence, NWW and Olson provide opposing hypotheses regarding the effects of interest group activity and of political institutions. At level II the hypotheses H-O 1 and H-NWW 1 suggest the following alternative effects of interest group activity and political institutions on economic institutions:

H-O 1: Countries exhibiting a larger number of special interest organization feature more sclerotic economic institutions (including badly-enforced property rights and contract laws, larger government sectors focusing on rent-creation instead of public good provision as well as more rigid and rent-generating regulations).

H-NWW 1: Countries exhibiting a larger number of special interest organizations operating within open political institutions feature more open economic institutions (including impartially-enforced property rights and contract laws, larger government sectors focusing on public good provisions instead of rent-creation as well as absence of rigid and rent-generating regulations).

At Level I the hypothesis H-O 3 and H-NWW 3 summarize the direct and indirect effects of political institutions and interest group activity on economic performance and crisis resilience. They state:

H-O 3: Countries exhibiting a larger number of special interest organization should show deeper and longer-lasting economic crisis.

H-NWW 3: Countries exhibiting a larger number of special interest organizations operating within open political institutions should show milder and shorter economic crisis.

The task of the following chapter is to contrast the above-stated, partly opposing hypotheses with the empirical evidence from concrete case of the Great Recession during the years 2008 to 2012.

3. The Empirical Approach to Studying the Determinants of Crisis Resilience

This chapter functions as a link between the theoretical arguments presented in the previous chapter 2 and the empirical analysis which follows in chapter 4.

The first part of this chapter, section 3.1, provides a short overview of a complementary strand of empirical literature that investigates the relationships between the explanatory variables of interest (economic institutions, political institutions and interest group activity) and economic growth. As argued in chapter 1 and following Olson's and NWW's accounts, economic growth is another performance dimension of adaptive efficiency besides crisis resilience. Hence, looking at the growth literature should provide some guidance on how to approach the empirical analysis of crisis resilience in section 4, and it should already give some hints about the expectable results. Furthermore, the results of the growth literature are important plausibility benchmarks for the results of the subsequent analysis regarding the determinants of crisis resilience.

The second part of this chapter, section 3.2, outlines the empirical approach taken in this thesis to investigate the relationships between the variables of interest (economic institutions, political institutions and interest group activity) and crisis resilience. Unfortunately, previous research regarding this questions is very scarce. Therefore, as discussed in section 3.2, the approach taken in this thesis builds closely on another strand of literature that investigates the mainly non-institutional determinants of crisis resilience during the Great Recession and extends that analysis by adding further explanatory variables representing institutions and interest group activity.

3.1 Review of the Empirical Literature on Institutions, Interest Groups and Growth

Before turning to the outline of the empirical approach in section 3.2, this section 3.1 summarizes the complementary literature on the institutional and organizational determinants of economic growth. I order this review according to the two levels of analysis outlined in section 2.1. With reference to the first level of analysis, I first give an overview of (1) the literature investigating the relationship between *economic institutions* and growth, then, turn to (2) the relationship between *political institutions* and growth and, finally, summarize (3) the literature analyzing the potential effects of *interest group activity* on growth. With reference to the second level of analysis, I review (4) the literature examining the relationship between *political institutions* and *economic institutions*.[80] As the amount of previous research regarding each level of

[80] To my knowledge, there do not exist any empirical papers which analyze the relationship between interest group activity and economic institutions according to Olson's arguments. Considering that institutional sclerosis due to interest group activity is an important building block of Olson's theory, this lack of empirical research is a surprising gap within the Olson-related empirical literature.

R. Fritzsch, *Adaptive Efficiency During the Great Recession*,
Wirtschaft und Politik, https://doi.org/10.1007/978-3-658-27409-2_3

analysis is very large, this section focuses on general empirical tendencies based on seminal papers and other more detailed literature reviews.

(1) The first strand of the growth literature, which analyzes the effects of *economic institutions*, builds on neoclassical growth models, which understands output growth as a function of capital growth, labor growth, technological progress and human capital accumulation (Solow, 1956; Mankiw et al., 1992). Institutional economics, in turn, tries to explain the fundamental causes of these determinants of growth. According to North & Thomas (1973, p. 2), physical and human capital accumulation as well as technological innovations "are not causes of growth; they *are* growth", and the quality of institutions, in turn, explains the rate of advancement of these factors.[81] By putting institutions at the center of the analysis, institutional economics tries to mitigate certain prediction failures of neoclassical growth models, such as the inability to explain why many low-income countries exhibit lower growth rates than high-income countries (which contradicts the convergence hypothesis entailed by neoclassical growth models).[82] Starting in the 1980's and the 1990's, economic institutions were included systematically in growth regressions. These early studies, however, suffered from limited data quality, as indicators often captured both economic *and* political institutions at once.[83] As more indicators became available, an increasing literature emerged that reported significantly positive associations between economic institutions (usually market-creating institutions such as property rights and contract laws) and economic growth.[84] One methodological issue in these studies was the question whether significant coefficients between economic institutions and economic performance actually imply causality, as the causation might also run the other way allowing countries with good economic performance to afford better economic institutions. One seminal work which tackles this issue is Acemoglu et al. (2001). Looking at formerly colonized countries, these authors argue that settler mortality rates determined whether colonizers introduced extractive economic institutions or institutions of private property. Therefore, the settler mortality rate functions as an instrument variable that is theoretically related to the explanatory variable 'current institutions' but theoretically unrelated to the dependent variable 'current development'. Applying this technique, the authors conclude that good institutions *cause* better economic development.

---

81 In this earlier work, North & Thomas (1973, pp. 1-3) do not consequently use the phrase "institutions" but also other labels such as "efficient economic organization".

82 Keefer & Knack (1997), for example, show that the ability of poor countries to catch up (to grow faster than richer countries) depends on the security of property rights, the rule of law and the extent of corruption.

83 Kormendi & Meguire (1985) and Scully (1988), for example, use an index constructed by Gastil (1980), which includes political rights, civil liberties and properties of economic systems. Barro (1991) uses a count of coups and revolutions per year as an indicator for political stability. For a critique of both approaches see Knack & Keefer (1995).

84 For literature reviews see Aron (2000) and Ugur (2010). Important earlier studies include Knack & Keefer (1995), Mauro (1995) or Hall & Jones (1999).

While the earlier studies on the institutional prerequisites of economic growth focused primarily on market-creating institutions such as property rights and contract laws, more recent studies try to disentangle the effects of various types of economic institutions. Several authors, for example, analyze the effects of the different components of the 'Economic Freedom of the World Index' from the Fraser Institute or the 'Index of Economic Freedom' from the Heritage Foundation. While they mainly confirm the evidence from earlier studies by pointing out the positive effects of property rights and contract laws on economic development, they provide only inconclusive evidence regarding the effects of other aspects of economic freedom. Especially indices representing limited government size and trade openness are in some regressions even negatively related to economic growth. Indices representing sound money and absence of complex regulation usually show positive coefficients but are only partially significant.[85]

Following this short review, there exists considerable evidence regarding the positive effect of economic institutions on economic growth, most importantly of market-creating institutions such as secure property rights and contract laws. Results regarding other institutional features such as the size of government, freedom to trade or the extent of regulations are more ambiguous.

(2) A second strand of empirical literature analyzes the relationship between *political institutions* and economic growth. Theoretical positions range from the claim that democracy promotes growth by "constraining kleptocratic dictators, reducing social conflict or preventing politically powerful groups from monopolizing lucrative economic opportunities" (Acemoglu et al., 2014, pp. 4-5) to democracy-inhibits-growth arguments especially due to rent-creating redistributions in democracies (Meltzer & Richard, 1981).[86] Throughout the very large empirical literature, no clear picture emerges, as there exist results supporting either view.[87] Furthermore, even assuming there is positive associations between democracy and growth, it is not clear whether these associations reflect reverse causality running from higher levels of development to democracy (Lipset, 1959; Wu & Davis, 1999). In a meta-study of 483 regression estimates in 84 papers, Doucouliagos & Ulubaşoğlu (2008, p. 62) state "that 15% of the estimates are negative and statistically significant, 21% of the estimates are negative and statistically insignificant, 37% of the estimates are positive and

---

[85] See, for example Carlsson & Lundsstrom (2002), Berggreen & Jordahl (2005), Dawson (2006) or Rode & Coll (2012). For a survey see De Haan (2006).

[86] See also Irvin & Stansbury (2004) for a review of the potential drawbacks of citizen participation in public decision-making. Many of these argument also apply to democracy, in general.

[87] Important papers arguing that democracy leads to lower growth rates are Barro (1996), who finds negative net effects after controlling for rule of law, market freedom or high human capital, Tavares & Wacziarg (2001), who analyze different channels of influence and Gerring et al. (2005), who provide evidence that overall effects of democracy on growth are negative. Papers arguing that democracy fosters growth include Sala-i-Martin (1997), Rodrik & Wacziarg (2005), Persson & Tabellini (2007) and Acemoglu et al. (2014).

statistically insignificant, and 27% of the estimates are positive and statistically significant." Other literature reviews come to similar conclusions or find a slight tendency towards support for the claim that democracy promotes growth. One issue that stands out is that negative or insignificant coefficients of democracy variables often depend on the inclusion of certain control variables such as the quality of human capital or secure property rights (Knack & Keefer, 1995; Barro, 1996). Usually, democracy is positively related to growth when the respective control variables are excluded from the regressions, but coefficients turn negative or insignificant once human capital and economic institutions are controlled for. One possible interpretation of these effects is that democracy has indirect positive effects on growth because it promotes the accumulation of human capital (through the better provision of public education) and because democracies credibly enforce property rights and contract laws. Beyond these indirect effects, however, democracy does not promote growth.[88]

(3) Investigations regarding Mancur Olson's arguments almost entirely focus on growth rates as dependent variables, whereas they pay little attention to Olson's account of interest group activity affecting crisis resilience.[89] Within the growth-related literature, most studies aggregate steps 2 and 3 or 1, 2 and 3 of Olson's line of argument (as illustrated in section 2.2.1) by regressing the dependent variable 'growth' either against 'interest group activity'[90] or against 'the long-lasting stability of a society'[91]. The authors, therefore, analyze the two levels of analysis I and II together. According to literature reviews, results of both types of regression are mixed but weakly supportive of Olson's hypotheses, indicating that political stability and interest group activity have a negative impact on growth rates.[92]

Besides disregarding crisis resilience as the dependent variable, the existing literature is limited in other ways, as well. It, first, stands out that no study considers measures of institutional quality as dependent variables, although Olson makes clear predictions about the sclerotic institutional consequences of interest group activity. Furthermore, most of the existing studies are restricted to OECD countries, although, as stressed above and by other scholars (Heckelman, 2007), Olson's theory applies just as well to

---

88 See, for example, Borner et al. (2004, p. 56) or Sunde (2006). The latter conducts a literature review and concludes that especially the human-capital channel and the economic-institutions channel are relevant for understanding the positive effects of democracy on economic performance.

89 To my knowledge, there does not exist such an analysis. Heckelman (2007), who provides a comprehensive review of the empirical literature testing Olson's theory, mentions a few studies which consider dependent variables other than growth rates (such as income inequality or financial development). However, none of these refer to crisis resilience.

90 See, for example, Knack & Keefer (1997), Mc-Callum & Blais (1987), Heckelman (2000) or Knack (2003).

91 See, for example, Choi (1983), Weede (1984) or Tang & Hedley (1998).

92 Literature reviews about the very extensive amount of studies can be found particularly in Heckelman (2007) but also in Bischoff (2007) and Horgos & Zimmermann (2009).

less developed countries.[93] Hence, there are at least two important gaps in the Olson-related empirical literature, which can be approached with this thesis: the first involves looking at crisis resilience as the dependent variable and the second involves taking the two steps of Olson's argument separately (first, from the organizational strength of interest groups to institutional sclerosis and, second, from sclerotic economic institutions to lower crisis resilience). Furthermore, this analysis can be applied to less developed countries just as well as to developed countries, although, following Heckelman (2007),[94] the two groups of countries should be studied separately.

(4) The final strand of related literature, which corresponds to the second level of analysis according to the framework developed in section 2.1, investigates the determinants of institutional quality.[95] Some explanatory variables considered in these studies include cultural variables referring to the origin of the legal system and the preponderance of certain religions, social cohesion variables referring to inequality and ethnic diversity or incidental variables capturing the existence of natural rents, the level of development and trade openness. As dependent variables for institutional quality, some authors use composite measures that include economic and political institutions (Alsons & Garcimartin, 2013; Aixalá Pasto & Fabro Esteban, 2008). Furthermore, other authors regress political institutions on other political institutions and economic institutions on other economic institutions (Straub, 2000). Both approaches are inadequate from the viewpoint of the theoretical framework developed in chapter 2, as economic and political institutions need to be separated. Only few studies investigate the effects of political institutions on economic institutions. Studies which run such regressions come to the conclusion that democratic political institutions are indeed associated with 'good' economic institutions. Borner et al. (2004), for example, show that the strength of the state (especially in less developed countries) and the democratic commitment of the state both support high-quality economic institutions (especially secure property rights and contract laws); Islam & Montenegro (2002) report a positive association between checks and balances in the political system and measures of economic institutions (although they do not establish causality);[96] and Asongu & Kodila-Tedica (2016) show that those Sub-Sahara African countries with more democratic political institutions provide a better protection of property rights.

---

93 The few studies which analyze non-OECD countries include Chan (1987), Tang & Hedley (1998) or Knack (2003).

94 Heckelman (2007) stresses that developed and more stable countries should not be mixed with less developed and more unstable countries, as the number and strength of interest groups necessary for causing institutional sclerosis differs in both types of societies.

95 See La Porta et al. (1999), Straub (2000), Islam & Montenegro (2002), Alonso & Garcimartin (2013), Borner et al. (2004), Aixalá Pasto & Fabro Esteban (2008) and Asongu & Kodila-Tedica (2016).

96 When they measure the dependent variable representing 'good economic institutions' through indicators from the International Country Risk Guide, the 'checks and balances' variable is positive and significant. When using indicators from the World Governance Indicators Database, on the other hand, associations with political institutions are insignificant.

3.2 Outline of the Empirical Approach to Testing the Determinants of Crisis Resilience

While there exists an extensive literature studying the relationships between the variables of interest and output growth, only very few studies analyze the potential effects of institutions or interest group activity on crisis resilience. Notable exceptions include Rodrik (1999), Acemoglu et al. (2003), Giannone et al. (2011) and Bjornskov (2016). Furthermore, there are some papers which are relevant for certain aspects of the intended analysis in this thesis, as they investigate the effects of labor market institutions, financial institutions or government size during an economic crisis.[97] Of the related literature, especially Giannone et al. (2011) and Bjornskov (2016) are important points of reference. Bjornskov (2016), on the one hand, uses explanatory variables that conform to the variables of interest outlined in chapter 2, but he uses different dependent variables by looking at different crisis episodes through time. Giannone et al. (2011), on the other hand, investigate the determinants of the output decline during the years 2008 and 2009, thereby having the same object of investigation as this thesis. They, however, focus primarily on financial institutions and financial factors as explanatory variables without considering other economic institutions.

Giannone et al.'s (2011) paper and the closely related literature analyzing the determinants of output decline during the years 2008 and 2009 serve as main points of departure for the empirical analysis in chapter 4. That literature runs regressions with measures of crisis incidence as dependent variables and a variety of pre-crisis vulnerabilities as explanatory variables, including trade linkages, financial linkages or financial vulnerabilities. Apart from a few exceptions, the authors of these papers do not consider institutions or interest group activity as explanatory variables. Hence, their regressions take the general form:

$$Y_i = \propto + \beta \; Vuln_i + u_i \qquad (1)$$

Y_i is a vector measuring crisis incidence in different countries during the years 2008 to 2009, $Vuln_i$ is a matrix of different pre-crisis vulnerabilities, and u_i is the vector of country-specific residuals. In sections 4.1 and 4.2, I review that literature in detail and formulate a version of equation (1). Then, in sections 4.3 and 4.4, I add the explanatory variables of interest to assess the potential effects of economic institutions, political institutions and interest group activity.

In section 4.1, I first review the potential ways to define the dependent variable Y_i, that represents crisis resilience. Extending the scope of analysis of these papers, I do not solely construct a dependent variable for the downturn years 2008 and 2009 but also consider the subsequent years 2010 to 2012 during which the recovery took place in most countries.[98] Both periods capture different performance dimensions of crisis

[97] I discuss these papers in detail in the respective subsections in chapter 4.

[98] I discuss the timing of measurement of the dependent variables in section 4.1.2.

resilience and adaptive efficiency. While the development during the recession period 2008 to 2009 represents a country's ability to resist the original shock, the development during the recovery period 2010 to 2012 represents its ability to quickly resume a new growth path. Furthermore, I construct a third dependent variable covering the entire 5-year period 2008 to 2012 including the downturn and the recovery. Hence, in section 4.1, I specify the three dependent variables $Y_{i,08\text{-}09}$, $Y_{i,10\text{-}12}$ and $Y_{i,08\text{-}12}$.

Next, in section 4.2, I review the related literature with regard to non-institutional explanatory variables and formulate control models that include the most important pre-crisis vulnerabilities. Unfortunately, this choice of control models is associated with a high degree of model uncertainty because the related literature suggests a variety of potential variables representing each source of vulnerability. Therefore, any choice of a control model might open the door to criticism of allegedly picking the control variables that lead to the desired results. I address this problem by considering all relevant control variables together. To do this, I first apply principal component analysis to combine all variables representing the same source of vulnerability to single components. I, therefore, collapse a large number of original variables into a much smaller number of principal components. Then, I use these principal components (each representing one source of vulnerability) as new control variables.[99] Hence, in section 4.2.2, I formulate controls models that have the following general form:

$$Y_{i,08-12} = \propto + \beta\ Vuln_{i,07} + u_i \quad \text{(2a)}$$

$$Y_{i,08-09} = \propto + \beta\ Vuln_{i,07} + u_i \quad \text{(2b)}$$

$$Y_{i,10-12} = \propto + \beta\ Vuln_{i,07} + u_i \quad \text{(2c)}$$

$Y_{i,08\text{-}09}$, $Y_{i,10\text{-}12}$ and $Y_{i,08\text{-}12}$ are vectors of dependent variables as defined in section 4.1, $Vuln_{i,07}$ are matrices of the relevant pre-crisis vulnerabilities, and u_i are vectors of country-specific residuals. As it turns out, the pre-crisis vulnerabilities that affect the depth of the downturn during the years 2008 and 2009 are partly different from the vulnerabilities that affect the strength of the recovery 2010 to 2012. Therefore, $Vuln_{i,07}$ differs according to the time period covered by the dependent variable.

As the explanatory variables of interest are not pre-crisis vulnerabilities but institutions and interest group activity, I next add these variables to equations (2a), (2b) and (2c). In section 4.3, I first consider different economic institutions and run regressions that take the following form:

$$Y_i = \propto + \beta\ Vuln_{i,07} + \gamma\ Econ\ Inst_{i,07} + u_i \quad \text{(3)}$$

Y_i are vectors of the different measures of crisis resilience ($Y_{i,08\text{-}09}$, $Y_{i,10\text{-}12}$ and $Y_{i,08\text{-}12}$), $Vuln_{i,07}$ are matrices of the relevant pre-crisis vulnerabilities, $Econ\ Inst_{i,07}$ are different

[99] As robustness checks I also test whether the results change when using original variables as control variables. I discuss this approach in more detail in section 4.2.2.

vectors of economic institutions following Olson's and NWW's arguments, and u_i are vectors of country-specific residuals. In each of the sections 4.3.1 to 4.3.6, I consider one institution at a time. Thus, $Econ\ Inst_{i,07}$ in section 4.3.1 includes measures of impartially-enforced property rights and contract laws; in section 4.3.2 to 4.3.4 it contains measures of business, labor and financial regulations; and in section 4.3.5 it consists of variables representing government size. Furthermore, in section 4.3.6, I consider additional explanatory variables not discussed by Olson and NWW representing the exchange rate regime.[100] Finally, in section 4.3.7, I run regressions that include all relevant economic institutions together.

Before turning to political variables, three short notes are necessary about sections 4.3.1 to 4.3.7. First, for each institution $Econ\ Inst_{i,07}$ there exists a variety of potential measures, each capturing slightly different aspects of the respective institution. Instead of selecting one measure, I report the coefficients of all relevant variables. Besides avoiding criticism of allegedly picking the measure that entails the 'desired' results, this approach also provides a first robustness check. Second, I do not assess statistically whether the correlations between explanatory and dependent variables actually represent *causal* effects from the former to the latter, as this involves complications that go beyond the scope of this thesis, such as finding suitable instruments. I nevertheless try to minimize the problem of reverse-causality by using 2007-values of the explanatory variables, thereby excluding the possibility that the severity of the crisis affected the institutional variables (for example by stimulating reforms). Furthermore, following the discussion in chapter 2, there are strong theoretical arguments in favor of economic institutions having causal effects on crisis resilience.[101] Ultimately, however, the interpretation of the causality behind reported correlations remains partly open and is, therefore, a potential path for future research. Third, I do not consider explanatory variables representing fiscal or monetary policy. Although I do acknowledge that such policies are relevant for overcoming an economic crisis, I decided to leave the respective variables out of the analysis (or in the error term of the regressions) because they entail serious endogeneity problems. Other than institutions, fiscal and monetary policy responses depend strongly on the severity of the downturn. Therefore, it is much more difficult to avoid reverse causality. To keep the empirical analysis manageable, and because monetary and fiscal policies are not the main focus of this thesis, I leave the assessment of those variables to future research.

After analyzing the potential effects of economic institutions on crisis resilience, in section 4.4 I turn to variables representing political institutions and interest group activity. As, following the theoretical framework developed in chapter 2, these

---

[100] This variable might be relevant as it affects countries' abilities to adjust external prices, which is an alternative adjustment mechanism to the internal adjustments discussed by Olson and NWW.

[101] I further discuss causality issues in the respective sub-section and when interpreting the regression results.

variables can affect economic performance either directly (through discretionary policies) or indirectly (through supporting efficiency-enhancing economic institutions), I try to disentangle both channels. Beginning with potential indirect effects, I first run regressions featuring resilience-enhancing economic institutions as dependent variables. They take the following form:

$$Econ\ Inst_{i,07} = \propto + \beta\ Control_i + \gamma\ Pol\ Inst_{i,07} + u_i \tag{4}$$

$$Econ\ Inst_{i,07} = \propto + \beta\ Control_i + \varepsilon\ Org_{i,07} + u_i \tag{5}$$

$Econ\ Inst_{i,07}$ are resilience-enhancing economic institutions according to the results of the regressions in section 4.3, $Control_i$ are cultural or societal control variables that may have an impact on the choice of economic institutions,[102] $Pol\ Inst_{i,07}$ and $Org_{i,07}$ are the explanatory variables of interest whose potential effects on resilience-enhancing economic institutions I want to assess, and u_i are country-specific error terms. The two coefficients γ and ε represent the associations between the explanatory political variables and resilience-enhancing economic institutions. Following the theoretical arguments, these associations have to be interpreted differently. While Olson's argument implies that interest group activity (represented by $Org_{i,07}$) has a unidirectional causal effect on economic institutions, the associations between political and economic institutions following NWW's argument is based on a double balance between the two institutional features.

The second step of the analysis in section 4.4 involves adding the two explanatory variables $Pol\ Inst_{i,07}$ and $Org_{i,07}$ to equations (2) to assess the potential effects of political institutions and interest group activity on crisis resilience. I, therefore run regressions that do not include economic institutions as explanatory variables:

$$Y_i = \propto + \beta\ Vuln_{i,07} + \delta\ Pol\ Inst_{i,07} + u_i \tag{6}$$

$$Y_i = \propto + \beta\ Vuln_{i,07} + \theta\ Org_{i,02} + u_i \tag{7}$$

By not including economic institutions in these regressions, the coefficients δ and θ indicate the directions and strengths of the *overall* relationships between the two political variables of interest and crisis resilience. These relationships may include direct effects *and* indirect effects that are mediated through the choice of resilience-enhancing economic institutions according to equations (4) and (5). Next, I run two regressions that also include economic institutions:

$$Y_i = \propto + \beta\ Vuln_{i,07} + \gamma\ Econ\ Inst_{i,07} + \delta\ Pol\ Inst_{i,07} + u_i \tag{8}$$

$$Y_i = \propto + \beta\ Vuln_{i,07} + \gamma\ Econ\ Inst_{i,07} + \theta\ Org_{i,02} + u_i \tag{9}$$

The coefficients δ and θ indicate the directions and strength of the direct effects of political institutions and interest group activity on crisis resilience that are not

[102] I derive these control variables from the literature regarding the determinants of institutional quality reviewed in section 3.1. For a more detailed discussion see appendix 57.

mediated through supporting resilience-enhancing economic institutions. By comparing these coefficients to the coefficients of equations (6) and (7), it is possible to disentangle potential direct and indirect effects of political institutions and interest group activity on crisis resilience and to compare them to the hypotheses derived from Olson's and NWW's theoretical accounts.

Before turning to the empirical analysis in the next chapter, two more general remarks are necessary regarding the sample and the method.

First, the sample I will consider only contains countries that have a yearly GDP above ten billion USD,[103] that do not depend heavily on oil exports[104] and that were not involved in internal or external armed conflicts during the years 2008 to 2012.[105] I also drop Turkmenistan from the sample due to very limited data availability regarding the majority of control and explanatory variables. Finally, anticipating the results from section 4.2.3, I exclude Luxembourg because that country (being a major financial center) features extraordinarily high values of financial control variables, which makes it unsuitable for principal component analysis (which I use for combining control variables).[106] Overall, following these criteria, 84 countries remain in the sample.[107]

Besides running regressions with all 84 countries, I also divide the sample into a group of 32 developed countries and 52 less developed countries based on the classification made by the International Monetary Fund (2016) between advanced economies and non-advanced economies.[108] This IMF distinction roughly represents the distinction

[103] I exclude small economies to ensure comparability. Identification of country size is based on the indicator 'GDP (current US$)' from the World Development Indicators Database (indicator code: NY.GDP.MKTP.CD).

[104] I try to exclude countries whose GDP development is heavily affected by oil-price movements. Identification of major oil-exporting countries is based on the indicator 'oil rents (% of GDP)' from the World Development Indicators Database (indicator code: NY.GDP.PETR.RT.ZS). I exclude countries whose oil rents contributed to more than 10 % of its GDP before the onset of the crisis in 2007.

[105] I try to exclude countries whose GDP development is heavily affected by non-economic factors. Identification of armed conflicts is based on the Armed Conflict Database Version 17.2 from the Uppsala Conflict Data Program (UCDP) and the International Peace Research Institute, Oslo (PRIO). I only consider conflicts with high intensity (more than 1.000 battle-related deaths per year). For further information on the dataset see Gleditsch et al. (2002) and Allansson et al. (2017).

[106] For details see section 4.2.3.

[107] See Appendix 1 for details on the selection of the sample.

[108] Throughout the literature there does not exist a classification based on strict, objective criteria (Nielsen, 2011). The IMF (2016, pp. 205-206) points out that its own classification evolved over time and has the objective to "facilitate analysis by providing a reasonably meaningful method of organizing data". Other potential classifications such as the one based on the Human Development Index, which distinguishes between highly developed and less developed countries, overlap strongly with the IMF classification (Nielsen, 2011). The classification of countries in this thesis is explained in Appendix 1.

between open access economies and limited access economies.[109] I divide the sample because I would like to assess whether, following NWW (2009, p. 139), certain institutions indeed work differently in open access and in limited access orders and because Olson's and NWW's accounts suggest that both country groups should be assessed separately.

Second, throughout the empirical analysis, I use OLS to estimate the size of the effects of interest. In the regressions that are central for the argument in section 4.3.7 and 4.4, I test for heteroscedasticity using the White test,[110] check for model miss-specifications using the RESET test[111] and assess the normality of the residuals through the Jarque-Bera test.[112] Given the very large amount of preliminary regressions in sections 4.3.1 to 4.3.6 and 4.4.1 to 4.4.2, which lead to the final specifications in sections 4.3.7 and 4.4.3, I do not undertake a detailed analyses of all OLS model assumptions in the those sections.[113] I only consider the critical model assumption of no perfect multicollinearity throughout the entire empirical analysis by reporting correlations amongst independent variables. Furthermore, I use heteroscedasticity-robust standard errors in all regressions to avoid incorrect p-values. Throughout the regressions, especially the assumption of normally-distributed residuals is violated in some instances. As, however, that model assumption is not crucial for receiving unbiased results, I do not take non-normally distributed residuals to be general qualifications of the empirical findings. Furthermore, in almost all regressions I use sample sizes above 30, which, according to a variety of textbooks,[114] is usually large enough for the central-limits theorem to hold.[115] As, however, 30 is not a sufficient size in every particular case (Wooldridge, 2006, p. 183), I furthermore show in section 4.3.7

[109] It is necessary to point out that the 32 developed countries are open access *economies* not general open access *societies*, as the two countries Singapore and Hong Kong are not democracies (which is a necessary condition of an open access political system) but feature open access economic institutions (scoring very high in almost all economic freedom indices). I decided to adopt a classification of countries according to economic criteria because the main part of this thesis - section 4.3 - analyses the effects of economic institutions on crisis resilience. Putting Singapore and Hong Kong in the less developed group throughout section 4.3 would be an undue misclassification. When analyzing the effects of political factors in section 4.4, however, I pay specific attention to the cases of these two countries and to the results that emerge when classifying them differently.

[110] The test goes back to White (1980). For a textbook illustration see also Hill et al. (2008, p. 215).

[111] The test goes back to Ramsey (1969). For textbook explications see Hill et al. (2008, pp. 151-152) or Wooldridge (2006, pp. 308-309). I use the versions of the RESET test with squared predicted values as additional explanatory variables.

[112] The test goes back to Jarque & Bera (1980). See also Hill et al. (2008, pp. 89-90).

[113] I report potential violation of model assumptions, in detail, in tables 41, 43, 45, 50, 51 and 56 as well as in appendices 48, 49, 51, 52, 53, 55, 56, 64, 65, 69, 75, 76 and 77.

[114] See, for example, Hill et al. (2008, p. 33), Stock & Watson (2007, p. 52) or Wooldridge (2006, p. 183). Others, such as Backhaus et al. (2011, p. 96) state that sample sizes of 40 are usually large enough.

[115] The central limits theorem states that, if the other OLS model assumption hold and if the sample size is sufficiently large (see the previous footnote), the least squares estimators have a distribution that approximates a normal distribution. See Hill et al. (2008, p. 33).

that the main findings regarding the small sub-sample of 32 developed countries do not change when excluding the outlier (Greece) that is responsible for non-normally-distributed residuals.

4. The Empirical Analysis of Adaptive Efficiency during the Great Recession 2008 to 2012

As outlined in the previous section, the empirical analysis in this chapter contains four main parts. The first part, section 4.1, is dedicated to defining the three dependent variables $Y_{i,08-12}$, $Y_{i,08-09}$ and $Y_{i,10-12}$. Next, section 4.2 deals with the selection of control variables and control models. Then, section 4.3 assesses the potential effects of economic institutions on crisis resilience. Finally, section 4.4 analyzes the way political institutions and interest group activity are related to economic institutions and crisis resilience.

4.1 The Definition of the Dependent Variables

This section deals with the definition of the dependent variables $Y_{i,08-12}$, $Y_{i,08-09}$ and $Y_{i,10-12}$, which represent the severity of the recession and the strength of the recovery. In order to derive such indicators, I first provide a short review and discussion of different ways to define crisis intensity throughout the related literature in section 4.1.1. Then, in section 4.1.2, I explain the resilience measures I employ in this thesis and report the resilience scores of all countries within the utilized sample.

4.1.1 Literature Review and Discussion of Potential Dependent Variables

There are at least two important strands of literature that use measures of crisis intensity and, therefore, provide points of reference for the definition of the dependent variables. First, there is an extensive literature which aims at detecting early-warning indicators to help predicting potential economic crises.[116] Second, and more importantly, there exists a considerable amount of research papers trying to explain the intensity of a *specific* economic crisis, such as the one studied in this thesis.[117] Following these two strands of literature, the various ways to measure crisis intensity can be classified along two dimensions, as depicted in figure 5: first, regarding the *scale of the crisis intensity variable* and, second, regarding the *type of crisis measurement*. Below, I explain each distinction, starting with (1) the scale of the crisis intensity variable and, then, turning to (2) the type of measurement.

[116] Reviews of this literature can be found in Kaminsky et al. (1998), Abiad (2003) and Frankel & Saravelos (2012).

[117] See, for example, Berglöf et al. (2010), Berkman et al. (2012), Blanchard et al. (2010), Claessens et al. (2010), Frankel & Saravelos (2012), Giannone et al. (2011), Groot et al. (2011), Lane & Milesi-Ferretti (2011) and Rose & Spiegel (2010, 2011, 2012).

R. Fritzsch, *Adaptive Efficiency During the Great Recession*,
Wirtschaft und Politik, https://doi.org/10.1007/978-3-658-27409-2_4

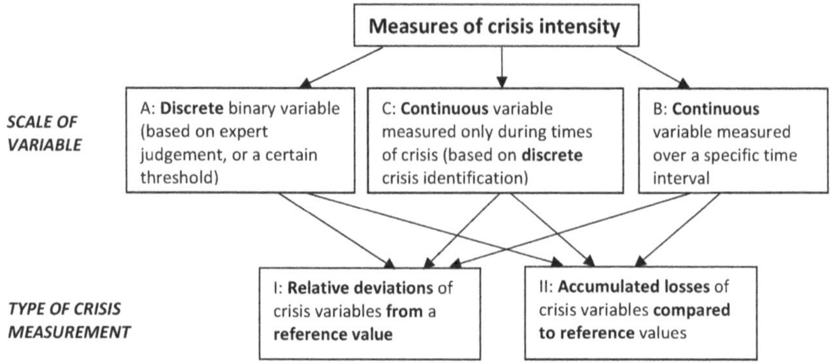

Figure 5: Classification of crisis intensity measures in the related literature.

(1) Crisis intensity variables may be scaled in three different ways: as discrete variables (A), as continuous variables (B), or as mixed variables with a continuous scale based on discrete crisis identification (C).

Discrete variables (A), which are more common in the early-warning literature, usually report crisis occurrence and crisis timing as binary yes/no variables. The decision whether a crisis variable takes the value 1 (crisis) or 0 (no crisis) depends either on expert judgments[118] or on the question whether an underlying crisis variable (which may be measured in various ways according to the second dimension, the *type of crisis measurement*) exceeds a certain crisis threshold.[119] The most serious disadvantage of this approach is the loss of information about the actual severity of the crisis. Countries barely missing the crisis threshold remain in the no-crisis group together with unaffected economies, while other countries that perform just slightly worse move into the crisis group together with economies that are severely affected. Another disadvantage of this approach stems from the necessity to define specific crisis thresholds adequately, which is always somewhat arbitrary.

The second approach to specify crisis intensity is via continuous variables (B). It is the most common approach in papers studying cross-country variations of crisis intensity during a specific economic crisis such as the Great Recession.[120] This method avoids having to define exact thresholds and offers the advantage that small differences

[118] Caprio & Klingebiel (2002, p. 31), who compile a frequently updated list of systematic banking crises, base the identification of the crisis period on the judgement of "finance experts familiar with the countries".

[119] Examples include Frankel & Rose (1996, p. 352), who define a currency crisis "as a nominal depreciation of the currency of at least 25% that is also at least a 10% increase in the rate of depreciation", or Eichengreen et al. (1994), who identify an exchange market crisis whenever an index consisting of interest rates, reserve loss and currency depreciation is two standard deviations above its mean.

[120] All papers cited in footnote 117 use this approach.

among units of analysis (countries) become visible. Scholars who follow this approach simply measure crisis intensity in terms of a certain underlying crisis definition variable over the same time interval for all countries. This approach, however, has the disadvantage that it includes all countries, irrespective of whether they actually faced an economic crisis or not. Furthermore, measuring crisis variables over a fixed time interval is an inadequate approach if downturns or recoveries in different countries occur at different points in time.

The mixed approach (C) tries to combine the advantages of the two methods explained above. Similar to the second approach (B), scholars specify crisis intensity as a continuous variable. This variable, however, only takes values different from zero during times of crisis. The identification of crisis occurrence, in turn, depends on expert judgment or on the passing of certain thresholds for the beginning and the end of a crisis, which resembles the first approach (A).[121] Although this mixed approach leads to a continuous dependent variable, it doesn't mitigate the problem of having to define crisis thresholds. Furthermore, measuring crisis intensity of different countries over different time intervals still makes meaningful comparisons difficult.

(2) The second dimension along which measures of crisis intensity can be distinguished is according to *the type of crisis measurement*. While some scholars measure crisis intensity as the *relative deviation* of a crisis variable from a reference value (I) at the end of the relevant time period, others define it as the *accumulated deviations* of a crisis variable from a reference value during the whole time interval, thereby capturing the accumulated economic costs of a crisis (II). Common to both approaches is the need to define a reference value for comparisons, which represents the hypothetical no-crisis situation. The underlying crisis variable in both cases can either be a single variable or an index.

The most common way to measure crisis intensity in terms of (I) *relative deviations* from a reference value is relating GDP to its pre-crisis level, its pre-crisis trend or its pre-crisis forecast. Other potential variables underlying crisis measurement are changes of unemployment rates, currency depreciations and drops in demand, consumption or industrial production.[122] Furthermore, some authors define crises in

---

[121] Babecky et al. (2011, 2013) employ this approach by constructing a continuous 'index of real economic costs' (IRC). This index only takes a value different from zero if another binary index, the 'crisis occurrence index' (COI), indicates that an economic crisis actually existed. This 'crisis occurrence index' is based on the crisis identification by other scholars. Furthermore, Laeven & Valencia (2008) build a database in which crisis identification is based on subjective assessments, quantitative data and systematic literature reviews. As they complement crisis identification with further information on the depth of the crisis, their approach may be classified as *mixed*, as well.

[122] Berglöf et al. (2010), Frankel & Saravelos (2012), Giannone et al. (2011), Groot et al. (2011), Lane & Milesi-Ferretti (2011) all use actual growth rates during the years 2008 and 2009 as dependent variables (thereby relating GDP to its pre-crisis level). Additionally to looking at simple growth rates, Berglöf et al. (2010) and Claessens et al. (2010) also consider deviations of growth rates from trend growth, Groot et al (2011) consider changes in unemployment rates, Frankel & Saravelos (2012)

terms of indices capturing a broader range of variables at once.[123] This general approach works well for shorter time periods capturing only downturns *or* only recoveries, but it has disadvantages during longer time periods including both downturns *and* recoveries, as it disregards different trajectories of variable movements. To illustrate this problem, figure 6 shows two hypothetical paths of a crisis variable (e.g. GDP or a crisis index).

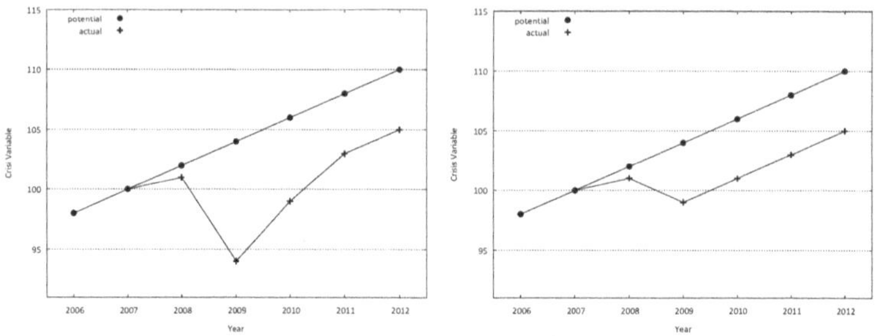

Figure 6: Two hypothetical trajectories of a crisis variable representing a deep and a mild recession.

The upper straight graphs in both cases represent a reference value for comparisons such as a pre-crisis trend value or a pre-crisis forecast, and the lower graphs represent actual movements of the variable in question. In the final year 2012, the crisis variables in both hypothetical cases take the same value (105). Calculating the relative deviation of this actual value (105) either from the trend value of the year 2012 (110) or from the pre-crisis value of the year 2007 (100) yields the same crisis intensity scores. Figure 6, however, illustrates that the losses in the first case at the left panel were much larger during the downturn than in the second case at the right panel. Using a relative-deviation measure based on 2012-values does not capture this information.

The accumulated-loss approach tries to remedy this loss of information. It aims at capturing the economic costs of a crisis by accumulating the deviations of the crisis variable from the reference values over the whole time interval in question.[124] Applying

look at changes in industrial production, equity market returns and currency exchange rates, and Lane & Milesi-Ferretti (2011) examine changes in growth rates, consumption growth and private demand growth during the years 2008 and 2009. Berkman et al. (2012) and Blanchard et al. (2010) compare actual growth rates in 2008 and 2009 to growth forecasts before the crisis.

[123] Rose & Spiegel (2010) create an index based on changes in GDP, the stock market, country credit ratings and exchange rates. Babecky et al. (2011, 2013) focus on real variables. They consider a simple average of the real GDP gap, increases of unemployment above its long-term trend and increases in the government's budget deficit.

[124] Some papers calculate the accumulated loss as the sum of the deviations of actual growth from trend growth. Examples are Bordo et al. (2001, p. 55), who calculate output losses "by cumulating – from the onset to the recovery – the difference between pre-crisis trend growth and actual growth", and IMF (1998, p. 78), who add up "the differences between trend growth and actual growth in the years following the crisis until the time when output growth returned to its trend". Instead of comparing growth rates, other papers compare GDP to its pre-crisis level or its pre-crisis

this approach to figure 6, for example, would mean summing up all five vertical deviations of the actual values from their respective potential values for the years 2008 to 2012. Using this approach is more common when looking at longer time periods. But even then, it exhibits disadvantages of its own because earlier developments affect the crisis intensity measure more strongly than later developments, thereby overstating the importance of the former vis-à-vis the latter. To illustrate this problem, figure 7 displays two different hypothetical paths of a crisis variable.

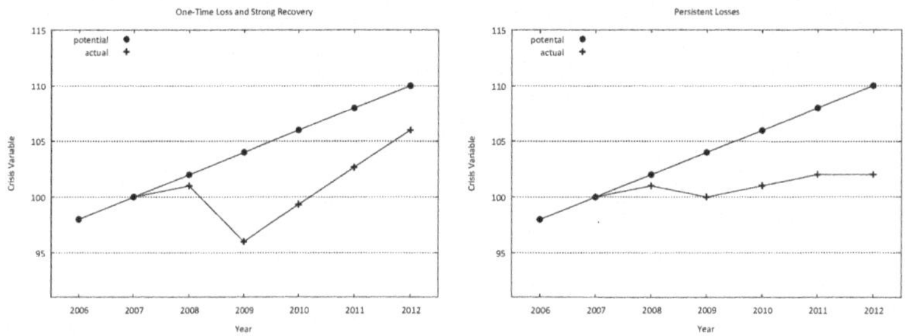

Figure 7: Two hypothetical trajectories of a crisis variable representing strong initial losses and persistent losses during the entire time period.

Both hypothetical countries fall eight points below their pre-crisis trend at one point in time during the period in question. The country at the left panel loses eight points with respect to its pre-crisis trend already in the second year of the crisis 2009 but recovers strongly thereafter, almost returning back to the pre-crisis trend in the final year 2012. The second hypothetical country, on the other hand, departs further from its pre-crisis trend every year, ending up eight points below its pre-crisis trend in the final year 2012. Although both hypothetical countries sustain the same output decline of eight points and although the first country ends up in a much better final position, it still features higher accumulated losses because the strong initial losses in 2009 also affect the deviation from the pre-crisis trend in the subsequent years 2010 and 2011.[125]

4.1.2 Operationalizing the Dependent Variables Representing Crisis Resilience

In the empirical analysis of this thesis, I define the dependent variables representing crisis resilience as *continuous* variables measured over fixed time intervals (B) based on *relative-deviations* (I) of the actual *Gross Domestic Product (GDP)* from potential

trend. Cecchetti et al. (2009) measure the cumulative output loss by adding up relative deviations of GDP from its pre-crisis level during the crisis interval. Boyd et al. (2005) calculate the cumulated deviations of actual output from its pre-crisis trend. Hoggarth et al. (2001) add up the deviations of actual growth from trend growth and the deviation of actual output levels from trend levels.

[125] In the hypothetical case depicted in figure 7, the crisis variable of the country at the left panel takes the values 100, 101, 96, 99.33, 102.66 and 106, which leads to accumulated losses of -25 points. The second country features scores of 100, 101, 100, 101, 102 and 102, which leads to accumulated losses of -24 points.

values. Below, I first (1) motivate this choice and, then, (2) define the actual explanatory variables I will use throughout the subsequent empirical analysis.

(1) First, I focus on the *Gross Domestic Product* as the underlying crisis variable because it is the most fundamental expression of economic performance and because the main reference literature focuses on the same variable.[126] Although, it would be interesting to consider additional dependent variables such as changes of unemployment rates or inequality, as well, I leave these investigations to future research because they would heavily inflate the already extensive empirical analysis in this thesis.

Second, I construct *continuous* variables as measures of crisis intensity and measure them over the same fixed time interval (instead of only during times of crisis occurrence, as in approach C). By proceeding this way, I avoid having to define thresholds for the beginning and the end of the crisis, which is always somewhat arbitrary. Furthermore, the potential disadvantages of using continuous variables over fixed time periods are less relevant for the particular case of the Great Recession, mainly out of two reasons. First, the economic distress affected most countries nearly at the same time during the years 2008 and 2009 (Blanchard et al., 2010; Berglöf et al, 2010; Claessens et al., 2010). Hence, there is less need to look at different time intervals in different countries. Second, the need to distinguish crisis countries from no-crisis countries is less relevant for the research question posed in this thesis. If a country avoided to fall below a certain crisis threshold (however it is defined), while others suffered recessions, I do not want to exclude the former from the sample but rather ask the question *why* it performed better. Finally, the related papers studying the determinants of cross-country crisis incidence use continuous variables measured over a fixed time interval, as well. To make the regression results of this thesis comparable to the results from that reference literature, I follow the same approach.

Third, I use the *relative-deviations* approach instead of the accumulated-loss approach. As both approaches have advantages and disadvantages, each choice is associated with certain trade-offs. I decided to calculate crisis resilience in terms of relative deviations of GDP from a reference value mainly because the related literature proceeds the same way. Following that lead facilitates the comparability of empirical findings.[127]

Hence, I construct three different dependent variables based on relative deviations of actual GDP from reference values. One variable represents the downturn period 2008 to 2009, one the period of potential recovery 2010 to 2012 and one the entire period 2008 to 2012. Before, however, turning to the definitions of these three crisis variables, the choice of the time intervals needs a short explanation.

Starting with the downturn, the more exact timing in most countries was the time period stretching from the last quarter of 2008 to the second quarter of 2009

[126] See footnote 117.

[127] In fact, I experimented with both approaches, and both dependent variables are highly correlated and feature very similar results.

(Blanchard et al., 2010; Berglöf et al, 2010). Accordingly, some authors look at quarterly data to capture only that shorter time period (Blanchard et al., 2010). I, nevertheless, use annual data covering the whole two-year period from the beginning of 2008 until the end of 2009 out of several reasons. First, although there was a high degree of simultaneity of crisis occurrence in most countries, the exact timing still varied slightly. Especially some advanced economies were affected already in the first half of 2008, while others entered the recession only in 2009 (Claessens et al., 2010). Looking at the broader time span of two years assures that all losses are captured, irrespective of the exact timing in each country. Second, using annual data increases the sample size due to better data availability. Third, using annual data also avoids complications from different seasonal adjustments for different geographical areas. Finally, the bigger part of the reference literature uses annual data as well. Proceeding the same way, again, facilitates comparison of empirical findings.[128]

Next, looking at the three years 2010 to 2012 as the period of potential recovery is a somewhat arbitrary but not unreasonable choice. First, starting in 2010 (and not, for example, in the second half of 2009) assures that the initial downturn is already finished in the great majority of countries. Second, calculations of business cycle durations show that three years is a reasonable time interval. Everts (2006) for example calculates that upswings (in terms of GDP) in Great Britain lasted on average 19 quarters (4.75 years). Hence, looking at a three-year period should be short enough not to contain the next slowdown but still long enough to capture sufficient variation amongst countries.[129]

(2) Following the previous discussion, I illustrate the construction of the three measures of crisis resilience for the three time periods based on figure 8, which displays the movement of the German GDP from 2007 to 2012. The fluctuating curve (black dots) displays the actual GDP movements, measured in billions of the national currency at a constant price level.[130] The output decline in the years 2008 and 2009 and the partial recovery in the subsequent years 2010 to 2012 are apparent. The straight line on the top (white triangles) displays the long-term trend based on average growth rates during the previous 10 years.[131] This curve represents potential German GDP if there had been no crisis. The third, straight curve on the bottom (white squares) displays a crisis-adjusted trend with the same average growth rate as before the crisis at a lower level. It portrays a hypothetical situation in which the country suffered the losses it actually did in 2008 and 2009 but then continued to grow at its pre-crisis average growth rates during the years 2010 to 2012. This line represents a

[128] Authors who also look at the entire two-year period include Lane & Milesi-Ferretti (2011), Giannone et al. (2011), Berglöf et al. (2010) and Claessens et al. (2010) with their third indicator.

[129] Furthermore, one of the few papers studying the determinants of post-crisis recovery also uses a three year period. See Jovanovic (2012).

[130] The base year is 2010. The data source is the IMF's World Economic Outlook Database.

[131] Again, I use data from the IMF's World Economic Outlook Database.

discriminating benchmark between countries that recovered some of the losses from the years 2008 and 2009 and countries that did not. Figure 8 shows that Germany performed better than this benchmark during the years 2010 to 2012, thereby regaining some of the initial losses from 2008 and 2009.

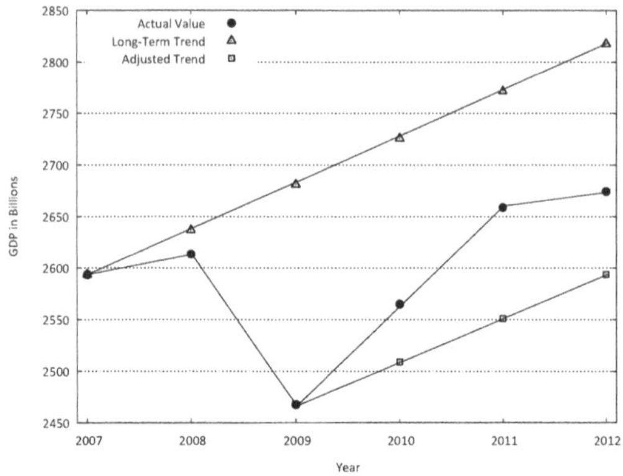

Figure 8: Actual values and trends of German GDP, 2007-2012 (in billions of local currency at constant prices).

Based on figure 8, I define the three crisis resilience variables in terms of GDP as follows:[132]

- The first variable '$GDP_{08\text{-}12}$' measures the relative deviation of actual GDP from its long-term trend value in 2012 according to the following formula:

  $$'GDP_{08-12}' = (\text{Actual GDP}_{12} - \text{Trend GDP}_{12})/(\text{Trend GDP}_{12})$$

  Lower values indicate worse crisis resilience because actual GDP in 2012 is further below the counterfactual long-term trend. This approach is similar to Abiad et al. (2009).[133]

- The second variable '$GDP_{08\text{-}09}$' measures the relative deviation of actual GDP from its long-term trend value in 2009. Its calculation is analogous to that of the previous variable, only for a shorter time interval:

  $$'GDP_{08-09}' = (\text{Actual GDP}_{09} - \text{Trend GDP}_{09})/(\text{Trend GDP}_{09})$$

  As before, lower values mean worse crisis resilience during the downturn 2008 and 2009 because they indicate heavier losses during that period. This variable

[132] Calculations of the three different dependent variables are based on data from the IMF's World Economic Outlook Database. GDP is measured in the national currency at constant prices. For Serbia, calculations of the long-term trend start in 1999 instead of 1998 due to lack of data for the first year.

[133] They, however, choose a post-crisis window of 7 years to capture medium-term output losses. Furthermore, they use a different approach for calculating the pre-crisis trend, as they consider the time period that starts ten years and ends three years before the onset of the crisis.

is similar to crisis intensity variables used by Lane & Milesi-Ferretti (2011), Claessens et al. (2010) and Berglöf et al. (2010) when considering a large sample of countries.[134]

- The third variable '$GDP_{10\text{-}12}$' measures the relative deviation of GDP in the year 2012 from the adjusted trend value, according to the formula:

$$'GDP_{10-12}' = (\text{Actual GDP}_{12} - \text{Adj. Trend GDP}_{12})/(\text{Adj. Trend GDP}_{12})$$

Positive values of this variable indicate that the country recovered some of its previous losses during the years 2010 to 2012 by growing faster than before the crisis and moving closer to its pre-crisis growth path. A value of zero implies that losses from 2008 and 2009 remained permanent. The economy neither moved back towards its former trend nor sustained further losses. Rather, it re-established pre-crisis growth rates at a lower level. Negative values indicate that the economy featured lower growth rates during the years 2010 to 2012 than before the crisis, moving further away from its pre-crisis trend and sustaining further losses. This approach resembles that of Jovanovic (2012), who relates post-crisis growth rates to average pre-crisis growth rates.

Before reporting the scores, one more remark is necessary to explain why all measures compare actual values to some type of long-term trend instead of pre-crisis values. Using the trend as a benchmark aims at ensuring comparability of a wider range of countries with different growth fundamentals. In line with the convergence hypothesis,[135] for example, emerging and developing economies often grow faster than highly developed countries. During the years 2008 and 2009 the former faced similar declines of growth rates as the latter. However, because many of them came from higher initial rates, their output growth during these years often did not turn negative.[136] Just looking at simple growth rates, which is analogous to using GDP 2007 as a benchmark, would provide a distorted picture, as countries with higher pre-crisis growth rates would appear to have been affected less severely by the crisis. Following the previous definitions, table 1 depicts the scores for all 84 countries in the sample ordered according to the scores for the period 2008 to 2012.

[134] Lane & Milesi-Ferretti (2011) follow this approach but use a different reference period for calculating counterfactual trend growth. In other specifications, they use simple growth rates during the years 2008 to 2009 as dependent variables but control for pre-crisis trends. Claessens et al. (2010) define one of their dependent variables as the difference between 2008/09 growth and pre-crisis growth. Berglöf et al. (2010) proceed the same way when they use a large worldwide sample of heterogeneous countries. Finally, Berkman et al. (2012) and Blanchard et al. (2010) compare actual growth rates in 2008 and 2009 to growth forecasts from before the crisis

[135] In its simplest form, the hypothesis of unconditional convergence states that poorer countries grow faster than richer countries because, having a lower initial capital stock and based on the assumption of diminishing returns of capital, they face higher marginal productivity of capital. For an overview of the convergence literature, see Islam (2003).

[136] For a good illustration of this point see Blanchard et al. (2010).

Country	Resilience 2008-12	Resilience 2008-09	Resilience 2010-12
Uruguay	22,67	8,78	12,77
Ghana	21,24	4,02	16,55
Ethiopia	18,65	7,55	10,32
Indonesia	17,26	6,42	10,19
Lebanon	15,19	13,00	1,94
Zambia	12,62	5,67	6,58
Peru	10,18	1,71	8,33
Paraguay	9,81	-1,10	11,03
Cote d'Ivoire	9,59	4,24	5,13
Panama	8,38	-1,10	9,59
Bolivia	7,51	2,85	4,53
Nepal	4,46	2,91	1,51
Kenya	4,38	-3,51	8,18
Colombia	4,17	-0,98	5,20
Brazil	3,22	-1,02	4,28
Philippines	2,20	-2,93	5,28
Bangladesh	0,91	-0,59	1,51
Tanzania	0,54	-0,90	1,45
Uganda	0,02	4,06	-3,89
Malaysia	-0,01	-5,05	5,31
Morocco	-0,67	0,95	-1,61
Chile	-0,91	-5,58	4,95
India	-0,96	-1,86	0,91
Argentina	-1,55	-7,39	6,31
Israel	-1,82	-3,20	1,42
Singapore	-2,00	-9,18	7,91
Cameroon	-2,18	-2,70	0,54
China	-2,66	-1,00	-1,68
Thailand	-3,09	-6,47	3,62
Poland	-4,00	-1,78	-2,26
Vietnam	-4,66	-2,38	-2,34
Mexico	-4,76	-8,75	4,38
Guatemala	-4,80	-3,58	-1,26
Australia	-4,85	-2,71	-2,20
Germany	-4,90	-7,91	3,28
Turkey	-5,23	-11,69	7,32
Japan	-5,63	-8,34	2,95
Switzerland	-5,97	-4,69	-1,35
Senegal	-6,00	-2,99	-3,10
Botswana	-6,32	-10,54	4,71
Hong Kong	-6,43	-7,75	1,43
South Africa	-7,91	-5,55	-2,50
Korea, Rep.	-7,97	-5,91	-2,18
Honduras	-8,19	-6,76	-1,54
Jordan	-8,44	0,88	-9,25
Belgium	-8,52	-6,15	-2,53
Canada	-9,32	-7,92	-1,51
Austria	-9,32	-7,22	-2,27
Dominican Rep.	-9,53	-6,70	-3,04
France	-9,87	-7,23	-2,85
New Zealand	-9,96	-6,68	-3,52
El Salvador	-10,17	-7,32	-3,08
Belarus	-10,50	-4,21	-6,57
Costa Rica	-10,52	-8,75	-1,94
Jamaica	-10,56	-6,58	-4,26
United States	-11,11	-8,69	-2,65
Tunisia	-11,42	-2,15	-9,48
Denmark	-12,45	-9,48	-3,29
Netherlands	-12,94	-7,34	-6,04
Georgia	-13,61	-13,35	-0,31
Italy	-13,74	-9,23	-4,97
Sweden	-13,76	-11,94	-2,07
United Kingdom	-13,78	-10,28	-3,91
Slovak Republic	-13,86	-9,30	-5,02
Albania	-14,54	-2,95	-11,95
Portugal	-15,82	-6,72	-9,76
Czech Republic	-15,84	-9,20	-7,32
Serbia	-15,97	-5,92	-10,68
Romania	-16,70	-6,94	-10,49
Cyprus	-18,26	-6,66	-12,43
Finland	-20,04	-14,20	-6,81
Bulgaria	-20,35	-8,73	-12,73
Hungary	-20,96	-12,44	-9,72
Bosn. & Herzegov.	-22,07	-7,21	-16,01
Spain	-22,42	-9,71	-14,08
Slovenia	-23,59	-12,50	-12,68
Croatia	-24,47	-12,13	-14,05
Iceland	-24,63	-12,30	-14,06
Lithuania	-29,17	-23,18	-7,80
Ukraine	-30,84	-22,58	-10,67
Estonia	-32,49	-29,20	-4,65
Ireland	-33,27	-19,76	-16,84
Greece	-37,38	-11,70	-29,08
Latvia	-39,56	-28,87	-15,03

Table 1: Resilience scores for all 84 countries in the sample.

The listing already shows that the most severely affected countries are predominantly emerging economies from Eastern Europe and advanced economies such as Greece, Ireland, Iceland and Spain. The countries with the best resilience scores, on the other hand, are emerging and developing economies located in Latin America, Africa or East Asia. Some of them even feature higher growth rates during the years 2008 to 2012 than before the crisis (as indicated by positive scores). These patterns of crisis scores conform to those in related papers.[137] At first sight, they seem to contradict NWW's hypothesis that open access orders show better crisis resilience than limited access orders (at least for the particular case of the Great Recession) because the least-affected countries are predominantly limited access orders. Advanced economies, on the other hand, either performed very badly or take medium positions.

Of course, every crisis has unique causes, which affect different countries to varying degrees, irrespective of their institutional structures and the organizational strength of interest groups. Therefore, the next section tries to identify control variables for non-institutional and non-organizational factors, which may explain part of the performance deviation of different countries during the years 2008 to 2012. Controlling for those factors is necessary to isolate the effects of the institutional and organizational variables that are of interest for the research question of this thesis.

4.2 The Selection of Control Variables and Control Models

The main reference point for the derivation of non-institutional and non-organizational control variables is the literature investigating the determinants of the cross-county variation of crisis intensity during the years 2008 and 2009.[138] Only one paper that I am aware of analyzes the factors promoting economic recovery during the years 2010 to 2012.[139] Following these papers, it is possible to group potential control variables according to certain transmissions channels through which the economic crisis spread from its point of origin, the US real-estate market, to the real economies of different countries throughout the world. Each transmission channel represents one potential source of contagion that needs to be controlled for to isolate the effects of institutions and interest group activity. In section 4.2.1, I first present a short review of the non-institutional explanatory variables which are most often found to be significantly related to crisis intensity throughout the related literature. Then, in section 4.2.2, I select the control variables and define the control models that I will use throughout the subsequent empirical analysis.

4.2.1 Literature Review of Potential Control Variables

Within the literature studying the cross-country variation of crisis incidence, authors distinguish three main transmission channels: (1) a *financial linkages channel*, (2) a *financial vulnerability channel* and (3) a *trade channel*.[140] Furthermore, most authors

---

[137] See, for example, Berkman et al. (2012, p. 45, figure 1), Gray et al. (2010, p. 6), Lane & Milesi-Ferretti (2011) or Verick & Islam (2010, p. 20-22).

[138] See footnote 117.

[139] Jovanovic (2012), however, mainly focuses on explanatory variables representing monetary and fiscal policies.

[140] The labeling of the transmission channels differs within the related literature. The identification of three distinct channels used here follows Berkman et al. (2012, p. 44) who distinguish a "*channel [of] financial linkages*", a "*trade channel*" and a channel "*of underlying vulnerabilities of the financial structure*". Claessens et al. (2010, p. 281) refer to three similar transmission channels,

use some *fundamental control variables* (4) in their analyses. Below, I present the most important non-institutional and non-organizational explanatory variables with reference to these transmission channels and, finally, (5) provide a short summary that is the point of departure for the selection of control variables in section 4.2.2.

(1) The *financial linkages channel* refers to the existence of so-called 'toxic' assets linked to the US housing market in the balance sheets of domestic banks in the respective country. The underlying values of these derivative assets were receivables from high-risk loans to US subprime debtors, who had financed their new homes through borrowed money. When large numbers of these original debtors, whose loans had been bundled to mortgage-backed securities and distributed to banks in various countries, defaulted on their repayments and interest obligations, banks throughout the world had to write off the values of these assets in their balance sheets. Furthermore, as many banks faced losses in their equity due to these write-offs, they were forced to sell other healthy assets, as well, in order to comply with compulsory equity ratios. This, in turn, caused an increasing supply of assets in financial markets and, therefore, a general drop in financial asset prices, leading to a further deterioration of bank's balance sheets. As financial corporations became aware of each other's increasing financing problems (especially after the bankruptcy of Lehman Brothers in September 2008) interbank financing slowed down drastically. These troubles in financial markets affected the real economies in many countries mainly due to tighter financing conditions for investors and consumers, who faced scarcer supply of loans and higher financing costs due to higher risk premiums (credit crunch).[141]

Following this short illustration, the real economies of countries with more financial linkages to the United States and other crisis countries should have suffered more severely during the Great Recession (Berkman et al., 2012). To measure such cross-country financial linkages, most authors use the 'ratio of external assets and liabilities to GDP'. Lane & Milesi-Ferretti (2011), however, stress that the effects from such linkages may be ambivalent, as they also provide a source of risk diversification and, therefore, may have cushioned the negative effects from asset value declines. Accordingly, these authors as well as Giannone et al. (2011) fail to find robust relationships between the 'ratio of foreign assets and liabilities to GDP' and 'crisis

---

whereas other authors classify them differently. Blanchard et al. (2010, p. 263), for example, distinguish between two separate shocks – *"the collapse in trade"* and *"the sharp decline in financial flows"*, the latter covering aspects of financial linkages and vulnerabilities together. Lane & Milesi-Ferretti (2011, pp. 81-82) mention four channels - a channel of *"exposure to U.S. assets backed by sub-prime mortgages"*, a channel working through *"the global collapse in trade"* and two related channels covering financial vulnerabilities. They, hence, split the financial vulnerabilities channel into two sub-channels, one referring to *"a global increase in risk aversion"* and another one operating *"through the reliance on those financial systems that got hit hardest by the crisis"*. Most of these differences however remain differences of labeling. The actual explanatory variables used by all authors are quite similar.

[141] For instructive illustrations of the sequence of events leading to the Great Recessions see, for example, Bricongne et al. (2009), Brunnermeier (2009) or Verick & Islam (2010).

intensity'. Berglöf et al. (2010), who use the same measure for financial linkages, confirm this result in a large worldwide sample. They do, however, find a significant negative relationship between output developments and the 'ratio of financial assets and liabilities to GDP' when they interact the linkages variable with a dummy for transition economies and when they restrict their sample to 59 emerging economies. This indicates that financial linkages may have played a role in non-advanced countries.

(2) The *financial vulnerability channel* refers to countries' vulnerabilities to the deterioration of worldwide financing conditions due to pre-crisis financial deepening, high current account deficits or large short-term external debts. In the years prior to the crisis, some countries had financed parts of their consumption and investment via the accumulation of large private debts. Often, this credit-based consumption and investment caused current account deficits as it relied on imports and loans from abroad.[142] When financing conditions throughout the world became less favorable, credit-based consumption and investment turned out to be more costly and declined.[143] This forced countries who had previously relied on the expansion of domestic private credits and on borrowing from abroad to adjust their economic activities more heavily, including re-allocations of productive factors from heavily-affected domestic sectors (such as the construction sector) to export-oriented sectors or reductions of prices and wages in accordance with downwardly adjusted expectations (Deutsche Bundesbank, 2014, pp. 25-26). Furthermore, highly leveraged economic actors were more vulnerable to falling asset prices or to the general contraction of economic activity than other actors, forcing them to cut back on consumption and investment more strongly to counteract balance sheet problems.[144]

Variables most frequently used to represent financial vulnerabilities are 'credit to deposit ratios', 'short-term debt to GDP ratios', 'ratios of private credit to GDP', pre-crisis changes of the 'ratio of private credit to GDP' and 'current account balance to GDP ratios'. Especially the last two variables turn out to be significantly related to the severity of the crisis in several papers. Increases of the 'ratio of private credit to GDP' represent the rapid and often unsustainable financial deepening prior to a crisis, which is likely to entail heavier adjustments and stronger liquidations of unsustainable activities in accordance with Schumpeter's previously presented account of business

---

[142] See, for example, Deutsche Bundesbank (2014, pp. 22-25) or Unger (2015). The latter shows empirically that the build-up of current account deficits in EMU countries is mainly driven by private credit demand from non-financial sectors in deficit countries. Hence, pre-crisis financial deepening and current account deficits are strongly connected.

[143] Unger (2015), for example, shows that the correction of current account deficits in the majority of deficit countries was accomplished through cutting back loans to private actors.

[144] Mian & Sufi (2014), for example, show that the economic contraction in the US were strongest in those geographic areas in which households faced strong balance-sheet problems. The authors show that the housing-net-worth channel explains large parts of the non-tradeable employment reductions in US counties, as households with balance-sheet problems had to cut back on consumption more heavily.

cycles. Accordingly, Lane & Milesi-Ferretti (2011) in various samples, Berglöf et al. (2010) in large worldwide samples, Claessens et al. (2010) in a sample of 58 countries and Berkman et al. (2012) in various samples of developing countries all report significant and negative relationships between pre-crisis financial deepening and crisis resilience. The second vulnerability variable that is often found to be significantly related to the severity of the crisis is the 'current account balance to GDP ratio'. While increases of the 'ratio of private credit to GDP' indicate financial deepening in general, high current account deficits suggest that pre-crisis economic expansion had relied on borrowing from abroad. Besides being an expression of external financial vulnerabilities, high current account deficits are also potential signs of poor economic competitiveness, as they reveal that domestic demand for foreign goods is higher than foreign demand for domestic goods. In times of crises, poor competitiveness can cause extensive liquidations of unprofitable activities, or it may require swift and strong adjustments of prices and quantities, which entail the costs of adaption pointed out in section 2.4. Accordingly, most papers such as Lane & Milesi-Ferretti (2011), Blanchard et al. (2010), Claessens et al. (2010), Rose & Spiegel (2011) and Giannone et al. (2011) find 'current account balance to GDP ratios' to be robustly and positively related to crisis resilience in various samples of developed and emerging countries.

Other variables representing financial vulnerabilities such as 'credit to deposit ratios' or 'short-term external debt to GDP ratios' are also negatively related to economic performance in several papers.[145] The only potential vulnerability variable that does not feature significant coefficients is the 'ratio of private credit to GDP'. Berglöf et al. (2010), however, do not interpret this variable as an indicator of financial vulnerabilities but rather as a sign of high financial development. They report positive coefficients for this variable, thereby suggesting that financial development helped to reduce crisis intensity. Giannone et al. (2011) confirm the significant and positive relationship between this variable and performance during the crisis, whereas Claessens et al. (2010) report insignificant coefficients.

While most previously-cited papers find several significant associations between vulnerability variables and crisis resilience, Rose & Spiegel (2010, 2011 and 2012) are skeptical about the existence of robust links between financial indicators and crisis incidence. In their 2011-paper, they show that the significance levels of most coefficients (including those of pre-crisis financial deepening) are sensitive to model specifications. The authors only report significant and positive coefficients for the 'current account to GDP ratio' and significantly negative coefficients for the 'ratio of short-term external debt to GDP' in most of their specifications.

(3) The *foreign trade channel* refers to the decline of exports due to a general contraction of worldwide economic activity and the consequential drop of demand

145 Berglöf et al. (2010) report negative coefficients of 'credit to deposit ratios'. Rose & Spiegel (2011) and Blanchard et al. (2010) find negative associations between 'ratios of short-term external debt to GDP' and crisis resilience. Berkman et al. (2012) report negative coefficients for both variables.

from abroad (Berkman et al., 2012, p. 4; Bricongne et al., 2009, p. 31). Furthermore, output contractions due to lower export demand may have been stronger for exporters of manufactured goods, as the demand for durables normally behaves more pro-cyclical than the demand for other goods. Demand for primary products, on the other hand, remained rather stable (Lane & Milesi-Ferretti, 2011).

Accordingly, most authors consider explanatory variables representing the relative importance of trade and the composition of exports. In a broad sample of 121 countries and in various specifications, Berkman et al. (2012) find that emerging and developing economies with strong trade linkages, measured by the 'exports to GDP ratio', were more severely affected by the crisis. Furthermore, they find evidence that the composition of trade mattered, too, as high shares of manufacturing products and low shares of soft commodities in exports were associated with worse performance. Berglöf et al. (2010) use a similar measure for export composition in a large worldwide sample. They report a significant positive relationship between the 'ratio of commodity exports to total exports' and output performance during the crisis. In a broad, worldwide sample, Lane & Milesi-Ferretti (2011) find no robust effects of trade-openness and trade-composition variables on GDP growth during the crisis.[146] Claessens et al. (2010) and Giannone et al. (2011) use the 'ratio of exports and imports to GDP' as a measure for trade openness. While the former authors report negative and significant coefficients for the relationship between trade openness and performance during the crisis, the latter do not find significant results. Blanchard et al. (2010) consider two trade variables: the 'exports to GDP ratio' and the 'unexpected trading partner growth' (the export-weighted difference between the growth of trading partners and their growth forecast) for a sample of 29 emerging economies. They report both variables to have a significant effect on economic performance, the sign of the 'export to GDP ratio' being negative and the sign of the 'unexpected trading partner growth' being positive. Rose & Spiegel (2011), on the other hand, cannot find robust results for the latter variable.

(4) The most commonly-used fundamental control variable in the related literature is 'GDP per capita', which represents a country's overall level of development. Lane & Milesi-Ferretti (2011), Berkman et al. (2012) and Rose & Spiegel (2011) all report significant negative coefficients for this variable in most of their specifications. Giannone et al. (2011) and Claessens et al. (2010), on the other hand, report mostly insignificant relationships between 'GDP per capita' and their measures of crisis intensity.

---

[146] They don't actually use the ratio of manufactured exports to total exports but rather the ratio of manufactured goods to GDP. Both variables, however, can be expected to capture similar effects – assuming that countries produce and export larger shares of those products to whose production they have a comparative advantage.

(5) Table 2 summarizes the previous review of potentially-relevant non-institutional control variables.

Channel	Potential control variables	LM [147]	BKPZ [148]	GMGG [149]	BGRW [150]	RS [151]	BDF [152]	CDIL [153]
1. Financial Linkages	Ratio of foreign assets and liabilities to GDP	/	/,-	/	/			
2. Financial Vulnerability	Credit to deposit ratio		-		-			
	Ratio of private credit to GDP		+	+		/		/
	Pre-crisis increase of the private credit to GDP ratio	-	-		-	/		-
	Current account balance to GDP ratio	+		+		+	+	+
	Short-term external debt to GDP ratio				-	-	-	
3. Foreign Trade	Exports to GDP ratio				-		-	
	Ratio of exports and imports to GDP	/		/				-
	Ratio of manufactured exports to total exports[154]	/			-			
	Ratio of soft commodity exports to total exports		+		+			
	Export-weighted trading partner growth	+				/	+	
4. Fundamental Variables	GDP per capita	-	-	/		-		/,-

Table 2: Summary of potentially-relevant control variables according to the previous literature review (the sign '/' indicates that relationships were insignificant; the signs '+' and '-' mean significant positive or negative associations; the combination '/,-' indicates that some specifications were insignificant and others were significantly negative).

[147] From Lane & and Milesi-Ferretti (2011) I consider the results of the multivariate analysis in tables 6a and 6b, which use output as dependent variable.

[148] From Berglöf et al. (2010) I consider the results of the multivariate analysis covering the larger sample displayed in table 5.

[149] From Giannone et al. (2011) I consider the results of the OLS regressions in tables 2 and 3.

[150] From Berkman et al. (2012) I consider the results of the multivariate analyses covering larger samples of developing and emerging countries as displayed in tables 2, A5 and A4.

[151] I consider all results from Rose and Spiegel (2010, 2011 and 2012).

[152] I consider all results from Blanchard et al. (2010).

[153] From Claessens et al. (2010) I consider the results of the multivariate analyses in table 4 using the decline of growth rates as dependent variable.

[154] Lane & and Milesi-Ferretti (2011) use the 'ratio of manufactured output to total GDP' instead of the 'ratio of manufactured exports to total exports'.

Table 2 shows that the variables most often found to be significantly associated with crisis intensity are 'current account balance to GDP ratios', increases in 'private credit to GDP ratios' and 'GDP per capita', thereby indicating the important role of financial vulnerabilities and overall economic development. Other variables representing financial vulnerabilities, like 'credit to deposit ratios' and 'short-term debt to GDP ratios', also exhibit significant signs in most regression. 'Private credit to GDP ratios', on the other hand, are not robustly related to crisis incidence, presumably because this variable represents financial development instead of financial vulnerabilities. Similar to the general development variable 'GDP per capita', it partly exhibits positive signs. Financial linkages appear to be mainly irrelevant for explaining crisis incidence, as the 'financial assets and liabilities to GDP ratios' are insignificant in most of the reviewed papers. Regarding trade linkages, the review indicates that the composition of trade was more important than the extent of trade, as the 'ratio of manufactured exports to total exports' and the 'ratio of soft-commodity exports to total exports' are mainly significant. Of the three variables representing the extent of trade the 'export-weighted partner growth' shows the strongest association with crisis incidence. This, however, may have explanations other than trade linkages. Besides representing the effects from trading partners' output declines, 'export-weighted partner growth' could also reflect other communalities amongst certain groups of countries, as trading partners are often geographically proximate countries who share similar fundamental features such as history, culture, climate, access to the sea, education levels or even institutions.

Based on this literature review, the next section deals with the construction of control models that represent the unequal exposure of different countries to the original shock.

4.2.2 Selecting Control Variables

In this section, (1) I first run bivariate regressions of the dependent variables constructed in section 4.1 against potential control variables and report correlations amongst these control variables. By doing this, I hope to gain a first overview of significant relationships. Then, (2) I employ principal component analysis to combine different control variables to single components of which each represents a different channel of contagion. Finally, (3) I use these components as new explanatory variables to formulate models that control for all relevant non-institutional and non-organizational determinants of crisis severity. These control models are the points of departure for the empirical analysis in section 4.3.

(1) Table 3 depicts the results of bivariate OLS regressions between each potential control variable and each dependent variable in the three samples of countries.[155]

[155] The definitions of all control variables and the data sources are listed in appendix 2. For all variables, I consider 2007-values, as the information of interest are countries' pre-crisis situations and

	Dep. Var.: $GDP_{08\text{-}12}$			Dep. Var.: $GDP_{08\text{-}09}$			Dep. Var.: $GDP_{10\text{-}12}$		
	All	Deve-loped	Emerging & Developing	All	Deve-loped	Emerging & Developing	All	Deve-loped	Emerging & Developing
(FA + FL) / GDP	**-0.67** **0.02^{**}** **R^2: 0.06**	0.08 0.79 R^2: 0.00	-1.52 0.44 R^2: 0.01	**-0.40** **0.02^{**}** **R^2: 0.07**	0.00 0.98 R^2: 0.00	0.03 0.98 R^2: 0.00	-0.30 0.10 R^2: 0.03	0.07 0.73 R^2: 0.00	-1.67 0.18 R^2: 0.04
Priv. Cred. / GDP	**-0.09** **0.00^{***}** **R^2: 0.13**	0.02 0.58 R^2: 0.01	-0.09 0.12 R^2: 0.05	**-0.04** **0.00^{***}** **R^2: 0.09**	0.03 0.25 R^2: 0.04	-0.03 0.33 R^2: 0.02	**-0.05** **0.00^{***}** **R^2: 0.11**	-0.00 0.87 R^2: 0.00	-0.06 0.11 R^2: 0.05
Increase (Priv. Cred. / GDP)[156]	**-0.30** **0.00^{***}** **R^2: 0.35**	**-0.17** **0.00^{***}** **R^2: 0.33**	**-0.54** **0.00^{***}** **R^2: 0.40**	**-0.14** **0.00^{***}** **R^2: 0.22**	**-0.07** **0.04^{**}** **R^2: 0.13**	**-0.24** **0.00^{***}** **R^2: 0.27**	**-0.18** **0.00^{***}** **R^2: 0.33**	**-0.12** **0.00^{***}** **R^2: 0.34**	**-0.31** **0.00^{***}** **R^2: 0.33**
Credit / Deposit	**-0.07** **0.00^{***}** **R^2: 0.13**	**-0.06** **0.04^{**}** **R^2: 0.14**	-0.04 0.10 R^2: 0.05	**-0.04** **0.00^{***}** **R^2: 0.12**	**-0.04** **0.05^{**}** **R^2: 0.13**	-0.02 0.15 R^2: 0.04	**-0.03** **0.01^{***}** **R^2: 0.09**	-0.03 0.15 R^2: 0.07	-0.02 0.17 R^2: 0.04
S.T. Ext. Debt / GDP	**-0.04** **0.03^{**}** **R^2: 0.05**	0.01 0.50 R^2: 0.02	-0.14 0.27 R^2: 0.02	**-0.02** **0.01^{**}** **R^2: 0.07**	0.00 0.82 R^2: 0.00	-0.05 0.48 R^2: 0.01	-0.01 0.22 R^2: 0.02	0.01 0.41 R^2: 0.02	-0.10 0.24 R^2: 0.03
Current Acc. Balance / GDP	**0.59** **0.00^{***}** **R^2: 0.16**	**0.78** **0.00^{***}** **R^2: 0.55**	**0.58** **0.00^{***}** **R^2: 0.16**	**0.18** **0.05^{**}** **R^2: 0.05**	**0.34** **0.00^{***}** **R^2: 0.26**	0.13 0.22 R^2: 0.03	**0.46** **0.00^{***}** **R^2: 0.26**	**0.53** **0.00^{***}** **R^2: 0.52**	**0.47** **0.00^{***}** **R^2: 0.26**
Exports / GDP	-0.04 0.34 R^2: 0.01	0.05 0.27 R^2: 0.04	-0.12 0.18 R^2: 0.04	-0.05 0.06^{*} R^2: 0.04	-0.00 0.95 R^2: 0.00	-0.08 0.10^{*} R^2: 0.05	0.01 0.81 R^2: 0.00	0.05 0.06^{*} R^2: 0.11	-0.04 0.47 R^2: 0.01
Trade / GDP	-0.03 0.17 R^2: 0.02	0.02 0.42 R^2: 0.02	**-0.10** **0.03^{**}** **R^2: 0.09**	-0.03 0.05^{*} R^2: 0.05	-0.00 0.76 R^2: 0.00	-0.04 0.08^{*} R^2: 0.06	-0.01 0.71 R^2: 0.00	0.02 0.11 R^2: 0.08	**-0.06** **0.04^{**}** **R^2: 0.08**
Manuf. Exp. / Total Exp.	**-0.17** **0.00^{***}** **R^2: 0.11**	0.15 0.07^{*} R^2: 0.11	**-0.24** **0.00^{***}** **R^2: 0.21**	**-0.11** **0.00^{***}** **R^2: 0.13**	0.02 0.69 R^2: 0.01	**-0.12** **0.00^{***}** **R^2: 0.18**	-0.06 0.09^{*} R^2: 0.03	**0.15** **0.01^{***}** **R^2: 0.20**	**-0.12** **0.01^{***}** **R^2: 0.13**
Com. Exp. / Total Exp.	**0.25** **0.00^{***}** **R^2: 0.15**	-0.09 0.50 R^2: 0.02	**0.22** **0.01^{***}** **R^2: 0.15**	**0.12** **0.00^{***}** **R^2: 0.11**	-0.05 0.58 R^2: 0.01	**0.09** **0.03^{**}** **R^2: 0.09**	**0.13** **0.00^{***}** **R^2: 0.10**	-0.06 0.58 R^2: 0.01	**0.13** **0.01^{**}** **R^2: 0.12**
GDP per Capita	**-0.27** **0.00^{***}** **R^2: 0.16**	0.16 0.19 R^2: 0.06	**-1.22** **0.01^{***}** **R^2: 0.13**	**-0.15** **0.00^{***}** **R^2: 0.15**	0.12 0.11 R^2: 0.08	**-0.76** **0.00^{***}** **R^2: 0.17**	**-0.13** **0.01^{***}** **R^2: 0.09**	0.05 0.54 R^2: 0.01	-0.49 0.12 R^2: 0.05

Table 3: Coefficients of bivariate OLS regressions between potential control variables and dependent variables (second row: p-values of two-sided significance tests; number of asterisks: significance levels of 10%*, 5%** and 1%***; significant results at 5% level are bold; third row: R^2).

Furthermore, table 4 shows the correlations amongst all potential control variables, thereby indicating which variables might belong to similar channels of contagion. From the variables depicted in table 2, I consider all but the 'export-weighted partner

vulnerabilities. To calculate the 'increase of the private credit to GDP ratio' I consider the time period 2002 to 2007.

[156] I calculate the increase of the 'private credit to GDP ratio' during the years 2002 to 2007.

growth' because, as mentioned above, the interpretation of that variable entails too many ambiguities.[157]

	(FA + FL) / GDP	Priv. Cred. / GDP	Increase (Priv. Cred. / GDP)	Credit / Deposit	S.T. Ext. Debt / GDP	Current Acc. Balance / GDP	Exports / GDP	Trade / GDP	Manuf. Exp. / Total Exp.	Com. Exp. / Total Exp.	GDP per Capita
(FA + FL) / GDP	1	**0.52**	**0.22**	0.10	**0.93**	**0.28**	**0.66**	**0.63**	0.18	**-0.29**	**0.65**
Priv. Cred./ GDP	**0.52**	1	**0.49**	**0.41**	**0.51**	0.08	0.16	0.12	0.19	**-0.32**	**0.77**
Increase (Priv. Cred. / GDP)	**0.22**	**0.49**	1	**0.52**	0.20	**-0.50**	-0.19	-0.16	0.08	-0.02	**0.41**
Credit / Deposit	0.10	**0.41**	**0.52**	1	0.12	-0.16	0.04	0.05	0.11	-0.02	**0.31**
S.T. Ext. Debt / GDP	**0.93**	**0.51**	0.20	0.12	1	**0.28**	**0.63**	**0.60**	0.18	**-0.28**	**0.67**
Current Acc. Balance / GDP	**0.28**	0.08	**-0.50**	-0.16	**0.28**	1	**0.42**	**0.29**	**0.27**	-0.02	0.21
Exports / GDP	**0.66**	0.16	-0.19	0.04	**0.63**	**0.42**	1	**0.98**	**0.32**	**-0.24**	0.22
Trade / GDP	**0.63**	0.12	-0.16	0.05	**0.60**	**0.29**	**0.98**	1	**0.29**	**-0.27**	0.16
Manuf. Exp. / Total Exp.	0.18	0.19	0.08	0.11	0.18	**0.27**	**0.32**	**0.29**	1	**-0.66**	**0.27**
Com. Exp. / Total Exp.	**-0.29**	**-0.32**	-0.02	-0.02	**-0.28**	-0.02	**-0.24**	**-0.27**	**-0.66**	1	**-0.31**
GDP per Capita	**0.66**	**0.77**	**0.41**	**0.31**	**0.67**	0.21	0.22	0.16	**0.27**	**-0.31**	1

Table 4: Correlations amongst potential control variables (significant correlations at 5% level are bold).

These first-step analyses already provide some tentative insights about the relevance of certain transmission channels and control variables.

- The coefficients of the measure representing *financial linkages*, the 'foreign assets and liabilities to GDP ratio', provide no clear picture. They have the expected negative signs only when taking all 84 countries into account. When, however, considering the sub-samples of 32 developed countries or 52 less developed countries, coefficients are partly positive. The only two coefficients that are significantly different from zero are those for the time periods 2008 to 2012 and 2008 to 2009 when considering the entire sample of all 84 countries.

[157] In fact, I constructed a variable for 'export-weighted trading partner growth' that turned out to be highly significant for explaining crisis resilience but was uncorrelated to the other two trade variables, the 'exports to GDP ratio' and the 'trade to GDP ratio'. I interpret these findings to indicate that 'export-weighted trading partner growth' indeed represents effects other than trade linkages, potentially even effects related to institutional similarities amongst close trading partners.

- Amongst the potential measures representing the *financial vulnerabilities channel*, especially the increase of the 'private credit to GDP ratio' and the 'current account balance to GDP ratio' are highly significant and show the expected signs (more severe economic downturns are associated with pre-crisis financial deepening and negative current account balances). While the increase of private credit is significant across all periods and sub-samples, the current account played an important role especially in the sub-group of developed countries and during the recovery period 2010 to 2012. Of the other three measures representing financial vulnerabilities (the 'private credit to GDP ratio', the 'ratio of short-term external debt to GDP' and the 'credit to deposit ratio'), only the 'credit to deposit ratio' shows the expected sign in all regressions. Furthermore, according to table 4, the five variables representing financial vulnerabilities show only partially significant correlations with one another, thereby indicating that they might not represent the same channel.
- The potential effects from *trade linkages* are weak. Coefficients for the 'exports to GDP ratio' and the 'trade to GDP ratio' show the expected negative signs only when considering the entire sample of 84 countries and the sub-sample of 52 less developed countries, although most coefficients miss conventional significance levels. Nevertheless, the results indicate that trade linkages are associated with a slightly higher crisis intensity in the sub-group of less developed countries. In the sub-group of 32 developed countries the two trade linkages variables are consistently insignificant.
- The *composition of trade* appears to be more important than the *extent* of trade. Interestingly, potential effects in developed countries are opposite to those in emerging and developing countries. While high shares of manufactured exports and low shares of commodity exports are associated with higher output in the sub-group of 32 developed countries, the same variables show a negative association with output in the sub-sample of 52 emerging and developing countries. However, only the results in the latter sub-group are significantly different from zero. When considering the entire sample of 84 countries, results correspond to those in less developed countries, as there is a significantly negative association between high shares of manufactured exports and crisis resilience, especially during the initial downturn 2008 and 2009.
- A similar picture emerges for 'GDP per capita'. On the one hand, coefficients for the sub-sample of 32 developed countries are positive, though insignificant. On the other hand, coefficients for the sub-sample of 52 emerging and developing countries are negative, being more distinct and significant during the initial recession period 2008 to 2009. Looking at the entire sample of 84 countries shows that more developed countries with higher 'GDP per capita' showed a deeper economic crisis than less developed countries. Finally, according to table 4, high 'GDP per capita' is positively correlated with many financial variables,

especially the 'foreign assets and liabilities to GDP ratio', the 'ratio of short-term external debt to GDP' and the 'ratio of private credit to GDP', thereby indicating that the latter three variables also represent a high degree of economic development.

These results from the bivariate regressions provide support for the notion that financial vulnerabilities intensified the crisis in both developed and less developed countries. Effects of the other variables are more ambiguous. While high ratios of manufactured exports and high development levels appear to have slightly mitigated the crisis in developed countries, the same variables are significantly related to a deeper economic crisis within the sub-sample of 52 less developed countries and within the entire dataset of 84 countries.

(2) Besides controlling for single variables, I would also like to control for many variables at the same time to cover all relevant channels of contagion in a single model. The most obvious way to do that – picking one variable for each channel and using these variables simultaneously in a multivariate regression analysis – is problematic for several reasons. First, the bivariate regressions as depicted in table 3 indicate that some channels of contagion that were mentioned throughout the related literature, such as the *financial linkages channel* or the *trade channel*, may not be relevant for explaining the severity of the crisis. As mentioned above, the coefficients of the 'foreign assets and liabilities to GDP ratio', the 'export to GDP ratio' and the 'trade to GDP ratio' don't consistently feature the expected signs and are mainly insignificant. Second, the coefficients of the bivariate regression do not provide a clear answer to the question which variables best represent each channel of contagion and should therefore be picked as control variables. Sometimes, two or more variables perform similarly well in explaining changes in output.[158] Increases in the 'ratio of private credit to GDP' and the 'current account balance to GDP ratio', for example, are both highly significant in most regressions. Third, the assignment of the variables to channels of contagion as suggested by the related literature might not be adequate. On the one hand, there are cases when two variables which supposedly belong to the same channel of contagion are uncorrelated, indicating that they in fact represent two distinct effects. Examples are the 'ratio of short-term external debt to GDP' and the 'credit to deposit ratio' as part of the *financial vulnerabilities channel*. On the other hand, other variables supposedly belonging to different channels, are highly correlated, indicating that they may actually represent similar effects. 'GDP per capita', for example, shows a high correlation with some financial vulnerability variables. Finally, including too many variables in one model may cause statistical problems such as a reduction of degrees of freedom or multicollinearity when control variables are highly correlated.

[158] Claessens et al. (2012) note in a similar way that many variables are highly correlated, which makes it difficult to distinguish different channels of contagion.

One way to alleviate the abovementioned problems is applying principal component analysis.[159] This multivariate analysis method has the ability to structure the information contained in all potential control variables by identifying those variables which are highly correlated, separating them from all other variables and combining them to a small number of principal components. Components (whose scores are weighted averages of original variables) can, then, function as new control variables instead of the original variables. Applying this approach circumvents the problem of having to select variables which best represent certain channels. Rather, the approach uses the information contained in *all* relevant variables at the same time. Furthermore, principal component analysis allows a statistical reassessment of the grouping of original variables according to certain channels of contagion that is suggested by the related literature. Ideally, the selected components should roughly represent the channels of contagion identified by other papers. From a statistical point of view, using components instead of original variables as explanatory variables has the advantage of reducing the large number of original variables to a smaller number of principal components, thereby saving degrees of freedom.

Table 5 shows the rotated loadings of all four extracted components, which reflect the correlations between original variables and extracted components.

	Component 1: International Linkages of Trade & Finance	Component 2: Economic & Financial Development	Component 3: Financial Vulnerabilities	Component 4: Industrial Orientation of the Economy
Trade / GDP	**0.97**	0.02	-0.05	0.18
Exports / GDP	**0.95**	0.10	-0.14	0.16
(FA + FL) / GDP	**0.68**	**0.65**	0.00	0.04
S.T. Ext. Debt / GDP	**0.65**	**0.66**	-0.01	0.03
GDP per Capita	0.11	**0.92**	0.10	0.18
Priv. Cred. / GDP	0.05	**0.84**	0.27	0.19
Increase (Priv. Cred. / GDP)	-0.10	0.42	**0.81**	-0.09
Current Acc. Balance / GDP	0.24	0.33	**-0.77**	0.08
Credit / Deposit	0.07	0.26	**0.67**	0.08
Manuf. Exp. / Total Exp.	0.16	0.11	-0.09	**0.89**
Com. Exp. / Total Exp.	-0.11	-0.15	-0.05	**-0.87**

Table 5: Factor loadings of all explanatory variables (loadings with larger values than ±0.5 are bold).[160]

[159] For a textbook discussion see Backhaus et al. (2011, pp. 329-394).

[160] I carried out an explorative principal component analysis following mainly the instructions from Backhaus et al. (2011). SPSS offers standardized commands for each step.

1. All original variables were first standardized to make variables with different units of measurement comparable (by, first, subtracting the variable mean from each value and, then, dividing by the variable's standard deviation). After standardization, original variables have an average of 0 and a standard deviation of 1 across all countries

One important task when applying principal component analysis is the interpretation of the extracted components. I put forward the following interpretation:

- Component 1 is most positively correlated to the 'exports to GDP ratio', the 'trade to GDP ratio' and two financial variables reflecting the amount of external financial positions that often go along with trade. I label this component *'international linkages of trade and finance'* (subsequently: 'international linkages').
- Component 2 is positively correlated with 'GDP per capita' and the three financial variables associated with high financial development (size and openness)–the 'foreign assets and liabilities to GDP ratio', the 'ratio of private credit to GDP' and the 'ratio of short-term external debt to GDP'. It is, furthermore, slightly correlated with other financial variables. I label this component *'economic and financial development'* (subsequently: 'economic development').
- Component 3 represents *'financial vulnerabilities'* as it is positively correlated to the increase of the 'private credit to GDP ratio' and the 'credit to deposit ratio'. Furthermore, it features a negative correlation with the 'current account balance to GDP ratio' – a variable of which higher values reflects lower financial vulnerabilities.
- Component 4 is positively correlated to the 'ratio of manufactured exports to total exports' and negatively correlated to the 'ratio of commodity exports to total exports'. I label this component *'industrial orientation of trade and the economy'* (subsequently: 'industrial orientation'). High values indicate an orientation towards the production and export of manufactured goods and low values indicate an orientation towards the production and export of simple commodities (agricultural products, fuels and mining products).

These extracted components partly confirm the choice and grouping of explanatory variables suggested by the related literature. Most variables representing financial

2. Overall, there was one missing value across the all 11 variables and 84 countries. I replaced it by the mean of the respective variable. The other option - eliminating the respective country (United Kingdom) from the entire sample – would have entailed a higher price considering the already small sample of 32 developed countries. Furthermore, as depicted in Appendix 3, the factor loadings would have been fairly the same when eliminating the UK.
3. The sample is appropriate for applying principal component analysis. The measure of sampling adequacy (MSA) as suggested by Kaiser, Meyer & Olkin (also known as KMO criterion) is 0.66.
4. Regarding the choice of the number of components, I followed the Kaiser criterion, selecting only those components with eigenvalues above 1.
5. As the method of component rotation I employed the orthogonal Varimax method.
6. As the method for estimating the scores of the four principal components I used regression analysis as provided by SPSS. Following that method, the scores for each component across all countries are standardized with an average of 0 and a standard deviation of 1.

vulnerabilities (with the exception of the 'short-term external debt to GDP ratio'), for example, belong to one component. Furthermore, following Berkman et al. (2012), it is necessary to distinguish variables representing developed financial sectors such as the 'private credit to GDP ratio', from variables representing financial vulnerabilities such as *increases* in the 'private credit to GDP ratio'. Similarly, the analysis suggests that the extent of trade needs to be distinguished from the composition of trade. However, the extracted components also suggest some re-grouping of variables as compared to the related literature. Most importantly, some financial linkages variables (the 'financial assets and liabilities to GDP ratio' and the 'short-term external debt to GDP ratio') and both trade variables ('exports to GDP ratio' and 'trade to GDP ratio') load on the same component, suggesting that international trade and international financial linkages are two sides of the same medal.

(3) After extracting four components out of the eleven original variables, I now use the scores of these four components as independent variables for explaining crisis resilience during the three time periods 2008 to 2012, 2008 to 2009 and 2010 to 2012 for the three samples of 84 countries, 32 developed countries and 52 less developed countries.[161] Table 6 displays the coefficients of the OLS regressions when using the extracted components as explanatory variables after eliminating insignificant variables with p-values above 0.1 from the regressions.[162]

	Dep. Var.: $GDP_{08\text{-}12}$			Dep. Var.: $GDP_{08\text{-}09}$			Dep. Var.: $GDP_{10\text{-}12}$		
	All	Deve-loped	Emerging & Dev.	All	Deve-loped	Emerging & Dev.	All	Deve-loped	Emerging & Dev.
Constant	-7.53 0.00***	-16.41 0.00***	-4.20 0.00***	-5.91 0.00***	-11.43 0.00***	-3.74 0.00***	-2.05 0.00***	-5.00 0.00***	-0.70 0.42
Financial Vulnerabilities	-7.55 0.00***	-6.36 0.00***	-6.45 0.01***	-3.26 0.00***	-3.30 0.00***	-2.14 0.07*	-4.77 0.00***	-3.97 0.00***	-4.53 0.00***
Economic Development	-2.83 0.00***	2.27 0.10*		-1.61 0.01***	1.82 0.09*		-1.32 0.04**		
Industrial Orientation	-4.42 0.00***		-3.88 0.00***	-2.42 0.00***		-1.95 0.01***	-1.99 0.00***		-1.90 0.00***
International Linkages	-1.47 0.03**			-1.33 0.00***	-1.03 0.07*				
N	84	32	52	84	32	52	84	32	52
R^{2*}	0.51	0.57	0.40	0.37	0.41	0.20	0.44	0.43	0.38

Table 6: Control models with principal components (second row: p-values of two-sided significance tests; number of asterisks: significance levels of 10%*, 5%** and 1%***).

The only component that is significantly different from zero in all specifications is 'financial vulnerabilities' suggesting that these vulnerabilities aggravated the initial downturn and retarded the recovery in developed and less developed countries alike. 'Economic development' played a more ambiguous role, as coefficients in the sub-

[161] For a short explanation on how to calculate component scores based on regression analysis see Backhaus et al. (2011, pp. 364-366, 380-383).

[162] I use generous p-value thresholds of 0.1 only for the selection of control variables to assure that I don't miss potential biases in later regressions when the actual variables of interest are included.

group of 32 developed countries are significantly positive in two cases and coefficients for the entire sample of 84 countries are significantly negative. This indicates that within the sub-group of developed countries, a high level of development made economies more resilient, especially during the contraction 2008 and 2009. Overall, however, more developed countries suffered larger output losses. Trade composition mattered mainly in emerging and developing economies, as countries with a stronger 'industrial orientation' were less resilient to the original shock and also recovered more slowly. 'International linkages' only played a minor role, being associated with a deeper recession within developed countries during the period 2008 to 2009 and within the entire sample during the periods 2008 to 2012 and 2008 to 2009.

Throughout the empirical analysis that follows in the next sections, the control models depicted in table 6 will be the points of departure. I, however, will not solely rely on these models to control for initial vulnerabilities because control variables based on principal component analysis entail some complications of their own. First, related papers mainly use *original* variables for explaining the downturn and the recovery during the economic crisis. Therefore, using control variables based on principle components complicates the comparability of the results. Second, principal component analysis involves some degree of subjective decision-making and leaves room for interpretations. Using original variables would make the results less vulnerable to critics who challenge the subjective decisions and interpretations put forward with regard to the previous analysis. Third, transforming the original variables into principal components involves a loss of information. Although the application of components allows the use of more information from *a variety of variables* at the same time, some information from *every single* variable is lost.

Finding control models with no drawbacks is impossible. I try to deal with this problem by considering both principal components *and* original variables as control variables. First, I use the control models with principal components as depicted in table 6 throughout the entire empirical analysis. By doing this, I control for a wide variety of different vulnerabilities at the same time without losing many degrees of freedom. Doing this, furthermore, allows a clear and efficient presentation of the results without overloading the analysis with countless models each controlling for different variables. Second, to make my empirical analysis less vulnerable to criticism associated with principle component analysis, I also conduct additional robustness checks controlling for five original variables, one at a time. The variables I will consider are the increase of the 'private credit to GDP ratio', the 'current account balance to GDP ratio', the 'trade to GDP ratio', the 'ratio of manufactured exports to total exports' and 'GDP per capita'. These five original variables represent the four transmission channels suggested by the principal component analysis. Regarding each component, I selected the original variable which performed best in the bivariate regressions depicted in table 3. Only for the financial vulnerabilities channel I picked two variables – the increase of the 'private credit to GDP ratio' and the 'current account balance to GDP ratio' – because they are both highly significant and because most of the related papers use them as well. As running these robustness checks with original variables for all combinations of explanatory and dependent variables would still heavily overload the analysis, I undertake them only whenever the bivariate regressions or the regression controlling for principle components feature significant relationships. To maintain a clear and efficient presentation, I furthermore display most results of these robustness checks in the appendices and discuss them only briefly in the main part of this thesis.

4.3 The Empirical Analysis Part I: Economic Institutions and Crisis Resilience

After defining the dependent variables in section 4.1 and selecting control models in section 4.2, this section contains the empirical analysis of the associations between economic institutions and crisis resilience during the Great Recession. In the first five sub-sections 4.3.1 to 4.3.5, I consider the individual roles of the economic institutions outlined by Olson and NWW – rule of law including impartially-enforced property rights and contract laws (in section 4.3.1), regulations of businesses, labor and financial markets (in sections 4.3.2, 4.3.3 and 4.3.4) and government size (in section 4.3.5). Additionally to these institutions, I analyze the potential effects of exchange rate regimes (in section 4.3.6) because adjustments of external prices and wages are potential substitutes for internal adjustments that depend on complex regulations. I organize each sub-section 4.3.1 to 4.3.6 in the same way. First, I provide a short literature review of theoretical arguments that substantiate those of Olson and NWW. Then, I discuss the data sources for the indices representing each institution. Finally, each sub-section finishes with a presentation and discussion of the empirical results. After considering each institution individually in sub-sections 4.3.1 to 4.3.6, section 4.3.7 investigates correlations amongst various institutional variables and assesses the combined effects of related institutions on crisis resilience and adaptive efficiency during the Great Recession.

The statistical analysis in each sub-section 4.3.1 to 4.3.6 always proceeds the same way. In the first step, I conduct bivariate regressions of the dependent variables representing crisis resilience against the respective institutional variables. For each of the three time periods, there will be three separate regressions, one for the whole sample of 84 countries, one for the sub-sample of 32 developed countries and one for the sub-sample of 52 emerging and developing economies. These nine bivariate regressions will provide first tentative insights into the potential effects of each institution on crisis resilience, differentiated according to time periods and country groups. In the next step, I conduct another nine multivariate regression, now including the control variables based on principle component analysis, as depicted in table 6. These nine regressions provide further information about significant relationships after controlling for all relevant initial economic vulnerabilities at the same time. For those time periods and sub-samples with significant coefficients, I run additional regressions which control for only one principal component or one original control variable at a time. Besides being robustness checks, these regressions also provide information on the most relevant individual control variables that influence the significance of the institutional variables.

Before proceeding to the individual assessment of institutional variables, one more issue has to be addressed regarding the interpretation of significant coefficients. The analysis below assumes that economic performance during the crisis depends on two factors: initial vulnerabilities and economic institutions. The coefficients of the institutional variables after controlling for pre-crisis vulnerabilities can be interpreted as the effects of economic institutions on adaptive efficiency during the years 2008 to 2012. Besides these effects on adaption *during* the crisis period, however, economic institutions may also have another impact on crisis resilience via another channel – by affecting the initial vulnerabilities *before* the crisis started. Potential examples are financial institutions affecting pre-crisis financial deepening or regulations affecting international competitiveness and therefore the current account balance. This means that if coefficients of institutional variables are significant in bivariate regressions but insignificant when controlling for initial vulnerabilities, this only indicates that they had no direct effect during the recession period. If, however, initial vulnerabilities and institutions are correlated, such results may still indicate an effect of economic institutions that was mediated through pre-crisis vulnerabilities. Whether such interpretations are adequate depends on theoretical consideration in each individual case. At this point it is only necessary to mention this issue, as I will pick it up again throughout the analysis below.

4.3.1 Rule of Law and Crisis Resilience

The first institution under consideration is rule of law. In the economic realm, rule of law refers mainly to the impartial enforcement of property rights and contract laws. Property rights include the rights to use, to alter, to derive income from and to transfer property. Contract laws involve specifications of rules regarding the conclusion and the permitted terms of contracts. Both aspects require a strong judicial system and a strong police who protect private actors against violations of rights and contracts by other private actors or by public authorities. This, however, creates a dilemma, as the authorities responsible for property rights protection and contract enforcement (courts and police) are closely tied to potential violators of the same rights and laws – the government and other state authorities. Weingast (1995, p. 1) describes this dilemma as follows: "A government strong enough to protect property rights and enforce contracts is also strong enough to confiscate the wealth of its citizens". Furthermore, public authorities may also be subject to corruption by affiliated private actors and therefore act in a partial way when dealing with private disputes about property or contracts. Hence, the quality of the rule of law depends on the ability of states to solve the above-stated dilemma by enforcing property rights and contract laws in an impartial way, even against the immediate interests of other state authorities or of affiliated private actors.

Discussion and Hypotheses

As outlined by Olson (2000) and North (1990), rule of law is an essential prerequisite for sophisticated economic transactions involving long-term economic activity or complex terms of cooperation. Secure property rights, for example, are relevant for long-term investment projects, as they ensure that investors are able to reap the benefits of their investments. Without assurances, such projects would be much riskier and therefore less likely to take place. Similarly, transparent and impartially-enforced contract laws reduce ex-ante uncertainties and make cooperation amongst contract partners more likely, especially when the terms of cooperation are complicated, such as in cases of long-term cooperation, when a large number of actors is involved or when the exact type of performance depends on various contingencies (Olson, 2000, pp. 174-180, 183-189).

Increasing the scope of feasible transactions matters during all phases of the business cycle. During times of economic crises, however, low transaction costs are particularly important, as uncertainties in the business environment are even higher than usual.[163] In such situations, well-enforced property rights and contract laws should increase the predictability of the cooperative behavior of contract partners and have a stabilizing effect on investment and economic activity (Lipford, 2007). Badly-enforced property rights and contract laws, on the other hand, potentially intensify the uncertainties associated with a difficult business environment. Dawson (2010, p. 178), for example, argues that "weak institutions leave economic cooperation to rely on trust, in which case shocks may lead to a breakdown of cooperation and economic collapses". Such breakdowns of cooperation and economic activity reduce the output potential of an economy but may also depress aggregate demand if higher uncertainties induce consumers and companies to cut back consumption expenditures and investments.

Besides cushioning economic downturns, secure property rights and contract laws may also facilitate recoveries because widening the scope of feasible transactions increases the potential for innovations in still-growing sectors that offer a destination for unemployed factors of production. Bjornskov (2016, p. 14) puts forward such an argument with regard to the benefits of economic freedom (which includes rule of law). He argues that "low freedom particularly leads to fewer actual and potential entrepreneurial firms. Entrepreneurs are arguably specifically important during the recovery period of a crisis, as firms and jobs have been destroyed and both new and existing firms have incentives to soak up unemployed resources". Without secure property rights and contract laws, high uncertainties may induce entrepreneurs to withhold investment projects or to abstain from engaging in new contracts, thereby reducing the scope of potentially innovative activity. Higgs (1997, p. 563) puts forward a similar argument regarding the slow recovery during the Great Depression. He argues "that the insufficiency of private investment from 1935 to 1940 reflected the pervasive

[163] Baker et al. (2016, p. 1600), for example, show that their index of policy-related economic insecurity for the United States is considerably higher after 2008 than before the crisis.

uncertainty among investors about the security of their property rights in their capital and its prospective returns".

Following these arguments, secure property rights and contract laws should have positive effects on crisis resilience especially by supporting two out of the three aspects of adaptive efficiency outlined in chapter 2. First, less uncertainty in the business environment should avoid costly and unnecessary changes of organizational structures and channels of cooperation amongst economic actors. Second, better predictability of the potential gains from cooperation and investment projects should increase the scope of innovative activity that offers new opportunities for economic expansions and employment for factors of production.

Past empirical research about this issue is very scarce. Bjornskov (2016) investigates the relationship between rule of law and crisis resilience in two samples including various crisis episodes in different countries. In both samples, one capturing crisis episodes in less developed countries and one capturing crisis episodes worldwide, he reports only insignificant coefficients. Berglöf et al. (2010), who consider rule of law as an explanatory variable in their analysis of crisis intensity during the years 2008 to 2009, also do not report significant results. Other authors, investigate whether rule of law has an impact on output variability measured by the standard deviation of growth rates. Lipford (2007), Dawson (2010) and Campbell & Snyder (2012) provide evidence that rule of law significantly reduces the variability of economic output, suggesting smaller output reductions during downturns.

Although the previous empirical evidence is inconclusive, the hypothesis that follows from chapter 2 based on Olson's and NWW's accounts and from the short discussion of related theoretical arguments in this section states:

- Countries with higher degrees of rule of law should have performed better during the Great Recession than countries with lower degrees of rule of law.

Data Sources

Below, I use four different indices as explanatory variables representing rule of law, impartially-enforced property rights and contract laws as well as absence of corruption:

- The first measure is the simple average of the two indices 'property rights' and 'freedom from corruption' published by the Heritage Foundation. These two indices aim at providing "an assessment of the ability of individuals to accumulate private property, secured by clear laws that are fully enforced by the state" and "assess the perception of corruption in the business environment" (Beach & Kane, 2008, p. 41). The 'property rights' index relies on expert judgments by the authors, whereas the 'freedom from corruption' index mirrors the scores of the 'corruption perception index' from Transparency International, which is based on a variety of different data sources (Beach &

Kane, 2008, pp. 51-53). Both indices can take values between 0 and 100. Values of the composite measure averaging the scores of both indices range from 18 (Vietnam) to 93.5 (Iceland) within the sample used in this thesis.

- The second measure labeled 'legal system and property rights' from the Fraser institute is a simple average of nine different items related to rule of law and the control of corruption. These items are derived from the Global Competitiveness Report, the International Country Risk Guide and the Doing Business Database of the World Bank. The index focuses on the "[p]rotection of persons and their rightfully acquired property" including aspects of contract enforcements and legal impartiality (Gwartney & Lawson, 2009, p. 7). It can take values between 0 and 10. Within the sample used in this thesis, the country with the lowest score is Côte d'Ivoire with 2.84, and the country with the highest score is Finland with 9.14.
- The third measure is the simple average of the two indices 'rule of law' and 'control of corruption' from the World Governance Indicators Database. These indices are the most comprehensive measures available, as they aggregate information from a wide variety of surveys and expert judgements from up to 31 different data sources (Kaufmann et al., 2010 p. 29). The 'rule of law' index most narrowly represents the aspects of the legal system discussed above, "capturing perceptions of the extent to which agents have confidence in and abide by the rules of a society, and in particular the quality of contract enforcement, property rights, the police, and the courts, as well as the likelihood of crime and violence" (Kaufmann et al., 2010, p. 4). The 'control of corruption' index is complementary to those narrow aspects of rule of law, as it refers to the way the abovementioned provisions are immune to being corrupted by special interest groups. It captures "perceptions of the extent to which public power is exercised for private gain, including both pretty and grand forms of corruption, as well as 'capture' of the state by elites and private interest" (Kaufmann et al., 2010, p. 4). Both indices take values of standard normal variables with 0 means and a standard deviation of 1. Values of the composite measure of 'rule of law and control of corruption' range from -1.28 (Côte d'Ivoire) to 2.26 (Denmark).
- The fourth measure is a simple average of four out of five components of the index 'public institutions' from the Global Competitiveness Report. These four components are labeled 'property rights', 'ethics and corruption', 'undue influence' and 'security'.[164] I do not include the fifth component labeled 'government efficiency' because it captures properties belonging to the extent of regulations and government size that I will analyze below. Within the sample

[164] For a list of the components included in the index see Schwab & Porter (2008, p. 39). The detailed questions of the Executive Opinion Survey, which are the base of the index construction, are also listed in Schwab & Porter (2008, pp. 364-377).

used in this thesis, values for the constructed index range from 2.30 (Paraguay) to 6.18 (Denmark).

All four explanatory variables are highly correlated, indicating that they capture very similar aspects of the legal system and rule of law (see appendix 4). The lowest correlation of 0.89 exists between the combined 'property rights and corruption' index from the Heritage Foundation and the index 'legal system and property rights' from the Fraser Institute. All other correlations are higher than 0.9.

Results

Table 7 depicts the coefficients when regressing the dependent variables for the three time periods against the rule of law variables in three different samples of countries. The results show that, when considering the entire sample of 84 countries, rule of law is negatively and significantly related to economic performance in most of the specifications. Countries with lower rule of law scores performed better than countries with higher scores. This effect was stronger during the initial downturn 2008 to 2009 than during the recovery period 2010 to 2012. When considering only the sub-sample of 32 developed countries, however, the coefficients point into a different direction, now indicating that developed countries with high degrees of rule of law performed better during the crisis (most importantly due to a stronger recovery 2010 to 2012) than developed countries with low degrees of rule of law. As the coefficients for the sub-group of 52 less developed countries are mainly insignificant, this suggests that the negative coefficients in the entire sample of 84 countries are mainly driven by the performance difference between developed and less developed countries, the former featuring higher degrees of rule of law but worse performance than the latter.

	Dep. Var.: GDP_{08-12}			Dep. Var.: GDP_{08-09}			Dep. Var.: GDP_{10-12}		
	All	Deve-loped	Emerging & Dev.	All	Deve-loped	Emerging & Dev.	All	Deve-loped	Emerging & Dev.
Her. Prop. Rights & Free from Cor.	**-0.16** **0.00*****	**0.28** **0.02****	-0.00 1.00	**-0.11** **0.00*****	0.11 0.13	-0.07 0.36	-0.05 0.12	**0.20** **0.03****	0.07 0.38
Fras. Leg. Syst. & Prop. Rights	**-3.17** **0.00*****	3.35 0.09*	**-2.51** **0.02****	**-1.89** **0.00*****	1.03 0.30	**-1.25** **0.04****	**-1.36** **0.00*****	2.69 0.07*	-1.27 0.15
WGI Rule of Law & Contr. of Cor.	**-4.66** **0.00*****	**6.41** **0.03****	-2.91 0.40	**-2.97** **0.00*****	2.94 0.14	-2.47 0.17	**-1.81** **0.01****	**4.17** **0.05****	-0.46 0.82
GCI Control of Cor.	**-3.12** **0.00*****	**5.54** **0.02****	-0.54 0.80	**-1.87** **0.00*****	2.73 0.09*	-0.35 0.75	-1.30 0.09*	**3.39** **0.03****	-0.12 0.94

Table 7: Coefficients of rule of law indices as explanatory variables in bivariate regressions (second row: p-values of two-sided significance tests; number of asterisks: significance levels of 10%*, 5%** and 1%***; significant results at 5% level are bold).

Figure 9 reinforces this interpretation. It plots the rule of law scores (based on the Heritage variable) of all 84 countries against the measure of crisis resilience during the period 2008 to 2012. Performance scores above 0 mean that countries achieved higher average growth rates during those years than before the crisis, and scores below 0 indicate declines of average growth rates as compared to pre-crisis rates. The scatterplot shows that developed countries (white circles) feature higher degrees of rule of law but also suffered deeper economic crises than less developed countries (black dots). While the fitted line has a negative slope when considering the entire sample of 84 countries, it has a positive slope for the sub-group of 32 developed countries. Plots for the other three rule of law variables look very similar (see appendix 5).

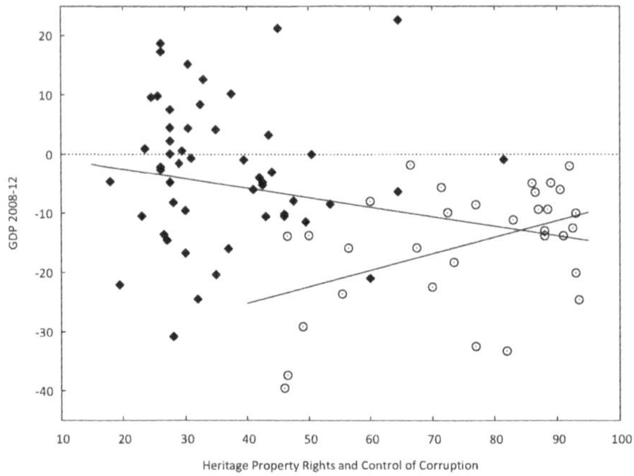

Figure 9: Scatterplot of '$GDP_{08\text{-}12}$' against Heritage 'property rights and corruption' (black dots: less developed countries; white circles: developed countries; downward-sloping line: fitted values for the entire sample; upward-sloping line: fitted values for the sub-sample of developed countries).

The preliminary results from the bivariate regressions contradict the hypothesis stated above that rule of law improves crisis resilience, but they provide tentative support for a qualified hypothesis that such a relation holds in developed countries. When controlling for initial vulnerabilities, however, the coefficients of explanatory rule of law variables turn insignificant, as depicted in table 8.

	Dep. Var.: $GDP_{08\text{-}12}$			Dep. Var.: $GDP_{08\text{-}09}$			Dep. Var.: $GDP_{10\text{-}12}$		
	All	Deve-loped	Emerging & Dev.	All	Deve-loped	Emerging & Dev.	All	Deve-loped	Emerging & Dev.
Her. Prop. Rights & Free from Cor.	-0.09 0.28	0.18 0.21	-0.06 0.54	-0.12 0.05*	-0.02 0.87	-0.09 0.17	0.02 0.60	0.14 0.07*	0.03 0.63
Fras. Leg. Syst. & Prop. Rights	-0.82 0.33	1.29 0.51	-0.13 0.91	-0.89 0.15	-0.97 0.44	-0.29 0.70	0.03 0.94	2.08 0.07*	-0.19 0.79
WGI Rule of Law & Contr. of Cor.	-2.66 0.16	2.93 0.38	-1.14 0.65	-2.61 0.06*	-0.67 0.78	-1.69 0.32	-0.18 0.82	2.79 0.12	0.52 0.65
GCI Control of Cor.	0.03 0.98	2.94 0.24	-0.68 0.68	-0.23 0.83	0.51 0.80	-0.30 0.80	0.23 0.75	2.24 0.05*	0.45 0.69

Table 8: Coefficients of rule of law indices as explanatory variables in multivariate regressions with control models according to table 6 (second row: p-values of two-sided significance tests; number of asterisks: significance levels of 10%*, 5%** and 1%***; significant results at 5% level are bold).

Table 8 depicts the coefficients of the rule of law variables from multivariate OLS regressions that include the control variables established in section 4.2 based on principle component analysis. While most coefficients clearly fall short of being significant, they come close to meeting the p-value threshold of 0.05 in two cases: first, during the initial downturn 2008 to 2009 when considering the entire sample of 84 countries and, second, during the recovery period 2010 to 2012 when considering only the sub-group of 32 developed countries.

The next step involves a deeper analysis of the question why coefficients of the rule of law variables turn insignificant when controlling for initial vulnerabilities. Specifically, it is interesting to know which particular control variables render the coefficients of the explanatory variables insignificant in multivariate regressions. I thereby focus on the entire sample of 84 countries during the downturn period 2008 to 2009 and the sub-sample of 32 developed countries during the recovery period 2010 to 2012.

Starting with the entire sample of 84 countries, table 9 depicts the simple correlations between explanatory rule of law variables and the different control variables (including principal components and original variables). Almost all correlations are positive and particularly high between rule of law variables and the two development variables ('economic development' and 'GDP per capita'). This indicates that countries with high degrees of rule of law are also highly developed. As high development levels are associated with worse crisis resilience within the sample of 84 countries (see tables 3 and 6), these correlations suggest that the loss of significance of rule of law variables in multivariate regressions depends most importantly on the inclusion of 'economic development'.

	WGI Rule of Law and Control of Corruption	Heritage Property Rights and Freedom from Corruption	Fraser Legal System and Property Rights	GCI Public Institutions
Financial Vulnerabilities	0.06	-0.01	0.13	-0.02
Increase (Priv. Cred. / GDP)	**0.28**	**0.25**	**0.28**	0.22
Current Acc. Balance / GDP	**0.23**	**0.27**	0.17	**0.28**
Economic Development	**0.79**	**0.81**	**0.70**	**0.76**
GDP per Capita	**0.90**	**0.88**	**0.82**	**0.82**
International Linkages	0.18	0.18	**0.23**	**0.23**
Trade / GDP	**0.26**	**0.25**	**0.31**	**0.31**
Industrial Orientation	**0.22**	0.15	**0.26**	0.19
Manuf. Exp. / Total Exp.	**0.29**	**0.24**	**0.29**	**0.25**

Table 9: Correlations between rule of law variables and control variables in the entire sample (significant correlations at 5% level are bold).

Table 10 reinforces this interpretation. The first nine columns depict the coefficients of multivariate regression of '$GDP_{08\text{-}09}$' against 'property rights and corruption' (based on Heritage data) and one control variable at a time. Especially the inclusion of 'GDP per capita' in regression 5 considerably reduces the magnitude and the significance level of the 'property rights and corruption' coefficients. Similarly, regressions 10 and 11, which depict the coefficients when considering the explanatory variable and significant control variables based on principle components, show that 'property rights and corruption' and 'economic development' both turn insignificant when included together. As both variables are correlated and highly significant when used alone, this suggests that they indeed capture similar effects. Results of other measures of rule of law during the same time period 2008 to 2009 (appendix 6) and for the entire time period 2008 to 2012 (appendix 7) look very similar. For the time period 2010 to 2012 results point into the same direction but are more sensitive to the choice of explanatory and control variables (appendix 8).

	Dependent Variable: 'GDP_{08-09}'; Sample: All 84 Countries										
	(1)	(2)	(3)	(4)	(5)	(6)	(7)	(8)	(9)	(10)	(11)
Constant	-0.03	-0.38	2.19	2.72	-2.13	-0.44	0.83	-0.77	2.79	0.12	-1.07
	0.98	0.81	0.20	0.42	0.41	0.79	0.65	0.63	0.13	0.97	0.49
Her. Prop. Rights	-0.11	-0.08	-0.14	-0.17	-0.04	-0.11	-0.10	-0.10	-0.09	-0.12	-0.09
& Free from Cor.	0.00***	0.00***	0.00***	0.01**	0.62	0.00***	0.00***	0.00***	0.00***	0.05*	0.00***
Financial	-3.28									-3.28	-3.28
Vulnerabilities	0.00***									0.00***	0.00***
Increase (Priv.		-0.12									
Cred. / GDP)		0.02**									
Current Acc.			0.28								
Balance / GDP			0.00***								
Economic				1.62						0.65	
Development				0.33						0.64	
GDP					-0.11						
per Capita					0.24						
International						-0.86				-0.81	-0.92
Linkages						0.17				0.12	0.05*
Trade /							-0.02				
GDP							0.15				
Industrial								-2.06		-2.00	-2.09
Orientation								0.00***		0.00***	0.00***
Manuf. Exp. /									-0.09		
Total Exp.									0.00***		
N	84	84	84	84	84	84	84	84	84	84	84
R^{2*}	0.33	0.27	0.23	0.13	0.14	0.13	0.13	0.20	0.20	0.40	0.41

Table 10: Multivariate regressions of 'GDP_{08-09}' against Heritage 'property rights and corruption' and one additional control variable in the entire sample (second row: p-values of two-sided significance tests; number of asterisks: significance levels of 10%*, 5%** and 1%***).

These results entail the question about an adequate interpretation. On the one hand, the loss of significance after the inclusion of 'GDP per capita' or 'economic development' could mean that rule of law is irrelevant for explaining the depth of the recession. On the other hand, rule of law may be one of the features that made highly developed countries more vulnerable to the crisis (for example by making the economic survival of companies subject to impartial economic competition instead of political discretion insulating them from a contracting business environment). No matter which interpretation the reader prefers, the negative coefficients clearly contradict the hypothesis that rule of law has a general positive effect on crisis resilience.

According to table 7, however, there may be a positive relationship between rule of law and crisis resilience in the sub-group of 32 developed countries, especially during the recovery period 2010 to 2012. This would provide some tentative support for a qualified hypothesis that rule of law improves crisis resilience when countries are already highly developed. To investigate why positive coefficients turn insignificant when controlling for pre-crisis vulnerabilities (in table 8), table 11 depicts the simple correlations between rule of law variables and different control variables in the sub-sample of 32 developed countries. Countries with higher levels of rule of law also feature better current account balances, higher levels of development and lower levels of industrial orientation of the economy.

	WGI Rule of Law and Control of Corruption	Heritage Property Rights and Freedom from Corruption	Fraser Legal System and Property Rights	GCI Public Institutions
Financial Vulnerabilities	-0.19	-0.20	-0.13	-0.20
Increase (Priv. Cred. / GDP)	0.07	0.05	0.06	0.06
Current Acc. Balance / GDP	**0.50**	**0.49**	**0.43**	**0.51**
Economic Development	**0.73**	**0.72**	**0.63**	**0.71**
GDP per Capita	**0.80**	**0.76**	**0.70**	**0.75**
International Linkages	0.12	0.14	0.14	0.15
Trade / GDP	0.10	0.13	0.13	0.15
Industrial Orientation	**-0.42**	**-0.41**	**-0.44**	**-0.40**
Manuf. Exp. / Total Exp.	-0.23	-0.22	-0.26	-0.24

Table 11: Correlations between rule of law variables and control variables in the sub-sample of developed countries (significant correlations at 5% level are bold).

Especially the positive correlations of the rule of law variables with the 'current account balance to GDP ratio' is relevant for explaining why the rule of law coefficients turn insignificant in some regressions. As explained before, positive current account balances mean that countries exported more goods than they imported, relied less heavily on capital inflows from abroad and, hence, featured lower financial vulnerabilities than countries with current account deficits. As all rule of law variables are positively related to the 'current account balance to GDP ratio', controlling for the latter variable (or for the principal component 'financial vulnerabilities', which includes current account deficits) reduces the significance level of the rule of law variables.

To show that this is the case, table 12 depicts the coefficients of multivariate regression including the Heritage variable 'property rights and corruption' together with one control variable at a time for the recovery period 2010 to 2012 (when results are more pronounced). Especially the inclusion of the 'current account balance to GDP ratio' in regression 3 drastically reduces the magnitude and the significance level of the 'property rights and corruption' coefficient. The same effects are less pronounced when controlling for the component 'financial vulnerabilities' that is partially based on current account deficits. Results for the other measures of rule of law (appendix 9) and for the entire period 2008 to 2012 (appendix 10) are very similar.

	Dependent Variable: 'GDP_{10-12}'; Sample: 32 Developed Countries								
	(1)	(2)	(3)	(4)	(5)	(6)	(7)	(8)	(9)
Constant	-15.81 0.02**	-18.90 0.00***	-8.95 0.13	-30.68 0.00***	-24.34 0.00***	-19.96 0.01***	-21.65 0.00***	-30.26 0.00***	-34.96 0.00***
Her. Prop. Rights & Free from Cor.	0.14 0.07*	0.21 0.01***	0.06 0.43	0.38 0.01***	0.37 0.02**	0.19 0.03**	0.18 0.03**	0.30 0.00***	0.25 0.00***
Financial Vulnerabilities	-3.58 0.00***								
Increase (Priv. Cred. / GDP)		-0.13 0.00***							
Current Acc. Balance / GDP			0.49 0.00***						
Economic Development				-3.89 0.02**					
GDP per Capita					-0.25 0.07*				
International Linkages						0.62 0.44			
Trade / GDP							0.02 0.04**		
Industrial Orientation								5.00 0.00***	
Manuf. Exp. / Total Exp.									0.19 0.00***
N	32	32	32	32	32	32	32	32	32
R^{2*}	0.52	0.55	0.50	0.31	0.27	0.16	0.20	0.45	0.48

Table 12: Multivariate regressions of 'GDP_{10-12}' against Heritage 'property rights and corruption' and one additional control variable in the sub-sample of developed countries (second row: p-values of two-sided significance tests; number of asterisks: significance levels of 10%*, 5%** and 1%***).

As before, the question arises whether the insignificant coefficients of rule of law variables when controlling for the 'current account balance to GDP ratio' or 'financial vulnerabilities' mean that rule of law is irrelevant for explaining the strength of the economic recovery during the years 2010 to 2012 in developed countries. Another plausible interpretation of these results is that higher degrees of rule of law contributed to healthier current accounts prior to the crisis, for example by improving these countries' productivity and international competitiveness (through innovative products and technologies) vis-à-vis deficit countries, thereby stimulating exports and creating less need to finance imports through foreign credit.[165] Furthermore, deficient

[165] This effect is particularly relevant within the European Monetary Union were a divergence of competitiveness could not be counterbalanced by exchange rate adjustments. However, it is debated within the literature whether differences in competitiveness are indeed relevant for explaining imbalances. While some authors put forward this view (Belke & Dreger, 2013; Zemanek et al., 2009), other authors claim that current account imbalances were caused not by differences

institutions (including badly-enforced property rights and contract laws or high degrees of corruption) in current account deficit countries may have contributed to misallocations of resources to unsustainable investment projects (Eichengreen, 2010).[166] Following this interpretation, competitive countries, which had experienced less pre-crisis capital inflows, had to make fewer painful adjustments during the crisis and recovered more quickly than deficit countries, which had to reduce prices and wages to regain competitiveness or cut back unsustainable investment projects and consumption activities. Hence, based on the premises that well-enforced property rights and contract laws promote productivity and international competitiveness and that they prevent misallocations of resources, there may have been an indirect positive effect of rule of law on crisis resilience that was mediated through better current account balances.

From the previous discussion I conclude that rule of law clearly did not improve crisis resilience within the sample of 84 countries. Highly developed countries with high degrees of rule of law even performed worse than less developed countries with low degrees of rule of law, especially during the initial downturn 2008 to 2009. These negative effects of rule of law variables are closely related to negative effects of development variables. Both variables show a strong positive correlation and at least one of them turns insignificant when using them alongside each other to explain crisis resilience in multivariate regressions. It is, therefore, unclear which of the two variables is responsible for this negative association with crisis resilience. Regardless of the answer to this question, the regression results suggest rejecting the hypothesis that rule of law had a generally positive effect on crisis resilience.

The results for the sub-sample of 32 developed countries, on the other hand, indicate that rule of law had a positive effect on crisis resilience within that sub-group of countries, especially during the recovery period 2010 to 2012. This finding, however, depends on the interpretation of the relationship between the rule of law variable and the current account variable. If rule of law contributed to healthier current accounts (for example, because of better competitiveness and fewer misdirected investments), it had a positive effect on crisis resilience that was mediated through the current account balance. This potential effect of rule of law on crisis resilience, however, works through a different channel than suggested by the previous theoretical discussion, as it refers to avoiding the build-up of imbalances *before* the recession instead of quicker adaptions *during* the crisis.

---

in competitiveness but rather by wage restraint and lower domestic demand in surplus countries (Uxó et al., 2011).

[166] Similarly, Gaulier & Vicard (2012) argue that misallocations of investment in non-tradable sectors in EU periphery countries contributed to the build-up of current account deficits.

4.3.2 Business Regulations and Crisis Resilience

The regulation of businesses by state authorities plays an ambiguous role for economic policy. On the one hand, many regulations such as restrictions of permitted economic activities, administrative requirements, licensing restrictions or tax laws fulfil legitimate social and economic ends, such as mitigating various forms of market failures.[167] On the other hand, these regulations can be instruments for rent-seeking attempts by interest groups, as they constitute entry barriers for potential competitors, thereby limiting competition and creating opportunities for non-competitive price setting (Krueger, 1974; Posner, 1975). In the subsequent discussion, I focus on the rent-creating effects of business regulations. By this, however, I do not mean to negate the legitimate role of regulations for other purposes; the latter are simply less relevant for the analysis of crisis resilience. An overall assessment of the optimal extent of business regulations would have to be based on both issues.

Two consequences of rent-creating business regulation are specifically important for the discussion of adaptive efficiency during a recession: first, price floors for goods and services and, second, barriers to market entry. According to Olson (1982, pp. 66-69), both are the concurrent consequences of rent-seeking efforts, as distributional coalitions try to create rents by fixing prices of goods and services above market-clearing levels. Thereby, each member of the coalition sells a smaller amount of goods and services at higher prices than they would normally do under competitive conditions. In order to secure high economic rents from such price floors, the coalition members have to prevent new competitors from entering the market – often by means of regulations such as licensing restrictions, administrative requirements or legal restrictions of certain activities. Permitting new competitors to enter the market would either drive prices back down to market-clearing levels or it would reduce the amount of goods and services each member of the coalition could sell. Hence, price floors and entrance barriers to markets are usually two sides of the same medal.

Discussion and hypothesis

According to the arguments outlined during the discussion of Olson's account in chapter 2, sclerotic markets featuring entrance barriers and inflexible prices entail slower decision-making by economic actors, a smaller number of competitors and more inflexible market participants. Thus, when an economic shock requires changes in prices and quantities or engagement in new activities, adjustments take place more slowly in sclerotic markets than in competitive markets with a larger number of presumably more flexible competitors. Retarded modifications of prices, quantities and activities, in turn, reduce the scope of innovative activity and slows down the re-allocation of factors of production to their best uses. Below, I discuss both effects,

[167] For a short overview of potential reasons for regulations see Stiglitz & Rosengard (2015, pp. 82-99). Even scholars with an outspoken pro-market attitude such as Hayek (1981, pp. 67-93) acknowledge that there are legitimate regulations by the government (although he also points out their limits).

starting with obstructions of innovative activity and then turning to slow factor re-allocations.

First, restricted market entry and inflexible prices may reduce the scope of innovative activity. The generation of innovations depends on the number and the capabilities of economic actors who engage in, what Hayek (1981, pp. 100-102) labels, an economic discovery procedure. According to that account, a market order with flexible prices and open access to competition enables market participants to freely use their personal knowledge to pursue their own personal plans. Economic success or failure determines which plans should be further pursued and which plans should be abandoned. This trial-and-error process amongst a wide variety of plans and coordination through flexible prices enable the best possible use of knowledge in society[168] and, hence, promote innovations. Regulations, which restrict new competitors from freely engaging in certain activities, interfere with this discovery procedure, as they reduce the number of market participants searching for new solutions to a society's problems, inhibit innovative competitors from entering markets and protect established and potentially inflexible companies from being eliminated by competitive forces. Burda (2013) puts forward a similar argument regarding the Great Recession: "Product market reforms, [...] the establishment and consistent application of rule of law, the banishment of corruption, increasing competition in all walks of economic life – [are] all measures which tend to make it easier for new entrants to engage in economic activity and expand the current set of economic alternatives. These measures also destroy rents in protected, regulated sectors which may have taken decades to accumulate. Current debates over market access to the 'free professions' in Italy and the issuance of new licenses in the transport sector in Greece are two particularly salient examples, but there are many, many more."

Second, inflexible prices and entry restrictions may slow down the re-allocation of productive factors to their most productive uses. If outside competitors cannot invest in protected markets, this restricts the potential for output expansion to already established companies. Furthermore, following Olson's (1982, pp. 53-58) argument, protected companies make their decisions more slowly than companies who are accustomed to a competitive business environment. Thus, although there may be a potential for renewed growth in certain sectors, a limited number of presumably more inflexible companies needs more time to redirect unemployed capital and labor to these uses. Other authors argue along similar lines. Bjornskov (2016), for example, states: "As a crisis hits an economy, a substantial share of resources become unemployed, which creates profit opportunities for entrepreneurs to the extent that these resources become cheaper. Yet, whether or not this happens and at which speed existing firms and new entrants can reallocate resources depends on the regulatory framework. Licensing requirements and similar business regulations constitute entry barriers that prevent entrepreneurs from seizing legal opportunities and thereby

---

[168] See also Hayek (1945).

limiting the economic and social losses during crises." Furthermore, the re-allocation of productive factors to their best uses may also be inhibited by price rigidities which disable prices from fulfilling their signaling function (Hayek, 1945, pp. 526-528).

There are, however, also voices that warn against the adverse effects of too much flexibility in goods markets. Blanchard et al. (2014), for example, point out that product market reforms should be chosen carefully during a recession, as increasing competition and productivity improvements may have adverse labor market effects if higher productivity is not accompanied by a proportionate increase in aggregate demand. Similarly, Schumpeter (1996 [1943], p. 95) points out the potentially negative effects of very flexible prices, stating that "under the conditions created by capitalist evolution, perfect and universal flexibility of prices might in depression further destabilize the system".

Previous empirical evidence regarding the effects of business regulation on crisis resilience is rather scarce. Giannone et al. (2012) consider business freedom as an explanatory variable for explaining the depth of the recession during the years 2008 to 2009. In two regression using a worldwide sample of 89 countries they report negative but insignificant coefficients. Bjornskov (2016) uses a broader measure of 'regulatory efficiency' based on data from the Heritage Foundation, which includes 'business freedom', 'labor market freedom' and 'financial freedom' as an independent variable for explaining crisis resilience in a sample of 212 different crisis episodes in 121 countries. Departing from Giannone et al. (2012), he provides evidence that better 'regulatory efficiency' is significantly associated with less severe downturns and quicker recoveries. Similarly, Dawson (2010) and Campbell & Snyder (2012) investigate the potential effects of overall regulatory quality (including regulations of business, labor and finance) on output volatility. They, too report negative associations between the variable 'regulatory efficiency' and output volatility, though the coefficients remain insignificant.

Following this short discussion and based on the theoretical arguments presented in chapter 2, there are two competing hypotheses regarding the effects of business regulations on crisis resilience. The first is based on Olson's and NWW's views, and the second follows the arguments focusing on structural stability:

- Countries with fewer business regulations that constitute market entrance barriers and price floors should have performed better during the Great Recession than countries with stricter regulations.
- Countries with stricter business regulations that reduce competition and price flexibility should have performed better during the Great Recession than countries with fewer regulations.

Data Sources

Below, I consider five different indices as measures for business regulations: the index labeled 'regulatory quality' from the Worldwide Governance Indicators Database, the 'business freedom' index from the Heritage Foundation, the 'business regulation' index from the Fraser Institute, an index labeled 'competition' provided by the Global Competitiveness Database and a summary index from the Doing Business Database. Most of these indices aggregate information from similar data sources including surveys, expert judgements and objective data. While some of the items explicitly refer to entrance barriers and price controls, others only capture the extent of business regulations in general, also including regulations that serve legitimate social and economic purposes. Below, I simply assume that, other things being equal, more business regulations entail more opportunities for rent-creation, barriers to market entry and price fixing.

- The first index is based on the Doing Business Database, which provides objective data about the ease of doing business in different countries. I calculate the average of the scores from the nine available areas including the difficulty of 'starting a business', 'dealing with construction permits', 'registering property', 'getting credit', 'protecting minority investors', 'paying taxes', 'trading across borders', 'enforcing contracts' and 'resolving insolvency'. Each area includes items measuring the time, costs and obstacles associated with each activity. The scores of each area in the Doing Business Database measure the distance of each country's regulatory environment from the best-practice institutional environment (World Bank, 2016, pp. 163-168). Potential scores of the index range from 0 (farthest away from best practice in each area) to 100 (best practice in each area). Actual scores of the overall index range from 36.48 (Senegal) to 91.46 (Singapore).
- The second index from the Heritage Foundation labeled 'business freedom' is based on the same data from the Doing Business Database. It aggregates information from three out of the nine available areas listed above, including the difficulty of 'starting a business', of 'dealing with construction permits' and of 'resolving insolvency' (Beach & Kane, 2008, pp. 42-43). Besides having a narrower scope than the first index, the Heritage Foundation also uses a slightly different aggregation approach than the Doing Business Report, relying on relative deviations from average values. Potential scores can take values between 0 and 100. Actual scores within the sample used in this thesis range from 41 (Cameroon) to 99.9 (New Zealand).
- The third index from the Global Competitiveness Database labeled 'competition' is based on subjective data from the Executive Opinions Survey gathered by the World Economic Forum and on objective data from the Doing Business Database. It is a weighted average of 14 items capturing the prevalence

of a competitive business environment that is not marked by market dominance, burdensome regulations and extensive trade restrictions.[169] The index can take values between 1 and 7. Actual scores within the sample used in this thesis range from 3.38 (Bolivia) to 5.89 (Singapore).

- The fourth index labeled 'regulatory quality' from the Worldwide Governance Indicators Database is the most comprehensive index. It aggregates information from a variety of survey data sources including the Executive Opinions Survey that also feeds the Global Competitive Database. One potential disadvantage of this index is the non-consideration of objective data. According to the authors, this index represents "the ability of the government to formulate and implement sound policies and regulations that permit and promote private sector development" (Kaufmann et al., 2010, p. 4). It takes values of a standard normal variable with the mean 0 and a standard deviation of 1 ranging from -1.43 (Belarus) to 2.00 (Hong Kong).
- The fifth index labeled 'business regulation' from the Fraser Institute's Economic Freedom of the World Index aggregates data from different sources including the Doing Business Database and the Executive Opinion Survey that feeds the Global Competitiveness Report. According to the authors, the index is "designed to identify the extent to which regulations and bureaucratic procedures restrain entry and reduce competition. In order to score high in this [...] index, countries must allow markets to determine prices and refrain from regulatory activities that retard entry into business and increase the cost of producing products. They must also refrain from 'playing favorites' this is, from using their power to extract financial payments and reward businesses at the expense of others" (Gwartney & Lawson, 2009, p. 8). The index can take values between 0 and 10. Actual values range from 3.43 (Cameroon) to 8.01 (Singapore).

All five indices capture the prevalence of entrance barriers and price controls to different degrees and based on different data sources. While some indices have a narrower scope and concentrate on domestic entrance barriers (such as the Heritage index or the Fraser index), others also consider entry barriers for foreign competitors (such as the Doing Business Summary index). Regarding data sources, some indices rely primarily on objective data (such as the Doing Business Index), others mix this information with items based on answers of business executives to survey questions (such as the WGI 'regulatory quality' index). Despite their differences, however, all five indices are positively correlated (the smallest correlation between two different indices being 0.67) and therefore capture similar aspects of business regulations.[170]

---

[169] These 14 items are listed in Schwab & Porter (2008, pp. 40). For a detailed description of the data and the wording of the survey questions see Schwab & Porter (2008, pp. 422-434).

[170] The correlation coefficients amongst the five different variables are depicted in appendix 10.

Results

Table 13 depicts the coefficients of the bivariate regressions of the business regulation variables against crisis resilience. When considering the entire dataset of 84 countries, coefficients are negative and mostly significant, especially during the initial downturn 2008 to 2009. Hence, countries with open goods markets show more pronounced downturns than highly regulated countries, thereby contradicting the first hypothesis stated above that business freedom supports crisis resilience. In the sub-set of 32 developed countries, on the other hand, coefficients partly support that hypothesis, as more open goods markets are associated with better economic performance during the recovery period 2010 to 2012 (three out of five variables feature positive and significant coefficients, while the other two miss conventional significance levels only slightly). Coefficients for the sub-set of 52 emerging and developing countries are inconclusive and mostly insignificant.

	Dep. Var.: GDP_{08-12}			Dep. Var.: GDP_{08-09}			Dep. Var.: GDP_{10-12}		
	All	Deve- loped	Emerging & Dev.	All	Deve- loped	Emerging & Dev.	All	Deve- loped	Emerging & Dev.
Heritage Busi- ness Freedom	**-0.30** **0.00*****	0.32 0.09*	-0.16 0.33	**-0.20** **0.00*****	0.05 0.57	-0.13 0.18	-0.10 0.05*	**0.30** **0.05****	-0.01 0.89
Fraser Business Regulation	-2.70 0.07*	2.27 0.30	0.67 0.75	**-2.15** **0.03****	-0.72 0.56	0.10 0.94	-0.55 0.50	3.28 0.07*	0.74 0.52
WGI Regulatory Quality	**-6.82** **0.00*****	9.96 0.07*	**-5.95** **0.04****	**-4.29** **0.00*****	2.96 0.32	**-4.01** **0.00*****	**-2.71** **0.00*****	8.08 0.05*	-1.96 0.29
GCI Competition	**-5.25** **0.01****	**9.79** **0.02****	1.42 0.69	**-3.75** **0.00*****	2.16 0.31	-1.00 0.59	-1.55 0.27	**8.65** **0.01****	0.18 0.94
Doing Business Summary	**-0.31** **0.00*****	**0.44** **0.02****	0.08 0.70	**-0.24** **0.00*****	0.06 0.44	-0.16 0.19	-0.07 0.22	**0.43** **0.02****	0.10 0.39

Table 13: Coefficients of business regulation indices as explanatory variables in bivariate regressions (second row: p-values of two-sided significance tests; number of asterisks: significance levels of 10%*, 5%** and 1%***; significant results at 5% level are bold).

These results suggest that the negative association between open goods markets and economic performance in the entire sample of 84 countries is again likely to be driven by intergroup differences between the two sub-groups of countries, as developed countries show a much higher degree of business freedom and lower crisis resilience than less developed countries.

Figure 10, which plots 'business freedom' based on Heritage data against 'GDP_{08-12}', reinforces this interpretation. Black dots mark emerging and developing countries, and white circles represent developed countries. It shows high resemblance to figure 9 that relates crisis resilience to rule of law. Less developed countries feature stricter business regulations and better economic performance, whereas developed countries have more open goods markets but face a deeper economic crisis. While the fitted line for the entire sample slopes downward, the fitted line within the sub-group of developed countries has a positive slope. Scatterplots for other measures of business regulation, as depicted in appendix 12, look much alike.

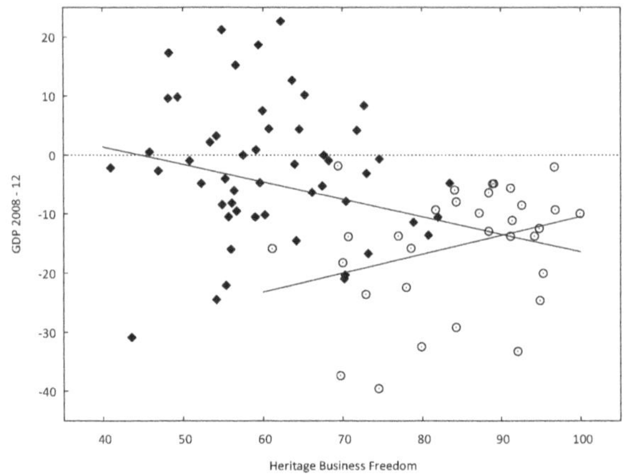

Figure 10: Scatterplot of 'GDP_{08-12}' against Heritage 'business freedom' (black dots: less developed countries; white circles: developed countries; downward-sloping line: fitted values for the entire sample; upward-sloping line: fitted values for the sub-sample of developed countries).

The next step involves controlling for initial vulnerabilities. Table 14 depicts the coefficients of the business regulation variables in multivariate regressions including control variables based on principle components.

	Dep. Var.: GDP_{08-12}			Dep. Var.: GDP_{08-09}			Dep. Var.: GDP_{10-12}		
	All	Deve-loped	Emerging & Dev.	All	Deve-loped	Emerging & Dev.	All	Deve-loped	Emerging & Dev.
Heritage Business Freedom	-0.10 0.30	0.11 0.52	-0.02 0.86	**-0.15** **0.05****	-0.18 0.08*	-0.08 0.41	0.04 0.37	**0.24** **0.05****	0.07 0.39
Fraser Business Regulation	1.13 0.51	0.50 0.71	2.08 0.26	-0.29 0.82	-2.30 0.21	0.75 0.58	1.33 0.07*	**3.15** **0.01*****	1.51 0.13
WGI Regulatory Quality	**-4.47** **0.03****	1.59 0.73	-2.41 0.29	**-3.91** **0.01*****	-3.64 0.41	**-2.66** **0.04****	-0.68 0.45	5.38 0.12	0.29 0.82
GCI Competition	-0.66 0.79	2.37 0.49	1.56 0.60	-1.88 0.33	-2.15 0.46	0.41 0.85	0.91 0.42	5.64 0.08*	1.40 0.41
Doing Business Summary	0.07 0.58	0.18 0.31	0.07 0.66	-0.20 0.05*	-0.15 0.25	-0.10 0.40	0.11 0.05*	**0.34** **0.03****	**0.18** **0.02****

Table 14: Coefficients of business regulation indices as explanatory variables in multivariate regressions with control models according to table 6 (second row: p-values of two-sided significance tests; number of asterisks: significance levels of 10%*, 5%** and 1%***; significant results at 5% level are bold).

In table 14, two aspects stand out. First, the coefficients for the entire sample of 84 countries are now insignificant in the majority of regressions during time periods 2008 to 2012 and 2008 to 2009. Second, the coefficients of the business regulation variables in the sub-group of 32 developed countries during the time period 2010 to 2012 remain positive and significantly different from zero in three out of five regressions, barely missing conventional significance levels in the other two regressions. Formerly significant coefficients in that sub-sample during the entire time period 2008 to 2012 now turn insignificant.

These changes of significance levels when controlling for initial vulnerabilities resemble those of the rule of law coefficients after the inclusion of the same control variables. As indicated in the previous section, rule of law coefficients in the sample of 84 countries turn insignificant when controlling for 'economic development' or 'GDP per capita'; and they turn insignificant in the sub-sample of 32 developed countries when including the 'current account balance to GDP ratio' or 'financial vulnerabilities' as control variables. Below, I analyze whether the same relations apply to the coefficients of the business regulation variables, starting with the entire sample of 84 countries and then turning to the sub-sample of 32 developed countries.

Table 15 shows the correlations between the business regulation variables and important control variables in the entire sample of 84 countries. Correlations are always positive but particularly high between business regulation variables and control variables representing economic development, thereby indicating that countries with more open goods markets are also more highly developed.

	Heritage Business Freedom	Fraser Business Regulation	WGI Regulatory Quality	GCI Competition	Doing Business Summary
Financial Vulnerabilities	0.10	0.08	0.12	-0.01	0.06
Increase (Priv. Cred. / GDP)	**0.27**	0.18	**0.30**	0.15	**0.24**
Current Acc. Balance / GDP	0.12	0.11	0.12	**0.26**	0.21
Economic Development	**0.70**	**0.50**	**0.71**	**0.66**	**0.71**
GDP per Capita	**0.80**	**0.57**	**0.84**	**0.74**	**0.80**
International Linkages	0.18	**0.29**	**0.24**	**0.37**	**0.26**
Trade / GDP	**0.24**	**0.35**	**0.31**	**0.44**	**0.33**
Industrial Orientation	0.19	0.14	**0.29**	**0.23**	**0.23**
Manuf. Exp. / Total Exp.	**0.26**	0.13	**0.34**	**0.32**	**0.32**

Table 15: Correlations between business regulation variables and control variables in the entire sample (significant correlations at 5% level are bold).

Table 16 depicts the coefficients of the 'business freedom' index from the Heritage Foundation in regressions against '$GDP_{08\text{-}09}$' when controlling for one non-institutional variable at a time. The results show that the coefficient of 'business freedom' turns insignificant when controlling for 'GDP per capita'. Furthermore, in regressions 4 and 10 the formerly significant variable 'economic development' now turns insignificant due to the inclusion of 'business freedom'. Results are very similar when using other explanatory variables for business regulation (see appendix 13) or when looking at the entire time period 2008 to 2012 (see appendix 14). When including business regulation variables and development variables in one regression, one of them turns insignificant, thereby suggesting that both variables capture similar effects.

	Dependent Variable: 'GDP_{08-09}'; Sample: All 84 Countries										
	(1)	(2)	(3)	(4)	(5)	(6)	(7)	(8)	(9)	(10)	(11)
Constant	7.06	6.24	10.28	11.92	5.87	7.80	8.85	6.78	9.79	4.30	4.53
	0.04**	0.06*	0.01***	0.04**	0.30	0.03**	0.01**	0.06*	0.00***	0.42	0.19
Heritage Busi-	-0.19	-0.16	-0.22	-0.25	-0.16	-0.20	-0.19	-0.18	-0.17	-0.15	-0.15
ness Freedom	0.00***	0.00***	0.00***	0.00***	0.10*	0.00***	0.00***	0.00***	0.00***	0.05**	0.00***
Financial	-2.97									-3.03	-3.03
Vulnerabilities	0.00***									0.00***	0.00***
Increase (Priv.		-0.11									
Cred. / GDP)		0.02**									
Current Acc.			0.23								
Balance / GDP			0.01***								
Economic				1.09						-0.06	
Development				0.32						0.94	
GDP					-0.05						
per Capita					0.44						
International						-0.80				-0.94	-0.93
Linkages						0.20				0.05**	0.04**
Trade /							-0.01				
GDP							0.18				
Industrial								-1.90		-2.00	-1.99
Orientation								0.00***		0.00***	0.00***
Manuf. Exp. /									-0.08		
Total Exp.									0.00***		
N	84	84	84	84	84	84	84	84	84	84	84
R^{2*}	0.34	0.31	0.24	0.18	0.17	0.18	0.18	0.23	0.23	0.40	0.41

Table 16: Multivariate regressions of 'GDP_{08-09}' against Heritage 'business freedom' and one additional control variable in the entire sample (second row: p-values of two-sided significance tests; number of asterisks: significance levels of 10%*, 5%** and 1%***).

As in section 4.3.1, there are different potential interpretations regarding the causality between business regulations and economic development. On the one hand, the loss of significance of the business regulation variables in some regressions could mean that open goods markets are unrelated to the depth of the recessions and that other aspects of economic development made countries vulnerable to the crisis. On the other hand, open goods markets could be one of the features that made actors in developed countries respond more drastically to the crisis (for example, because they were exposed to a more competitive business environment). Hence, these results contradict the first hypothesis stated above that more business freedom generally promotes crisis resilience, while they provide tentative support for the second hypothesis.

The regression results in tables 13 and 14, furthermore, suggest that business freedom may be related to *better* crisis resilience in highly developed countries. To investigate this relationship in detail, table 17 depicts the simple correlations between business regulation variables and relevant control variables in the sub-sample of 32 developed countries. The correlation coefficients indicate that countries with less-regulated goods markets have higher current account surpluses, feature higher levels of development, higher GDP per capita and lower degrees of industrial orientation.

	Heritage Business Freedom	Fraser Business Regulation	WGI Regulatory Quality	GCI Competition	Doing Business Summary
Financial Vulnerabilities	-0.14	-0.02	-0.22	-0.35	-0.18
Increase (Priv. Cred. / GDP)	0.08	0.12	-0.01	0.18	-0.01
Current Acc. Balance / GDP	**0.37**	0.34	**0.48**	**0.54**	**0.42**
Economic Development	**0.66**	**0.49**	**0.64**	**0.43**	**0.53**
GDP per Capita	**0.65**	**0.47**	**0.68**	**0.44**	**0.47**
International Linkages	0.10	**0.37**	**0.37**	**0.49**	0.30
Trade / GDP	0.07	**0.34**	**0.33**	**0.49**	0.28
Industrial Orientation	**-0.46**	**-0.52**	**-0.47**	**-0.35**	**-0.43**
Manuf. Exp. / Total Exp.	-0.27	**-0.37**	-0.25	-0.12	-0.26

Table 17: Correlations between business regulation variables and control variables in the sub-sample of developed countries (significant correlations at 5% level are bold).

Especially the positive correlations with the 'current account balance to GDP ratio' are relevant for explaining why the coefficients of some business regulation variables lose significance when controlling for initial vulnerabilities. Because countries with more open goods markets feature positive (or less negative) current account balances and because both variables are positively related to crisis resilience, considering them together reduces the significance of business regulation variables. Table 18 illustrates this effect using the example of the index 'business freedom' from the Heritage Foundation. This variable is highly significant for explaining crisis resilience in most regressions, but it turns insignificant when controlling for the 'current account balance to GDP ratio'. It also loses some significance when controlling for 'financial vulnerabilities', which is partly based on the current account variable. Similar effects arise when considering other business regulation variables as explanatory variables (see appendix 15). When conducting the same analysis with 'GDP_{08-12}' as dependent variable, results are similar but much weaker, suggesting that business regulation mattered mainly for the strength of the recovery (see appendix 16).

These relations are again very similar to those of rule of law variables, and again there exist different possible interpretations. On the one hand, business regulation variables may be coincidently correlated with the 'current account balance to GDP ratio'. In that case, the fact that they turn insignificant when controlling for the current account balance would mean that open goods markets are irrelevant for explaining crisis resilience. Another plausible interpretation is that countries with high degrees of goods market openness entered the crisis with healthier current account balances partly *because* they were more competitive and had accumulated less negative imbalances than highly regulated countries.[171] Following that interpretation, having open goods markets helped developed countries to avoid unsustainable current account deficits before the crisis and painful adaptions during the crisis, thereby facilitating their

[171] Goods market openness may have positive effects on competitiveness and current account balances due to the same reasons as rule of law. For a short discussion of these arguments, see again the previous section.

economic recovery. If that is indeed the case, the fact that the business regulation variables turn insignificant when controlling for the current account balance means that the positive effects of open goods markets on crisis resilience are mediated through healthier current accounts before the onset of the crisis.

	Dependent Variable: 'GDP$_{10-12}$'; Sample: 32 Developed Countries								
	(1)	(2)	(3)	(4)	(5)	(6)	(7)	(8)	(9)
Constant	-25.22 0.02**	-31.15 0.01***	-15.12 0.10*	-41-68 0.01***	-36.74 0.01**	-30.37 0.02**	-32.51 0.01**	-45.44 0.00***	-44.26 0.00***
Heritage Business Freedom	0.24 0.05**	0.33 0.01***	0.12 0.24	0.45 0.02**	0.42 0.03**	0.29 0.05**	0.29 0.04**	0.45 0.00***	0.35 0.01***
Financial Vulnerabilities	-3.70 0.00***								
Increase (Priv. Cred. / GDP)		-0.13 0.00***							
Current Acc. Balance / GDP			0.48 0.00***						
Economic Development				-2.30 0.12					
GDP per Capita					-0.13 0.25				
International Linkages						0.74 0.32			
Trade / GDP							0.02 0.01**		
Industrial Orientation								4.64 0.00***	
Manuf. Exp. / Total Exp.									0.17 0.01***
N	32	32	32	32	32	32	32	32	32
R^{2*}	0.52	0.53	0.51	0.20	0.16	0.14	0.19	0.39	0.40

Table 18: Multivariate regressions of 'GDP$_{10-12}$' against Heritage 'business freedom' and one additional control variable in the sub-sample of developed countries (second row: p-values of two-sided significance tests; number of asterisks: significance levels of 10%*, 5%** and 1%***).

I conclude that goods market openness shows a very similar relationship with crisis resilience as rule of law. In the entire sample of 84 countries, openness is negatively related to economic performance, especially during the initial downturn 2008 to 2009. The coefficients, however, partly turn insignificant when controlling for development levels. Hence, highly developed countries with more open goods markets showed worse performance than less developed countries with stricter regulations. This contradicts the hypothesis that business freedom generally promotes crisis resilience and provides tentative support for the opposite hypothesis.

There does, however, exist some evidence in favor of a qualified hypothesis that business freedom promotes crisis resilience within the sub-group of developed countries. In that group, most business regulation variables show significant and positive coefficients in bivariate and multivariate regressions. These coefficients, however, consistently turn insignificant when controlling for the 'current account balance to GDP ratio'. The question whether or not these regression results support the qualified hypothesis depends on the interpretation of the relationship between business freedom and the current account balance. From the (arguable) assumption that open goods markets contributed to healthier current account balances (for example by making countries more competitive and avoiding misdirected investments), it follows that business freedom had a positive effect on crisis resilience in developed countries that was mediated through healthier current accounts. Such an effect, however, would be different from the one suggested by the theoretical discussion, as it refers to avoiding pre-crisis imbalances instead of facilitating adjustments during the recession.

4.3.3 Labor Regulations and Crisis Resilience

Labor market regulations are probably the most complex institutions affecting a country's economic performance during an economic crisis. They include a wide variety of institutional features such as different types of employment protection legislation, wage-setting regimes or unemployment benefit provisions. What makes the study of labor market institutions so challenging is the wide variety of potential interactions amongst different types of regulations. While some institutions are functional substitutes having similar effects on economic outcomes, others are complements reinforcing each other's impact.[172] Furthermore, different labor market regulations may affect crisis resilience via various channels, sometimes having opposing effects on aggregate demand and aggregate supply.

Throughout the theoretical discussion and empirical analysis below I consider three different types of labor market institutions:

- *Employment protection legislation* includes regulations affecting the protection of employees against job losses, which create barriers to enter or exit labor markets. Examples of such regulations are advanced notice periods for dismissals, severance pay requirements, complicated dismissal procedures (including priority rules or the mandatory involvement of third parties), strong legal restrictions for dismissals in general or regulations of fixed-term contracts and temporary employment.
- *Wage setting institutions* include all regulations that affect the determination of wages. Most important for the assessment of crisis resilience are regulations of collective bargaining which affect the level of wage bargaining (firm level,

[172] Some authors, for example, study potential interactions of inflexible wage-setting regimes and flow restrictions stemming from employment protection legislation (Abbritti & Weber, 2010). Others discuss the effects of different combinations of benefit systems and flow restrictions (Blanchard et al., 2014). For a general approach to studying interactions amongst different institutions see Hall & Soskice (2001).

sectorial level or national level) or the degree of coordination by the state, trade unions and employer's associations.[173]

- *Unemployed support provisions* include passive and active labor market policies. While the former are mostly monetary benefits for people who have lost their jobs, the latter are measures such as re-training offers for unemployed people to facilitate re-employment in new companies or sectors.

These three institutions roughly correspond to the institutions discussed by Olson and NWW, as they represent barriers to exit and entry (employment protection legislation), potentially inflexible prices (wage-setting institutions) and public good provisions (unemployment support). Another important labor market institution which I cannot include into the empirical analysis is the flexibility of working hours.[174] Almost all authors studying the relationship between labor market institutions and crisis resilience during the Great Recession mention that short-time working schemes had a positive impact on crisis resilience.[175] This institution can be understood as a functional substitute for employment protection legislation. While the latter affects external flexibility by facilitating or inhibiting dismissals, short-time working schemes have an impact on internal flexibility, allowing firms to reduce working hours per employee while maintaining the same number of employed people. Unfortunately, there are (to my knowledge) no indicators available for this particular type of labor market regulation.[176]

Furthermore, slightly departing from part of the related literature, I do not consider interactions amongst the three institutional features listed above. Instead, in accordance with the theoretical account outlined in chapter 2, I assess broad tendencies along the basic distinction between open and flexibility-enhancing institutions versus rigid and flexibility-inhibiting institutions.

Finally, it is important to point out that labor market regulations fulfil a wide variety of legitimate purposes such as mitigating discrepancies of bargaining power between employers and employees or providing social support for unemployed people. This section analyzes *only* the relationship between labor market institutions and crisis resilience. An overall assessment of the desirability of each institution would have to

[173] Another institution directly affecting wages are statutory minimum wages. According to Blanchard et al. (2014), however, these are less relevant for crisis resilience but rather affect the natural rate of unemployment.

[174] A common term for this type of flexibility is "internal numerical flexibility". See, for example, Eichhorst et al. (2009).

[175] See, for example, Eichhorst et al. (2010), Leschke & Watt (2010) or Blanchard et al. (2014).

[176] The indicator 'flexibility of hours' provided by the Fraser Institute which is based on the Doing Business Labor Database comes closest to measuring short-time working schemes. Looking closer at the variable, however, shows that it only indicates the flexibility of extending working hours, not of reducing them.

be based on the effects on different social targets – the ability to overcome an economic crisis just being one of them.[177]

Discussion and hypotheses

Subsequently, I discuss the potential effects of the three aspects of labor market regulation on crisis resilience, starting with (1) employment protection legislation and then turning to (2) wage-setting institutions and (3) unemployment support.

(1) Employment protection legislation reduces the flows of labor into and out of unemployment (Martin & Scapetta, 2012). On the one hand, strong protection makes it more difficult and costly for businesses to dismiss employees and, therefore, reduces the rate of people who become unemployed. On the other hand, strict employment protection also reduces the rate of unemployed people who find new jobs if employers anticipating high dismissal costs are less willing to hire new people unless they are very sure that their need for additional labor is permanent. While such labor flow restrictions do not necessarily increase the natural rate of unemployment,[178] their impact on the evolution of unemployment during an economic crisis is more distinct. During a recession, more businesses face pressure to lay off employees, making the *positive* impact of employment protection legislation on job stability in such times more pronounced than during normal times. However, high uncertainty during an economic crisis is also likely to amplify the *negative* effects of employment protection on job creation, as businesses can be less secure about the permanence of their need for additional labor. Correspondingly, there exists a fair amount of theoretical and empirical research showing that stricter employment protection legislation is associated with smaller employment volatility,[179] with smaller employment losses during the first phase of a recession and with retarded job creation thereafter.[180]

---

[177] One review paper summarizing the effects of different labor market institutions on a variety of performance indicators including efficiency and equity dimensions is Betcherman (2013).

[178] Blanchard & Portugal (2001), for example, show that long-term unemployment rates in Portugal and the United States during the years 1983 to 1998 were roughly equal at 6.5 percent, even though Portugal had much more rigid employment protection legislation. These institutions, the authors argue, only led to smaller flows into and out of unemployment and therefore an unemployment duration that was three times as large in Portugal as in the U.S.

[179] Abbritti & Weber (2010) show theoretically and empirically for 19 OECD countries that more rigid employment protection is associated with less volatile unemployment rates. Gnocchi et al. (2015) investigate the effect of employment protections reforms on employment volatility. Also considering 19 OECD countries, they provide evidence that countries which eased employment protection faced significant increases in the volatility of employment.

[180] Bernal-Verdugo et al. (2012) investigate the relationship between labor market flexibility and the dynamics of unemployment following different economic crises for a sample of 97 countries. Although they use a broader composite index of labor market flexibility, their results are nevertheless instructive. They find that more rigid labor market institutions are associated with a less pronounced initial impact but also with a slower recovery.

Through their ambiguous effect on unemployment, employment protection legislation may also have ambiguous effects on output during an economic crisis. On the one hand, stabilized employment during the downturn may also stabilize aggregate demand since fewer people have to fear job losses and income reductions (Tridico, 2013). On the other hand, sluggish creation of new jobs and retarded re-allocation of labor may constrain economic recovery, as it takes more time until the production factor labor is put back to its best and full use again (Blanchard et al., 2014). This underutilization of labor not only reduces the output potential and aggregate supply but, following Olson's (1982, pp. 196-209) argument, also aggregate demand because involuntarily-unemployed people receive lower factor incomes. Furthermore, being out of work for a long time period can downgrade the skills of unemployed workers and discourage them from searching for employment, thereby reducing the availability of the labor and the overall output potential (Blanchard & Summers, 1986, p. 28). Based on these arguments, strict employment protection legislation mainly affects two out of three aspects of adaptive efficiency outlined in chapter 2. First, these regulations may have a positive effect on the ability to resist unnecessary adaptions, as they stabilize employment, labor income and aggregate demand during the initial downturn. Second, strong employment protection may also have a negative effect on the ability to reallocate labor to its most productive uses by making necessary labor adjustments more costly and difficult.

Past empirical research regarding the effects of employment protection on crisis resilience is mainly inconclusive. On the one hand, Tridico (2013) provides some evidence that, overall, there is a positive effect of rigid employment protection on economic performance during the years 2007 to 2011.[181] On the other hand, the papers cited in the previous section, which assess the effects of overall regulations (including regulations of labor, business and finance) on crisis resilience, come to different conclusions as they report positive effects of overall flexibility.[182] Furthermore, other research points towards a negative relationship between strong employment protection legislation and output volatility (Merkl & Schmitz, 2011),[183] which entails less severe downturns but also retarded recoveries.

Following the arguments summarized above and the short review of previous empirical research, there are two competing hypotheses regarding the effects of employment protection legislation on crisis resilience:

---

181 Tridico (2013) bases his judgement on a dependent variable which focuses mainly on labor market effects, as it includes absolute unemployment rates and the elasticity of GDP with respect to unemployment. As, however, almost the entire variability of his dependent variable depends to the variability of the unemployment rate, his conclusions have to be interpreted as labor market effects (not output effects) of employment protection.

182 However, only Bjornskov (2016) reports significant coefficients.

183 Rumler & Scharler (2011) also report negative but insignificant coefficients regarding the same relationship.

- Countries with less rigid employment protection legislation which promote flexible adjustments of labor should have performed better during the Great Recession than countries with more rigid employment protection.
- Countries with more rigid employment protection legislation which limit job losses during the downturn should have performed better during the Great Recession than countries which allow flexible adjustments.

(2) The next institutions under consideration are wage-setting institutions. The predictions regarding their impact on crisis resilience are also ambivalent. Disagreement exists especially about the question whether wages are more responsive to altered circumstances under centralized and coordinated wage-bargaining regimes or under decentralized and fragmented regimes. By responsiveness most authors mean downward adjustability, although wage reductions can also have negative effects during a crisis.[184] However, lowering wages may indeed be an appropriate strategy for countries who suffer from poor competitiveness and large current account deficits but cannot adjust external prices due to fixed exchange rates. For these countries, improving competitiveness through lowering wages should lead to higher export demand, lower unemployment and quicker recovery (Deutsche Bundesbank, 2014). Wage flexibility is also relevant for changing relative wages to adapt to firm-, sector- or region-specific shocks (Blanchard et al. 2014). Furthermore, following Olson's (1982, pp. 196-209) argument illustrated in chapter 2, lowering wages can stabilize employment and therefore aggregate demand by allowing firms who face an adverse shock to employ more people than at wages far above market-clearing levels. Finally, reducing relative wages in badly-affected sectors of the economy and increasing them in other sectors can facilitate the re-allocation of labor towards its most productive uses by providing the respective price signals. Hence, following these arguments, wage flexibility may have positive effects on two aspects of adaptive efficiency outlined in section 2, as it presumably stabilizes economic activity and facilitates the re-allocation of labor.

However, the question remains under which kind of bargaining regime wages are most responsive to economic shocks. On the one hand, authors who follow a corporatist view argue that highly centralized and coordinated wage bargaining leads to more wage flexibility, as unions serving a larger number of people focus on overall economic welfare instead of the interests of a few members (Abbritti & Weber, 2010). This argument follows Olson's (1982, pp. 47-53) account of encompassing organizations serving the interests of the general public much better than small interest groups. Furthermore, centralized and coordinated wage bargaining may help to solve a

[184] If, for example, lowering wages entails deflationary tendencies, this can have adverse consequences for over-indebted actors, as deflation increases the real value of their debt. Following the debt-deflation theory of Fisher (1933), this may lead to distress selling, bankruptcies, pessimism, output reductions and a prolonged economic contraction. One way to counteract such tendencies is expansionary monetary policy to avoid deflation.

coordination problem by permitting a simultaneous reduction of several wages at once. This potentially facilitates a reduction of overall wage levels if workers are more willing to accept wage cuts when their relative wages remain unchanged (Blanchard et al., 2014). This last argument, however, only holds if there is a need for a reduction of *overall* wage levels. If, on the other hand, there have to be adjustments of *relative* wages between different sectors, centralized and coordinated wage bargaining may be much more problematic (Blanchard et al., 2014; Cazes et al., 2012). This can be understood following Olson's other argument (1982, pp. 53-58) about the slow decision-making within distributional coalitions. Analogously to price negotiations, centralized negotiations about relative wages can be expected to take more time than decentralized wage setting. If this is the case, it takes much more time for wages to adjust, in the meantime entailing all the negative economic effects that were explained in the previous paragraph. Related to the ambiguous predictions following Olson's account, Calmfors & Driffill (1988, p. 15) argue that the relationship between centralization of wage bargaining and economic performance may be hump-shaped (regimes with high and low centralization show better results than intermediate regimes) because "organized interests may be most harmful when they are strong enough to cause major disruptions but not sufficiently encompassing to bear any significant fraction of the costs for society".

Empirical research regarding the effects of decentralized wage bargaining on crisis resilience is scarce, as most papers focus on the potential effects of wage bargaining institutions on unemployment or wage inequalities.[185] Rumler & Scharler (2011), who investigate the relationship between coordination of wage bargaining and output volatility, report inconclusive results. Starting from the hypothesis of a *negative* relationship between coordination of wage bargaining and volatility of the output gap, they report *positive* coefficients in some of their specifications. Overall, however, they conclude that output volatility and coordinated wage bargaining are not robustly related. Following the ambiguous theoretical arguments and the limited empirical research, there are two competing hypotheses regarding the effects of centralized and coordinated wage-setting institutions on crisis resilience.

- Countries with decentralized and fragmented wage-setting regimes should have performed better during the Great Recession, as decentralized wage setting facilitates the necessary wage adjustments.
- Countries with centralized and coordinated wage-setting regimes should have performed better during the Great Recession, as coordinated wage setting facilitates the necessary wage adjustments.

(3) The final labor market institution under consideration is the support system for unemployed people. Similar to the other institutions, theoretical predictions about its effects on crisis resilience are ambiguous. On the one hand, some authors argue that

[185] For a review see Cazes et al. (2012).

generous unemployment support has negative effects on employment and the re-allocation of labor by providing an attractive outside option to being employed (Abbritti & Weber, 2010). This, according to the argument, reduces the incentives for employees to accept lower wages and to search for new employment,[186] thereby entailing negative effects on the output potential due to a slower re-allocation of labor to its most productive uses. These negative effects are particularly pronounced if benefits do not decrease with the duration of unemployment (Blanchard et al., 2014). This argument about the negative effects of unemployment support is in line with Olson's (1982) pessimistic account of redistributions.

On the other hand, active and passive labor market programs may also have positive effects on the re-allocation of labor to its best uses because financial support alleviates the pressure on unemployed people to accept the next-best work offer and gives them more time to search for adequate employment. Furthermore, active labor market programs may actively promote re-employment in sectors that were less severely affected by the economic crisis. Both mechanisms improve the qualitative matching of employers and employees and are likely to have positive effects on the output potential. Finally, unemployment support can provide people who lost their jobs with the financial means to maintain a similar level of consumption, thereby stabilizing aggregate demand (Tridico, 2013). These last arguments are also in line with NWW's (2009) optimistic account of redistribution, which associates higher government spending on public goods in open access orders with less frequent and less severe recessions, although, as indicated in chapter 2, the authors do not discuss the mechanisms behind these stabilizing effects.

Previous empirical research regarding the effects of unemployment support is limited. Merkl & Schmitz (2011) report a positive association between the generosity of unemployment support and output volatility, thereby suggesting amplifying effects during the downturn and the recovery. Tridico (2013) assesses the overall effects of active and passive labor market policies on crisis resilience. His scatterplot shows a positive association between spending on labor market policies and his 'crisis management index', thereby suggesting that generous unemployment support improves crisis resilience.[187]

Thus, following the ambiguous arguments and the limited empirical research, there are two competing hypotheses regarding the effects of generous unemployment support on crisis resilience.

---

[186] Rothstein (2011), for example, provides evidence that more generous unemployment benefits had a significant but small effect on the duration of unemployment during the Great Recession (higher benefits leading to longer duration).

[187] As indicated in footnote 181, however, Tridico's (2013) measure focuses mainly on labor market effects instead of effects on output.

- Following the argument that unemployment support reduces incentives to accept lower wages and to search for new jobs, it should have a negative effect on crisis resilience.
- Following the arguments that unemployment support improves the quality of matching in the labor market and stabilizes consumption, it should have a positive effect on crisis resilience.

Data sources

There exists a wide variety of indicators measuring different regulatory aspects of the labor market. Unfortunately, most indices only cover developed countries. The two main data sources providing information about a larger number of countries are the Labor Market Regulation Database provided by the World Bank Doing Business Report and the Business Executives Survey that feeds the Global Competitiveness Report. Both databases are complementary to each other as the former includes objective information and the latter contains subjective opinions of business leaders. Most secondary indices use the information from these two data sources; so do the three indices I consider (the 'labor freedom' index from the Heritage Foundation, a version of the 'labor regulation' index from the Fraser Institute and the index on 'labor market flexibility' from the Global Competitiveness Report). All three indices combine information on employment protection legislation and wage-setting institutions. They hence combine the first two aspects of labor market institutions discussed above.[188] Following their lead, I use three indices that capture employment protection legislation and wage-setting institutions together:

- The first index labeled 'labor freedom' from the Heritage Foundation "is a composite measure of the ability of workers and businesses to interact without restriction by the state" (Beach & Kane, 2008, p. 41). It combines objective information from the Doing Business Labor Database on the magnitude of the minimum wage, the rigidity of working hours, the difficulty of firing redundant employees and the costs associated with firing them (putting equal weights on each of the four items).[189] Potential values range from 0 (low flexibility) to 100

[188] Although it would be possible to disentangle the different items referring to employment protection legislation and centralized wage setting, I decided to use composite indicators of labor market flexibility out of three main reasons: First, this degree of differentiation is analogous to the degree of differentiation I relied on when analyzing business regulations in the previous section. There, I also considered indicators capturing entry restrictions and price rigidities together. Second, disentangling the effects of entry restrictions and price rigidities in labor markets would inflate the analysis below. Third, correlations amongst the items show that rigid employment protection and centralized wage setting are highly correlated (0.61 between the two respective items derived from the Business Executives Survey). Thus, given the small sample size, it would be hard to distinguish the individual effects of both aspect of labor market institutions.

[189] For a detailed description of the index construction see Beach & Kane (2008, pp. 53-54).

(high flexibility). Actual values within the considered sample range from 28.5 (Paraguay) to 99.9 (Denmark and Georgia).

- The second index labeled 'flexibility' in the labor market from the Global Competitiveness Indicators Database consists of the four items 'cooperation in labor-employer relations', 'hiring-and-firing practices', 'flexibility of wage determination'[190] and 'redundancy costs', which are based on answers to survey questions to the Executive Opinions Survey. It, hence, captures aspects of employment protection and wage determination. The index can take values between 1 (low flexibility) and 7 (high flexibility). Actual scores within the sample considered in this thesis range from 3.02 (Argentina) to 6.20 (Singapore).
- The third index corresponds to the index 'labor regulation' from the Fraser Institute. Departing from that index, however, I only use 6 out of 7 items to construct a composite measure of labor market flexibility.[191] These 6 items are based on objective data from the Doing Business Labor Database and answers to survey questions from the Executive Opinions Survey. They include information on the 'minimum wage', on 'hiring-and-firing regulations', on 'centralized collective bargaining', on 'mandated costs of hiring' and on 'mandated costs of worker dismissal'.[192] Potential values of the index range from 0 (low flexibility) to 10 (high flexibility). Actual values within the considered sample range from 3.94 (Bolivia) to 9.23 (Singapore).

Furthermore, I consider two measures for the third aspect of labor market institutions – the generosity of unemployment support.[193]

- The first index labeled 'gross replacement rates' from the Fondazione Rodolfo De Benedetti measures "the ratio of unemployment insurance benefits a worker receives relative to the worker's last gross earning" during the first two years of unemployment (Aleksynska & Schindler, 2011, p. 5). It is the only measure

[190] According to the survey question, inflexible wage determination means "set by a centralized bargaining process", while flexible wage determination is "up to each individual company" (Schwab & Porter, 2008, p. 439).

[191] I do not consider the item 'conscription', which indicates the duration of mandatory military service. I exclude this item because it is a strongly normative aspect of labor market freedom that is largely irrelevant for labor market adjustments during a crisis. From a flexibility perspective, the fact that a small proportion of the population (usually young men) is employed in the military is equivalent to stable employment of any other small group of people in any other government branch. This item, however, has a very high impact on the overall index of labor market regulation, as it varies between 0 and 10 while the other items do not show such a high variation. Excluding that item, therefore, reduces noise alongside the *relevant* aspects of labor market regulation.

[192] For detailed information on the data construction see Gwartney & Lawson (2009, pp. 199-200).

[193] I also considered to use another index measuring the ratio of public spending on active and passive labor market policies relative to GDP. Such a measure, however, suffers from strong endogeneity as spending on unemployment support during the crisis is likely to be correlated with the severity of the crisis in the respective country.

available for a large sample of countries, including developed and less developed countries alike. It, however, also has a variety of limitations. First, the *gross* replacement rate (benefits relative to gross earnings) is a much rougher measure for unemployment support than the *net* replacement rate (benefits relative to net earnings after tax). Second, gross replacement rates provide no information on the number of people who are actually covered. Hence, especially in less developed countries with large informal sectors this measure is likely to be an inaccurate representation of benefit generosity. Finally, gross replacement rates are available only for the time period 1980 to 2005. I use the scores of the year 2005 as proxies for the benefit generosity at the beginning of the crisis because I assume that institutions are fairly stable over time. While the last limitation should not provide a major problem (as benefit generosity in 2005 probably doesn't differ considerably from benefit generosity in 2007), the first two limitations suggest a lot of caution when interpreting the potential effects of gross replacement rates, especially in less developed countries.

- The second index is based on OECD data on average 'net replacement rates' for four types of family situations (single person without children, couple without children, single person with two children, couple with two children) and two types of earning levels (families who either do or do not qualify for cash housing assistance and other social assistance). The net replacement rate measures the percentage of net income that is maintained after losing a job. I calculate simple averages with equal weights across the four family types and two types of earning levels. Unfortunately, data for this measure is only available for a small number of developed countries.

The correlations coefficients among the five explanatory variables show that those measures which presumably represent the same institutions are indeed strongly related. As depicted in appendix 17, all three flexibility variables show correlation coefficients between 0.69 and 0.84, and the two variables capturing benefit generosity show a correlation coefficient of 0.49.

Results

Below, I first (1) analyze the potential effects of the three composite variables capturing employment protection and wage determination before (2) turning to the two variables representing the generosity of unemployment benefits.

(1) Table 19 depicts the coefficients of the bivariate regression with the three indices of overall labor market flexibility as explanatory variables. What stands out are the opposite signs in the two sub-groups of countries. In emerging and developing countries, on the one hand, open labor markets are associated with worse performance, during the entire crisis period 2008 to 2012 and during the recovery period 2010 to 2012, although only the coefficient of the Fraser variable is significantly different from zero. In developed countries, on the other hand, countries with flexible

labor markets showed better performance than countries with rigid employment protection and wage determination during the same time periods.

	Dep. Var.: GDP_{08-12}			Dep. Var.: GDP_{08-09}			Dep. Var.: GDP_{10-12}		
	All	Deve-loped	Emerging & Dev.	All	Deve-loped	Emerging & Dev.	All	Deve-loped	Emerging & Dev.
Heritage Labor Freedom	-0.10 0.16	**0.23** **0.01*****	-0.16 0.09*	-0.06 0.16	0.10 0.10*	-0.05 0.39	-0.04 0.40	**0.16** **0.02****	-0.11 0.11
GCI Labor Flexibility	0.82 0.63	**3.76** **0.05****	-1.28 0.58	-0.02 0.98	0.64 0.34	0.89 0.57	1.01 0.49	**3.49** **0.04****	-2.21 0.22
Fraser Labor Regulation	-1.43 0.09*	**2.15** **0.03****	**-3.53** **0.00*****	-0.81 0.07*	0.51 0.22	-1.16 0.17	-0.59 0.34	**1.84** **0.03****	**-2.44** **0.00*****

Table 19: Coefficients of labor market flexibility indices as explanatory variables in bivariate regressions (second row: p-values of two-sided significance tests; number of asterisks: significance levels of 10%*, 5%** and 1%***; significant results at 5% level are bold).

Figure 11 visualizes these relations by plotting 'labor freedom' based on Heritage data against 'GDP_{08-12}'. White circles mark developed countries, and black dots represent less developed ones. The fitted lines for both sub-groups show the negative relationship between open labor markets and economic performance in the sub-group of less developed countries and the positive relationship between the same variables in developed countries (although only the slope of the latter relationship is significantly different from zero). Scatterplots using the other two labor regulation variables look similar (appendix 18).

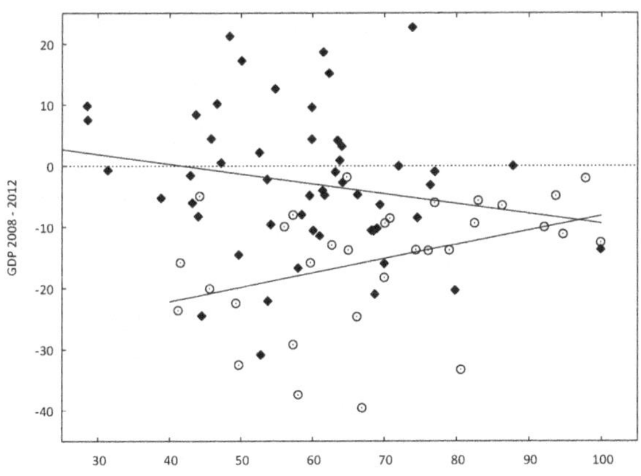

Figure 11: Scatterplot of 'GDP_{08-12}' against Heritage 'labor freedom' (black dots: less developed countries; white circles: developed countries; downward-sloping line: fitted values for the sub-sample of emerging and developing countries; upward-sloping line: fitted values for the sub-sample of developed countries).

I, next, control for initial vulnerabilities in terms of principal components. The results depicted in table 20 show that the association between open labor markets and economic performance in the entire sample of 84 countries and in the sub-sample of 52 less developed countries are insignificant. In the sub-sample of 32 developed countries, on the other hand, open labor markets exhibit a significantly positive association with the strength of the recovery in 2010 to 2012 for two out of three explanatory variables, while the third variable misses conventional significance levels only slightly. During the entire crisis period 2008 to 2012, however, labor flexibility variables turn insignificant when controlling for initial vulnerabilities.

	Dep. Var.: GDP_{08-12}			Dep. Var.: GDP_{08-09}			Dep. Var.: GDP_{10-12}		
	All	Deve-loped	Emerging & Dev.	All	Deve-loped	Emerging & Dev.	All	Deve-loped	Emerging & Dev.
Heritage Labor Freedom	0.04	0.10	-0.00	0.03	0.03	0.00	0.02	**0.10**	-0.01
	0.47	0.17	0.97	0.50	0.64	0.91	0.67	**0.05****	0.91
GCI Labor Flexibility	2.30	2.16	-0.34	1.05	0.04	1.21	1.28	**2.96**	-1.56
	0.12	0.12	0.88	0.21	0.97	0.48	0.26	**0.02****	0.25
Fraser Labor Regulation	-0.27	0.77	-1.82	-0.08	-0.08	-0.55	-0.12	1.27	-1.29
	0.66	0.29	0.07*	0.84	0.90	0.47	0.79	0.05*	0.09*

Table 20: Coefficients of labor market flexibility indices as explanatory variables in multivariate regressions with control models according to table 6 (second row: p-values of two-sided significance tests; number of asterisks: significance levels of 10%*, 5%** and 1%***; significant results at 5% level are bold).

These results indicate that there exists no significant association between flexible labor markets and crisis resilience when considering the entire sample of 84 countries or the sub-sample of 52 less developed countries. Tables 19 and 20 do, however, provide tentative support for a qualified hypothesis that links flexible labor markets to better recovery in the sub-group of 32 developed countries. This corresponds closely to the results obtained when analyzing rule of law or business regulations. I, next, investigate whether this association remains significant when controlling for original variables. Following the experience in the previous sections, especially the association with the current account balance is of particular interest.

As a first step, table 21 depicts the correlation coefficients between the three labor market flexibility variables and each potential control variable. Only a few correlations with 'economic development', 'GDP per capita', 'international linkages', the 'trade to GDP ratio' and 'industrial orientation' are significant. Most importantly, correlations with the 'current account balance to GDP ratio' are positive, though slightly insignificant.

	Heritage Labor Freedom	GCI Labor Flexibility	Fraser Labor Regulation
Financial Vulnerabilities	-0.22	-0.10	-0.20
Increase (Priv. Cred. / GDP)	-0.08	0.03	-0.07
Current Acc. Balance / GDP	0.30	0.29	0.29
Economic Development	**0.39**	**0.35**	0.31
GDP per Capita	**0.35**	0.25	0.28
International Linkages	0.23	**0.36**	0.34
Trade / GDP	0.23	**0.37**	**0.36**
Industrial Orientation	**-0.38**	-0.32	-0.33
Manuf. Exp. / Total Exp.	-0.26	-0.19	-0.17

Table 21: Correlations between labor market flexibility variables and control variables in the sub-sample of developed countries (significant correlations at 5% level are bold).

As expected from the analysis in the previous two sections, the 'current account balance to GDP ratio' is again the crucial control variable affecting the magnitude and significance level of the coefficients of the explanatory variables. Table 22 shows that the coefficient of Heritage 'labor freedom' is consistently positive and significant except when controlling for the 'current account balance to GDP ratio'.

	Dependent Variable: 'GDP_{10-12}'; Sample: 32 Developed Countries								
	(1)	(2)	(3)	(4)	(5)	(6)	(7)	(8)	(9)
Constant	-11.96 0.00***	-12.72 0.00***	-9.71 0.01**	-17.13 0.00***	-16.36 0.00***	-15.88 0.00***	-17.03 0.00***	-23.82 0.00***	-31.60 0.00***
Heritage Labor Freedom	0.10 0.05**	0.14 0.01***	0.07 0.14	0.18 0.02**	0.16 0.03**	0.15 0.02**	0.14 0.02**	0.24 0.00***	0.22 0.00***
Financial Vulnerabilities	-3.66 0.00***								
Increase (Priv. Cred. / GDP)		-0.12 0.00***							
Current Acc. Balance / GDP			0.49 0.00***						
Economic Development				-0.78 0.52					
GDP per Capita					-0.01 0.91				
International Linkages						0.52 0.47			
Trade / GDP							0.02 0.05**		
Industrial Orientation								4.40 0.00***	
Manuf. Exp. / Total Exp.									0.19 0.00***
N	32	32	32	32	32	32	32	32	32
R^{2*}	0.46	0.41	0.51	0.09	0.08	0.09	0.12	0.32	0.42

Table 22: Multivariate regressions of 'GDP_{10-12}' against Heritage 'labor freedom' and one additional control variable in the sub-sample of developed countries (second row: p-values of two-sided significance tests; number of asterisks: significance levels of 10%*, 5%** and 1%***).

Results for the other two labor regulation variables during the recovery period 2010 to 2012 (appendix 19) and for all three explanatory variables during the entire period 2008 to 2012 (appendix 20) are very similar, although they slightly miss conventional significance levels in some specifications.

As regarding rule of law and business regulations, the question remains how to interpret these results. On the one hand, insignificant coefficients might indicate that open labor markets are irrelevant for explaining economic recovery if the positive correlation between labor market flexibility and healthy current accounts is coincidental. On the other hand, based on the assumption that open labor markets make countries more competitive and avoid the build-up of unsustainable imbalances (Berger & Nitsch, 2010), the results could also indicate that labor market openness has an indirect positive effect on the strength of the recovery that is mediated through healthier pre-crisis current accounts.

(2) After analyzing the first two aspects of labor market regulation together, I now turn to the third aspect – *the generosity of unemployment benefits*. Table 23 depicts the coefficients of 'gross replacement rates' and 'net replacement rates'.

	Dep. Var.: $GDP_{08\text{-}12}$			Dep. Var.: $GDP_{08\text{-}09}$			Dep. Var.: $GDP_{10\text{-}12}$		
	All	Deve-loped	Emerging & Dev.	All	Deve-loped	Emerging & Dev.	All	Deve-loped	Emerging & Dev.
FRDB Gross Replacement Rate	**-32.09** **0.00*****	3.84 0.70	**-62.49** **0.00*****	**-14.08** **0.00*****	10.315 0.09*	**-29.37** **0.01****	**-19.17** **0.00*****	-5.97 0.38	**-35.57** **0.00*****
OECD Net Replacement Rate		0.16 0.24			0.09 0.27			0.08 0.42	

Table 23: Coefficients of unemployment benefit indices as explanatory variables in bivariate regressions (second row: p-values of two-sided significance tests; number of asterisks: significance levels of 10%*, 5%** and 1%***; significant results at 5% level are bold).

Within the entire sample and the sub-group of 52 less developed countries, high 'gross replacement rates' are significantly and negatively related to economic performance during all three time periods. Disregarding the potential inaccuracy of the explanatory variable, these results indicate that less developed countries with generous unemployment support faced deeper recessions than less developed countries with little or no unemployment support. Within the sub-group of 32 developed countries (where the two measures are likely to be more accurate), on the other hand, coefficients are positive but insignificant.

Figure 12 visualizes these relationships by plotting 'gross replacement rates' against '$GDP_{08\text{-}12}$'. White circles mark developed countries, and black dots represent less developed ones. The downward-sloping fitted line represents the negative coefficient of 'gross replacement rates' within the sub-group of less developed countries, and the nearly horizontal line indicates the insignificant association between unemployment benefits and economic performance in developed countries.

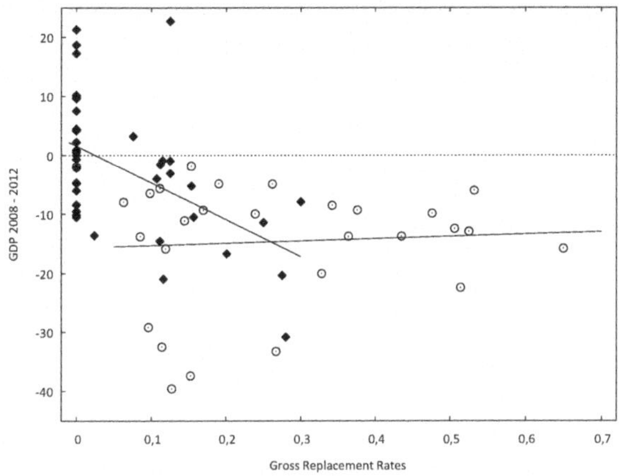

Figure 12: Scatterplot of 'GDP_{08-12}' against 'gross replacement rates' (black dots: less developed countries; white circles: developed countries; downward-sloping line: fitted values for the sub-sample of emerging and developing countries; nearly horizontal line: fitted values for the sub-sample of developed countries).

After controlling for initial vulnerabilities, the relationship between generous unemployment support and economic performance in less developed countries remains consistently negative, although the coefficient slightly misses conventional significance levels during the downturn period 2008 to 2009. In developed countries, on the other hand, generous unemployment protection appears to have cushioned the downturn 2008 and 2009, although only the coefficient of the 'gross replacement rate' is significant, whereas the more accurate measure 'net replacement rates' remains insignificant. In the entire sample, coefficients turn insignificant during the time periods 2008 to 2012 and 2008 to 2009.

	Dep. Var.: GDP_{08-12}			Dep. Var.: GDP_{08-09}			Dep. Var.: GDP_{10-12}		
	All	Deve-loped	Emerging & Dev.	All	Deve-loped	Emerging & Dev.	All	Deve-loped	Emerging & Dev.
FRDB Gross Re-placement Rate	-10.43 0.15	7.39 0.23	**-41.24** **0.01*****	-0.29 0.95	**9.49** **0.05****	-20.98 0.07*	**-10.17** **0.02****	-3.39 0.49	**-22.55** **0.01****
OECD Net Re-placement Rate		0.06 0.57			0.07 0.24			0.06 0.51	

Table 24: Coefficients of unemployment benefit indices as explanatory variables in multivariate regressions with control models according to table 6 (second row: p-values of two-sided significance tests; number of asterisks: significance levels of 10%*, 5%** and 1%***; significant results at 5% level are bold).

The next step involves a more detailed analysis of the control variables that affect the significance of the results. As a first step, table 25 depicts the correlations between 'gross replacement rates' and the relevant control variables in all three samples. It shows that more developed countries with higher GDP per capita grant higher unemployment benefits. Furthermore, generous unemployment support is positively correlated with pre-crisis financial deepening (the increase of the 'ratio of private credit to GDP') in the entire sample and the sub-sample of less developed countries.

	Gross Replacement Rates		
	All Countries	Developed Countries	Emerging & Dev. Countries
Financial Vulnerabilities	0.15	0.09	0.25
Increase (Priv. Cred. / GDP)	**0.36**	0.20	**0.35**
Current Acc. Balance / GDP	0.04	0.02	-0.23
Economic Development	**0.60**	0.34	0.05
GDP per Capita	**0.69**	**0.43**	**0.43**
International Linkages	-0.06	-0.26	0.09
Trade / GDP	-0.01	-0.28	0.14
Industrial Orientation	**0.32**	0.03	0.25
Manuf. Exp. / Total Exp.	**0.35**	-0.02	0.29

Table 25: Correlations between 'gross replacement rates' and control variables in all three samples of countries (significant correlations at 5% level are bold).

Next, table 26 shows that the negative relationship between generous unemployment support and economic performance in the entire sample is for the most part robust to changes of control variables. Only when including 'gross replacement rates' together with 'economic development' or 'GDP per capita' in regressions 4, 5 and 10, one of the variables turns insignificant. Given the positive correlation between high development levels and generous unemployment support, these results suggest that both variables indeed capture similar effects. These findings correspond closely to the findings in previous sections regarding the relationship between other economic institutions, high development levels and crisis resilience – when considered together, either the coefficient of the development variable or the institutional variable turns insignificant. Results in the two sub-periods 2008 to 2009 and 2010 to 2012, as depicted in appendix 21, look very much alike.

When considering the sub-sample of emerging and developing countries, results are also very similar (see appendix 22). During the entire time period 2008 to 2012 the coefficient of the explanatory variable are consistently significant, and during the two sub-periods 2008 to 2009 and 2010 to 2012 they are significant in most specifications.

	Dependent Variable: 'GDP$_{08-12}$'; Sample: All Countries										
	(1)	(2)	(3)	(4)	(5)	(6)	(7)	(8)	(9)	(10)	(11)
Constant	-3.92	-1.10	-0.76	-2.07	-1.95	-2.54	0.31	-3.66	2.08	-6.17	-4.76
	0.02**	0.47	0.64	0.26	0.30	0.14	0.90	0.02**	0.51	0.00***	0.00***
Gross Replace-	-25.72	-16.28	-33.35	-36.02	-23.61	-32.87	-32.16	-25.22	-26.07	-10.43	-20.50
ment Rates	0.00***	0.01***	0.00***	0.00***	0.01***	0.00***	0.00***	0.00***	0.00***	0.15	0.00***
Financial	-7.29									-7.89	-7.12
Vulnerabilities	0.00***									0.00***	0.00***
Increase (Priv.		-0.37									
Cred. / GDP)		0.00***									
Current Acc.			0.63								
Balance / GDP			0.00***								
Economic				1.12						-2.58	
Development				0.58						0.02**	
GDP					-0.11						
per Capita					0.22						
International						-1.86				-1.70	-1.83
Linkages						0.10				0.01***	0.01***
Trade /							-0.03				
GDP							0.09*				
Industrial								-3.70		-3.44	-3.30
Orientation								0.00***		0.00***	0.00***
Manuf. Exp. /									-0.12		
Total Exp.									0.03**		
N	71	71	71	71	71	71	71	71	71	71	71
R^{2*}	0.46	0.46	0.36	0.16	0.17	0.18	0.18	0.23	0.20	0.55	0.54

Table 26: Multivariate regressions of 'GDP$_{08-12}$' against 'gross replacement rates' and one additional control variable in the entire sample (second row: p-values of two-sided significance tests; number of asterisks: significance levels of 10%*, 5%** and 1%***).

In developed countries, where 'gross replacement rates' and 'net replacement rates' should be more accurate representations of benefit generosity, coefficients of both explanatory variables are positive but mainly insignificant. Only during the downturn period 2008 to 2009 are 'gross replacement rates' positively related to economic performance in a few specifications (see appendix 23).

Hence, the previous regressions provide support for the hypothesis that more generous unemployment benefits are negatively related to crisis resilience in the entire sample and in less developed countries. In developed countries, on the other hand, there does not exist such a negative relationship, as coefficients are even positive (though mainly insignificant). Especially the differing results in the two sub-groups of countries are in accordance with NWW's argument that redistributions in limited access orders have a different character than redistributions in open access orders, which may be regarded as public goods. At the same time, these findings contradict Olson's pessimistic account that redistributions are generally detrimental to adaptive efficiency and economic performance. However, as pointed out above, the limitations of the measure 'gross replacement rates' – especially in less developed countries – suggest treating these results with a lot of caution.

Overall, the regressions considering labor market regulations as explanatory variables provide moderate support for the qualified hypotheses that open exit and entry as well as decentralized wage bargaining facilitated economic recovery in developed countries – two hypotheses which are in line with Olson's and NWW's accounts. This finding, however, does not hold in the entire sample or in the sub-sample of emerging and developing countries. Furthermore, regressions assessing the effects of generous unemployment benefits provide some support for NWW's argument that redistributions have less of a common good character in limited access orders than in open access orders. Due to limited data quality, however, it is important not to over-interpret the latter regression results.

4.3.4 Financial Regulations and Crisis Resilience

Financial market institutions govern the way banks and other financial corporations are permitted to operate. They include various kinds of regulations and supervision provisions such as definitions of permitted banking activities, minimum capital requirements, disclosure obligations to facilitate private monitoring of risk positions, entry restrictions for domestic and foreign banks, the granting of supervisory powers to public agencies, deposit insurance schemes or direct credit provision by the state. Most of these regulations serve the purpose of making financial sectors more stable and securing a steady flow of funding to companies and households. The assessment of credit market institutions is, therefore, central to the question posed in this thesis. Similar to the other institutions discussed before, financial regulations serve a wide range of purposes besides providing financial stability. It is thereby possible that the same institutions which provide stability may impede the attainment of other objectives such as promoting maximum economic growth during booms. In this thesis, I only focus on the effects of credit market regulation on the depending variable 'crisis resilience' and disregard effects on other potential objectives.

Discussion and Hypotheses

Financial market regulations are not the main concern of Olson's and NWW's theories of adaptive efficiency. Throughout the literature discussing the causes of the Great Recession, however, these institutions play a prominent role, as many authors attribute the severity of the crisis to lax regulations of the financial sector.[194] Following these arguments, low capital requirements for banks, deregulation of permitted bank activities, insufficient supervision by public agencies and naïve reliance on private rating agencies facilitated those financial activities which triggered and aggravated the economic crisis. These activities included the provision of credit to subprime debtors, the diffusion of these positions to banks throughout the world and the concealment of their underlying default risks. When the crisis unfolded, highly indebted households

[194] See, for example, Stiglitz (2009), Crotty (2009), Krugman (2009, pp. 190-192) or Verick & Islam (2010). Similarly, Diaz-Alejandro (1985) links financial crises in some Latin American countries to previous financial liberalizations.

and highly leveraged banks holding toxic assets in their balance sheets had to make more painful adjustments to avoid defaults or bankruptcies. Households cutting back on consumption and banks restraining credit provisions, in turn, aggravated the economic crisis by reducing aggregate demand in terms of private consumption and credit-based investment.[195] Hence, arguments in favor of stricter financial regulations refer to the third aspect of adaptive efficiency outlined in chapter 2 – the avoidance of avoidable adjustment of economic activity. Examples of such avoidable adjustment are insolvencies of actually healthy businesses due to temporarily restrained credit provisions by crisis-ridden banks or liquidations of unsustainable house construction projects, which should not have been undertaken in the first place.

In general, however, theoretical arguments about the role of financial sector regulations on crisis resilience point into varying directions. For example, while some authors argue that high capital requirements have positive effects on crisis resilience by providing banks with financial buffers against losses from asset depreciations, other authors dispute the ability of those regulations to fulfil their purpose because they induce banks to take up riskier assets to maintain high profits (Furlong & Keeley, 1989; Blum, 1999; Santos, 2001). Disagreement also exists regarding the role of restrictions of permitted banking activities such as underwriting and managing securities, insurances or mortgage obligations. On the one hand, these restrictions may promote economic stability by inhibiting the origination and distribution of highly risky and in-transparent positions, whereas, on the other hand, they may increase default risks by keeping banks from diversifying their sources of revenue (John et al., 1994; Claessens & Klingebiel, 2001). Likewise, high market entry requirements for banks promote stability if they prevent fraudulent banks from entering the market, whereas the same requirements create instability if they restrict the number and diversity of competitors (see Barth et al., 2004). Finally, the desirability of public credit provision and public financial sector supervision as opposed to private credit provision and monitoring by private rating agencies depends on authors' perceptions of the effectiveness and benevolence of government activity in general. While some authors emphasize the need for public engagement and supervision to keep banks from taking up extensive risks, other authors stress the destabilizing role of self-interested and badly informed public decision makers (see Barth et al., 2004).

Previous empirical studies also come to diverging conclusions regarding the effects of financial market regulations on economic stability. One important study regarding the time period before the Great Recession by Barth et al. (2004) analyzes the impact of banking regulation and supervision on banking development, banking efficiency and banking stability. In their study the authors show that the likelihood of suffering a banking crisis increases with stricter activity restrictions, stricter regulations of foreign bank entry and generous deposit insurance schemes, thereby indicating that stricter

[195] For an instructive summary of the sequence of events leading from the financial crisis to the economic crisis see Bricongne et al (2009).

regulations reduce crisis resilience.[196] In a similar study regarding the time period during the Great Recession, however, Caprio et al. (2010) come to different conclusions. In their analysis, restrictions of banking activities are *positively* related to crisis resilience, thereby contradicting the findings from the previous study, which had found a negative association between the same variables. Furthermore, the authors find a negative relationship between transparency requirements and economic stability, indicating that reliance on private monitoring intensified the crisis. Giannone et al. (2011) who investigate the relationship between financial market regulation and crisis resilience during the years 2008 to 2009 show that countries with more liberalized financial sectors suffered a deeper economic crisis.

The previous discussion shows that there are competing theoretical arguments and inconclusive empirical results regarding the effects financial market regulation on crisis resilience. Hence, there are two competing hypotheses.

- Following the argument that financial regulations inhibit excessive risk-taking and the build-up of financial vulnerabilities, stricter financial market regulation should have promoted crisis resilience during the Great Recession.
- Following the argument that government intervention is neither well-informed nor benevolent, stricter financial regulations should have reduced crisis resilience during the Great Recession by interfering with market forces.

Data Sources

In the empirical analysis below, I consider three composite measures of overall financial market regulation:

- The first index is the 'credit market regulations' index provided by the Fraser Institute. It is a composite index that takes values between 0 and 10 based on the four components 'ownership of banks', 'foreign bank competition', 'private sector credit' and 'interest rate controls / negative real interest rates'. The index takes high values if the percentage of bank deposits held in privately-owned (as opposed to publicly-owned) banks is high, if foreign banks are permitted to enter the market, if the extent of government borrowing relative to borrowing by the private sector is low and if interest rates are positive and determined primarily by the market (Gwartney & Lawson, 2009, pp. 198-199). Actual values of this index range from 5.11 (Ethiopia) to 10 (in a variety of mostly developed countries).
- The second index is based on the Bank Regulation and Supervision Database provided by Barth et al. (2013). This database contains information on various types of regulatory and supervisory practices including regulations of bank

[196] Other types of financial sector regulations like minimum capital requirements, official supervisory powers and transparency requirements to facilitate private monitoring are unrelated to financial sector stability in their analysis.

entry, restrictions of permitted activities, transparency obligations, strong supervisory powers by public agencies, high capital adequacy obligations and a high proportion of public banks. I construct a composite index that takes values between 0 and 1. While low values indicate strict regulations and strong government involvement, high values indicate lose regulations and little government involvement. To construct the index, I first normalize each of the six items to take values between 0 (strictest regulation within the sample) and 1 (least strict regulation within the sample) and then calculate a simple average of all six items.[197] Actual values of the new index range from 0.17 (Indonesia) to 0.66 (Hong Kong).

- The third index labeled 'financial freedom' provided by the Heritage Foundation is "a measure of banking security as well as independence from government control" (Beach & Kane, 2008, p. 41). It can take values between 0 and 100 depending on authors' personal judgements about regulations of financial services, the extent of state intervention in banks, the difficulties of opening and operating financial organizations and government influence on the allocation of credit (Beach & Kane, 2008, p. 50). Higher values indicate more open financial systems. Actual values range from 10 (Belarus) to 90 (in a variety of mostly developed countries).

All three variables are positively and significantly correlated. As shown in appendix 25, however, these correlations are smaller (between 0.48 and 0.67) than those amongst the previously-analyzed institutions. Hence, the three indices possibly capture different aspects of financial sector openness.

Results

The results from the bivariate regressions as depicted in table 27 are fairly straight forward. Coefficients for the entire worldwide sample are always negative and significant, coefficients for the sub-group of 32 developed countries are always insignificant, and coefficients for the sub-group of 52 less developed countries are always negative and significant when using the index 'credit market regulation' from the Fraser Institute or the composite index from the Bank Regulation and Supervision Database. The negative association between financial openness and crisis resilience in less developed countries is more pronounced during the initial downturn 2008 to 2009 than during the recovery period 2010 to 2012, thereby indicating that countries with open financial markets faced a deeper downturn than highly regulated countries. These results indicate that the negative association between financial openness and crisis resilience in the entire sample is mainly driven by the sub-group of 52 less developed countries and by inter-group differences.

---

197 For a detailed description of the index construction see appendix 24.

	Dep. Var.: GDP_{08-12}			Dep. Var.: GDP_{08-09}			Dep. Var.: GDP_{10-12}		
	All	Deve-loped	Emerging & Dev.	All	Deve-loped	Emerging & Dev.	All	Deve-loped	Emerging & Dev.
Fraser Credit Market Regulation	**-5.74** **0.00*****	0.45 0.88	**-4.90** **0.00*****	**-3.37** **0.00*****	-0.92 0.37	**-2.62** **0.00*****	**-2.45** **0.00*****	1.51 0.58	**-2.25** **0.01****
BRS Summary Index	**-49.76** **0.00*****	14.52 0.32	**-55.45** **0.01****	**-27.55** **0.00*****	6.64 0.43	**-27.36** **0.01*****	**-22.71** **0.01*****	9.76 0.38	-27.70 0.06*
Heritage Financial Freedom	**-0.28** **0.00*****	-0.08 0.59	-0.15 0.16	**-0.17** **0.00*****	-0.10 0.16	-0.08 0.14	**-0.11** **0.01****	0.01 0.92	-0.07 0.31

Table 27: Coefficients of financial regulation indices as explanatory variables in bivariate regressions (second row: p-values of two-sided significance tests; number of asterisks: significance levels of 10%*, 5%** and 1%***; significant results at 5% level are bold).

Figure 13 shows a scatterplot relating financial openness according to the Fraser index to economic performance during the entire period 2008 to 2012. Less developed countries are marked by black dots and developed countries by white circles. It shows that the negative slope of the fitted line for the entire sample (continuous) resembles the fitted line for the sub-sample of less developed countries (dotted). Scatterplots for the other two measures of financial openness are very similar (see appendix 26).

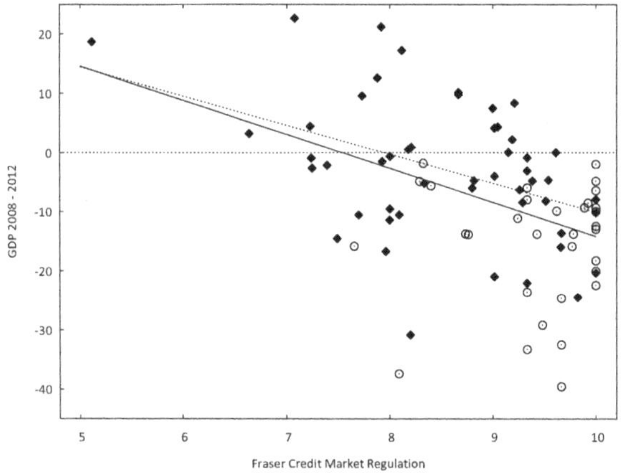

Figure 13: Scatterplot of 'GDP_{08-12}' against Fraser 'credit market regulation' (black dots: less developed countries; white circles: developed countries; dotted line: fitted values for sub-sample of emerging and developing countries; continuous line: fitted values for the entire sample).

When controlling for initial vulnerabilities, results hardly change. Coefficients for the entire sample are negative and significant during the periods 2008 to 2012 and 2008 to 2009, coefficients for the sub-group of 32 developed countries are insignificant, and coefficients for the sub-group of 52 less developed countries are negative and mainly significant for the periods 2008 to 2012 and 2008 to 2009.

	Dep. Var.: GDP_{08-12}			Dep. Var.: GDP_{08-09}			Dep. Var.: GDP_{10-12}		
	All	Deve-loped	Emerging & Dev.	All	Deve-loped	Emerging & Dev.	All	Deve-loped	Emerging & Dev.
Fraser Credit Market Regulation	**-2.36** **0.02****	0.38 0.87	**-2.59** **0.02****	**-1.70** **0.00*****	-0.53 0.71	**-1.86** **0.00*****	-0.52 0.46	1.85 0.41	-0.62 0.42
BRS Summary Index	**-30.56** **0.00*****	2.78 0.77	**-41.89** **0.01*****	**-16.64** **0.00*****	3.88 0.68	**-25.34** **0.01*****	**-13.88** **0.01*****	1.39 0.84	-15.50 0.09*
Heritage Financial Freedom	**-0.16** **0.03****	0.01 0.95	-0.19 0.05*	**-0.12** **0.01*****	-0.05 0.39	-0.11 0.06*	-0.04 0.39	0.09 0.37	-0.08 0.20

Table 28: Coefficients of financial regulation indices as explanatory variables in multivariate regressions with control models according to table 6 (second row: p-values of two-sided significance tests; number of asterisks: significance levels of 10%*, 5%** and 1%***; significant results at 5% level are bold).

Robustness checks with a variety of control variables mainly confirm these results. First, table 29 depicts regressions of 'GDP_{08-12}' against the Fraser 'credit market regulation' index and one control variable at a time for the entire sample. It shows that the coefficients of 'credit market regulation' remain significant in all specifications.

	Dependent Variable: 'GDP_{08-12}'; Sample: All Countries								
	(1)	(2)	(3)	(4)	(5)	(6)	(7)	(8)	(9)
Constant	28.70 0.00***	31.10 0.00***	44.49 0.00***	40.17 0.00***	33.50 0.01***	44.37 0.00***	43.79 0.00***	37.75 0.00***	42.42 0.00***
Fraser Credit Market Regulation	-4.10 0.00***	-4.05 0.00***	-5.68 0.00***	-5.39 0.00***	-4.34 0.00***	-5.87 0.00***	5.85 0.00***	-5.12 0.00***	-5.08 0.00***
Financial Vulnerabilities	-6.43 0.00***								
Increase (Priv. Cred. / GDP)		-0.25 0.00***							
Current Acc. Balance / GDP			0.59 0.00***						
Economic Development				-1.03 0.41					
GDP per Capita					-0.16 0.02**				
International Linkages						0.37 0.74			
Trade / GDP							0.00 0.82		
Industrial Orientation								-3.54 0.00***	
Manuf. Exp. / Total Exp.									-0.11 0.02**
N	82	82	82	82	82	82	82	82	82
R^{2*}	0.44	0.42	0.36	0.19	0.23	0.18	0.18	0.26	0.22

Table 29: Multivariate regressions of 'GDP_{08-12}' against Fraser 'credit market regulation' and one additional control variable in the entire sample (second row: p-values of two-sided significance tests; number of asterisks: significance levels of 10%*, 5%** and 1%***).

Results for the other two financial regulation variables (appendix 27) and for the two sub-periods 2008 to 2009 (appendix 28) and 2010 to 2012 (appendix 29) look very much alike. They are insignificant only in a few specifications when using the Heritage variable during the time period 2010 to 2012. Notably, in those regressions which include financial freedom variables and development variables alongside each other, the latter usually turn insignificant.

As financial freedom and economic development are positively correlated (see table 30), loss of significance of the development variable when considered alongside financial freedom offers a potential explanation why highly developed countries faced a deeper economic crisis: Possibly, they were less resilient to the economic shock because they featured more open and less-regulated financial sectors.

	Fraser Credit Market Regulation	BRS Summary Index	Heritage Financial Freedom
Financial Vulnerabilities	**0.25**	0.10	0.20
Increase (Priv. Cred. / GDP)	**0.27**	0.12	**0.35**
Current Acc. Balance / GDP	-0.01	-0.01	-0.09
Economic Development	**0.33**	**0.26**	**0.45**
GDP per Capita	**0.46**	**0.42**	**0.54**
International Linkages	**0.32**	0.20	0.19
Trade / GDP	**0.38**	**0.25**	0.20
Industrial Orientation	0.17	0.07	-0.05
Manuf. Exp. / Total Exp.	**0.25**	0.10	0.02

Table 30: Correlations between financial freedom variables and control variables in the entire sample (significant correlations at 5% level are bold).

In the sub-group of 52 less developed countries, results resemble those within the entire sample of 84 countries, although they are not robust during the time period 2010 to 2012 and depend on the choice of the explanatory variable for financial freedom. As depicted in appendices 31, 32 and 33, especially the coefficients of the Heritage variable are insignificant across most specifications during all three time periods. Furthermore, the positive correlation coefficients between financial freedom variables and pre-crisis financial deepening (appendix 30), as well as the loss of significance when running regressions including both variables together, suggest that the potential negative effects of financial freedom on crisis resilience are partly mediated through higher financial vulnerabilities.

To conclude, the empirical analysis in this section showed that financial freedom and less stringent financial regulations are associated with worse crisis resilience in the entire sample of 84 countries and within the sub-group of 52 less developed countries, especially during the downturn period 2008 to 2009. Overall, these results support and partly qualify the results obtained by Giannone et al. (2011), who provide evidence that financial freedom aggravated the impact of the economic crisis in a large worldwide sample of 102 countries. The previous analysis confirmed this negative relationship within the entire sample of 84 countries but showed that it doesn't apply to developed countries, where financial freedom and crisis resilience are unrelated.

4.3.5 Government Size and Crisis Resilience

The public sector engages in a wide range of economic activities, including the maintenance of a legal system, regulations of goods-, labor- and capital markets, the direct provision of public goods or redistributive transfers and subsidies. The relevance of government activity, which usually accounts for 25 to 55 percent of overall economic activity, for crisis resilience stems from its partial autonomy from developments in the private sector.[198] The provision of public goods and services, for example, doesn't primarily depend on consumers' willingness to pay and therefore on short-term fluctuations of demand. Rather, it is based on political discretion and takes into account issues such as perceived fairness, perceived merit, public good considerations or demands from powerful interest groups. This partial autonomy of public spending entails a potentially stabilizing effect during a crisis, as public spending may expand while private economic activity contracts.

Discussion and Hypotheses

As illustrated in chapter 2, Olson and NWW have different views regarding the effectiveness of government activity. While Olson stresses the general rent-generating character of government activity, NWW point out the public good orientation in open access orders, whereas they tend to agree with Olson's pessimistic account of government spending in limited access orders. Although both accounts link government size to certain economic outcomes, neither Olson nor NWW offer a detailed discussion of the theoretical link between government size and crisis resilience.

Authors, who argue that government activity is a stabilizing force, often resort to Keynesian arguments of demand stabilization through counter-cyclical fiscal policies.[199] Such counter-cyclical measures can either take the form of discretionary stimulus packages, or they can be based on automatic stabilizers. Examples for discretionary measures are extraordinary transfers to adversely affected groups (such as house owners and banks) or public investment projects (for example into infrastructure). The most important automatic stabilizers are social transfer payments, which normally increase during recessions, and tax revenues, which normally decrease, especially when tax rates rise progressively with income. Proponents of countercyclical policies argue that they stabilize aggregate demand by substituting public for private demand and by cushioning the reductions of household's disposable incomes and

---

[198] For an instructive overview of government activities and government expenditure relative to GDP across countries see Stiglitz & Rosengard (2015, pp.26-58).

[199] For a standard textbook discussion of the effects of fiscal policies during a recession see, for example, Blanchard (2005, pp. 151-155, 553-574).

company revenues through government transfers and reduced tax burdens.[200] Empirical research partially supports these arguments, especially regarding the resilience-enhancing effects of automatic stabilizers. Dolls et al. (2012), for example, estimate that automatic stabilizers provided a demand stabilization of up to 30 % in EU countries and up to 20 % in the US during the Great Recession. The magnitude of such automatic stabilizers, in turn, is often associated with larger government sectors. Fatás & Mihov (2001, p. 8), for example, argue that "government size can be a proxy for the overall level of stabilization provided by fiscal policy", and Rodrik (1998, p. 1011) perceives "larger government spending [...] as performing an insulation function, insofar as the government sector is the 'safe' sector (in terms of employment and purchases from the rest of the economy) relative to other activities, and especially compared to tradables".[201] Related empirical research also supports these arguments showing that larger government sectors are often associated with lower output volatility (Galí, 1994; Fatas & Mihov, 2001; Domenech & Fatas, 2008).[202] Hence, the arguments put forward by these authors refer to the third aspect of adaptive efficiency – the ability to avoid unnecessary adjustments of economic activity. The more heavily governments step in to replace temporarily depressed private demand, the fewer companies are forced out of business and the fewer people become unemployed, which potentially helps avoiding further demand reductions through multiplier effects.

Authors who are skeptical about the beneficial effects of government activity on crisis resilience either dispute the positive impact of counter-cyclical fiscal policies in general, or they point out the inability and unwillingness of many governments to actually implement such policies. The first type of skepticism focuses on the distortionary character of government spending and on the crowding-out of private investment by public investment through discretionary fiscal measures (Cwik & Wieland, 2011; Pană, 2013). Especially proponents of very limited governments stress "a tendency of government failure whereby the state becomes inefficient, bureaucratic, and even harmful to productivity. Government expenditures necessarily compete with private agents and interfere in market prices by overstimulating demand and potentially diverting resources" (Beach & Kane, 2009, p. 46). Following this argument, inefficient government activity affects the first two aspects of adaptive efficiency, as it impedes innovative activity and slows down the re-allocation of productive resources to their best uses.

---

[200] See Spilimbergo et al. (2009), although they point out that appropriate measures may differ according to the specific situation of each country.

[201] Rodrik (1998), however, also states that more volatile economies have larger government sectors to insulate themselves against further output fluctuations. Thus, both effects (higher volatility leading to larger governments and larger governments leading to less volatility) cancel each other out.

[202] Other papers such as Debrun et al. (2008) provide empirical evidence that the negative relationship between government size and output volatility vanishes when considering more recent data.

The second type of skepticism towards the role of government activity for promoting crisis resilience refers to the inability and unwillingness of most governments to actually run effective policies. Hence, authors putting forward such arguments acknowledge the potential positive effects of counter-cyclical fiscal measures but point out the pro-cyclical spending behavior in many countries. One explanation of pro-cyclicality are implementation lags of fiscal policies, which may turn into action only with some delay when economic recovery is already on its way. Most authors, however, attribute the pro-cyclicality of government spending either to more intense borrowing constraints during bad times (Gavin & Perotti, 1997; Kaminsky et al., 2004) or to rent-seeking by special interest groups during good times (Talvi & Végh, 2005; Alesina et al., 2008). Furthermore, they argue that both problems are more prevalent in less developed countries. Empirical evidence reinforces this thesis, showing that fiscal policy is indeed pro-cyclical in less developed countries and a-cyclical or counter-cyclical in highly developed ones (Gavin & Perotti, 1997; Talvi & Végh, 2005; Alesina et al., 2008). Especially this latter finding is in accordance with the distinction NWW make about the nature of government activity in the two types of social orders.

Hence, the arguments summarized above and the discussions of Olson's and NWW's accounts in chapter 2 entail the following two competing hypotheses.

- Following NWW's account, larger government sectors should be associated with worse crisis resilience in less developed countries and with better crisis resilience or no performance differences during the Great Recession in developed ones.
- Following Olson's generally pessimistic view on government spending, larger government sectors should be associated with worse crisis resilience during the Great Recession.

Data Sources

In the empirical analysis below, I use three different explanatory variables measuring government size. While the first variable is a broader measure that captures different aspects of government activity, the other two variables have a narrower scope measuring government size relative to GDP.

- The index 'size of government: expenditures, taxes and enterprises' (subsequently: 'size of government') provided by the Fraser Institute captures "the extent to which countries rely on the political process to allocate resources and goods and services" (Gwartney & Lawson, 2009, p. 7). The index aggregates information on overall government consumption, on transfers and subsidies, on direct government production and investment as well as on the top marginal tax rate. Potential values range from 0 (high government involvement) to 10 (little government involvement). Actual scores within the sample used in this thesis range from 3.66 (Sweden) to 9.30 (Hong Kong).

- The item 'general government consumption spending as a percentage of total consumption' (subsequently 'government consumption') by the Fraser Institute is a subcomponent of the previous index. It measures government size in a narrower sense than the composite index. The index takes values between 0 (high percentage of government consumption) and 10 (low percentage of government consumption). Actual scores range from 1.16 (Botswana) to 9.72 (Bangladesh).
- The Index 'government size' from the Heritage Foundation also provides scores for the magnitude of government expenditures relative to GDP. It is, therefore, closely related to the previous index but uses a slightly different approach to calculate scores (Beach & Kane, 2008, p. 46). Potential values range from 0 (high percentage of government expenditures) to 100 (low percentage of government expenditures). Actual scores range from 3.6 (Sweden) to 96.1 (Guatemala).

All three indices are highly correlated. As depicted in appendix 34, correlation coefficients range from 0.74 to 0.76. Therefore, the three indices are likely to capture similar aspects of government size.

Results

The results of the bivariate regression as depicted in table 31 are straight forward. When considering the entire sample of 84 countries, smaller governments are significantly related to better crisis resilience across all three measures during all three time periods (as indicated by positive coefficients). A similar picture emerges for the sub-group of 52 emerging and developing countries, although coefficients are not always significant, especially when using the broader measure of government involvement 'size of government' from the Fraser Institute. Coefficients for the sub-group of 32 developed countries are always insignificant and partially negative.

	Dep. Var.: GDP_{08-12}			Dep. Var.: GDP_{08-09}			Dep. Var.: GDP_{10-12}		
	All	Deve-loped	Emerging & Dev.	All	Deve-loped	Emerging & Dev.	All	Deve-loped	Emerging & Dev.
Fraser Size of Government	**2.83** **0.00*****	0.31 0.78	2.07 0.12	**1.33** **0.00*****	-0.07 0.92	0.79 0.22	**1.64** **0.00*****	0.40 0.64	1.40 0.12
Fraser Government Consumption	**2.53** **0.00*****	-0.33 0.76	**1.98** **0.03****	**1.45** **0.00*****	-0.27 0.63	**1.18** **0.01*****	**1.15** **0.00*****	-0.12 0.88	0.83 0.16
Heritage Govern-ment Spending	**0.26** **0.00*****	-0.03 0.75	**0.33** **0.00*****	**0.11** **0.00*****	-0.05 0.27	**0.12** **0.01*****	**0.15** **0.00*****	0.02 0.72	**0.22** **0.00*****

Table 31: Coefficients of government size indices as explanatory variables in bivariate regressions (second row: p-values of two-sided significance tests; number of asterisks: significance levels of 10%*, 5%** and 1%***; significant results at 5% level are bold).

Figure 14 depicts a scatterplot relating the variable 'size of government' to crisis resilience during the time period 2008 to 2012. The plots show that the positive relationships between explanatory and dependent variables are driven by the sub-group of less developed countries (black dots) and by the inter-group difference between developed (white circles) and less developed countries. The latter usually feature smaller governments, as indicated by higher scores of the Fraser variable, and better crisis resilience than the former. The scatterplots for the other two variables representing government size look very similar (see appendix 35).

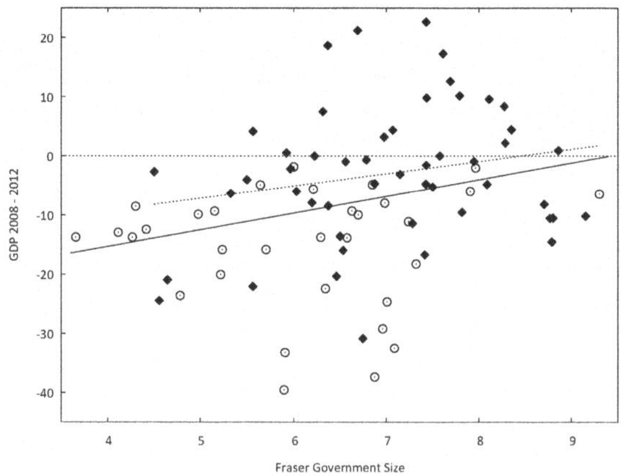

Figure 14: Scatterplot of '$GDP_{08\text{-}12}$' against Fraser 'size of government' (black dots: less developed countries; white circles: developed countries; dotted line: fitted values for sub-sample of emerging and developing countries; continuous line: fitted values for the entire sample).

When controlling for initial vulnerabilities, the picture doesn't change very much, although some coefficients now turn insignificant (see table 32).

	Dep. Var.: $GDP_{08\text{-}12}$			Dep. Var.: $GDP_{08\text{-}09}$			Dep. Var.: $GDP_{10\text{-}12}$		
	All	Deve-loped	Emerging & Dev.	All	Deve-loped	Emerging & Dev.	All	Deve-loped	Emerging & Dev.
Fraser Size of Government	1.20 0.06*	0.26 0.67	1.30 0.22	0.55 0.13	0.44 0.45	0.47 0.42	0.72 0.12	0.39 0.52	0.94 0.19
Fraser Government Consumption	**1.30** **0.01****	-0.67 0.36	**1.62** **0.02****	**0.89** **0.01*****	-0.06 0.88	**1.00** **0.01****	0.44 0.17	-0.48 0.49	0.65 0.13
Heritage Government Spending	**0.12** **0.00*****	-0.03 0.58	**0.20** **0.01*****	0.04 0.09*	-0.02 0.69	0.07 0.14	**0.08** **0.01*****	0.01 0.76	**0.14** **0.00*****

Table 32: Coefficients of government size indices as explanatory variables in multivariate regressions with control models according to table 6 (second row: p-values of two-sided significance tests; number of asterisks: significance levels of 10%*, 5%** and 1%***; significant results at 5% level are bold).

Especially, the coefficients of the broader measure 'size of government' now miss conventional significance levels in all specifications, as do some coefficients of the two narrower measures during the two sub-periods 2008 to 2009 and 2010 to 2012. When, however, considering the narrower measures during the time period 2008 to 2012, coefficients confirm the positive relationship between limited government and better crisis resilience within the entire sample of 84 countries and the sub-sample of 52 less developed countries. Coefficients for the sub-group of 32 developed countries remain insignificant.

The next step involves a deeper analysis of the question which control variables affect the significance of the government size variables. First, table 33 depicts the correlations between the three explanatory variables and control variables. It shows that limited governments are associated with low economic development, low GDP per capita and small industrial sectors. These results are in accordance with Wagner's "law of increasing expansion of public, and particularly state, activities", which states that government involvement increases as countries industrialize and show higher income levels (Wagner, 1958 [1883], p. 8).

	Fraser Size of Government	Fraser Government Consumption	Heritage Government Spending
Financial Vulnerabilities	-0.09	-0.11	-0.21
Increase (Priv. Cred. / GDP)	-0.15	**-0.30**	**-0.33**
Current Acc. Balance / GDP	-0.07	-0.13	0.07
Economic Development	**-0.27**	**-0.48**	**-0.45**
GDP per Capita	**-0.38**	**-0.59**	**-0.64**
International Linkages	0.15	0.01	0.13
Trade / GDP	0.10	-0.06	0.05
Industrial Orientation	**-0.26**	**-0.33**	**-0.33**
Manuf. Exp. / Total Exp.	**-0.30**	**-0.32**	**-0.32**

Table 33: Correlations between government size variables and control variables in the entire sample (significant correlations at 5% level are bold).

The correlations suggest that the government size may be related to economic development and crisis resilience in a similar way as rule of law, business freedom and financial freedom. As smaller government sectors and lower development levels usually go together and as both are associated with better crisis resilience, the respective variables are likely to capture similar effects. Table 34, which depicts the coefficients of multivariate regressions of crisis resilience against the 'size of government' index and different control variables, reinforces this interpretation, as the inclusion of GDP per capita in regression 5 reduces the magnitude and significance level of the 'size of government' index. Similarly, regressions 10 and 11 show that the inclusion of the development variable renders the coefficient of the 'size of government' index slightly insignificant. When using the other two government size indices as explanatory variables, as depicted in appendix 36, results are very similar. Then, however, the development variables instead of the government size variables turn insignificant when including both variables together. The same effects are visible when looking only at the two sub- periods 2008 to 2009 (appendix 37) and 2010 to 2012 (appendix 38). These empirical findings are consistent with the interpretation that small government size and low development levels capture similar effects.

Dependent Variable: 'GDP$_{08-12}$'; Sample: All Countries											
	(1)	(2)	(3)	(4)	(5)	(6)	(7)	(8)	(9)	(10)	(11)
Constant	-23.40 0.00***	-18.06 0.00***	-26.84 0.00***	-23.82 0.00***	-14.46 0.03**	-28.31 0.00***	-24.35 0.00***	-21.50 0.00***	-16.03 0.02**	-15.75 0.00***	-19.56 0.00***
Fraser Size of Government	2.34 0.00***	2.01 0.00***	3.14 0.00***	2.41 0.00***	1.57 0.07*	3.07 0.00***	3.02 0.00***	2.06 0.01***	2.11 0.01***	1.20 0.06*	1.77 0.00***
Financial Vulnerabilities	-7.17 0.00***									-7.30 0.00***	-7.24 0.00***
Increase (Priv. Cred. / GDP)		-0.27 0.00***									
Current Acc. Balance / GDP			0.63 0.00***								
Economic Development				-1.96 0.11						-2.37 0.02**	
GDP per Capita					-0.22 0.00***						
International Linkages						-2.06 0.08*				-1.69 0.01***	-1.82 0.02**
Trade / GDP							-0.04 0.06*				
Industrial Orientation								-3.70 0.00***		-3.99 0.00***	-3.80 0.00***
Manuf. Exp. / Total Exp.									-0.13 0.03**		
N	82	82	82	82	82	82	82	82	82	82	82
R^{2*}	0.40	0.36	0.26	0.08	0.16	0.09	0.10	0.14	0.11	0.53	0.50

Table 34: Multivariate regressions of 'GDP$_{08-12}$' against Fraser 'size of government' and one additional control variable in the entire sample (second row: p-values of two-sided significance tests; number of asterisks: significance levels of 10%*, 5%** and 1%***).

Results for the sub-group of less developed countries are more ambiguous. As depicted in appendices 39, 40 and 41, the significance of the government size variables depends on the choice of the explanatory variable. While the Fraser index 'size of government' is mainly insignificant during all three time periods, the indices 'government consumption' from the Fraser Institute and the index 'government spending' from the Heritage Foundation are partly significant.

Overall, the previous empirical analysis provides support for the hypothesis that smaller governments are associated with better economic performance when considering the entire sample. Furthermore, there exists weaker evidence in favor of the same hypothesis within the sub-group of 52 less developed countries, as significance levels in that group depend on the choice of explanatory variables. Finally, in line with the argument made by NWW, this relationship does not hold within the sub-group of 32 developed countries, where stronger government involvement apparently does not have negative effects on crisis resilience.

4.3.6 Exchange Rate Regimes and Crisis Resilience

The final institution under consideration is the exchange rate regime. Although neither Olson nor NWW discuss this institution, I still include it in the analysis as it is highly relevant for adaptive efficiency during an economic crisis.

There are many possible ways to classify exchange rate regimes.[203] Subsequently, I follow the classification made by Frankel (2003) or Tavlas et al. (2008) and distinguish three broad categories: hard pegs, soft pegs and floating regimes.

- Hard pegs include monetary unions (many countries adopt a single currency under the supervision of a common central bank as in the case of the EMU), dollarization or euroization (countries completely adopt another currency like the US Dollar or the Euro as their legal tender) and currency boards (central banks guarantee to exchange domestic currency for an anchor currency at a fixed rate, and they ensure conversion at all time by keeping a sufficiently large amount of foreign currency reserves). All cases have in common that there is a strong institutional commitment not to alter exchange rates in any case.
- Soft pegs include regimes in which central banks commit to maintaining certain exchange rates without, however, providing a strong institutional commitment. Hence, the exchange rate targets in these regimes are open to alterations if circumstances change. Under adjustable peg arrangements target bands are usually narrow and altered infrequently to larger degrees. Under crawling band arrangements target bands are usually wider and frequently altered to smaller degrees.
- Floating regimes include managed floating arrangements and free floating arrangements. Under the former, monetary authorities try to influence exchange rates either to smooth elsewise volatile rates or to correct rates that are perceived to be out of equilibrium. Under free floating arrangements exchange rates are solely determined by supply and demand. In both cases, there is no target zone as under pegs.

Discussion and Hypotheses

There exists an extensive literature studying the advantages and disadvantages of exchange rate arrangements both theoretically and empirically. In those papers, authors come to varying conclusions regarding the preferability of different regimes. Many authors even insist that there is not one perfect choice for all types of economies (Frankel, 2003; Wagner, 2000). Subsequently, I summarize broader tendencies without aiming at the highest possible level of differentiation amongst different types of economies. Overall, I present four important arguments about the relationship between exchange rate regimes and crisis resilience: two in favor of flexible rates, one

---

[203] Tavlas et al. (2008) provide a good overview of classification issues. They especially point out problems regarding the distinction between de jure and de facto regimes.

in favor of fixed rates and one putting forward the so-called bipolar view that intermediate regimes are more crisis-prone than either flexible or fixed rates.[204]

The first potential advantage of flexible exchange rates stems from their propensity to avoid the build-up of external imbalances and to correct imbalances once they occur. As argued in the literature regarding the Great Recession (Deutsche Bundesbank, 2014) and as indicated by the significant coefficients of the 'current account balance to GDP ratio' in section 4.2.2, external imbalances were an important cause of output losses during the years 2008 to 2012. Pegged exchange rates can provoke the build-up of such imbalances by creating the illusion of low exchange rate risks and therefore leading to excessive borrowing from abroad (Angkinand & Willet, 2006). Furthermore, flexible rates may also facilitate the adjustment of imbalances, once they occur. As they allow external-deficit countries to devaluate their currencies relative to external-surplus countries, they help these countries to improve external price competitiveness and stimulate export demand. Higher demand from abroad, in turn, increases export revenues and stimulates the re-allocation of factors of production to export-orientated sectors. In the case of fixed exchange rates, the improvements of external competitiveness would have to be accomplished through the reduction of domestic prices and wages, which is usually much more complicated (Friedman, 1953; Gosh, 2014). Hence, following this argument, flexible exchange rates function as an external counterpart to flexible prices and wages within a country. By generating the respective price signals, they affect the second aspect of adaptive efficiency - the quick re-allocation of factors of production to their most efficient uses.

The second argument in favor of flexible exchange rates stems from their relation to monetary policy, as countries with inflexible exchange rates have a much more limited scope for executing an independent monetary policy than countries with flexible rates (Wagner, 2000; Frankel 2003). In countries with fixed rates (which allow free international capital flows), central banks have to subordinate their main policy instruments such as the base interest rate or open market operations to their goal of maintaining exchange rates at their target level. This means that central banks cannot freely use these instruments to curb aggregate demand during a boom and to stimulate aggregate demand during a crisis.[205] Lowering interest rates, for example, would induce capital exports to higher-interest countries, thereby reducing relative demand for the domestic currency and creating downward pressure on the exchange rates. Barnebek & Andersen (2014), for example, attribute Denmark's relatively bad crisis performance to its constrained monetary policy. Before 2008, the authors argue, inadequately low interest rates contributed to the overheating of Denmark's economy,

[204] More arguments about the general advantages and disadvantages of different exchange rate regimes besides their bearing on economic crisis can be found in Frankel (2003).

[205] This argument assumes that countries cannot fully restrict international capital mobility, as restrictions to international capital flows allow countries to maintain fixed exchange rates and to run an independent monetary policy at the same time.

leading to high wages and a loss of international competitiveness. When the crisis started, commitment to fixed exchange rates impeded the necessary monetary easing, which would have stimulated domestic demand and restored international competitiveness. Following this account, flexible exchange rates promote the third aspect of adaptive efficiency - the ability to avoid unnecessary adjustments of economic activity - because the more freedom central banks have to stimulate aggregate demand, the better they can counteract potential bankruptcies and job losses during a crisis.

Departing from the previous two arguments, other authors argue that fixed exchange rates stabilize output during an economic crisis, as they reduce exchange rate fluctuations that are unrelated to macroeconomic fundamentals (Wagner, 2000; Frankel, 2003).[206] For economic actors engaged in cross-border economic activity such financially-induced volatilities mean a higher degree of uncertainty and higher transaction costs. Exporters and importers, for example, have to deal with constantly-changing goods prices; and investors or debtors face fluctuating real values of positions that are denominated in foreign currencies. Fixed exchange rates can help to reduce such uncertainties and to avoid a volatility-induced decline of trade and investment.[207]

The previous argument, however, only holds if the fixing of exchange rates is credible. If the domestic currency comes under depreciation pressure (due to an economic downturn, for example) and private economic actors lose faith that the central bank possesses enough reserves to meet the increasing demand for a foreign currency, there exists the danger of capital flight or speculative attacks. This, in turn, adds to the already existing depreciation pressure and can create a self-fulfilling prophecy that forces the central bank to abandon the target parity and devaluate the domestic currency even further than would have been necessary under a floating regime. For this reason, authors putting forward the so-called bipolar view argue that intermediate regimes are more prone to currency crises than the two corner solutions – hard pegs and flexible rates (Eichengreen, 1994).[208]

---

206 During the Great Recession, for example, developments in the financial sector such as the so-called 'flight to safety' or the unwinding of carry trade led to a strong appreciation of the US Dollar, although the USA was the epicenter of the crisis and should have seen a depreciation of its currency (Kohler, 2010).

207 Rose (2000), for example, shows that exchange rate volatility between two countries has a negative effect on their bilateral trade. Having a common currency, on the other hand, has a positive effect on trade between two countries (See Frankel & Rose, 2002).

208 Although Eichengreen (1994) is often cited to be the origin of this argument, the view goes back at least as far as Friedman (1953, p. 164), who argued that "the system of occasional changes in temporarily rigid exchange rates seems to me the worst of two worlds: it provides neither the stability of expectations that a genuinely rigid and stable exchange rate could provide in a world of unrestricted trade and willingness and ability to adjust the internal price structure to external conditions nor the continuous sensitivity of a flexible exchange rate".

Previous empirical research comes to opposing conclusions and provides inconclusive evidence in favor of either one of the above-stated arguments. Although there are some authors pointing out a lower likelihood of a banking crisis in inflexible regimes (Domac & Martinez Peria, 2003),[209] the majority of authors provide evidence either in favor of flexible exchange rates (Gosh et al., 2014; Combes et al., 2016) or in favor of the bipolar view (Frankel, 2003; Angkinand & Willet, 2006). Other authors cast doubt on robust links between exchange rate regimes and crisis resilience by showing that the choice of the appropriate regime depends on other country-specific features (Aşıcı, 2011) or by providing evidence that exchange rate regimes are unrelated to the speed of current account adjustment (Chinn & Wei, 2013).

Following the arguments presented above and the inconclusive empirical results, there are three competing hypotheses regarding the relationship between exchange rate regimes and crisis resilience:

- The first two arguments entail the hypothesis that countries with floating exchange rates should have performed better during the Great Recession than countries with intermediate regimes or hard pegs.
- From the third argument it follows that countries with hard pegs should have performed better during the Great Recession than countries with intermediate regimes or floating exchange rates.
- The fourth argument leads to the hypothesis that countries with intermediate regimes should have performed during the Great Recession worse than countries with floating exchange rates or hard pegs.

Data Sources

The data source for constructing the indices is the IMF's De Facto Classification of Exchange Rate Regimes (IMF, 2008, pp. xiv-xv). Following this classification, countries belong to one out of eight different categories. Instead of using these eight categories, I re-classify each country to belong to one of the three broader categories 'peg', 'intermediate' and 'float'. Under the category 'peg' I combine countries with the IMF classifications 'exchange arrangement with no separate legal tender' and 'currency board arrangement'. Furthermore, I include all countries belonging to the European Monetary Union to this category.[210] As 'float' I classify countries that have the IMF

[209] The same authors, however, also provide evidence that countries with fixed rates face deeper crises than countries with flexible rates.

[210] The classification of the EMU countries is particularly difficult. Having the Euro as a common currency, these countries have fixed exchange rates to other EMU member states. Exchange rates to non-EMU countries, on the other hand, are flexible since the Euro floats freely as compared to other currencies. I classify the EMU countries to have fixed exchange rates out of three considerations. First, the main trading partners of most EMU countries are other EMU countries, meaning that the fixed rates to those countries weigh heavier than the flexible rates to non-EMU countries. Second, membership in the currency union disables EMU countries to pursue an

classifications 'independently floating' and 'managed floating with no pre-determined path' with the exception of the EMU countries. Finally, the category 'intermediate' includes all other regimes: 'conventional pegged arrangement', 'pegged exchange rates with horizontal bands', 'crawling peg' and 'crawling band'. All explanatory variables are dummies which can either take values of 0 or 1, depending on whether a country belongs to the respective regime or not.

Results

Table 35 displays the coefficients of the bivariate regressions without control variables. As only three developed countries are classified to have intermediate regimes, I don't run regressions with the 'intermediate' dummy for that sub-group of countries.

	Dep. Var.: GDP_{08-12}			Dep. Var.: GDP_{08-09}			Dep. Var.: GDP_{10-12}		
	All	Deve-loped	Emerging & Dev.	All	Deve-loped	Emerging & Dev.	All	Deve-loped	Emerging & Dev.
Floating Exchange Rates	**6.35** **0.02****	**9.42** **0.00*****	1.78 0.59	1.88 0.24	**4.55** **0.02****	-1.38 0.43	**4.89** **0.00*****	**5.78** **0.01****	3.18 0.13
Pegged Exchange Rates	**-12.59** **0.00*****	-6.60 0.07*	-9.02 0.16	**-6.08** **0.00*****	-2.36 0.30	-3.24 0.07*	**-7.18** **0.00*****	-4.77 0.06*	-6.19 0.24
Intermediate Regime	3.60 0.25		0.67 0.79	3.27 0.10*		2.46 0.18	0.41 0.81		-1.49 0.46

Table 35: Coefficients of exchange rate regime dummies as explanatory variables in bivariate regressions (second row: p-values of two-sided significance tests; number of asterisks: significance levels of 10%*, 5%** and 1%***; significant results at 5% level are bold).

Within the entire dataset of 84 countries, 'float' coefficients are positive and significant, while 'peg' coefficients are negative and mostly significant. This suggests that countries with flexible exchange rates performed better than countries with inflexible exchange rates. Within the sub-group of 32 developed countries, coefficients point towards the same positive relationship between exchange rate flexibility and crisis resilience. As coefficients within the sub-group of 52 less developed countries results are insignificant, the relationships in the entire dataset are likely to be driven by developed countries or by inter-group differences. Finally, the 'intermediate' dummy exhibits no significant coefficients, thus, providing no support for the bipolar hypothesis.

Figure 15 depicts the scatterplots relating exchange rate flexibility to economic performance during the time period 2008 to 2012 in both sub-groups of countries. While the left panel shows a positive relationship between flexible exchange rates and

individual monetary policy, which means that they face the same monetary policy constraints as other countries with hard pegs. Finally, I classify the EMU countries as hard pegs out of consistency considerations. Bosnia and Herzegovina, Bulgaria, Estonia and Lithuania, for example, have currency boards that guarantee the exchange to the Euro. They, hence, face the same constraints for external adjustment and monetary policy as EMU countries. Therefore, classifying them as hard pegs and EMU countries as free floating would be inconsistent.

crisis resilience in the sub-group of 32 developed countries, the right panel illustrates that no such relation exists in the sub-group of 52 less developed countries.

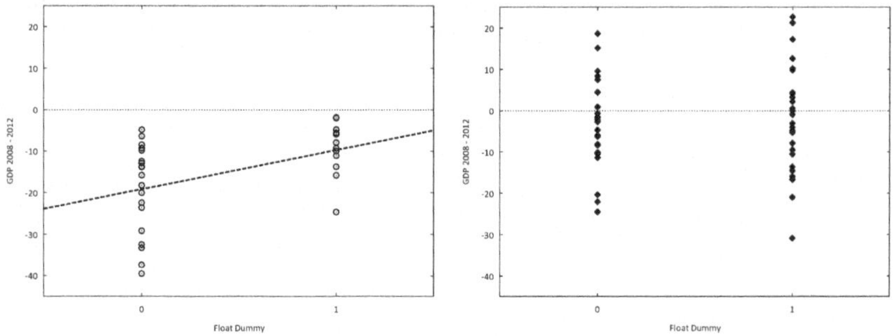

Figure 15: Scatterplot of '$GDP_{08\text{-}12}$' against the 'float' dummy (black dots in the right panel: less developed countries; white circles in the left panel: developed countries; upward-sloping line in the left panel: fitted values for the sub-sample of developed countries).

Next, table 36 depicts the coefficients of the three explanatory variables after controlling for non-institutional variables based on principal components. When considering the entire sample, countries with flexible exchange rates performed better than countries with inflexible rates during the time periods 2008 to 2012 and 2010 to 2012, although not all coefficients are significant. Within the sub-group of 32 developed countries, results look the same, however with consistently significant coefficients. All coefficients for the sub-group of 52 emerging and developing countries and for the time period 2008 to 2009 remain insignificant.

	Dep. Var.: $GDP_{08\text{-}12}$			Dep. Var.: $GDP_{08\text{-}09}$			Dep. Var.: $GDP_{10\text{-}12}$		
	All	Deve-loped	Emerging & Dev.	All	Deve-loped	Emerging & Dev.	All	Deve-loped	Emerging & Dev.
Floating Exchange Rates	2.64 0.18	**5.83** **0.02****	-0.05 0.99	-0.16 0.90	1.64 0.31	-2.14 0.20	**3.06** **0.02****	**4.12** **0.01****	2.08 0.21
Pegged Exchange Rate	**-6.16** **0.02****	**-5.56** **0.02****	-1.94 0.75	-2.43 0.15	-1.16 0.52	-0.52 0.78	**-4.15** **0.03****	**-4.52** **0.02****	-1.69 0.73
Intermediate Regime	1.70 0.52		0.61 0.83	2.25 0.22		2.40 0.17	-0.49 0.74		-1.70 0.32

Table 36: Coefficients of exchange rate regime dummies as explanatory variables in multivariate regressions with control models according to table 6 (second row: p-values of two-sided significance tests; number of asterisks: significance levels of 10%*, 5%** and 1%***; significant results at 5% level are bold).

Robustness checks with original control variables mainly confirm these results. Of particular interest are the positive associations between exchange rate flexibility and crisis resilience in the entire sample of 84 countries and in the sub-sample of 32 countries during the time periods 2008 to 2012 and 2010 to 2012. Correlations between explanatory variables and control variables are depicted in table 37 (for the entire sample of 84 countries) and appendix 42 (for the sub-sample of 32 developed countries). The positive correlations of the 'peg' dummy with variables representing development levels and industrial orientation in table 37 can likely be attributed to EMU member countries which are highly developed and classified as 'pegs'. Other correlations between explanatory and control variables are weak and mainly insignificant.

	Floating Exchange Rates	Pegged Exchange Rates	Intermediate Regime
Financial Vulnerabilities	-0.16	0.16	0.03
Increase (Priv. Cred. / GDP)	-0.05	0.16	-0.10
Current Acc. Balance / GDP	0.08	-0.11	0.01
Economic Development	0.03	**0.25**	**-0.28**
GDP per Capita	-0.04	**0.38**	**-0.32**
International Linkages	-0.16	0.19	-0.00
Trade / GDP	-0.17	**0.21**	-0.01
Industrial Orientation	-0.15	**0.24**	-0.07
Manuf. Exp. / Total Exp.	-0.15	**0.28**	-0.11

Table 37: Correlations between exchange rate regime dummies and control variables in the entire sample (significant correlations at 5% level are bold).

The simple insight from the robustness checks with control variables is that the coefficients of the 'peg' variable are consistently significant when considering the entire sample of 84 countries and the coefficients of the 'float' variable are consistently significant when considering the sub-sample of 32 developed countries. Positive float coefficients and negative 'peg' coefficients both indicate that countries with flexible exchange rates performed better than countries with inflexible rates.

Beginning with the entire sample of 84 countries, table 38 shows the consistently negative and significant association between pegs and crisis resilience during the entire time period 2008 to 2012. Results for the two sub-periods 2008 to 2009 and 2010 to 2012 are similar (see appendix 42). When using 'float' variables, coefficients are mainly positive and significant during the periods 2008 to 2012 and 2010 to 2012 but insignificant during the sub-period 2008 to 2009 (see appendix 43). Notably, the joint inclusion of 'peg' and 'economic development' variables usually renders the latter variables insignificant, thereby indicating that part of the negative association between high development levels and crisis resilience may be attributed to the stronger prevalence of pegs (due to EMU membership) in highly developed countries.

When analyzing the sub-group of 32 developed countries, the 'float' variable is positive and mainly significant during all three time periods (see appendix 45), whereas the 'peg' variable misses conventional significance levels in a few specifications during the entire crisis period 2008 to 2012 and in all specifications during the sub-period 2008 to 2009 (see appendix 46).

	Dependent Variable: 'GDP₀₈₋₁₂'; Sample: All Countries								
	(1)	(2)	(3)	(4)	(5)	(6)	(7)	(8)	(9)
Constant	-5.12 0.00***	-2.10 0.11	-3.21 0.02**	-4.75 0.00***	-2.12 0.22	-4.58 0.00***	-3.44 0.14	-4.98 0.00***	0.32 0.91
Peg	-10.10 0.00***	-10.07 0.00***	-11.41 0.00***	-11.67 0.00***	-9.53 0.00***	-12.40 0.00***	-12.20 0.00***	-10.71 0.00***	-10.71 0.00***
Financial Vulnerabilities	-6.87 0.00***								
Increase (Priv. Cred. / GDP)		-0.27 0.00***							
Current Acc. Balance / GDP			0.53 0.00***						
Economic Development				-1.59 0.17					
GDP per Capita					-0.19 0.00***				
International Linkages						-0.44 0.67			
Trade / GDP							-0.01 0.51		
Industrial Orientation								-3.30 0.00***	
Manuf. Exp. / Total Exp.									-0.12 0.03**
N	84	84	84	84	84	84	84	84	84
R^{2*}	0.45	0.44	0.29	0.18	0.23	0.16	0.23	0.23	0.21

Table 38: Multivariate regressions of '$GDP_{08\text{-}12}$' against the 'peg' dummy and one additional control variable in the entire sample (second row: p-values of two-sided significance tests; number of asterisks: significance levels of 10%*, 5%** and 1%***).

Overall, the results suggest that exchange rate flexibility mattered only partially – most importantly for the sub-group of 32 developed countries and during the recovery period 2010 to 2012 when flexible exchange rates facilitated a quick recovery. As results within the sub-sample of 52 less developed countries are insignificant, the negative association between pegs and crisis resilience within the entire sample is likely to be attributable to the low-performing EMU member countries, which are classified as pegs.

4.3.7 Summary – Economic Institutions and Crisis Resilience

After discussing each economic institution separately, I now bring together the findings from the previous sections to provide a consolidated picture about the relationships between economic institutions and crisis resilience. First, (1) I summarize the empirical results from the previous sections and point out those institutions which turned out to be significantly related to crisis resilience. Then, (2) I confront the hypotheses derived from Olson and NWW with these empirical findings. Interestingly, the economic institutions which turned out to be significantly related to crisis resilience only partially conform to those suggested by Olson and NWW. Finally, I run regression that explain crisis resilience in terms of a variety of economic institutions, beginning with (3) the entire sample of 84 countries and then turning to (4) developed and (5) less developed countries. As many of the significant institutions are correlated and their individual effects are difficult to separate, I partly combine significant and highly correlated institutional variables to indices and use *them* as explanatory variables. These variables, which capture a variety of economic institutions, will then function as dependent variables in the analysis of the political determinants of resilience-enhancing economic institutions (according to the second level of analysis) in section 4.4.

(1) Table 39 summarizes the findings from sections 4.3.1 to 4.3.6.

	Dep. Var.: GDP_{08-12}			Dep. Var.: GDP_{08-09}			Dep. Var.: GDP_{10-12}		
	All	Deve-loped	Emerging & Dev.	All	Deve-loped	Emerging & Dev.	All	Deve-loped	Emerging & Dev.
Rule of Law	--(d)	+(ca)		--(d)			-(d)	+(ca)	
Business Freedom	-(d)	+(ca)		--(d)				++(ca)	
Labor Market Freedom		++(ca)						++(ca)	
Low Unemploy-ment Benefit	+++(d)		+++	++(d)		++	+++(d)		++
Financial Freedom	---(d)		-(f)	---(d)		-(f)	-(d)		
Small Government	+++(d)		+(d)	++(d)		+(d)	++(d)		
Flexible Exchange Rates	++(d)	++		+(d)	+		+++(d)	+++	

Table 39: Summary of the empirical analysis in the sections 4.3.1 to 4.3.6 (the signs '±' indicate the direction of significant relationships. Subscripts in parenthesis mark common effects with non-institutional control variables; (d) represents common effects with 'GDP per capita' and 'economic development', (ca) represents common effects with the 'current account balance to GDP ratio', and (f) represents common effects with the increase of the 'private credit to GDP ratio' and 'financial vulnerabilities'. The number of signs represents the robustness of the relationship apart from common effects. Three signs indicate significant results across all considered institutional variables and specifications, two signs indicate significant results across all considered institutional variables and in most specifications, and one sign indicates significant results for some institutional variables).

Negative or positive signs indicate the directions of the relationships between the respective institutional variables and crisis resilience. Subscripts in parentheses mark non-institutional vulnerability variables that capture similar effects as the respective institutional variable. These non-institutional vulnerability variables ('GDP per capita', 'economic development', the 'current account balance to GDP ratio', increases in the 'private credit to GDP ratio' and 'financial vulnerabilities') are correlated with the respective institutional variables, and, when included together in one regression, at least one of the two coefficients loses considerable magnitude and significance. Hence, these relations between institutional and non-institutional variables raise causality issues about channels of influence and sources of vulnerabilities. Finally, based on the assumption that the common effects of the institutional and the non-institutional variables can indeed be attributed to the institutional variable, the number of signs indicates the robustness of these effects. Three signs indicate significant results (p-values of 5%) across all explanatory variables representing the respective institution and across all specifications controlling for non-institutional vulnerabilities (other than those marked in parentheses). Two signs indicate that the coefficients are mainly significant across all explanatory variables representing an institution but miss conventional significance levels in a few specifications when controlling for non-institutional vulnerabilities (other than those marked in parentheses). One sign indicates that coefficients are mainly significant for at least half of the explanatory variables representing an institution but insignificant for other explanatory variables representing the same institution.

From table 39, it first stands out that results differ considerably in developed and less developed countries, as there is not one single institution that affects crisis resilience in the same way in both sub-groups of countries. Therefore, it is necessary to discuss the findings for each sample, separately.

First, results within the entire sample of 84 countries are either driven by the results within one sub-group of countries (exchange rate flexibility in developed countries or unemployment benefits, financial market openness and government size in less developed countries) or by inter-group differences between developed and less developed countries. As pointed out throughout the previous sections, especially the associations between certain institutions (rule of law, business freedom, low unemployment benefits, financial freedom, small government sectors and flexible exchange rates) and economic development are highly relevant for understanding the significance of many institutional variables in different specifications. Whenever I jointly considered the respective institutional variables and the development variables in one regression, typically one coefficient lost magnitude and significance as compared to bivariate regressions. These results entailed the question whether highly developed countries faced deeper economic crises because they feature certain high-development institutions such as rule of law, open goods markets, generous unemployment support, open financial markets, larger governments and inflexible exchange rates (in EMU countries) or because of other properties associated with high economic development but unrelated to economic institutions. According to the first interpretation, the abovementioned economic institutions may have contributed to a deeper economic crisis.[211] According to the second interpretation, the significant

[211] Rule of law and business freedom, which are associated with a competitive business environment, may have forced companies to react more heavily to the economic shock. Open financial markets, which are associated with higher financial vulnerabilities, may have aggravated the impact of the financial turbulence that originated in the US financial sector. Government spending may have been pro-cyclical or distortionary. Finally, inflexible exchange rates especially in EMU countries may have contributed to the build-up and slow reduction of current-account imbalances.

relationships between economic institutions and crisis resilience may just be spurious because of another, non-institutional characteristic of highly developed countries.

Second, in the sub-group of 32 developed countries, economic institutions mattered primarily during the years 2010 to 2012, as the strength of the recovery is positively related to rule of law, open goods markets and open labor markets. However, the significance of the positive coefficients depends most importantly on the exclusion of the current account variable. As the abovementioned institutions are positively related to healthy current accounts and as healthy current accounts facilitated a quick and strong recovery, including both variables jointly in regressions usually rendered the institutional variables insignificant. In the respective sections, I pointed out the possible interpretation that the three economic institutions – rule of law, open goods markets and open labor markets - contributed to healthy current accounts and therefore had an indirect positive effect on the strength of the recovery. This interpretation is not uncontroversial but in line with a variety of related papers discussing the determinants of external imbalances.[212] Furthermore, within developed countries, there is strong evidence in favor of a positive relationship between crisis resilience and exchange rate flexibility, especially during the entire time period 2010 to 2012, indicating that external price flexibility improved crisis resilience, as well. Low unemployment support, unregulated financial markets and small government sectors are unrelated to economic performance during the entire time period under investigation.

Finally, within the sub-group of 52 less developed countries, crisis resilience is significantly related to the generosity of unemployment benefits during the entire time period, thereby indicating that countries which granted lower support to unemployed people performed better than those providing more generous benefits. As pointed out in section 4.3.3, however, these results need to be treated with caution due to measurement problems of the explanatory variable in less developed countries. Furthermore, the analyses in sections 4.3.4 and 4.3.5 provided evidence that countries with rigid financial regulations and smaller public sectors showed better performance than countries with open financial markets and larger public sectors – especially during the initial downturn 2008 to 2009. The analysis in section 4.3.4 also showed that the potential negative effects of open financial markets are related to higher financial vulnerabilities, suggesting that financial openness may have weakened crisis resilience by facilitating unsustainable financial deepening prior to the crisis. However, for both institutions (government size and financial openness) only two out of three measures showed significant coefficients. Finally, as opposed to developed countries, in the sub-group of 52 emerging and developing countries there exists no evidence that rule of law, business freedom or labor market freedom had any positive effect on crisis resilience.

---

[212] See, for example, Belke & Dreger (2013), Berger & Nitsch (2010), Eichengreen (2010) or Zemanek et al. (2009).

(2) These results only partially conform to the hypotheses derived from Olson's and NWW's accounts. In other parts, they call for qualifications. In particular, five findings stand out:

1. Non-sclerotic, open access institutions did not have a general positive effect on crisis resilience. Within the entire sample, variables representing rule of law, open goods markets and open financial markets even show a negative association with economic performance. This suggests that limited access institutions may have insulated less developed countries from the negative effects of this particular crisis, which is partially in accordance with structural stability arguments and the hypothesis H-S. At the same time, the empirical results contradict the hypotheses H-O 2 and H-NWW 2 and call for a specification of the circumstances under which Olson's and NWW's arguments are valid.
2. Non-sclerotic, open access institutions such as rule of law, open goods markets and open labor markets did, however, show a positive association with crisis resilience within the sub-group of developed countries. This finding suggests a qualification of the theoretical account presented in chapter 2, as it indicates that the positive association between non-sclerotic, open access institutions and crisis resilience (H-NWW 2 and H-O 2) only holds within developed countries. Furthermore, the close association between the effects of the respective economic institutions and the current account balance provides some hints about the potential channel of influence. Departing from the theoretical arguments presented in chapter 2, the empirical analysis suggests that open markets did not matter primarily by facilitating adjustment *during* the crisis but rather by avoiding mal-adjustments that caused current account imbalances in the years *before* the crisis.
3. Larger government sectors and more generous unemployment benefits play different roles in highly developed and less developed countries, being detrimental to crisis resilience only in the latter group. On the one hand, these findings support NWW's optimistic account of redistributions and government activity in open access orders, while they contradict Olson's pessimistic account for that group of countries. For less developed countries, on the other hand, the empirical results are in line with both NWW's and Olson's pessimistic views that redistributions and government activity mainly serve the rent-seeking interests of powerful groups and are therefore detrimental to economic performance.
4. Not all regulations are detrimental to economic performance. Most importantly, stricter financial regulations did not have negative effects in developed countries. They even showed a positive association with crisis resilience within the entire sample and partly within less developed countries. Although Olson and NWW did not put much focus on financial regulations, the empirical findings call for caution against over-generalizations regarding the

merits and demerits of regulations. Instead, it appears necessary to differentiate amongst different realms of regulatory activity.

5. Institutions work differently in developed and less developed countries. This finding partly conforms to NWW's account, which stresses the different character of government activity in open access orders and limited access orders. Expanding on that idea, other institutions, too, seem to work differently in the two types of orders.

Based on these findings, I next run regression which include all relevant institutional variables. Later, these regressions will function as points of departure for the analysis of the political determinants of crisis resilience in the final section 4.4.

Unfortunately, it is often not possible to include all individually significant institutional variables in one regression because many of them are highly correlated, thereby rendering coefficients insignificant when considering all variables together. I try to circumvent this problem by constructing simple indices of highly correlated institutional variables and use *them* as new explanatory variables.[213] I, therefore, do not try to disentangle the individual effects of each institution but, instead, assume that related institutions matter conjointly for explaining crisis resilience. Furthermore, combining different institutional variables to single indices has the side effect of saving degrees of freedom, which is particularly important in the small sample of 32 developed countries.

(3) Considering, first, the entire sample of 84 countries, table 40 depicts the correlations amongst significant explanatory variables based on data from the Fraser Institute.

	Fraser Legal System & Prop. Rights	Fraser Business Regulation	Gross Replacement Rates	Fraser Credit Market Regulation	Fraser Government Consumption	Pegs
Fraser Legal System & Prop. Rights	1	**0.70**	**0.60**	**0.46**	**-0.64**	**0.28**
Fraser Business Regulation	**0.70**	1	**0.27**	**0.46**	**-0.32**	0.19
Gross Replacement Rates	**0.60**	**0.27**	1	**0.30**	**-0.61**	**0.54**
Fraser Credit market Regulation	**0.46**	**0.46**	**0.30**	1	**-0.39**	**0.32**
Fraser Government Consumption	**-0.64**	**-0.32**	**-0.61**	**-0.39**	1	**-0.22**
Pegs	**0.28**	0.19	**0.54**	**0.32**	**-0.22**	1

Table 40: Correlations amongst significant institutional variables (mainly based on data from the Fraser Institute) in the entire sample (significant correlations at 5% level are bold).

[213] Departing from the approach in section 4.2, I do not combine original variables by using principal component analysis because I want to give equal weights to each institution.

Table 40 shows that all but one pair of institutional variables are significantly correlated. Little surprisingly, institutions that are associated with high economic development occur in combination: developed countries feature a high degree of rule of law, open goods markets, higher unemployment benefits, more open financial markets, larger government sectors and inflexible exchange rates.[214] Analogous correlations based on Heritage data, which are depicted in appendix 47, look very similar.

Based on these correlations, I next construct a simple index that combines the four institutional variables 'legal system and property rights', 'business regulation', 'credit market regulation' and 'government consumption' to one explanatory variable. It takes high values for countries with high degrees of rule of law, open goods markets, open financial markets and large public sectors, weighting each institutional feature equally. As all four institutions are associated with higher economic development, I label the index 'developed economic institutions'.[215] I do not include gross replacement rates in this index because of the previously expressed doubts about the accuracy of this variable and because it is not available for all countries in the sample. Furthermore, I consider the exchange rate regime separately because it shows weaker and partly insignificant correlations with the other four explanatory variables and because I want to differentiate the institutions affecting internal adjustments from those affecting external price flexibility.

Table 41 shows the results when regressing '$GDP_{08\text{-}12}$' against the newly-constructed index 'developed economic institutions' in a variety of specifications alongside the 'peg' variable and alongside different sets of control variables based on principle components (specifications 3 to 6) or original variables (specifications 7 to 10). Regardless of the specification, the 'developed economic institutions' index and the 'peg' variable remain negative and significant. This supports the previous finding that countries with rule of law, open goods markets, open financial markets, large government sectors and with inflexible exchange rates were more heavily affected by the economic crisis. Furthermore, as the coefficient of both variables remain significant when considered together, both appear to be independent sources of vulnerabilities. Interestingly, the control variables 'economic development' and 'GDP per capita' turn insignificant whenever included together with the 'developed economic institutions' variable (specifications 3, 4, 9, 10), which is consistent with the interpretation that highly developed countries where more heavily affected by the economic crisis due to

[214] The association with inflexible exchange rates may be coincidental, as EMU countries are highly developed and classified as pegged regimes.

[215] Thus, I construct the composite index according to the following formula:

*'developed economic institutions' = 1/4 * 'legal system and property rights' + 1/4 * 'business regulation' + 1/4 * 'credit market regulation' + 1/4 * (10 – 'government consumption')*

Government size enters the index with negative values because low scores of 'government consumption' indicate large public sectors.

developed institutions. Regressions for the two sub-periods 2008 to 2009 and 2010 to 2012, as depicted in appendix 48, show that the potential negative effects of developed economic institutions are more robust during the initial downturn than during the recovery period. This suggests that countries with developed economic institutions showed worse crisis resilience because they were less insulated from the initial shock during the years 2008 to 2009 than countries with low rule of law, highly regulated goods markets, highly regulated capital markets and small public sectors. The 'peg' variable, on the other hand, features significantly negative coefficients mainly during the years 2010 to 2012, indicating that inflexible exchange rates inhibited a strong recovery. These findings are reinforced by regressions that use an alternative 'developed economic institutions' index based on Heritage data (see appendix 49).

Dependent Variable: 'GDP_{08-12}'; Sample: All Countries										
	(1)	(2)	(3)	(4)	(5)	(6)	(7)	(8)	(9)	(10)
Constant	26.15 0.00***	21.41 0.00***	9.04 0.26	9.88 0.19	14.01 0.02**	11.83 0.04**	26.00 0.00***	22.76 0.00***	23.62 0.00***	23.28 0.00***
Fras. Developed Econ. Institutions	-5.38 0.00***	-4.28 0.00***	-2.66 0.03**	-2.57 0.03**	-3.45 0.00***	-2.87 0.00***	-3.52 0.00***	-3.00 0.00***	-3.03 0.01**	-3.11 0.01***
Peg		-9.00 0.00***		-5.88 0.03**		-6.12 0.01**		-4.93 0.05**		-5.02 0.03**
Financial Vulnerabilities			-6.94 0.00***	-6.57 0.00***	-6.79 0.00***	-6.49 0.00***				
Industrial Orientation			-3.57 0.00***	-2.99 0.00***	-3.33 0.00***	-2.88 0.00***				
Economic Development			-0.90 0.46	-0.36 0.74						
International Linkages			-0.87 0.25	-0.39 0.64						
Increase (Priv. Cred. / GDP)							-0.15 0.04**	-0.16 0.02**	-0.14 0.07*	-0.16 0.03**
Current Acc. Balance / GDP							0.57 0.00***	0.51 0.00***	0.60 0.00***	0.50 0.00***
Man. Exp. / Total Exp.							-0.18 0.00***	-0.16 0.00***	-0.18 0.00***	-0.16 0.00***
GDP per Capita									-0.05 0.56	0.01 0.87
N R^{2*}	82 0.21	82 0.29	82 0.54	82 0.57	82 0.54	82 0.58	82 0.58	82 0.59	82 0.57	82 0.59

Table 41: Multivariate regressions of 'GDP_{08-12}' against Fraser 'developed economic institutions', the 'peg' dummy and different sets of control variables in the entire sample (second row: p-values of two-sided significance tests; number of asterisks: significance levels of 10%*, 5%** and 1%***; residuals are not normally distributed in regressions 3, 4, 5, 6 and 7).

(4) Now turning to the sub-group of developed countries, table 42 shows the bivariate correlations amongst 'legal system and property rights', 'business regulation', 'labor regulation' (all based on data from the Fraser institute) and the 'float' dummy. Different aspects of openness are significantly and positively correlated, thereby illustrating that developed countries either feature many different aspects of open

markets at once or not at all. Correlations between flexible exchange rates and the other three variables are partly insignificant. Correlations among analogous variables from the Heritage Foundation and the Global Competitiveness Report are very similar (see appendix 50).

	Fraser Legal System & Prop. Rights	Fraser Business Regulation	Fraser Labor Regulation	Floating Exchange Rates
Fraser Legal System & Prop. Rights	1	**0.75**	**0.40**	0.22
Fraser Business Regulation	**0.75**	1	**0.45**	0.26
Fraser Labor Regulation	**0.40**	**0.45**	1	**0.51**
Floating Exchange Rates	0.22	0.26	**0.51**	1

Table 42: Correlations amongst significant institutional variables (mainly based on data from the Fraser Institute) in the sub-sample of developed countries (significant correlations at 5% level are bold).

I next combine the three institutional variables 'legal system and property rights', 'business regulation' and 'labor regulation' to one explanatory variable (using equal weights of 1/3). As the three institutions resemble important aspects of Olson-type unconstrained markets (only missing small public sectors) and NWW-type open access economies, I label the index 'open access economic institutions' and use it alongside the unchanged variable 'float' which represents external price flexibility.[216]

Table 43 depicts regressions of '$GDP_{10\text{-}12}$' against 'open access economic institutions', the 'float' dummy and different sets of control variables.[217] As control variables I use the 'financial vulnerability' component (regressions 3 and 4) or the two original financial vulnerability variables – increases in the 'private credit to GDP ratio' and 'current account balance to GDP ratio' (regressions 5 to 10). The results depicted in table 43 show that the significance of the index 'open access economic institutions' depends strongly on the inclusion of the 'current account balance to GDP ratio'. This again illustrates that the potential positive effects of the three open access institutions (rule of law, open goods markets and open labor markets) are closely related to current account balances. Furthermore, the 'float' and the 'open access economic institutions' variable are positively correlated (0.44) and lose significance when considered alongside each other, thereby indicating the positive effects of internal and external flexibility are difficult to separate. Results are very similar when regressing '$GDP_{10\text{-}12}$' against alternative indices of 'open access economic institutions' based on data from the Heritage Foundation or the Global Competitiveness Report instead of the Fraser

216 It is important to point out that both indices – 'developed economic institutions' in the entire sample and 'open access economic institutions' in developed countries - both capture similar institutions associated with open access and high development.

217 I look at the years 2010 to 2012 because the potential positive effects of open access economic institutions in developed countries were more pronounced during the recovery period.

Institute (see appendix 51). When using 'GDP_{08-12}' as the dependent variable, coefficients for all three indices are also similar but less significant (see appendix 52).

	Dependent Variable: 'GDP_{10-12}'; Sample: Developed Countries									
	(1)	(2)	(3)	(4)	(5)	(6)	(7)	(8)	(9)	(10)
Constant	-30.97 0.00***	-26.07 0.01**	-24.53 0.00***	-21.44 0.01**	-28.82 0.00***	-24.15 0.00***	-14.93 0.05**	-11.25 0.12	-20.62 0.00***	-16.91 0.01**
Fraser Open Access Economic Institutions	3.65 0.01**	2.73 0.05*	2.81 0.01**	2.21 0.05*	3.71 0.00***	2.83 0.01**	1.47 0.15	0.76 0.45	2.46 0.01**	1.74 0.06*
Float		3.64 0.09*		2.46 0.09*		3.48 0.01**		3.01 0.04**		3.20 0.02**
Financial Vulnerabilities			-3.62 0.00***	-3.50 0.00***						
Increase (Priv. Cred. / GDP)					-0.12 0.00***	-0.12 0.00***			-0.07 0.03**	-0.08 0.01***
Current Acc. Balance / GDP							0.48 0.00***	0.47 0.00***	0.27 0.06*	0.25 0.08*
N	32	32	32	32	32	32	32	32	32	32
R^{2*}	0.17	0.20	0.53	0.54	0.52	0.56	0.51	0.53	0.56	0.59

Table 43: Multivariate regressions of 'GDP_{10-12}' against Fraser 'open access economic institutions', the 'float' dummy and different sets of control variables in the sub-sample of developed countries (second row: p-values of two-sided significance tests; number of asterisks: significance levels of 10%*, 5%** and 1%***; residuals are not normally-distributed in regressions 2 to 10).

One potential problem in the above-depicted regressions is the non-normality of the residuals. Although the violation of this OLS model assumption does not lead to biased estimators, it might still entail wrong standard errors in the small sample of only 32 countries and therefore invalidate the results of the significance tests. I try to deal with this problem by running additional regressions excluding the outlier case (Greece) that is the main source of non-normality.[218] These regressions, which are depicted in appendix 53, feature similar coefficients and p-values as those shown in table 43 but have normally-distributed residuals. I, therefore, conclude that the non-normality of residuals does not invalidate the results displayed in table 43.

(5) Now turning to the sub-group of 52 less developed countries, table 44 depicts simple correlations among the three institutional variables (based on Fraser data) which turned out to be significantly related to crisis resilience in sections 4.3.1 to 4.3.6. Significant correlations exist only between 'gross replacement rates' and 'government consumption' indicating that countries with smaller government sectors also provide less generous unemployment benefits. 'Credit market regulation' is uncorrelated with the other two variables. When using data from the Heritage Foundation instead of the Fraser institute, correlations are similar (see appendix 54).

218 Greece showed particularly bad crisis resilience scores during the recovery period 2010 to 2012 (see also table 1) that cannot be fully explained for by the independent variables considered in this thesis.

	Gross Replacement Rates	Fraser Credit Market Regulation	Fraser Gov. Consumption
Gross Replacement Rates	1	0.09	**-0.42**
Fraser Credit Market Regulation	0.09	1	-0.19
Fraser Government Consumption	**-0.42**	-0.19	1

Table 44: Correlations amongst significant institutional variables (mainly based on Fraser data) in the sub-sample of less developed countries (significant correlations at 5% level are bold).

I next turn to regressions including the abovementioned explanatory institutional variables together. As before, I drop 'gross replacement rates' because of the previously expressed reservations about the accuracy of this measure (especially in less developed countries) and because the variable is not available for all countries in the sample. Departing from the approach taken before, I do not combine the remaining two variables to a composite index because they are uncorrelated. Instead, I simply run regressions with 'credit market regulation' and 'government consumption' as individual explanatory variables. Table 45 depicts the results when regressing 'GDP_{08-09}' against these two variables alongside different sets of relevant control variables.[219]

Dependent Variable: 'GDP_{08-09}'; Sample: Less developed Countries										
	(1)	(2)	(3)	(4)	(5)	(6)	(7)	(8)	(9)	(10)
Constant	9.88 0.12	4.33 0.55	7.75 0.24	3.76 0.60	6.94 0.27	7.79 0.24	11.06 0.08*	8.15 0.18	8.67 0.17	7.99 0.19
Fraser Credit Market Regulation	-2.29 0.00***	-1.71 0.01***	-1.97 0.00***	-1.57 0.01**	-1.72 0.00***	-2.07 0.00***	-1.97 0.00***	-1.45 0.02**	-1.67 0.01***	-1.44 0.01**
Fraser Government Consumption	0.93 0.02**	1.00 0.02**	0.78 0.04**	0.85 0.03**	0.77 0.04**	1.04 0.02**	0.76 0.05*	0.62 0.10	0.86 0.03**	0.64 0.11
Financial Vulnerabilities		-1.90 0.05*		-1.47 0.10						
Industrial Orientation			-1.82 0.01**	-1.56 0.02**						
Increase (Priv. Cred. / GDP)					-0.16 0.00***			-0.15 0.00***		-0.15 0.04**
Current Acc. Balance / GDP						0.13 0.05**			0.16 0.03**	0.02 0.84
Manuf. Exp. / Total Exp.							-0.07 0.04**	-0.06 0.02**	-0.08 0.01**	-0.06 0.02**
N	50	50	50	50	50	50	50	50	50	50
R^{2*}	0.24	0.29	0.32	0.35	0.36	0.26	0.29	0.40	0.33	0.39

Table 45: Multivariate regressions of 'GDP_{08-09}' against Fraser 'credit market regulation', Fraser 'government consumption' and different sets of control variables in the sub-sample of emerging and developing countries (second row: p-values of two-sided significance tests; number of asterisks: significance levels of 10%*, 5%** and 1%***; residuals in regressions 1, 3, 6, 8 and 9 are not normally-distributed).

219 I look at 'GDP_{08-09}' as dependent variable because results in the sub-group of less developed countries were more pronounced during the downturn.

While financial openness shows a robust negative association with crisis resilience in all specifications, the measure for small government sectors turns insignificant in specifications that control for the increase in the 'private credit to GDP ratio'. As depicted in appendix 55, the significance of the results depends on the choice of the explanatory institutional variables because the alternative measures from the Heritage Foundation are insignificant in most specifications. Results for the entire crisis period 2008 to 2012 are very similar but contingent on the choice of the explanatory variables, as well (see appendix 56). Interestingly, although the significance of the two institutional variables depends on the specifications and the choice of the explanatory variables, F-test show that the two institutional variables together are jointly significant across all possible specifications. Hence, emerging and developing countries with more open financial markets and larger government sectors showed worse performance than countries with the opposite institutional features.

Following the assessment of economic institutions in this section 4.3, the next section 4.4 focuses on the role of political factors for promoting these resilience-enhancing economic institutions and crisis resilience. The economic institutions identified to be resilience-enhancing in this section thereby function as dependent variables in those of the following regression which assess the determinants of institutional quality according to the second level of analysis.[220]

4.4 The Empirical Analysis Part II: Political Institutions, Interest Group Activity and Crisis Resilience

According to the theoretical considerations laid out in chapter 2, I consider two types of explanatory variables – open political institutions and interest group activity. Following the framework developed in chapter 2, these two variables may affect crisis resilience either directly by influencing the quality of discretionary policies or indirectly by supporting resilience-enhancing economic institutions. Therefore, I consider both possibilities. First, in section 4.4.1, I analyze the potential effects of open political institutions on resilience-enhancing economic institutions and on crisis resilience. Then, in section 4.4.2, I turn to an analogous assessment of the potential effects of interest group activity on the two dependent variables. Finally, in section 4.3, I summarize the previous results and confront them to Olson's and NWW's theoretical predictions.

[220] This approach departs from the related literature which analyzes the determinants of institutional quality. That literature simply postulates certain institutions to be of 'high quality' and uses them as dependent variables. Typically, authors consider the composite index of the World Governance Indicators (see Islam & Montenegro, 2002; Aixalá Pasto & Fabro Esteban, 2008; Alonso & Garcimartín, 2013). I depart from than approach and use dependent variables which capture those economic institutions which have actually turned out to be resilience-enhancing according to the empirical analysis in this section.

4.4.1 Political Institutions and Crisis Resilience

In this section, I discuss the potential effects of open political institutions on resilience-enhancing economic institutions and on crisis resilience. Following NWW's account, three features of political institutions are constitutive of an open and democratic political order: first, free elections, second, politically-relevant civil liberties and, third, constraints against the abuse of power.[221]

The first institutional feature refers to the question whether a country's executive and legislative bodies are selected in free elections or whether these bodies come to power through alternative recruitment processes which confine the rights to elect and to be elected to small groups of elites. Elections alone constitute a minimalist conception of democracy as they do not necessarily entail a high degree of fairness and openness.[222]

The second institutional prerequisite of an open political order, following NWW's account, is the enforcement of politically-relevant civil liberties. Specifically, the authors mention a free press and the freedoms of association, assembly, expression and conscience (NWW, 2009, p. 115). These liberties are important complements to elections as they affect the ability of citizens to form and express opinions and to establish organizations for the pursuit of common goals. Impediments to these liberties benefit those in power and, therefore, restrict the ability of an opposition to become a serious political competitor for incumbents. These first two institutional features are constitutive of what Dahl (1971) labels a *polyarchy*.[223]

The third institutional feature outlined by NWW are constraints against the abuse of power. Such constraints usually stem from constitutional provisions that oblige the different branches of government to work together in order to implement certain policies. The mentioning of this third institutional feature indicates that NWW advance

[221] Recalling the quote cited in section 2.3.2, NWW (2009, p. 115) mention a variety of institutions besides periodic elections. "Other institutions support rights, such as a free press, freedom of expression, freedom of religion and conscience, and the right to assemble. All open access orders have some form of division of powers and multiple veto points [...], sometimes explicit, as in the American Constitution's separation of powers system, and sometimes implicit, as in the coalition governments of Europe with separate ministries, a prime minister, a cabinet within which coalition members negotiate and approve legislation, and parliament necessary to pass legislation. All open access orders also have judicial and bureaucratic mechanism for enforcing citizen rights and contracts. And finally, they all have constitutions [...] that provide for the limit condition – limiting the stakes of power so that everything is not up for grabs in the next election".

[222] This first institutional feature is closely related to Schumpeter's (1996 [1943], p. 271) definition of the democratic method, which focuses on "free competition for free vote" but does not exclude the possibilities of "'unfair' and 'fraudulent' competition". See also Schmidt (2008, pp. 184-186).

[223] Dahl (1971, p. 3) lists eight institutional prerequisites of a polyarchy, which refer to elections and civil liberties. According to him, these institutional features affect the degree of public contestation and the inclusion of a large proportion of the population into the political decision-making process. See also Schmidt (2008, pp. 212-216).

a 'thicker' account of democracy that goes beyond Dahl's (1971) concept of a polyarchy.[224]

Discussion and Hypotheses

As argued in chapter 2, the political institutions outlined above may affect adaptive efficiency and crisis resilience either directly by stimulating efficiency-enhancing economic policies or indirectly by supporting resilience-enhancing economic institutions. Hence, the question arises whether the abovementioned institutions indeed have these two hypothesized effects. Below, I discuss three different views on this issue, the first pointing out the merits of democracy in accordance with NWW's account, the second focusing on the weaknesses of democracy and the third arguing that economic performance is unrelated to political institutions.[225]

According to NWW, open political institutions form a double balance with open economic institutions. Thereby, they promote crisis resilience through two separate processes. First, democracies produce better political decisions because they allow public debate and expose office holders to a competitive environment. This generates a political discovery procedure in which bad policies cannot prevail very long, as incompetent or self-interested decision makers are quickly eliminated by competitive forces. In autocratic regimes, on the other hand, distortionary policies are more prevalent, as uncontested power holders can create rents by restricting market entry through selectively-enforced property rights or selective regulations.[226] NWW's account is in line with arguments put forward by other authors such as Acemoglu & Robinson (2012), who argue that 'inclusive institutions' (their theoretical counterpart to NWW's 'open access institutions') constrain the ability of power holders to generate excessive rents through entrance barriers to lucrative economic activities. This not only entails higher growth rates but, following Acemoglu et al. (2003), also lower output volatility and less frequent economic crises.[227]

Second, according to NWW, democracies have a higher ability to provide credible commitments. This increases the probabilities of compromise amongst affected interest groups and of quick policy reactions. In a similar vein, Rodrik (1999) argues that countries with weak institutions of conflict management (including the absence of democratic rights) have bigger problems reacting to economic shocks because of

[224] Dahl (1971, p. 8), too, considers polyarchies to be only "relatively (but incompletely) democratized regimes".

[225] In the short discussion, I focus on arguments that are related to Olson's and NWW's accounts. For a comprehensive overview of the merits and weaknesses of democracy (including strongly normative arguments) see Schmidt (2008, pp. 453-471). Furthermore, Przeworski & Limongi's (1993) review of arguments about the effects of democracy on economic growth also applies to potential effects of democracy on crisis resilience.

[226] Acemoglu (2008), for example, argues that distortionary economic policies in autocracies are more often based on entrance barriers than on direct redistributions. The latter, according to him, are more prevalent in democracies.

[227] Unfortunately, the authors do not distinguish explicitly between political and economic institutions.

distributional conflicts over who should bear the main burden of the necessary adaptions.[228] Uncooperative strategies which do not aim at compromises, he argues, are more likely when there are fewer institutionalized constraints on the potential outcomes of distributional struggles. Then, the stakes are higher and the ex-ante likelihood of cooperative rival behavior is lower, thereby increasing the probability of infighting amongst antagonistic groups. Democratic institutions, on the other hand, which grant participation rights to a large proportion of the population and which provide constraints against the abuse of power, "can be viewed as the ultimate institutions of conflict management, in that they allow for differences among social groups to be resolved in a predictable, inconclusive, and participatory manner" (Rodrik, 1999, pp. 396-397).

Contrary to these two arguments, other authors argue that democracies generate worse economic policies and show delayed reactions to shocks. One common argument stems from the fear of a "tyranny of the majority" (Tocqueville, 1990, pp. 258-270).[229] In a literature survey, Przeworski & Limongi (1993) show that this view was particularly prevalent in the 19th century when a variety of political economists objected to the extension of suffrage because they feared that political participation of workers and peasants would endanger the protection of property rights. Hayek (2011 [1960], pp. 166-177) puts forward a similar argument. He points out that collective (democratic) decision-making may undermine a liberal order of if all aspects of life become subject to the short term will of the majority. This, according to him, not only entails a potential deterioration of property rights and other economic institutions but also inferior decision-making in general.[230] Furthermore, a variety of authors derive an argument of inferior policies in democracies from Olson's argument regarding the detrimental effects of interest group activity. Although Olson emphasizes that his theory also applies to autocracies and although he takes a clear pro-democratic stance in *Power and Prosperity*, he is frequently cited as a reference author for the deficits of

[228] Rodrik (1999), too, does not distinguish explicitly between political and economic institutions.

[229] It is, however, important to point out that, according to Tocqueville (1990, pp. 271-286), such a tyranny can be mitigated by various provisions, such as a decentralized administration and a strong legal system with competent (aristocratic) lawyers and judges. Overall, Tocqueville maintained an ambivalent position towards the merits and weaknesses of democratic regimes, which was not generally unfavorable towards democracy (see Schmidt, 2008, pp. 125-131).

[230] Hayek (2011 [1960], p. 176) argues: "We have no ground for crediting majority decisions with that higher, superindividual wisdom which, in a certain sense, the products of spontaneous social growth may possess. The resolutions of a majority [...] are bound, if anything, to be inferior to the decisions that the most intelligent members of the groups will make after listening to all opinions [...]. This will be even more true of the cumulative results emanating from the successive decisions of shifting majorities variously composed: the result will be the expression not of a coherent conception but of different an often conflicting motives and aims".

democratic decision-making involving a large number of interest groups.[231] Finally, contrary to the argument put forward by NWW (2009) and Rodrik (1999) that the availability of credible commitments in democracies facilitates the adaption to shocks, other authors argue that the existence of veto rights delays the necessary policy reactions due to a "war of attrition" between antagonistic interest groups (Alesina et al., 1991; Alesina et al., 2006).

Another group of authors argues that political institutions have inconclusive effects on economic institutions and on economic performance. Sah (1991) and Almeida & Ferreira (2002), for example, argue that the properties of autocratic rulers vary widely in terms of benevolence and competence. Therefore, unconstrained decision-making may lead to very good or very bad decisions, whereas institutionally constrained decision-making in democracies entails neither very good nor very bad results. Correspondingly, regimes with a small amount of veto players should show a higher variability of economic performance but no superior average performance. Furthermore, democratic political institutions may exert various mutually-offsetting influences, at once. Cox & McCubbins (2001), for example, argue that the existence of veto rights increases responsiveness to citizens' demands at the same time as it reduces decisiveness, thereby entailing a trade-off and inconclusive overall effects.

The empirical literature which investigates the relationship between political institutions and economic performance is mainly inconclusive. Following the theoretical framework in section 2, it may be divided into two strands, one assessing effects of political institutions on crisis resilience and the other analyzing effects on resilience-enhancing economic institutions. Results regarding the first strand are mixed. Although some papers show that democratic institutions promote crisis resilience,[232] others provide evidence in favor of the opposite position.[233] One paper which is very closely related to the intended analysis of this thesis is Essers (2012) who investigates the relationship between democracy and the decline of growth rates during the year 2009 as compared to pre-crisis growth. Focusing on a sample of emerging and developing countries and using similar control variables as the ones considered in this thesis, he provides evidence that democratic political institutions aggravated the severity of the crisis.

Next, previous empirical results regarding the second strand of literature point towards a positive relationship between democratic political institutions and the security of

---

[231] See for example Acemoglu et al. (2014, p. 4) or Schmidt (2008, p. 470). It, however, is to the credit of these authors that Olson himself remained sometimes ambiguous regarding the merits and weaknesses of democracy throughout his career (Rosser, 2007).

[232] See Rodrik (1999) and Cavallo & Cavallo (2010). Similarly, Acemoglu et al. (2002) provide evidence that more inclusive political institutions reduce output volatility.

[233] Alesina et al. (2006) for example provide evidence that countries with stronger constraints on the executive branch need more time for introducing stabilization policies during times of economic crises.

property rights and contract laws,[234] thereby providing support for NWW's account of a double balance between open political institutions and open economic institutions. However, the analysis in section 4.3 showed that these economic institutions feature a positive association with crisis resilience only within the sub-group of developed countries, whereas they were insignificant in less developed countries and negatively related to crisis resilience in the entire sample. In the latter two samples, other economic institutions such as low degrees of financial openness and small government sectors turned out to be more relevant. Hence, the question remains how open political institutions relate to *these* specific sets of resilience-enhancing economic institutions in different sub-samples of countries.

In summary, the theoretical arguments and empirical results in the related literature are mainly inconclusive. The hypothesis derived from NWW's account, which is also compatible with Rodrik (1999) and Acemoglu et al. (2002), states:

- Countries with democratic political institutions should have performed better during the Great Recession than countries with less democratic or autocratic political institutions.

As, following NWW, part of the positive effects of open political institutions on crisis resilience may be mediated through the choice of resilience-enhancing economic institutions, I furthermore consider the following hypothesis:

- Countries with democratic political institutions should feature more resilience-enhancing economic institutions than countries with less democratic or autocratic political institutions.

Data

In the empirical analysis below, I consider two different indicators representing the openness of political institutions as explanatory variables.

- First, the indicator 'voice and accountability' from the Worldwide Governance Indicators Database summarizes information from a wide variety of sources including surveys and expert judgements regarding "perceptions of the extent to which a country's citizens are able to participate in selecting their government, as well as freedom of expression, freedom of association, and a free media" (Kaufmann et al., 2010). The variable takes values of standard normal variables with a mean of 0 and a standard deviation of 1. Actual values within the sample used in this thesis range from -1.69 (Belarus) to 1.58 (Netherlands).
- Second, I construct an index based on data provided by Freedom House (2008), which relies on subjective expert judgements by the composers of the report. The index I use differs slightly from the Freedom House composite variable

[234] See Islam & Montenegro (2002), Borner et al. (2004) and Asongu & Kodila-Tedica (2016).

'political rights and civil liberties'. To make the index accord to the theoretical consideration put forward in this thesis, I only consider items referring to *political* institutions and disregard those referring to *economic* ones. Concretely, I drop the item 'personal autonomy and individual rights' as it captures the rights to choose an occupation, to own property and to run a business without being subject to discriminatory regulations. I add the scores of the remaining 6 sub-categories 'electoral process', 'political pluralism and participation', 'functioning of government', 'freedom of expression and belief', 'associational and organizational rights' and 'rule of law'.[235] The newly constructed variable can take values between 0 (no political rights and civil liberties) and 84 (maximum political rights and civil liberties). Actual scores within the sample used in this thesis range from 9 (Belarus) to 84 (Finland, Iceland and Sweden).

Both measures are highly correlated (showing a correlation coefficient of 0.96) and, hence, capture similar aspects of political institutions. Furthermore, I decided to disregard a third, commonly-used measure of open political institutions – the 'polity' index from the Polity IV Dataset – because it shows only very little variation, especially amongst democracies.[236]

Results

In this section, I, first, (1) analyze the relationships between open political institutions and resilience-enhancing, economic institutions and, then, (2) turn to the relationships between open political institutions and crisis resilience. The first part corresponds to the second level of analysis outlined in figures 1 and 4, analyzing the determinants of economic institutions, whereas the second part corresponds to the first level of analysis, analyzing the determinants of economic performance.

(1) According to the empirical results of section 4.3, crisis resilience is negatively related to the index 'developed economic institutions' (including rule of law, open goods markets, open financial sectors and large governments) within the entire sample; it is positively related to the index 'open access economic institutions' (including rule of law, open goods markets and open labor markets) within the sub-sample of 32 developed countries; and it is positively related to small government sectors and rigid financial regulations within the sub-sample of less developed countries (although not all results in the latter group are significant). I, hence, first analyze whether there exist significant relationships between these sets of economic institutions and open political institutions within the respective samples. Besides running bivariate regressions, I also control for a variety of social and cultural variables

[235] The rule of law questions refer to the enforcement of personal rights unrelated to economic activity.

[236] According to the 'polity' index, one third of all 84 countries receives the maximum score of 10 on a scale ranging from -10 to 10. Almost half of the countries score a 9 or higher, and two thirds score an 8 or higher (including quite diverse countries such as Albania, Austria, Bolivia, Bulgaria, Canada, India, Netherlands, Romania and the United Kingdom).

which are commonly used in regressions explaining the determinants of economic institutions.[237]

Looking first at the entire sample, figure 16 displays a scatterplot of the 'developed economic institutions' index based on Fraser data against the WGI 'voice and accountability' index.

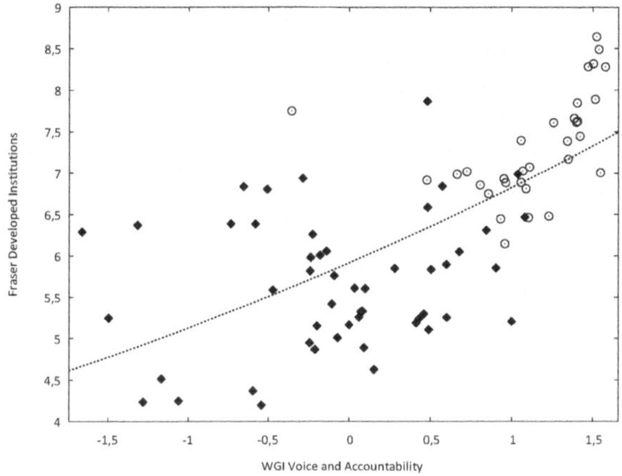

Figure 16: Scatterplot of Fraser 'developed economic institutions' against WGI 'voice and accountability' (black dots: less developed countries; white circles: developed countries; upward-sloping line: fitted values for the entire sample based on a log-linear model).

The plot shows that politically more open countries also tend to feature developed economic institutions (including rule of law, open goods markets, open financial markets and larger public sectors). Scatterplots using the index 'political rights and civil liberties' from Freedom House as indicators for open political institutions or the 'developed economic institutions' index based on Heritage data look very similar (see appendix 58). As most scatterplots show a slightly non-linear relationship between political openness and developed economic institutions, the fitted lines in figure 16 and in appendix 58 are based on log-linear models (taking the logarithm of the dependent variable 'developed economic institutions').

As the next step, I assess whether the positive relationship between open political institutions and developed economic institutions is robust to the inclusion of the cultural and social control variables explained in appendix 57. Table 46 shows the coefficients when regressing the logarithm of 'developed economic institutions' based on Fraser data against 'voice and accountability' and one additional control variable.[238]

[237] I list and explain these social and cultural control variables in appendix 57.

[238] I use log-linear models to account for the slightly non-linear relationship. This changes the interpretation of the coefficients (changes of the dependent variables are now percentage changes).

The positive relationship between open political institutions and developed economic institutions remains significant except when controlling for GDP per capita (which shows a positive correlation of 0.74 with 'voice and accountability'). A possible interpretation of these results is a virtuous circle between high economic development in terms of GDP per capita and institutional quality, as highly developed countries are able to support better institutions, and better institutions promote economic development (Alsonso & Garcimartín, 2013).[239] Results are very similar when considering the dependent variable 'developed economic institutions' based on Heritage data or the explanatory variable 'political rights and civil liberties' from Freedom House (see appendix 59).

	Dependent Variable: Log Fraser 'Developed Economic Institutions'; Sample: All Countries									
	(1)	(2)	(3)	(4)	(5)	(6)	(7)	(8)	(9)	(10)
Constant	1.77 0.00***	1.76 0.00***	1.82 0.00***	1.76 0.00***	1.82 0.00***	1.82 0.00***	1.78 0.00***	1.74 0.00***	1.85 0.00***	1.71 0.00***
WGI Voice & Accountability	0.14 0.00***	0.14 0.00***	0.12 0.00***	0.13 0.00***	0.14 0.00***	0.13 0.00***	0.14 0.00***	0.14 0.00***	0.13 0.00***	0.04 0.14
British Legal Origin		0.04 0.22								
French Legal Origin			-0.11 0.00***							
Percentage Protestants				0.10 0.12						
Percentage Catholics & Muslims					-0.10 0.04**					
Ethnic Fractionalization						-0.11 0.15				
Linguistic Fractionalization							-0.03 0.68			
Religious Fractionalization								0.06 0.41		
WB Inequality									-0.00 0.27	
GDP per Capita										0.01 0.00***
N	82	82	82	81	81	82	80	81	82	82
R^{2*}	0.42	0.43	0.50	0.43	0.45	0.44	0.41	0.42	0.43	0.58

Table 46: Multivariate regressions of log Fraser 'developed economic institutions' against WGI 'voice and accountability' and one additional control variable in the entire sample (second row: p-values of two-sided significance tests; number of asterisks: significance levels of 10%*, 5%** and 1%***).

These regression results are partly supportive and partly contradictory to NWW's theoretical framework. On the one hand, the positive association between democratic political institutions, developed economic institutions and high GDP per capita is mainly in line with NWW's account of a double balance between open access to the economy and open access to politics in richer countries. On the other hand, according

[239] This interpretation is also in line with NWW's (2009) account of a double balance between open economic and open political institutions in highly developed countries.

to the results in section 4.3, the index 'developed economic institutions' is not associated with *better* crisis resilience (as argued by NWW) but with *worse* performance during the Great Recession. Therefore, democratic political institutions are not positively related to *resilience-enhancing* but instead to *crisis-aggravating* economic institutions within the entire sample of 84 countries.

Next, turning to the sub-group of developed countries, the index 'open access economic institutions' (including rule of law, open goods markets and open labor markets) is associated with *better* crisis resilience. Hence, the question arises whether democratic political institutions show a positive association with this index in that group of countries, as well. Figure 17 visualizes the relationship between the index 'open access economic institutions' based on Fraser data and 'voice and accountability'.

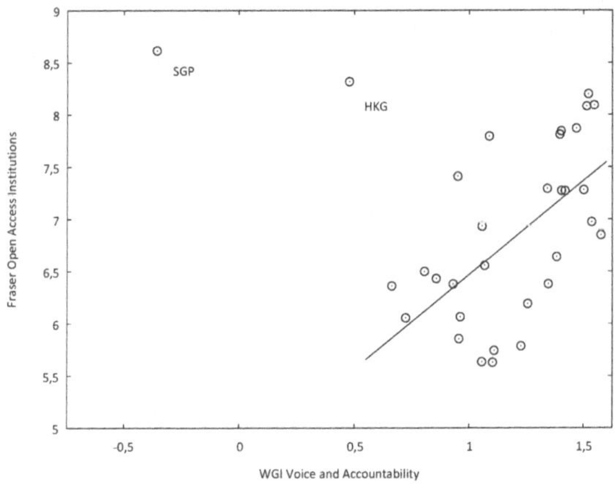

Figure 17: Scatterplot of Fraser 'open access economic institutions' against WGI 'voice and accountability' in the sub-group of developed countries (upward-sloping line: fitted values for the sub-group of 30 developed democracies after excluding Singapore and Hong Kong).

The plot shows that there are two outliers – Singapore and Hong Kong. Both countries are not democratic but feature open economic institutions. Without these two countries, there exists a clear positive relationship between 'voice and accountability' and resilience-enhancing 'open access economic institutions', as indicated by the fitted line for the remaining 30 countries. Scatterplots using the index 'open access economic institutions' based on Heritage data or 'political rights and civil liberties' as measure for political institutions provide a similar picture (see appendix 60).

According to table 47, this significant relationship between democratic political institutions and open economic institutions in the sub-sample of 30 developed democracies is robust to the inclusion of social and cultural control variables except GDP per capita. Hence, richer countries feature more open political institutions and more open economic institutions. As before, a plausible interpretation is a virtuous circle between open institutions and development. Appendix 61 shows that these results do not change when using the index 'open access economic institutions' based on Heritage data.

These results suggest that democracy is not a necessary prerequisite for the support of open economic institutions, as autocrats such as those in Singapore may just as well choose to uphold the respective economic institutions. Within democracies, however, it appears to make a difference whether a country just features basic democratic institutions or whether elections are fair and transparent, supported by strong civil liberties and complemented by constraints against the abuse of power. Hence, after excluding Singapore and Hong Kong from the sub-sample of developed countries, open political institutions (and, at the same time, higher GDP per capita) show a positive relationship with resilience-enhancing economic institutions.

	Dependent Variable: Fraser 'Open Access Economic Institutions'; Sample: Developed Democracies									
	(1)	(2)	(3)	(4)	(5)	(6)	(7)	(8)	(9)	(10)
Constant	4.67 0.00***	4.61 0.00***	5.00 0.00***	5.28 0.00***	5.06 0.00***	4.43 0.00***	4.60 0.00***	4.00 0.00***	3.16 0.01***	5.07 0.00***
WGI Voice & Accountability	1.80 0.00***	1.71 0.00***	1.72 0.00***	1.05 0.01***	1.81 0.00***	1.85 0.00***	1.81 0.00***	1.84 0.00***	1.97 0.00***	0.79 0.37
British Legal Origin		0.59 0.01***								
French Legal Origin			-0.90 0.00***							
Percentage Protestants				1.25 0.01***						
Percentage Catholics & Muslims					-1.06 0.00***					
Ethnic Fractionalization						0.74 0.24				
Linguistic Fractionalization							0.22 0.72			
Religious Fractionalization								1.32 0.01**		
WB Inequality									0.04 0.16	
GDP per Capita										0.02 0.14
N	30	30	30	30	30	30	30	30	30	30
R^{2*}	0.34	0.43	0.59	0.45	0.50	0.35	0.32	0.45	0.36	0.38

Table 47: Multivariate regressions of Fraser 'open access economic institutions' against WGI 'voice and accountability' and one additional control variable in the sub-sample of 30 developed democracies after excluding Singapore and Hong Kong (second row: p-values of two-sided significance tests; number of asterisks: significance levels of 10%*, 5%** and 1%***).

I, finally, assess the relationship between open political institutions and resilience-enhancing economic institutions in the sub-group of 52 less developed countries. Table 48 depicts the coefficients of bivariate regressions between the two measures of political openness and the variables representing financial openness and the size of the public sector, which turned out to be relevant in that sub-group of countries. The regressions show that political openness is associated with larger public sectors and open financial sectors. However, the results are only significant when using the two Heritage variables as measures for economic institutions. Furthermore, when controlling for standard control variables, as depicted in appendix 62, these relations to the two Heritage variables slightly miss conventional significance levels in some regressions, especially when controlling for GDP per capita. Hence, the negative relationship between political openness and resilience-enhancing economic institutions in the sub-group of 52 less developed countries is not robust to the choice of measures for the respective institutions and to the inclusion of control variables.

		Dependent Variables			
		Fraser Gov. Consumption	Heritage Gov. Spending	Fraser Credit Market Regulation	Heritage Financial Freedom
Explanatory Variables	WGI Voice & Accountability	-0.52 0.24	**-8.23** **0.03****	0.32 0.22	**7.95** **0.03*****
	Political Rights & Civil Liberties	-0.01 0.44	**-0.24** **0.05***	0.01 0.17	**0.27** **0.04****

Table 48: Coefficients of bivariate regressions between economic institutions as dependent variables and political institutions as explanatory variables (second row: p-values of two-sided significance tests; number of asterisks: significance levels of 10%*, 5%** and 1%***; significant results at 5% level are bold).

Summing up the previous results regarding the second level of analysis, open political institutions are (apart from a few outliers) associated with many features of developed and open economic institutions, such as rule of law, open goods markets, open labor markets, open financial markets and large public sectors. Almost all of these positive associations are contingent on the inclusion of GDP per capita as control variable. These results are mainly in line with NWW's argument that there exists a double balance between open access to politics and open access to the economy within highly developed countries as well as a double balance between limited access to politics to and limited access to the economy in less developed countries. However, as shown in section 4.3, the abovementioned economic institutions do not generally support crisis resilience. On the contrary, within the entire sample, the set of 'developed economic institutions' (rule of law, open goods markets, open financial markets and large public sectors) is associated with worse economic performance. Similarly, within the sub-group of 52 less developed countries, financial openness and large public sectors are also related to worse crisis resilience (although the results are partly insignificant). Only within the sub-sample of developed countries, there exists evidence in favor of a positive relationship between 'open access economic institutions' (rule of law, open goods markets and open labor markets) and crisis resilience. Hence, the hypothesis formulated above, which links democracy to resilience-enhancing economic institutions, only finds support within the sub-group of 30 developed democracies (excluding Singapore and Hong Kong from the group of developed countries).

(2) After assessing the relationship between political and economic institutions, the second part of the empirical analysis focuses on the overall relationship between political institutions and crisis resilience. As a first step, table 49 depicts the coefficients of the bivariate regressions. The results indicate that the association between open political institutions and crisis resilience is negative within the entire sample of 84 countries and within the sub-group of 52 less developed countries during the period 2008 to 2009. These negative coefficients are not surprising as the previous analysis showed that open political institutions are associated with crisis-aggravating economic institutions. Furthermore, in the sub-group of 32 developed countries, coefficients are significantly negative when using the variable 'political rights and civil liberties' as indicator for the openness of political institutions during the time period 2008 to 2012 and the sub-period 2010 to 2012. However, the significance of this variable is strongly driven by the two outliers Singapore and Hong Kong, which feature low degrees of political openness and good economic performance during the Great Recession. When excluding these two countries from the sample of developed countries, leaving a sample of 30 developed democracies, coefficients of both explanatory variables are now positive but insignificant.

	Dep. Var.: GDP_{08-12}				Dep. Var.: GDP_{08-09}				Dep. Var.: GDP_{10-12}			
	All	Developed		Emerg. & Developing	All	Developed		Emerg. & Developing	All	Developed		Emerg. & Developing
		N = 30	N = 32			N = 30	N = 32			N = 30	N = 32	
Voice & Account.	**-6.36** **0.00*****	8.51 0.31	-1.88 0.69	-2.49 0.31	**-3.99** **0.00*****	5.53 0.31	1.57 0.51	**-2.65** **0.02****	**-2.67** **0.00*****	4.03 0.41	-3.60 0.27	0.00 1.00
Pol. Rights Civ. Libert.	**-0.24** **0.00*****	0.19 0.79	**-0.28** **0.00*****	-0.06 0.43	**-0.16** **0.00*****	0.14 0.73	-0.03 0.49	**-0.09** **0.02****	**-0.09** **0.02****	0.10 0.84	**-0.27** **0.00*****	0.02 0.68

Table 49: Coefficients of political openness indices as explanatory variables and crisis resilience as dependent variables in bivariate regressions (second row: p-values of two-sided significance tests; number of asterisks: significance levels of 10%*, 5%** and 1%***; significant results at 5% level are bold).

The previous results suggest that the negative association between political openness and crisis resilience within the entire sample reflects inter-group differences between developed and less developed countries. Figure 18, which depicts a scatterplot relating 'voice and accountability' to 'GDP_{08-12}', supports this interpretation, as developed countries (white circles) show higher degrees of political openness and worse crisis resilience than less developed countries (black dots). The scatterplot using the alternative index 'political rights and civil liberties' as measure for political openness looks very similar (see appendix 63).

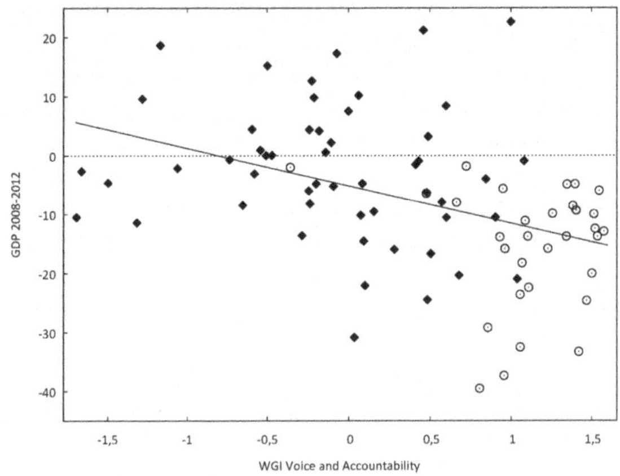

Figure 18: Scatterplot of '$GDP_{08\text{-}12}$' against WGI 'voice and accountability' in the entire sample (black dots: less developed countries; white circles: developed countries; downward-sloping line: fitted values for the entire sample).

One likely explanation for the negative relationship between political openness and crisis resilience is the specific nature of the Great Recession, which originated in the financial markets of highly developed countries. While almost all developed countries, which typically feature open political institutions and developed economic institutions, fell below their pre-crisis trend (as indicated by negative scores of '$GDP_{08\text{-}12}$'), some less developed countries were entirely unaffected by the crisis (as indicated by scores above 0).

To further investigate potential channels of influence, I next control for the relevant economic institutions (according to section 4.3) and for non-institutional pre-crisis vulnerabilities (according to section 4.2). I begin with the entire sample and then turn to the two sub-samples. Of particular interest is the question whether controlling for economic institutions affects the significance of political institutions.

First, table 50 depicts regressions for the entire sample of 84 countries, which explain '$GDP_{08\text{-}12}$' in terms of 'voice and accountability' as indicator for political openness, the 'developed economic institutions' index based on Fraser data, the 'peg' dummy and non-institutional control variables. The regressions show that political openness is significantly and negatively related to crisis resilience in bivariate regressions and when controlling for non-institutional vulnerabilities or the exchange rate regime (in regressions 1, 2, 3, 5 and 8). When, however, controlling for 'developed economic institutions' in regressions 4, 6, 7, 9 and 10, at least one of the indices 'voice and accountability' or 'developed economic institutions' turns insignificant. As both variables are positively related and as F-tests show that both together are jointly significant, these results indicate that the negative effects of political openness on crisis resilience are difficult to separate from the negative effects of developed economic institutions. Similar results emerge when using the variables 'political rights and civil liberties' or 'developed economic institutions' based on Heritage data as alternative measures for political and economic institutions (appendix 64) and when taking '$GDP_{08\text{-}09}$' as the dependent variable (appendix 65). When considering '$GDP10_{10\text{-}12}$' as dependent variable, coefficients of 'voice and accountability' and 'political rights and civil liberties' are mainly insignificant (appendix 66). Hence, politically more open countries with developed economic institutions (including high degrees of rule of law, open goods markets, open financial markets and larger public sectors) were more heavily affected by the Great Recession, mainly during the downturn period, than countries with the opposite institutional features.

Dependent Variable: '$GDP_{08\text{-}12}$'; Sample: All Countries										
	(1)	(2)	(3)	(4)	(5)	(6)	(7)	(8)	(9)	(10)
Constant	-5.16	-5.95	-5.77	16.89	-3.76	17.08	1.96	-5.07	4.10	6.43
	0.00***	0.00***	0.00***	0.07*	0.01***	0.05*	0.79	0.00***	0.58	0.35
Voice and	-6.36	-4.22	-4.71	-3.44	-4.45	-1.77	-3.77	-3.83	-2.63	-2.13
Accountability	0.00***	0.02**	0.00***	0.06*	0.00***	0.32	0.03**	0.00***	0.12	0.19
Fras. Dev. Econ.				-3.69		-3.51	-1.29		-1.53	-1.91
Institutions				0.01**		0.01**	0.28		0.19	0.09*
Peg					-8.85	-8.19		-4.33	-4.51	-5.10
					0.01***	0.01**		0.10	0.09*	0.04**
Financial		-7.08	-7.03				-6.76	-6.84	-6.55	-6.49
Vulnerabilities		0.00***	0.00***				0.00***	0.00***	0.00***	0.00***
Industrial		-3.83	-3.77				-3.49	-3.44	-3.11	-3.00
Orientation		0.00***	0.00***				0.00***	0.00***	0.00***	0.00***
Economic		-0.63								
Development		0.61								
International		-1.74	-1.77				-1.37	-1.36	-0.87	
Linkages		0.01***	0.01***				0.05**	0.09	0.27	
N	84	84	84	82	84	82	82	84	84	84
R^{2*}	0.17	0.56	0.56	0.23	0.23	0.29	0.57	0.57	0.57	0.57

Table 50: Multivariate regressions of '$GDP_{08\text{-}12}$' against WGI 'voice and accountability', Fraser 'developed economic institutions', the 'peg' dummy and different sets of control variables in the entire sample (second row: p-values of two-sided significance tests; number of asterisks: significance levels of 10%*, 5%** and 1%***; residuals are not normally-distributed in regressions 2, 3, 7, 8, 9 and 10).

Turning to the sub-group of developed countries, the bivariate regressions in table 49 showed mainly insignificant coefficients. Appendices 67 and 68 depict regressions of '$GDP_{10\text{-}12}$' against the two measures for open political institutions controlling for 'open access economic institutions', the 'float' dummy and 'financial vulnerabilities'. Results in these regressions, as well, do not indicate significant associations between open political institutions and crisis resilience. The partly significant negative coefficients of political openness variables depicted in appendix 67 are strongly driven by the two outliers Singapore and Hong Kong, which are not democratic but performed well during the Great Recession. When excluding these two countries from the sample, coefficients of the political openness variables turn positive (see appendix 68), which is not entirely surprising given the positive association between open political institutions and resilience-enhancing economic institutions in the sub-group of 30 developed democracies. However, these coefficients in the reduced sample are insignificant and turn negative when controlling for open economic institutions. Therefore, the positive association between open political institutions and resilience-enhancing economic institutions in developed democracies does not translate into an overall positive association between political openness and crisis resilience - possibly because positive indirect effects of open political institutions working through economic openness are counterbalanced by other negative effects.

Finally, turning to the sub-sample of 52 emerging and developing countries, I assess whether the negative association between the two measures of open political institutions and crisis resilience during the downturn period 2008 to 2009 (according to table 49) remains significant when controlling for the relevant economic institutions and for non-institutional pre-crisis vulnerabilities. Table 51 displays different regressions of 'GDP_{08-09}' against 'voice and accountability', the two Fraser indices 'government consumption' and 'credit market regulation' as well as the two principal components 'financial vulnerabilities' and 'industrial orientation'.

	Dependent Variable: 'GDP_{08-09}'; Sample: Emerging and Developing Countries							
	(1)	(2)	(3)	(4)	(5)	(6)	(7)	(8)
Constant	-3.36 0.00***	-10.44 0.00***	16.44 0.01***	8.76 0.17	-4.01 0.00***	-9.69 0.00***	8.61 0.12	2.04 0.75
WGI Voice and Accountability	-2.65 0.02**	-2.21 0.05*	-2.00 0.06*	-1.63 0.10	-2.75 0.01***	-2.36 0.03**	-2.32 0.03**	-2.00 0.06*
Fras. Gov. Consumption		1.03 0.02**		0.84 0.04**		0.83 0.03**		0.72 0.05*
Fras. Credit Market Regulation			-2.34 0.00***	-2.10 0.00***			-1.49 0.02**	-1.28 0.03**
Financial Vulnerabilities					-2.17 0.02**	-2.02 0.01***	-1.40 0.10	-1.55 0.04**
Industrial Orientation					-1.98 0.00***	-1.78 0.01***	-1.88 0.00***	-1.66 0.01**
N	52	50	50	50	52	50	50	50
R^{2*}	0.07	0.15	0.21	0.25	0.28	0.36	0.35	0.38

Table 51: Multivariate regressions of 'GDP_{08-09}' against WGI 'voice and accountability', Fraser 'credit market regulation', Fraser 'government consumption' and different sets of control variables in the sub-sample of less developed countries (second row: p-values of two-sided significance tests; number of asterisks: significance levels of 10%*, 5%** and 1%***; residuals are non-normally-distributed in regressions 1 and 3 to 8).

Table 51 shows that the coefficients of 'voice and accountability' slightly miss conventional significance levels in specifications which include variables representing economic institutions (2, 3, 4 and 8). Similar results emerge when using alternative measures for political and economic institutions, as depicted in appendix 69. Coefficients of 'voice and accountability' and 'political rights and civil liberties' are consistently negative, but they miss conventional significance levels in specifications that control for financial openness and government size. F-test, however, show that the three variables representing political openness, small government sectors and open financial markets are jointly significant in all possible combinations of indicators. Hence, although it is difficult to isolate individual effects of the three institutions, the regressions provide evidence that less developed countries featuring open political institutions, large government sectors and open financial institutions showed worse performance during the downturn period 2008 to 2009.

Overall, the results presented in this section challenge NWW's hypothesis that open political institutions promote crisis resilience, as these institutions are associated with more severe downturns in the entire sample of 84 countries and in the sub-sample of 52 less developed countries. The results, furthermore, suggest that the negative effects of open political institutions are closely associated with the negative effects of developed economic institutions (such as open financial institutions and large government sectors), as one of the respective variables typically turns insignificant when included together.

Only in developed democracies, there exists evidence in favor of a positive association between democracy and crisis resilience, as open political institutions are associated with resilience-enhancing economic institutions (after excluding the two developed autocracies Singapore and Hong Kong from the sample of developed countries). This relationship, however, does not translate into a significantly positive association between democracy and crisis resilience.

4.4.2 Interest Group Activity and Crisis Resilience

After looking at political institutions as explanatory variables, this section analyses potential effects of interest group activity on crisis resilience. The concept 'interest group activity' refers, very broadly, to the number of special interest groups in a given country. In the meaning used in this thesis, special interest groups are non-governmental, formal organizations that try to promote the particularistic interests of group members through the provision of goods (often in terms of favorable government legislation) that are to some extent non-excludable and non-rival for group members. Often, these goods in terms of selectively-beneficial government legislation are detrimental to the interests of non-members. Examples of special interest organizations are trade organizations, trade unions or lobby organizations. Examples of selectively beneficial government legislation are selective redistributions to interest group members or favorable regulations which fix prices or exclude competitors.[240]

[240] For a detailed discussion of the properties of interest groups with reference to Olson's theory see Murrell (1984).

Discussion and Hypotheses

As discussed in detail in chapter 2, Olson and NWW provide two opposing arguments regarding the influence of special interest groups on crisis resilience. In this section, I recapitulate their accounts only very briefly.

Olson (1982) argues that interest group activity is detrimental to economic performance and leads to lower growth rates and poorer crisis resilience. According to his argument, special interest groups exert a negative influence on economic performance and economic institutions. They do this by creating entrance barriers, fixing prices or obstructing innovative activities. Olson, furthermore, argues that the activities of opposing interest groups don't counterbalance each other's effects, as groups are not symmetrically organized. This latter argument follows from his theory of collective action which states that smaller and more homogenous groups face fewer difficulties to organize.

NWW (2009) explicitly disagree with Olson by arguing that a large number of interest groups can only emerge in open access orders. In those societies, they argue, interest groups fulfil important functions to make democratic competition work properly, such as monitoring office holders and other interest groups, proposing solutions to a society's most pressing problems or organizing support for policies which meet the interests of large proportions of society. Hence, large numbers of interest groups complement democratic political institutions. According to NWW (2009, p. 141) "[o]rganizations are the lifeblood of both political and economic competition. They are the vehicles through which economic and political entrepreneurs implement their ideas and affect the dynamics of the economy and polity". Furthermore, the authors disagree with Olson's account of asymmetrical power amongst interest groups. Drawing on Galbraith (1952), they argue that there is always a tendency towards an equilibrium of interests, as groups become active and defend open access whenever their interests are threatened by the activity of opposing groups. Hence, following NWW's arguments, larger numbers of well-organized interest groups should be associated with adaptively-efficient economic institutions that promote growth and crisis resilience.[241]

Past empirical research regarding the relationship between interest group activity, resilience-enhancing economic institutions and crisis resilience is very scarce. As pointed out in the literature review in chapter 3, most researchers who assess Olson's theory focus on economic growth as the dependent variable. Furthermore, the literature assessing the determinants of economic institutions and crisis resilience pays only little regard to Olson's arguments. NWW (2009, pp. 5 and 8) are an exception, as

---

[241] Another, closely related argument stems from Putnam et al. (1994), who argue that civic groups are promoters of generalized trust, which is conducive for economic prosperity and an important factor to make democracy work properly. For a comparison of Olson and Putnam including an empirical assessment, see Knack (2003).

they provide evidence that richer countries feature larger numbers of organizations as well as more moderate declines in growth rates during downturns. The three authors, however, do not control for other factors or investigate whether potential effects of interest group activity on crisis resilience may be mediated through specific economic institutions.

Following this short discussion, there are two opposing hypotheses regarding the effects of interest group activity on crisis resilience.

- Following Olson, a larger number of special interest organizations should be associated with worse crisis resilience.
- Following NWW, a larger number of special interest organizations should be associated with better crisis resilience.

Furthermore, Olson and NWW link the number of special interest groups to certain economic institutions, which are a mediating channel through which interest group activity affects economic performance.

- Following Olson, a larger number of special interest organizations should be associated with sclerotic and crisis-aggravating economic institutions.
- Following NWW, a larger number of special interest organizations should be associated with open and resilience-enhancing economic institutions.

Data

The data source for the interest group variable is the *World Guide to Trade Associations* (Zils, 2002), which lists trade organizations, trade unions and chambers of commerce in 185 countries around the world. The measure I use to proxy interest group activity is a simple count of organizations per million inhabitants. The use of this measure goes back to Murrell (1984), who however emphasizes that it "is obviously not an ideal measure of interest group activity or strength but lack of information precluded the construction of a better measure" (p. 153). The most important drawback of this variable is its focus on the *number* of organizations and its disregard of organizational *strength* in terms of membership or resources. Unfortunately, until today, no better measure has become available.[242] Another limitation of the variable derives from the year of its measurement. The latest issue of the *World Guide to Trade Associations* appeared in 2002, which is six years prior to the start of the downturn. I nevertheless use this data because I assume the number of interest groups to be fairly stable over time and because the year 2002 is close to the time period in which the economic institutions were chosen which existed in 2007 at the onset of the Great Recession.

[242] The measure is commonly used within the Olson-related literature (see McCallum & Blais, 1987; Heckelman, 2000; Coates & Heckelman, 2003). Other potential measures are based on membership in different organizations according to the World Values Survey (see, for example, Knack 2003). The latter, however, do not measure the number of organizations but rather count the number of members in the respective organizations.

The actual values of the constructed variable 'organizations per million inhabitants' within the sample used in this thesis range from 0.07 (China) to 205.02 (Austria). As some developed countries are extreme outliers with a very high number of organizations, I use logarithms of the variable, which range from -2.61 (China) to 5.32 (Austria).

Results

I, first, (1) analyze the relationship between interest group activity and resilience-enhancing economic institutions and, then, (2) turn to the relationship between interest group activity and crisis resilience. The first part corresponds to the second level of analysis outlined in chapter 2 (assessing the determinants of economic institutions), and the second part corresponds to the first level (analyzing the determinants of economic performance).

(1) According to the second level of analysis, I assess the relationships between interest group activity and the relevant economic institutions within the three samples. Beginning with the entire sample of 84 countries, figure 19 depicts a scatterplot relating the index 'developed economic institutions' based on Fraser data to the logarithm of 'organizations per million inhabitants'. The plot shows that countries with more special interest organizations feature more highly developed economic institutions including rule of law, open goods markets, open financial markets and larger public sectors. When considering the variable 'developed economic institutions' based on Heritage data instead of Fraser data, the relationship looks very similar (see appendix 70).

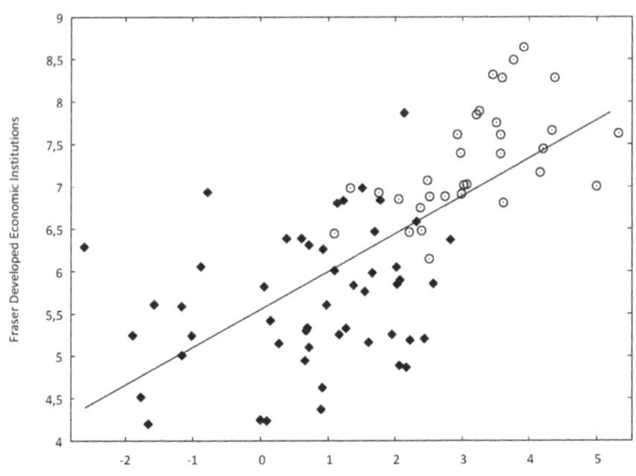

Figure 19: Scatterplot of Fraser 'developed economic institutions' against log 'organizations per million inhabitants' (black dots: less developed countries; white circles: developed countries; upward-sloping line: fitted values for the entire sample).

When controlling for different social and cultural variables, as depicted in table 52, the logarithm of 'organizations per million inhabitants' remains significant in all specifications except when controlling for 'GDP per capita', which is positively correlated with the interest group variable (0.68). These results show that countries with more interest groups - and at the same time higher GDP per capita - feature more highly developed economic institutions including rule of law, open goods markets, open financial markets and larger public sectors.

Dependent Variable: Fraser 'Developed Economic Institutions'; Sample: All Countries										
	(1)	(2)	(3)	(4)	(5)	(6)	(7)	(8)	(9)	(10)
Constant	5.55 0.00***	5.47 0.00***	5.98 0.00***	5.46 0.00***	6.03 0.00***	5.88 0.00***	5.55 0.00***	5.19 0.00***	6.57 0.00***	5.47 0.00***
Log Org. per Mio. Inhabitants	0.45 0.00***	0.45 0.00***	0.40 0.00***	0.41 0.00***	0.44 0.00***	0.40 0.00***	0.45 0.00***	0.45 0.00***	0.42 0.00***	0.12 0.14
WGI Voice and Accountability		0.29 0.11								
British Legal Origin			-0.77 0.00***							
French Legal Origin				1.00 0.02**						
Percentage Protestants					-0.95 0.00***					
Percentage Catho-lics & Muslims						-0.68 0.10*				
Ethnic Fractionalization							0.03 0.93			
Linguistic Fractionalization								0.82 0.03**		
Religious Fractionalization									-0.02 0.02**	
WB Inequality										0.01 0.00***
N	82	82	82	81	81	82	80	81	82	82
R^{2*}	0.46	0.47	0.58	0.49	0.54	0.47	0.46	0.49	0.50	0.62

Table 52: Multivariate regressions of Fraser 'developed economic institutions' against log 'organizations per million inhabitants' and one additional control variable in the entire sample (second row: p-values of two-sided significance tests; number of asterisks: significance levels of 10%*, 5%** and 1%***).

These results are mainly at odds with the hypothesis derived from Olson's account that more interest group activity is associated with sclerotic economic institutions. On the contrary, the index 'developed economic institutions' includes many aspects of open economic institutions such as rule of law or open goods markets. The only feature of the index that may be classified 'sclerotic' according to Olson's theory are larger public sectors.[243] The same results, on the other hand, mainly conform to NWW's argument that more interest group activity is associated with open economic institutions and

[243] The item 'government consumption', which indicates small public sectors, enters the index 'developed economic institutions' with a negative sign.

higher economic development. The picture does not change when using the dependent variable 'developed economic institutions' based on Heritage data (see appendix 71).

A similar picture emerges when considering the sub-sample of 32 developed countries and plotting the index 'open access economic institutions' against the logarithm of 'organizations per million inhabitants'. Figure 20 illustrates that countries with more special interest organization feature more open economic institutions including rule of law, open goods markets and open labor markets, thereby contradicting Olson's argument that interest group activity causes sclerotic economic institutions. The scatterplot using an alternative index for economic institutions based on Heritage data looks similar (see appendix 72).

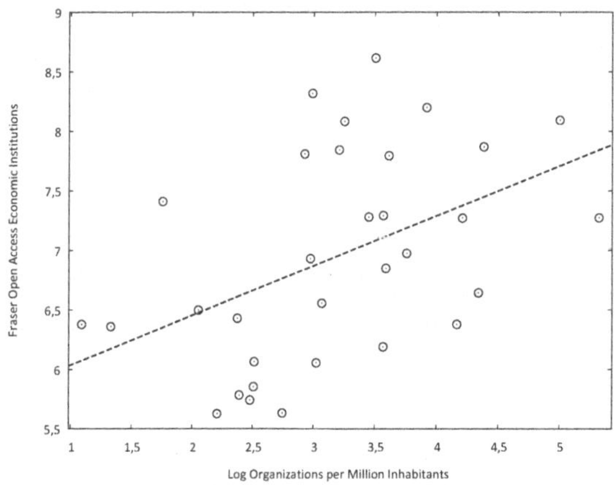

Figure 20: Scatterplot of Fraser 'open access economic institutions' against log 'organizations per million inhabitants' in the sub-group of developed countries (upward-sloping line: fitted values for the sub-group of 32 developed countries).

Table 53 reinforces the previous finding. It depicts regression results when explaining 'open access economic institutions' based on Fraser data in terms of the logarithm of 'organizations per million inhabitants' and one additional cultural or social control variable. It shows that the coefficients of the measure for interest group activity are positive and significant in all specifications except when controlling for 'GDP per capita'. This indicates that countries with more interest groups (and, at the same time, higher GDP per capita) feature more open economic institutions. These results, too, are at odds with Olson's argument that larger numbers of interest groups are associated with sclerotic economic institutions. On the contrary, they mainly support NWW's account of interest group activity in richer countries being associated with more open economic institutions. Results look very similar when using an alternative measure for economic institutions based on Heritage data, as depicted in appendix 73.

	Dependent Variable: Fraser 'Open Access Econ. Institutions'; Sample: Developed Countries									
	(1)	(2)	(3)	(4)	(5)	(6)	(7)	(8)	(9)	(10)
Constant	5.62 0.00***	5.51 0.00***	6.05 0.00***	5.69 0.00***	5.95 0.00***	5.56 0.00***	5.61 0.00***	4.72 0.00***	3.91 0.00***	5.63 0.00***
Log Org. per Mio. Inhabitants	0.42 0.00***	0.37 0.00***	0.36 0.00***	0.29 0.01***	0.44 0.00***	0.41 0.00***	0.42 0.00***	0.46 0.00***	0.42 0.00***	0.10 0.59
WGI Voice and Accountability		0.81 0.01***								
British Legal Origin			-0.96 0.00***							
French Legal Origin				1.29 0.00***						
Percentage Protestants					-1.19 0.00***					
Percentage Catholics & Muslims						0.33 0.63				
Ethnic Fractionalization							0.02 0.98			
Linguistic Fractionalization								1.63 0.00***		
Religious Fractionalization									0.05 0.02**	
WB Inequality										0.03 0.02**
N	32	32	32	31	31	32	32	32	32	32
R^{2*}	0.19	0.36	0.40	0.35	0.39	0.17	0.16	0.33	0.29	0.25

Table 53: Multivariate regressions of Fraser 'open access economic institutions' against log 'organizations per million inhabitants' and one additional control variable in the sub-sample of developed countries (second row: p-values of two-sided significance tests; number of asterisks: significance levels of 10%*, 5%** and 1%***).

Finally, turning to the sub-sample of 52 less developed countries, table 54 shows that the measure for interest group activity is negatively related to the measures for small government size and positively related to the measures for open financial markets. Hence, countries with more interest groups feature larger public sectors and more open financial sectors – two economic institutions which are negatively related to crisis resilience in emerging and developing countries according to the analysis in section 4.3. However, the coefficients of bivariate regressions depicted in table 54 are only significant for the two Heritage variables. When controlling for social and cultural variables, as depicted in appendix 74, coefficients remain significant only when using Heritage 'financial freedom' as dependent variable. When, however, considering Heritage 'government spending' as dependent variable, coefficients turn insignificant in some specifications, especially when controlling for GDP per capita. Hence, the relationship between the number of special interest organizations and resilience-enhancing economic institutions within the sub-group of less developed countries is not robust to the choice of dependent variables and to the inclusion of certain control variables.

		Dependent Variables			
		Fraser Gov. Consumption	Heritage Gov. Spending	Fraser Credit market Regulation	Heritage Financial Freedom
Explanatory Variable	Log Org. per Mio. Inhabitants	-0.18 0.45	**-3.31** **0.04****	0.20 0.13	**4.43** **0.01****

Table 54: Coefficients of bivariate regressions between economic institutions as dependent variables and log 'organizations per million inhabitants' as explanatory variable (second row: p-values of two-sided significance tests; number of asterisks: significance levels of 10%*, 5%** and 1%***; significant results at 5% level are bold).

Summing up the previous results regarding the second level of analysis, countries with larger numbers of special interest organizations do not feature more sclerotic economic institutions in Olson's terms. Within the entire sample and the sub-sample of developed countries, larger numbers of special interest organizations are even positively related to rule of law, open goods markets and open labor markets. The only institutional feature that shows the predicted association with interest group activity are larger public sectors within the entire sample and partly within the sub-sample of 52 less developed countries. Overall, the positive relationships between interest group activity and open or developed economic institutions (in association with high economic development in terms of GDP per capita) mainly support NWW's account.

(2) After assessing the relationship between interest group activity and economic institutions according to the second level of analysis, I now turn to the overall relationship between interest group activity and crisis resilience according to the first level of analysis. Table 55 depicts the coefficients of bivariate regressions relating crisis resilience to the logarithm of 'organizations per million inhabitants'. The table shows that only the results for the entire sample of countries are significantly negative across all three time periods. Results for the two sub-samples are consistently insignificant.

	Dep. Var.: GDP_{08-12}			Dep. Var.: GDP_{08-09}			Dep. Var.: GDP_{10-12}		
	All	Deve-loped	Emerging & Dev.	All	Deve-loped	Emerging & Dev.	All	Deve-loped	Emerging & Dev.
Log Org. per Mio. Inhabitants	**-2.77** **0.00*****	1.98 0.28	-1.17 0.41	**-1.62** **0.00*****	0.99 0.36	-0.61 0.45	**-1.24** **0.00*****	1.18 0.32	-0.55 0.50

Table 55: Coefficients of log 'organizations per million inhabitants' as explanatory variable in bivariate regressions with crisis resilience (second row: p-values of two-sided significance tests; number of asterisks: significance levels of 10%*, 5%** and 1%***; significant results at 5% level are bold).

Figure 21 visualizes the relationship between crisis resilience and the number of organizations for the entire sample of countries. The scatterplot shows that the negative association between 'GDP_{08-12}' and the logarithm of 'organizations per million inhabitants' is strongly driven by inter-group difference between less developed (black dots) and developed countries (white circles), as the former feature smaller numbers of interest groups but better crisis resilience scores than the latter. Within the two sub-groups, however, there is no significant relationship between both variables.

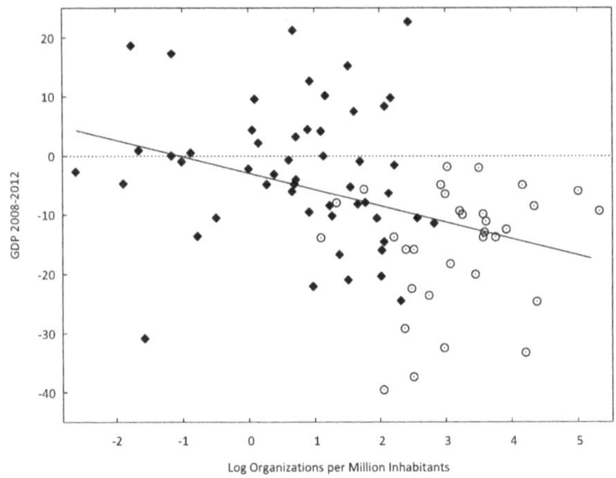

Figure 21: Scatterplot of 'GDP_{08-12}' against log 'organizations per million inhabitants' (black dots: less developed countries; white circles: developed countries; downward-sloping line: fitted values for the entire sample).

I, next, assess whether these findings prevail when controlling for economic institutions and non-institutional, pre-crisis vulnerabilities. Table 56 depicts the coefficients of the respective regressions for the entire sample of 84 countries.

	Dependent Variable: 'GDP_{08-12}'; Sample: All Countries								
	(1)	(2)	(3)	(4)	(5)	(6)	(7)	(8)	(9)
Constant	-2.89 0.13	-3.95 0.04**	-3.50 0.02**	22.06 0.01***	-2.34 0.21	21.76 0.01***	3.91 0.51	-3.18 0.04**	5.19 0.36
Log Org. per Mio. Inhabitants	-2.77 0.00***	-2.14 0.02**	-2.41 0.00***	-0.83 0.42	-1.72 0.04**	0.08 0.94	-1.89 0.02**	-1.92 0.00***	-1.33 0.10*
Fraser Dev. Econ. Institutions				-4.50 0.00***		-4.35 0.00***	-1.34 0.19		-1.51 0.12
Peg					-9.73 0.00***	-9.07 0.00***		-4.76 0.06*	-4.71 0.06*
Financial Vulnerabilities		-7.45 0.00***	-7.43 0.00***				-7.08 0.00***	-7.14 0.00***	-6.76 0.00***
Industrial Orientation		-4.06 0.00***	-4.01 0.00***				-3.67 0.00***	-3.60 0.00***	-3.22 0.00***
Economic Development		-0.45 0.73							
International Linkages		-0.81 0.29							
N	84	84	84	82	84	82	82	84	82
R^{2*}	0.12	0.55	0.56	0.21	0.20	0.28	0.57	0.57	0.59

Table 56: Multivariate regressions of 'GDP_{08-12}' against log 'organizations per million inhabitants', Fraser 'developed economic institutions', the 'peg' dummy and different sets of control variables in the entire sample (second row: p-values of two-sided significance tests; number of asterisks: significance levels of 10%*, 5%** and 1%***; residuals in regressions 2, 3, 7, 8 and 9 are not normally distributed).

The regressions show that the logarithm of 'organizations per million inhabitants' remains significantly negative except when considering it alongside the index 'developed economic institutions'. In specifications 4, 6, 7 and 9, which include both variables, at least one of the two turns insignificant. As both variables are positively related and as F-tests show that they are jointly significant, this indicates that the potential negative effects of interest group activity and developed economic institutions are difficult to separate. Results when considering the index 'developed economic institutions' based on Heritage data instead of Fraser data (appendix 75) or when looking at the sub-periods 2008 to 2009 (appendix 76) and 2010 to 2012 (appendix 77) are similar.[244]

When dividing the sample into 32 developed and 52 less developed countries, the story is fairly simple, as coefficients of the logarithm of 'organizations per million inhabitants' are consistently insignificant. Hence, interest group activity is unrelated to crisis resilience within both sub-groups of countries. This also means that the positive association between interest group activity and resilience-enhancing economic institutions within the sub-group of 32 developed countries does not translate into a positive overall relationship between interest group activity and crisis resilience.

Summing up the previous results, within the entire sample there is a negative association between the measure of interest group activity and crisis resilience, which is mainly driven by inter-group difference between developed and less developed countries. Although this finding is superficially consistent with Olson's account that more interest group activity is associated with worse crisis resilience, the empirical results contradict other parts of his theory. Especially the positive association between larger numbers of interest groups and the index 'developed economic institutions' is at odds with his account, as it indicates that the potential negative effects of interest-group activity are not mediated through sclerotic economic institutions. Furthermore, there is no significant relationship between the number of interest groups and crisis resilience in the two sub-samples of developed and less developed countries. In the sub-group of developed countries, the measure for interest group activity is even positively related to open access economic institutions, which is in line with NWW's account that countries with more interest groups feature more open economic institutions. However, in disaccord with their theoretical framework, these positive associations between interest group activity and open economic institutions do not translate into positive association between interest group activity and overall crisis resilience.

[244] When explaining the time period 2010 to 2012, however, the two explanatory variables 'developed economic institutions' and log 'organizations per million inhabitants' are not jointly significant. Therefore, the two variables matter more for explaining the downturn than for explaining the recovery.

4.4.3 Summary - Political Institutions, Interest Group Activity and Crisis Resilience

After analyzing the potential effects of political institutions and interest group activity, in this section I summarize the previous results. I begin with (1) the relationship between the two political variables and resilience-enhancing economic institutions according to the second level of analysis outlined in section 2. Then, I turn to (2) the relationship between both political variables and crisis resilience according to the first level of analysis. Finally, (3) I confront the results to the predictions derived from Olson's and NWW's theories.

(1) First, table 57 summarizes the empirical results regarding the associations between both political variables and economic institutions. The signs indicate the direction of the relationships (positive or negative); the numbers of signs indicates the robustness of the results;[245] and subscripts in parenthesis mark important factors that influence the significance of the coefficients.

	Entire Sample	Developed	Emerging & Developing	
Dependent Variable / Explanatory Variable	Developed Economic Institutions - *Rule of Law, Open Goods Markets, Open Financial Markets, Large Public Sectors* (Crisis-aggravating)	Open Access Economic Institutions - *Rule of Law, Open Goods Markets, Open Labor Markets* (Resilience-enhancing)	Open Financial Markets (Crisis-aggravating)	Small Public Sectors (Resilience-enhancing)
Open Political Institutions	$+++_{(d)}$	$+++_{(d,\ dem)}$	$+_{(d)}$	$-_{(d)}$
Interest Group Activity	$+++_{(d)}$	$+++_{(d)}$	$+_{(d)}$	

Table 57: Summary of the empirical analysis in the sections 4.4.1 and 4.4.2 according the second level of analysis (The signs ± indicate the direction of significant relationships. The subscript (d) means that significant results are contingent on the inclusion of the control variable 'GDP per capita', which represents high economic development. The subscript (dem) means that significant results depend on the exclusion of the two non-democracies Singapore and Hong Kong from the sample. The number of signs represents the robustness of the relationship. Three signs indicate significant results across all considered institutional measures and specifications, two signs indicate significant results across all considered institutional measures and most specifications, and one sign indicates significant results for some institutional measures).

It, first, stands out that the variables representing open political institutions and interest group activity show very similar results. According to NWW's account, this is not surprising, as both are joint features of open political orders.[246] Furthermore, all

[245] Three signs indicate significant relationships for all measures and specifications; two signs mean that the significance of the coefficients depends on the choice of control variables but is robust to the choice of explanatory and dependent variables; and one sign indicates that the significance of the coefficients depends on the choice of the explanatory and dependent variables.

[246] Appendix 78 shows that correlations between the respective variables are indeed positive and (apart from one exception) significant within the three sub-samples. Furthermore, appendix 79 visualizes the positive relationships between political openness and the number of interest groups by means of two scatterplots.

associations between the two measures of political openness and economic institutions are closely related to development levels in terms of GDP per capita. Hence, wealthier countries feature more open political institutions, larger numbers of interest groups and more open and developed economic institutions, at the same time.

Within the entire sample, the measures for open political institutions and interest group activity show robust positive relationships with the index 'developed economic institutions' (capturing rule of law, open goods markets, open financial markets and large public sectors). These developed economic institutions are, in turn, associated with worse crisis resilience within the entire sample. Hence, the results suggest negative indirect effects of both political openness variables on crisis resilience that are mediated through developed economic institutions.

Within the sub-sample of developed countries, results are different. When considering all 32 countries, open political institutions are unrelated to the measure 'open access economic institutions' (capturing rule of law, goods market openness and labor market openness) – especially due to the two outliers Singapore and Hong Kong, which are not democratic but economically open. Hence, according to these results, open political institutions are no *necessary* prerequisites for upholding open economic institutions. When, however, excluding the two outliers from the sample, there is a robust positive association between open political institutions and open economic institutions (that is contingent on the inclusion of GDP per capita). Furthermore, there is a significant positive relationship between interest group activity and open economic institutions (that is also contingent on the inclusion of GDP per capita) irrespective of the inclusion of Singapore and Hong Kong. Departing from the results within the entire sample, the measure 'open access economic institutions' is not associated with *worse* but with *better* crisis resilience within the sub-group of developed countries. Hence, in *those* countries, the results suggest positive indirect effects of open political institutions and interest group activity on crisis resilience, which are mediated through open economic institutions.

Finally, within the sub-sample of 52 less developed countries, open political institutions and interest group activity are positively related to open financial markets and negatively related to small public sectors. As, according to the empirical results of section 4.3, open financial markets are crisis-aggravating and small public sectors are resilience-enhancing, these results suggest negative indirect effects of political openness and interest group activity on crisis resilience. However, the relationships between both political variables and economic institutions are only significant when measuring the latter based on Heritage data.

(2) To assess whether the previous significant relationships translate into significant relationships between the two political variables and crisis resilience, table 58 summarizes the results regarding the first level of analysis. Again, the signs indicate the directions of the relationships (positive or negative); subscripts in parenthesis mark

common effects with control variables; and the number of signs indicates the robustness of the results (apart from the common effects indicated in parenthesis).[247]

	Dep. Var.: $GDP_{08\text{-}12}$			Dep. Var.: $GDP_{08\text{-}09}$			Dep. Var.: $GDP_{10\text{-}12}$		
	All	Deve-loped	Emerging & Dev.	All	Deve-loped	Emerging & Dev.	All	Deve-loped	Emerging & Dev.
Open Political Institutions	---(dei)			---(dei)		--(g, f)	---(dei)		
Interest group Activity	---(dei)			---(dei)			-(dei)		

Table 58: Summary of the empirical analysis in the sections 4.4.1 and 4.4.2 according the first level of analysis (The signs ± indicate the direction of significant relationships. Subscripts in parenthesis mark common effects with control variables; (dei) represents common effects with 'developed economic institutions', (g, f) represents common effects with measures for government size and open financial markets. The number of signs represents the robustness of the relationship. Three signs indicate significant results across all considered institutional measures and specifications, two signs indicate significant results across all considered institutional measures and most specifications, and one sign indicates significant results for some institutional measures).

First, within the entire sample, the measures for open political institutions and interest group activity are associated with worse crisis resilience across all time periods. However, the significance of the results depends on the inclusion of the index 'developed economic institutions'. When the political variables are considered alongside the 'developed economic institutions' index, one of both indices typically turns insignificance. F-tests, however, show that they are jointly significant. Hence, the negative effects of open political institutions and interest group activity on crisis resilience are closely related to negative effects of developed economic institutions. This entails the conclusion that wealthier countries featuring open political institutions, more interest group activity and developed economic institutions (including rule of law, open goods markets, open financial markets and larger government sectors) faced a deeper economic crisis than countries with the opposite institutional features.

Next, within the sub-group of developed countries, coefficients of the two political variables are insignificant. Hence, the positive associations between open political institutions, interest group activity and resilience-enhancing economic institutions (rule of law, open goods markets and open labor markets) do not translate into positive relationships between the two political variables and crisis resilience. This indicates that positive indirect effects of political openness, which are mediated through open economic institutions, are counterbalanced by other negative effects.

Finally, within the sub-group of 52 less developed countries, results are mainly insignificant. Only the variables for open political institutions feature partly significant coefficients in regressions explaining crisis resilience during the years 2008 to 2009, although these results are not robust to the inclusion of control variables representing open financial markets and small public sectors. F-test, however, indicate that the

[247] See the previous footnote.

three institutions together (open political institutions, open financial markets and small public sectors) are jointly significant in all specifications using different combinations of measures. Hence, there is moderate evidence that within that sub-group those countries faced a deeper downturn which featured open political institutions, open financial markets and larger public sectors.

(3) The previously summarized results regarding the potential effects of political institutions and interest group activity are mainly at odds with the theoretical predictions derived from Olson and NWW. The following five findings stand out.

1. Interest group activity is not associated with sclerotic economic institutions. On the contrary, countries with more interest groups feature more open economic institutions including rule of law, open goods markets, open labor market and open financial markets. Only the positive association between the number of interest groups and larger government sectors is in line with Olson's account. Hence, the results contradict most parts of the hypothesis H-O 1, which links interest group activity to sclerotic economic institutions.
2. More interest group activity is associated with worse crisis resilience within the entire sample. This is superficially in line with the hypothesis H-O 3. However, this negative relationship is not mediated through sclerotic economic institutions as predicted by Olson's theory (hypotheses H-O 1 and H-O 2). On the contrary, the potential negative effects of interest group activity cannot be separated from the negative effects of developed economic institutions (including rule of law, open goods markets, open financial markets and larger public sectors). Hence, negative coefficient of the interest group variable possibly reflect the negative effects from these economic institutions, which are more prevalent in politically open and developed countries that also feature more interest groups. Furthermore, within the two sub-groups of developed and less developed countries, coefficients of the interest group variables are consistently insignificant. Hence, overall, the empirical results contradict H-O 3, which links interest group activity to worse crisis resilience
3. Open political institutions are associated with open and developed economic institutions, such as rule of law, open goods markets, open labor markets, open financial markets and large government sectors. Exceptions are the two outliers Singapore and Hong Kong which feature open economic institutions despite being autocracies. The main tendencies, however, are in line with NWW's account and the hypothesis H-NWW 1, which states that there is a double balance between political openness and economic openness that is closely connected to higher economic development in terms of GDP per capita.
4. Open political institutions are associated with worse crisis resilience within the entire sample and partly within the sub-sample of less developed countries. This finding contradicts hypothesis H-NWW 3, which states that open political

institutions (in combination with more interest group activity) enhance crisis resilience. Open political institutions show a positive association with crisis resilience only within the sub-group of developed countries. As, however, coefficients of the respective variables are mainly insignificant and as the positive coefficients depend on the exclusion of two outliers Hong Kong and Singapore, these results do not provide support for the hypothesis H-NWW 3, which links political openness to better crisis resilience. Furthermore, the (insignificant) positive coefficients in the reduced sample of 30 developed democracies turn negative when controlling for open economic institutions, thereby suggesting that positive indirect effects of political openness that work through economic openness are counterbalanced by other negative effects.

5. The relationships between open political institutions, interest group activity and crisis resilience are closely related to effects of open and developed economic institutions. Within the entire sample, developed economic institutions are associated with *worse* crisis resilience, likely reflecting the specific nature of the Great Recession, which originated in the financial markets of developed countries. Accordingly, political openness also shows a negative association with crisis resilience in the entire sample. Within the sub-sample of developed countries, on the other hand, in which all countries were affected by the crisis, open economic institutions are related to *better* crisis resilience. Accordingly, political openness also shows a slightly positive, though insignificant, association with crisis resilience within that groups of countries. Hence, potential effects of political variables cannot be studied apart from the effects of related economic institutions.

This summary of the results regarding the relationship between political openness and crisis resilience now leads to the conclusion of this thesis.

5. Conclusion and Outlook

This thesis set out to investigate the question whether economic institutions, political institutions and the intensity of interest group activity affected countries' crisis resilience during the years 2008 to 2012. From the previous analysis, I conclude that they do - however in a different way than expected from the theoretical consideration laid out in chapter 2.

According to the theoretical framework developed in chapter 2, *crisis resilience* is one aspect of *adaptive efficiency*, which "denotes the ability of an economy to self-organize – that is, to suitably modify its structure" (Pelikan, 1986, pp. 4-5). This ability to efficiently modify economic structures (organizations and channels of cooperation amongst different actors), in turn, depends on *economic institutions, political institutions* and *interest group activity*. From Olson's and NWW's accounts and from the related literature I derived testable hypotheses regarding these effects and ordered them according to *two distinct levels of analysis*. While the first level refers to the determinants of *adaptions of economic actors* and therefore of *economic performance*, the second level refers to the *determinants of efficiency-enhancing economic institutions*. This distinction between two levels of analysis is particularly important when assessing the effects of political institutions and of interest group activity, as both may affect crisis resilience either directly through the promotion of resilience-enhancing discretionary policies or indirectly through the choice of resilience-enhancing economic institutions.

Starting with the effects of economic institutions on crisis resilience, which refer solely to the first level of analysis, both NWW and Olson argue that open markets featuring *well-enforced property rights and contract laws* as well as *limited regulations of goods and labor markets* promote adaptive efficiency and therefore also crisis resilience. The authors, however, disagree on the role of *large government sectors*. While Olson puts forward a generally pessimistic account of government activity, NWW point out the predominant public good orientation of governments in open access orders. Furthermore, in section 2.4, I pointed out that both accounts miss an important aspect of adaptive efficiency that entails partly alternative hypotheses. While Olson and NWW focus on the ability of an economy to generate *change* through constant *innovations* and *reallocations of productive factors to their best uses*, the missing aspects refers to the *avoidance of unnecessary structural adjustments* during bottlenecks.

The empirical results in section 4.3 provide full support for neither of these theoretical accounts. Within the entire sample of 84 countries, economic institutions associated with high economic development (rule of law, open goods markets, open financial markets and large government sectors) are related to worse economic performance. These results most likely reflect the specific nature of the Great Recession, which had its origin in the financial markets of highly developed countries. Similarly, within the sub-group of 52 emerging and developing countries, those faced deeper downturns

R. Fritzsch, *Adaptive Efficiency During the Great Recession*,
Wirtschaft und Politik, https://doi.org/10.1007/978-3-658-27409-2_5

which had open financial markets and larger government sectors. Only within the sub-group of 32 developed countries, the results conform to the theoretical predictions derived from NWW and Olson, as well-enforced property rights and contract laws, open goods markets and open labor markets are associated with better crisis resilience within that sub-group of countries. However, deviating from the two theories, these economic institutions did not promote crisis resilience by facilitating the adjustment to imbalances *during* the crisis, as indicated by insignificant coefficients whenever controlling for the current account balance. Rather, these institutions, which are correlated with positive current accounts, potentially helped avoiding the build-up of unsustainable imbalances in the years *before* the recession.

Hence, these empirical results call for qualifications of the theories presented in chapter 2. Apparently, facilitating adjustments during a crisis is not the only relevant way how institutions affect crisis resilience. Besides that, avoiding the 'infection' with a crisis in the first place appears to matter, as well. In the entire sample and the sub-sample of less developed countries, for example, institutions such as stricter financial regulations seem to be relevant for this aspect of crisis resilience. Furthermore, in developed countries, open access institutions appear to have promoted crisis resilience mainly through preventing the build-up of unsustainable external imbalance in the years before the crisis. Especially this last relationship offers interesting paths for future research, in particular regarding the channels through which open access economic institutions affected external imbalances. For this purpose, reconciliations of the empirical results with country case studies or other qualitative research should be very instructive. Furthermore, there needs to be further research regarding the question why certain institutions work differently in developed and less developed countries. For this purpose, again, country cases studies should provide further interesting insights, in particular about the actual adaption processes that were at work in different countries.

Next, turning to the *political* determinants of crisis resilience, Olson and NWW offer competing accounts regarding the role of political institutions and interest group activity. On the one hand, Olson emphasizes the detrimental effects of interest group activity on economic institutions, adaptive efficiency and crisis resilience through *rent seeking*. On the other hand, NWW argue that a large number of interest groups can only emerge in open political orders, which support open economic institutions, adaptive efficiency and crisis resilience by promoting *experimentation with new ideas* for a society's most pressing problems and by *providing credible commitments* to antagonistic groups.

The empirical results in section 4.4 are at odds with most of these predictions, as discussed in detail at the end of the previous section. In short, more interest group activity and open political institutions are related to open and developed economic institutions. This is mainly in line with NWW's theoretical framework but at odds with Olson's account. Within the entire sample this association of political openness with developed economic institutions translates into a negative association with crisis resilience, as economically developed countries faced a more severe crisis than less developed countries. However, given the empirical methods used in this thesis, the negative effects of open political institutions, larger numbers of interest groups and developed economic institutions turned out to be difficult to separate. Similarly, within the sub-sample of emerging and developing countries, open political institutions in association with open financial markets and large public sectors are also related to worse crisis resilience within that sub-group of countries. In developed countries all explanatory variables are insignificant for explaining the severity of the Great Recession. All these results contradict NWW's account that open political institutions promote adaptive efficiency and Olson's account that the negative effects of interest group activity a mediated through sclerotic economic institutions. Furthermore, the close accordance between the effects of the political order and related economic institutions suggest the former cannot be studied separately from the latter, thereby confirming the necessity of distinguishing two levels of analysis.

Although the analysis of one particular economic crisis, such as the one assessed in this thesis, could not lead to generalizable statements about the determinants of crisis resilience, it still offers interesting insights the relations of interest. Similarly, although the methodological approach did not permit a disentanglement of overlaying effects stemming from different institutions, it still provides a comprehensive overview of empirical regularities. These regularities amongst the variables of interest, In turn, suggest revisions of existing theoretical accounts and they indicate promising paths for further research. Especially, an in-depth analysis of the relationship between open access economic institutions and the current account balance in developed countries in the years prior to the crisis should provide additional insights into the institutional determinants of crisis resilience. Also of interest is the question why institutions work differently in developed and less developed countries. Furthermore, it would be interesting to study the impact of institutions and interest group activity on other performance dimensions besides output, such as poverty rates or unemployment, in order to identify potential trade-offs amongst different institutional set-ups. Finally, these insights have to be integrated into a revised theoretical framework which distinguishes between the institutional determinants of infection and of recovery and which takes into account differences between developed and less developed countries. For these potential paths of future research, I hope this thesis can be a useful point of departure.

Appendices

Appendix 1 – Classification of countries

The group of advanced economies based on the IMF (2016) distinction includes the following 39 countries: Austria, Australia, Belgium, Canada, Cyprus, Czech Republic, Denmark, Estonia, Finland, France, Germany, Greece, Hong Kong, Iceland, Ireland, Israel, Italy, Japan, Korea (South), Latvia, Lithuania, Luxemburg, Macao, Malta, Netherland, New Zealand, Norway, Portugal, Puerto Rico, San Marino, Singapore, Slovakia, Slovenia, Spain, Sweden, Switzerland, Taiwan, United Kingdom and United States of America.

Of those 39 countries, 7 are dropped from the sample. Malta and San Marino don't pass the 10-billion dollar GDP threshold, Norway is a mayor oil-exporting country, for Macao and Puerto Rico (being territories of the USA and China) no data is available regarding the most important institutions and for Taiwan (being a territory claimed by China) no data is available regarding some important control variables. Finally, Luxemburg is dropped from the sample because, being a mayor financial center, it features extraordinarily high values of some financial control variables which makes it unsuitable for the principal component analysis.

The 52 less developed countries which fulfil the selection criteria are: Albania, Argentina, Bangladesh, Belarus, Bolivia, Bosnia and Herzegovina, Botswana, Brazil, Bulgaria, Cameroon, Chile, China, Colombia, Costa Rica, Cote d'Ivoire, Croatia, Dominican Republic, El Salvador, Ethiopia, Georgia, Ghana, Guatemala, Honduras, Hungary, India, Indonesia, Jamaica, Jordan, Kenya, Lebanon, Malaysia, Mexico, Morocco, Nepal, Panama, Paraguay, Peru, Philippines, Poland, Romania, Senegal, Serbia, South Africa, Tanzania, Thailand, Tunisia, Turkey, Uganda, Ukraine, Uruguay, Vietnam and Zambia.

Of the countries passing the GDP threshold, I did not include the following countries because they had oil rents above 10 percent of their yearly GDP at the onset of the crisis in 2007: Algeria, Angola, Azerbaijan, Bahrain, Brunei Darussalam, Congo, Ecuador, Egypt, Equatorial Guinea, Gabon, Iran, Iraq, Kazakhstan, Kuwait, Libya, Nigeria, Oman, Qatar, Russia, Saudi Arabia, Sudan, Syria, Trinidad and Tobago, United Arab Emirates, Uzbekistan, Venezuela and Yemen

Furthermore, of the countries passing the GDP threshold, I did not include the following countries because they were involved in (high-intensity) internal or external armed conflicts during the considered crisis period 2008 to 2012: Iraq, Libya, Pakistan, Sri Lanka, Sudan, Syria, Yemen (Rep.). I, furthermore, exclude Turkmenistan due to very limited data availability.

R. Fritzsch, *Adaptive Efficiency During the Great Recession*,
Wirtschaft und Politik, https://doi.org/10.1007/978-3-658-27409-2

Appendix 2 – Control variables

Variable	Definition	Data Sources
(Foreign Assets + Foreign Liabilities) / GDP	• Sum of the stock of foreign assets and foreign liabilities (% of GDP) including portfolio equity positions, foreign direct investment positions, debt positions, financial derivatives and foreign exchange reserves • 2007-values	• Own calculation: all values in current USD • All Data: "External Wealth of Nations Database" • For detailed descriptions of the data see Lane, Milesi-Ferretti (2007).
Private Credit / GDP	• Private credit by deposit money banks and other financial institutions (% of GDP) • 2007-values	• Indicator directly taken from the "Global Financial Development Database" - Indicator Code: GFDD.DI.12 • Background paper see: Cihák et al (2012).
Increase of (Private Credit / GDP)	• Private credit by deposit money banks and other financial institutions (% of GDP) • 2007-values minus 2002-values	• Indicator directly taken from the "Global Financial Development Database" - Indicator Code: GFDD.DI.12 • Background paper see: Cihák et al (2012).
Credit / Deposit	• Bank Credit to Bank Deposits (%) • 2007-values • Missing data for UK	• Indicator directly taken from the "Global Financial Development Database" - Indicator Code: GFDD.SI.04 • Background paper see: Cihák et al (2012).
Short-Term External Debt / GDP	• Gross short-term external debt stocks (% of GDP) • Q4-2007-values • Missing Q4-2007-values for Cyprus, New Zealand, Panama and Slovakia where replaced by nearest possible value (Q1-2008 for Cyprus, Q4-2011 for New Zealand, Q3-2014 for Panama, and Q4-2014 for Slovakia)	• Own calculation: all values in current USD • Short-term debt (emerging countries): "World Development Indicators Database" - Indicator Code: DT.DOD.DSTC.CD • Short-term debt (developed countries): "World Bank Quarterly External Debt Statistics (SDSS)" - Indicator Code: DT.DOD.DSTC.CD.US • GDP: "World Bank Development Indicators" – Indicator Code: NY.GDP.MKTP.CD
Current Account Balance / GDP	• Current account balance (% of GDP) • 2007-values	• Indicator directly taken from the "World Bank Development Indicators Database" – Indicator Code: BN.CAB.XOKA.GD.ZS
Exports / GDP	• Exports of goods and services (% of GDP) • 2007-values	• Indicator directly taken from the "World Bank Development Indicators Database" – Indicator Code: NE.EXP.GNFS.ZS
Trade / GDP	• Sum of exports and imports of goods and services (% of GDP) • 2007 values	• Indicator directly taken from the "World Bank Development Indicators Database" – Indicator Code: NE.TRD.GNFS.ZS
Manufactured Exports / Total Exports	• Value of manufactured goods exports (% of total exports of goods and services) • 2007 values	• Own calculations: all values in current USD • Manufactured exports: World Trade Organization "Time Series on

		International Trade" – Total exports of manufactured goods; Indicator Code: MA; Partner Code: WL • Exports of goods and services: "World Bank Development Indicators Database" - Indicator Code: NE.EXP.GNFS.CD
Commodity Exports / Total Exports	• Combined value of agricultural product, fuels and mining product exports (% of total exports of goods and services) • 2007 values	• Own calculations: all values in current USD • Agricultural product exports: World Trade Organization "Time Series on International Trade" – Total exports of agricultural products; Indicator Code: AG; Partner Code: WL • Fuels and mining product exports: World Trade Organization "Time Series on International Trade" – Total exports of fuels and mining products; Indicator Code: MI; Partner Code: WL • Exports of goods and services: "World Bank Development Indicators Database" - Indicator Code: NE.EXP.GNFS.CD
GDP per Capita	• GDP per capita (current USD) • 2007 values	• Indicator directly taken from the "World Bank Development Indicators Database" – Indicator Code: NY.GDP.PCAP.CD

Appendix 2: Definitions and data sources of non-institutional control variables.

Appendix 3 – Principal component analysis without UK

	Component 1: "International Linkages of Trade & Finance"	Component 2: "Economic & Financial Development"	Component 3: "Financial Vulnerabilities"	Component 4: "Industrial Orientation of the Economy"
Trade / GDP	**0.96**	0.03	-0.06	0.19
Exports / GDP	**0.95**	0.06	-0.16	0.18
(FA + FL) / GDP	**0.75**	**0.57**	0.00	0.03
S.T. Ext. Debt / GDP	**0.75**	**0.57**	-0.01	0.03
GDP per Capita	0.18	**0.91**	0.10	0.17
Priv. Cred. / GDP	0.10	**0.84**	0.26	0.18
Increase (Priv. Cred. / GDP)	-0.07	0.41	**0.82**	-0.09
Current Acc. Balance / GDP	0.23	0.32	**-0.80**	0.08
Credit / Deposit	0.05	0.31	**0.63**	0.08
Manuf. Exp. / Total Exp.	0.13	0.12	-0.11	**0.89**
Com. Exp. / Total Exp.	-0.15	-0.14	-0.06	**-0.88**

Appendix 3: factor loadings of all explanatory variables when excluding the UK from the sample (loadings larger than 0.5 are bold).

Appendix 4 - Correlations amongst rule of law indices

	WGI Rule of Law & Control of Corruption	Fraser Legal System & Property Rights	Heritage Property Rights & Freedom from Corruption	GCI Public Institutions
WGI Rule of Law & Control of Corruption	1	**0.94**	**0.97**	**0.94**
Fraser Legal System & Property Rights	**0.94**	1	**0.89**	**0.94**
Heritage Property Rights & Freedom from Corruption	**0.97**	**0.89**	1	**0.93**
GCI Public Institutions	**0.94**	**0.94**	**0.93**	1

Appendix 4: Correlations amongst rule of law indices within the entire sample (all correlations are significant at conventional significance levels).

Appendix 5 – Scatterplots of 'GDP08-12' against different rule of law indices

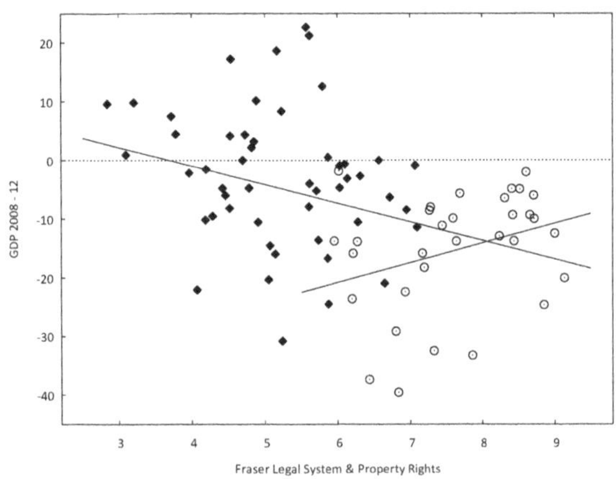

Appendix 5a: Scatterplot of '$GDP_{08\text{-}12}$' against Fraser 'legal system and property rights' (black dots: less developed countries; white circles: developed countries; downward-sloping line: fitted values for the entire sample; upward-sloping line: fitted values for the sub-sample of developed countries).

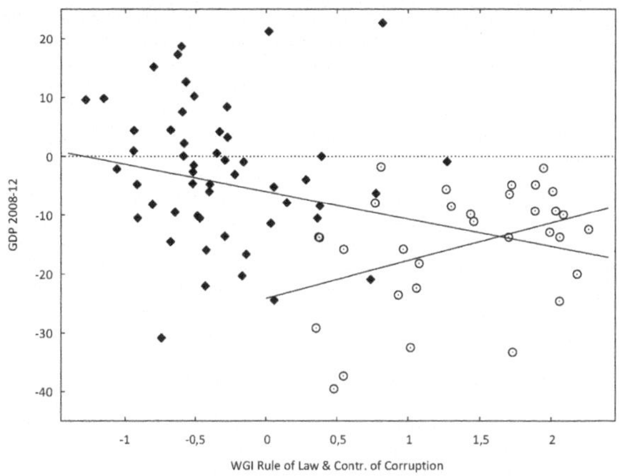

Appendix 5b: Scatterplot of 'GDP$_{08\text{-}12}$' against WGI 'rule of law and control of corruption' (black dots: less developed countries; white circles: developed countries; downward-sloping line: fitted values for the entire sample; upward-sloping line: fitted values for the sub-sample of developed countries).

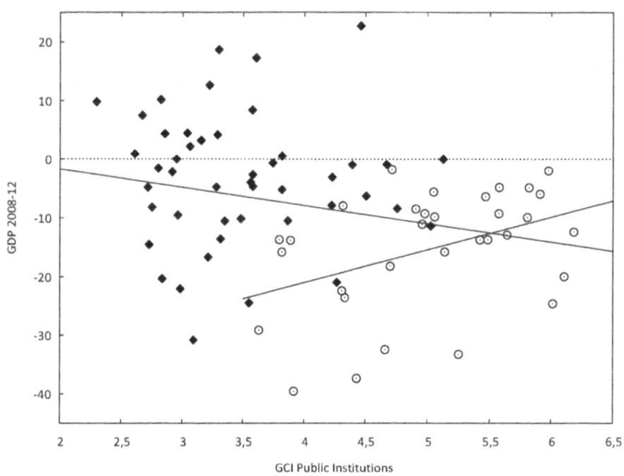

Appendix 5c: Scatterplot of 'GDP$_{08\text{-}12}$' against GCI 'public institutions' (black dots: less developed countries; white circles: developed countries; downward-sloping line: fitted values for the entire sample; upward-sloping line: fitted values for the sub-sample of developed countries).

Appendix 6 – 'GDP_{08-09}' against different rule of law indices in the entire sample

Dependent Variable: 'GDP_{08-09}'; Sample: All Countries											
	(1)	(2)	(3)	(4)	(5)	(6)	(7)	(8)	(9)	(10)	(11)
Constant	3.94	3.71	7.76	8.46	3.21	4.77	5.67	3.63	6.71	-0.68	1.04
	0.05	0.07*	0.00***	0.04**	0.37	0.02**	0.01**	0.09*	0.00***	0.85	0.61
Fras. Leg. Syst.	-1.64	-1.41	-2.14	-2.38	-1.38	-1.78	-1.73	-1.59	-1.57	-0.89	-0.94
& Prop. Rights	0.00***	0.00***	0.00***	0.00***	0.08*	0.00***	0.00***	0.00***	0.00***	0.15	0.06*
Financial	-2.82									-2.98	-2.92
Vulnerabilities	0.00***									0.00***	0.00***
Increase (Priv.		-0.10									
Cred. / GDP)		0.02**									
Current Acc.			0.26								
Balance / GDP			0.00***								
Economic				1.09						-0.54	
Development				0.37						0.61	
GDP					-0.05						
per Capita					0.45						
International						-0.72				-1.04	-0.94
Linkages						0.23				0.03**	0.06*
Trade /							-0.01				
GDP							0.21				
Industrial								-1.75			
Orientation								0.00***			
Manuf. Exp. /									-0.07	-2.03	-1.92
Total Exp.									0.01***	0.00***	0.00***
N	82	82	82	82	82	82	82	82	82	82	82
R^{2*}	0.32	0.29	0.26	0.17	0.16	0.17	0.17	0.22	0.21	0.39	0.39

Appendix 6a: Multivariate regressions of 'GD$_{P08-09}$' against Fraser 'legal system and property rights' and one additional control variable in the entire sample (second row: p-values of two-sided significance tests; number of asterisks: significance levels of 10%*, 5%** and 1%***).

	Dependent Variable: 'GDP₀₈₋₀₉'; Sample: All Countries										
	(1)	(2)	(3)	(4)	(5)	(6)	(7)	(8)	(9)	(10)	(11)
Constant	-5.01	-3.95	-3.95	-4.43	-4.47	-5.00	-3.73	-5.08	-1.50	-5.07	-5.20
	0.00***	0.00***	0.00***	0.00***	0.00***	0.00***	0.00***	0.00***	0.28	0.00***	0.00***
WGI Rule of	-2.80	-2.19	-3.52	-4.60	-2.26	-2.82	-2.76	-2.57	-2.41	-2.61	-2.20
Law & Cor.	0.00***	0.00***	0.00***	0.00***	0.24	0.00***	0.00***	0.00***	0.00***	0.06*	0.00***
Financial	-3.10									-3.11	-3.13
Vulnerabilities	0.00***									0.00***	0.00***
Increase (Priv.		-0.11									
Cred. / GDP)		0.02**									
Current Acc.			0.27								
Balance / GDP			0.00***								
Economic				2.06						0.47	
Development				0.18						0.72	
GDP					-0.04						
per Capita					0.67						
International						-0.80				-0.84	-0.92
Linkages						0.19				0.11	0.05*
Trade /							-0.01				
GDP							0.19				
Industrial								-1.86		-1.85	-1.94
Orientation								0.00***		0.00***	0.00***
Manuf. Exp. /									-0.08		
Total Exp.									0.00***		
N	84	84	84	84	84	84	84	84	84	84	84
R^{2*}	0.34	0.29	0.25	0.18	0.15	0.16	0.16	0.21	0.21	0.40	0.40

Appendix 6b: Multivariate regressions of '$GDP_{08\text{-}09}$' against WGI 'rule of law and control of corruption' and one additional control variable in the entire sample (second row: p-values of two-sided significance tests; number of asterisks: significance levels of 10%*, 5%** and 1%***).

	Dependent Variable: 'GDP_{08-09}'; Sample: All Countries										
	(1)	(2)	(3)	(4)	(5)	(6)	(7)	(8)	(9)	(10)	(11)
Constant	0.90 0.71	0.05 0.98	4.87 0.07*	2.08 0.64	-5.63 0.09*	0.29 0.91	1.53 0.55	-0.12 0.96	2.94 0.23	-5.36 0.22	-1.51 0.53
GCI Public Institutions	-1.79 0.00***	-1.26 0.02**	-2.57 0.00***	-2.08 0.07*	0.48 0.62	-1.64 0.00***	-1.55 0.01***	-1.52 0.01***	-1.46 0.01**	-0.23 0.83	-1.19 0.03**
Financial Vulnerabilities	-3.11 0.00***									-3.15 0.00***	-3.14 0.00***
Increase (Priv. Cred. / GDP)		-0.11 0.02**									
Current Acc. Balance / GDP			0.30 0.00***								
Economic Development				0.30 0.82						-1.18 0.31	
GDP per Capita					-0.16 0.00***						
International Linkages						-0.97 0.13				-1.28 0.01***	-1.07 0.04**
Trade / GDP							-0.02 0.11				
Industrial Orientation								-1.83 0.00***		-2.16 0.00***	-1.93 0.00***
Manuf. Exp. / Total Exp.									-0.07 0.01***		
N	78	78	78	78	78	78	78	78	78	78	78
R^{2*}	0.27	0.23	0.19	0.05	0.11	0.07	0.08	0.12	0.11	0.35	0.35

Appendix 6c: Multivariate regressions of 'GDP_{08-09}' against GCI 'public institutions' and one additional control variable in the entire sample (second row: p-values of two-sided significance tests; number of asterisks: significance levels of 10%*, 5%** and 1%***).

Appendix 7 – '$GDP_{08\text{-}12}$' against different rule of law indices in the entire sample

	Dependent Variable: 'GDP_{08-12}'; Sample: All Countries										
	(1)	(2)	(3)	(4)	(5)	(6)	(7)	(8)	(9)	(10)	(11)
Constant	0.80	-0.01	-6.82	1.80	-6.76	0.34	1.65	-0.62	5.34	-2.79	-0.84
	0.79	1.00	0.01**	0.75	0.13	0.91	0.65	0.83	0.14	0.55	0.75
Her. Prop. Rights	-0.16	-0.09	-0.24	-0.18	0.12	-0.15	-0.15	-0.14	-0.13	-0.09	-0.13
& Free from Cor.	0.00***	0.04**	0.00***	0.09*	0.37	0.00***	0.00***	0.01***	0.01**	0.28	0.00***
Financial	-7.58									-7.57	-7.57
Vulnerabilities	0.00***									0.00***	0.00***
Increase (Priv.		-0.28									
Cred. / GDP)		0.00***									
Current Acc.			-0.76								
Balance / GDP			0.00***								
Economic				0.66						-1.06	
Development				0.81						0.58	
GDP					-0.39						
per Capita					0.01**						
International						-0.80				-1.07	-0.90
Linkages						0.56				0.21	0.23
Trade /							-0.02				
GDP							0.49				
Industrial								-3.93		-4.09	-3.95
Orientation								0.00***		0.00***	0.00***
Manuf. Exp. /									-0.14		
Total Exp.									0.01**		
N	84	84	84	84	84	84	84	84	84	84	84
R^{2*}	0.43	0.35	0.33	0.07	0.15	0.07	0.07	0.16	0.14	0.52	0.52

Appendix 7a: Multivariate regressions of '$GDP_{08\text{-}12}$' against Heritage 'property rights and corruption' and one additional control variable in the entire sample (second row: p-values of two-sided significance tests; number of asterisks: significance levels of 10%*, 5%** and 1%***).

Dependent Variable: 'GDP_{08-12}'; Sample: All Countries											
	(1)	(2)	(3)	(4)	(5)	(6)	(7)	(8)	(9)	(10)	(11)
Constant	8.04	7.46	18.21	15.37	5.21	11.37	11.83	8.25	13.71	-2.65	3.42
	0.03**	0.04**	0.00***	0.01**	0.39	0.01***	0.01***	0.06*	0.00***	0.61	0.35
Fras. Leg. Syst.	-2.57	-2.00	-3.88	-3.77	-1.70	-3.12	-3.08	-2.60	-2.67	-0.82	-1.82
& Prop. Rights	0.00***	0.00***	0.00***	0.00***	0.17	0.00***	0.00***	0.00***	0.00***	0.33	0.00***
Financial	-6.90									-7.26	-7.05
Vulnerabilities	0.00***									0.00***	0.00***
Increase (Priv.		-0.25									
Cred. / GDP)		0.00***									
Current Acc.			0.72								
Balance / GDP			0.00***								
Economic				1.33						-1.89	
Development				0.49						0.21	
GDP					-0.15						
per Capita					0.16						
International						-0.36				-1.17	-0.83
Linkages						0.79				0.14	0.29
Trade /							-0.01				
GDP							0.75				
Industrial								-3.35		-4.06	-3.66
Orientation								0.00***		0.00***	0.00***
Manuf. Exp. /									-0.11		
Total Exp.									0.05**		
N	82	82	82	82	82	82	82	82	82	82	82
R^{2*}	0.44	0.38	0.39	0.14	0.15	0.13	0.13	0.20	0.17	0.52	0.51

Appendix 7b: Multivariate regressions of 'GDP_{08-12}' against Fraser 'legal system and property rights' and one additional control variable in the entire sample (second row: p-values of two-sided significance tests; number of asterisks: significance levels of 10%*, 5%** and 1%***).

	Dependent Variable: 'GDP$_{08-12}$'; Sample: All Countries										
	(1)	(2)	(3)	(4)	(5)	(6)	(7)	(8)	(9)	(10)	(11)
Constant	-6.16	-3.64	-3.26	-5.42	-3.41	-6.06	-4.96	-6.28	-0.61	-6.67	-6.47
	0.00***	0.01***	0.01***	0.00***	0.17	0.00***	0.05**	0.00	0.84	0.00***	0.00***
WGI Rule of	-4.24	-2.78	-6.17	-6.54	-0.82	-4.54	-4.47	-3.88	-3.78	-2.66	-3.28
Law & Cor.	0.00***	0.00***	0.00***	0.00***	0.79	0.00***	0.00***	0.00***	0.00***	0.16	0.00***
Financial	-7.30									-7.39	-7.36
Vulnerabilities	0.00***									0.00***	0.00***
Increase (Priv.		-0.27									
Cred. / GDP)		0.00***									
Current Acc.			-0.75								
Balance / GDP			0.00***								
Economic				2.38						-0.71	
Development				0.34						0.71	
GDP					-0.23						
per Capita					0.17						
International						-0.63				-0.98	-0.87
Linkages						0.65				0.25	0.25
Trade /							-0.01				
GDP							0.61				
Industrial								-3.56		-3.83	-3.70
Orientation								0.00***		0.00***	0.00***
Manuf. Exp. /									-0.13		
Total Exp.									0.03**		
N	84	84	84	84	84	84	84	84	84	84	84
R^{2*}	0.45	0.37	0.37	0.13	0.14	0.12	0.12	0.19	0.17	0.52	0.53

Appendix 7c: Multivariate regressions of 'GDP$_{08-12}$' against WGI 'rule of law and control of corruption' and one additional control variable in the entire sample (second row: p-values of two-sided significance tests; number of asterisks: significance levels of 10%*, 5%** and 1%***).

	Dependent Variable: 'GDP_{08-12}'; Sample: All Countries										
	(1)	(2)	(3)	(4)	(5)	(6)	(7)	(8)	(9)	(10)	(11)
Constant	3.82 0.34	1.81 0.67	14.43 0.00***	3.94 0.61	-9.80 0.14	3.82 0.44	4.81 0.34	2.09 0.66	7.02 0.15	-8.11 0.16	0.35 0.93
GCI Public Institutions	-2.95 0.00***	-1.68 0.06*	-5.01 0.00***	-2.97 0.11	1.79 0.34	-2.94 0.01***	-2.85 0.01**	-2.48 0.03**	-2.53 0.03***	0.03 0.98	-2.07 0.02**
Financial Vulnerabilities	-7.27 0.00***									-7.36 0.00***	-7.33 0.00***
Increase (Priv. Cred. / GDP)		-0.27 0.00***									
Current Acc. Balance / GDP			0.81 0.00***								
Economic Development				-0.20 0.92						-2.60 0.09*	
GDP per Capita					-0.33 0.00***						
International Linkages						-0.76 0.58				-1.42 0.07*	-0.95 0.24
Trade / GDP							-0.01 0.54				
Industrial Orientation								-3.38 0.01***		-4.05 0.00***	-3.54 0.00***
Manuf. Exp. / Total Exp.									-0.10 0.07*		
N	78	78	78	78	78	78	78	78	78	78	78
R^{2*}	0.43	0.36	0.37	0.05	0.13	0.05	0.05	0.12	0.08	0.51	0.50

Appendix 7d: Multivariate regressions of 'GDP_{08-12}' against GCI 'public institutions' and one additional control variable in the entire sample (second row: p-values of two-sided significance tests; number of asterisks: significance levels of 10%*, 5%** and 1%***).

Appendix 8 - 'GDP$_{10-12}$' against different rule of law indices in the entire sample

	Dependent Variable: 'GDP$_{10-12}$'; Sample: All Countries								
	(1)	(2)	(3)	(4)	(5)	(6)	(7)	(8)	(9)
Constant	0.32	-0.37	3.99	-2.82	-5.03	-0.15	0.01	-0.67	1.79
	0.86	0.83	0.03**	0.37	0.05**	0.94	1.00	0.74	0.46
Her. Prop. Rights	-0.04	0.01	-0.08	0.01	0.14	-0.04	-0.03	-0.03	-0.02
& Free from Cor.	0.11	0.79	0.00***	0.79	0.02**	0.26	0.28	0.44	0.47
Financial	-4.81								
Vulnerabilities	0.00***								
Increase (Priv.		-0.18							
Cred. / GDP)		0.00***							
Current Acc.			0.52						
Balance / GDP			0.00***						
Economic				-1.59					
Development				0.23					
GDP					-0.28				
per Capita					0.00***				
International						-0.04			
Linkages						0.97			
Trade /							-0.00		
GDP							0.89		
Industrial								-1.91	
Orientation								0.01	
Manuf. Exp. /									-0.06
Total Exp.									0.15
N	84	84	84	84	84	84	84	84	84
R^{2*}	0.37	0.31	0.30	0.01	0.13	-0.01	-0.01	0.05	0.02

Appendix 8a: Multivariate regressions of 'GDP$_{10-12}$' against Heritage 'property rights and corruption' and one additional control variable in the entire sample (second row: p-values of two-sided significance tests; number of asterisks: significance levels of 10%*, 5%** and 1%***).

	Dependent Variable: 'GDP$_{10-12}$'; Sample: All Countries								
	(1)	(2)	(3)	(4)	(5)	(6)	(7)	(8)	(9)
Constant	3.90 0.10	3.49 0.16	10.97 0.00***	6.89 0.08*	1.54 0.72	6.63 0.03**	6.19 0.04**	4.71 0.13	6.98 0.02**
Fras. Leg. Syst. & Prop. Rights	-0.97 0.01***	-0.58 0.11	-1.87 0.00***	-1.45 0.02**	-0.28 0.74	-1.41 0.00***	-1.44 0.00***	-1.10 0.03**	-1.19 0.02**
Financial Vulnerabilities	-4.55 0.00***								
Increase (Priv. Cred. / GDP)		-0.17 0.00***							
Current Acc. Balance / GDP			0.51 0.00***						
Economic Development				0.21 0.85					
GDP per Capita					-0.11 0.12				
International Linkages						0.35 0.71			
Trade / GDP							0.01 0.68		
Industrial Orientation								-1.56 0.04**	
Manuf. Exp. / Total Exp.									-0.04 0.35
N	82	82	82	82	82	82	82	82	82
R^{2*}	0.39	0.32	0.38	0.05	0.07	0.05	0.05	0.09	0.06

Appendix 8b: Multivariate regressions of 'GDP$_{10-12}$' against Fraser 'legal system and property rights' and one additional control variable in the entire sample (second row: p-values of two-sided significance tests; number of asterisks: significance levels of 10%*, 5%** and 1%***).

	Dependent Variable: 'GDP10-12'; Sample: All Countries								
	(1)	(2)	(3)	(4)	(5)	(6)	(7)	(8)	(9)
Constant	-1.50 0.04**	0.14 0.86	-0.48 0.48	-1.18 0.18	-0.12 0.93	-1.36 0.12	-1.71 0.30	-1.50 0.07*	0.12 0.96
WGI Rule of Law & Cor.	-1.79 0.00***	-0.95 0.09*	-3.08 0.00***	-2.86 0.01**	-0.42 0.80	-2.25 0.00***	-2.28 0.00***	-1.79 0.03**	-1.94 0.02**
Financial Vulnerabilities	-4.61 0.00***								
Increase (Priv. Cred. / GDP)		-0.17 0.00***							
Current Acc. Balance / GDP			0.52 0.00***						
Economic Development				0.83 0.53					
GDP per Capita					-0.11 0.21				
International Linkages						0.19 0.84			
Trade / GDP							0.00 0.81		
Industrial Orientation								-1.50 0.05**	
Manuf. Exp. / Total Exp.									-0.03 0.39
N	84	84	84	84	84	84	84	84	84
R^{2*}	0.40	0.33	0.39	0.06	0.07	0.05	0.05	0.09	0.06

Appendix 8c: Multivariate regressions of '$GDP_{10\text{-}12}$' against WGI 'rule of law and control of corruption' and one additional control variable in the entire sample (second row: p-values of two-sided significance tests; number of asterisks: significance levels of 10%*, 5%** and 1%***).

	Dependent Variable: 'GDP10–12'; Sample: All Countries								
	(1)	(2)	(3)	(4)	(5)	(6)	(7)	(8)	(9)
Constant	2.64 0.30	1.34 0.62	10.02 0.00***	1.21 0.82	-5.33 0.31	3.28 0.33	3.04 0.37	2.00 0.55	3.79 0.27
GCI Public Institutions	-1.19 0.04**	-0.37 0.53	-2.62 0.00***	-0.83 0.51	1.59 0.29	-1.34 0.08*	-1.36 0.08*	-1.02 0.21	-1.14 0.16
Financial Vulnerabilities	-4.65 0.00***								
Increase (Priv. Cred. / GDP)		-0.17 0.00***							
Current Acc. Balance / GDP			0.57 0.00***						
Economic Development				-0.64 0.62					
GDP per Capita					-0.19 0.01**				
International Linkages						0.18 0.85			
Trade / GDP							0.00 0.84		
Industrial Orientation								-1.52 0.05**	
Manuf. Exp. / Total Exp.									-0.03 0.46
N	78	78	78	78	78	78	78	78	78
R^{2*}	0.40	0.33	0.40	0.01	0.08	0.01	0.01	0.04	0.01

Appendix 8d: Multivariate regressions of '$GDP_{10\text{-}12}$' against GCI 'public institutions' and one additional control variable in the entire sample (second row: p-values of two-sided significance tests; number of asterisks: significance levels of 10%*, 5%** and 1%***).

Appendix 9 – 'GDP10-12' against different rule of law indices in developed countries

	Dependent Variable: 'GDP$_{10-12}$'; Sample: Developed Countries								
	(1)	(2)	(3)	(4)	(5)	(6)	(7)	(8)	(9)
Constant	-20.92 0.03**	-25.72 0.01**	-8.48 0.26	-34.91 0.02**	-32.17 0.03**	-25.19 0.03**	-26.68 0.02**	-42.11 0.00***	-45.49 0.00***
Fras. Leg. Syst. & Prop. Rights	2.08 0.07*	2.98 0.02**	0.50 0.60	4.08 0.04**	4.12 0.05*	2.55 0.07*	2.46 0.08*	4.55 0.01***	3.84 0.01***
Financial Vulnerabilities	-3.75 0.00***								
Increase (Priv. Cred. / GDP)		-0.13 0.00***							
Current Acc. Balance / GDP			0.51 0.00***						
Economic Development				-2.01 0.16					
GDP per Capita					-0.13 0.25				
International Linkages						0.68 0.41			
Trade / GDP							0.02 0.05**		
Industrial Orientation								4.87 0.00***	
Manuf. Exp. / Total Exp.									0.19 0.00***
N	32	32	32	32	32	32	32	32	32
R^{2*}	0.49	0.47	0.49	0.13	0.11	0.09	0.14	0.36	0.42

Appendix 9a: Multivariate regressions of 'GDP$_{10-12}$' against Fraser 'legal system and property rights' and one additional control variable in developed countries (second row: p-values of two-sided significance tests; number of asterisks: significance levels of 10%*, 5%** and 1%***).

	Dependent Variable: 'GDP10-12'; Sample: Developed Countries								
	(1)	(2)	(3)	(4)	(5)	(6)	(7)	(8)	(9)
Constant	-8.89 0.01***	-9.36 0.00***	-4.78 0.05*	-13.83 0.00***	-8.84 0.01***	-11.22 0.00***	-13.32 0.00***	-16.71 0.00***	-23.53 0.00***
WGI Rule of Law & Cor.	2.79 0.12	4.65 0.01**	0.09 0.95	8.02 0.02**	8.87 0.04**	3.98 0.05*	3.87 0.05*	6.82 0.00***	5.65 0.00***
Financial Vulnerabilities	-3.69 0.00***								
Increase (Priv. Cred. / GDP)		-0.13 0.00***							
Current Acc. Balance / GDP			0.53 0.00***						
Economic Development				-3.11 0.06*					
GDP per Capita					-0.24 0.11				
International Linkages						0.85 0.39			
Trade / GDP							0.02 0.04**		
Industrial Orientation								4.69 0.01***	
Manuf. Exp. / Total Exp.									0.18 0.00***
N	32	32	32	32	32	32	32	32	32
R^{2*}	0.47	0.47	0.48	0.18	0.17	0.09	0.14	0.34	0.39

Appendix 9b: Multivariate regressions of 'GDP_{10-12}' against WGI 'rule of law and control of corruption' and one additional control variable in developed countries (second row: p-values of two-sided significance tests; number of asterisks: significance levels of 10%*, 5%** and 1%***).

	Dependent Variable: 'GDP_{10-12}'; Sample: Developed Countries								
	(1)	(2)	(3)	(4)	(5)	(6)	(7)	(8)	(9)
Constant	-16.33 0.01**	-21.67 0.00***	-4.25 0.37	-33.99 0.00***	-29.27 0.00***	-21.81 0.01***	-23.39 0.00***	-34.54 0.00***	-39.30 0.00***
GCI Public Institutions	2.24 0.05*	3.72 0.00***	-0.08 0.93	6.15 0.01***	5.98 0.02**	3.20 0.03**	3.08 0.03**	5.43 0.00***	4.67 0.00***
Financial Vulnerabilities	-3.70 0.00***								
Increase (Priv. Cred. / GDP)		-0.13 0.00***							
Current Acc. Balance / GDP			0.53 0.00***						
Economic Development				-2.78 0.07*					
GDP per Capita					-0.17 0.17				
International Linkages						0.66 0.41			
Trade / GDP							0.02 0.05**		
Industrial Orientation								4.54 0.01***	
Manuf. Exp. / Total Exp.									0.18 0.00***
N	32	32	32	32	32	32	32	32	32
R^{2*}	0.46	0.46	0.48	0.16	0.13	0.09	0.13	0.32	0.39

Appendix 9c: Multivariate regressions of 'GDP_{10-12}' against GCI 'public institutions' and one additional control variable in developed countries (second row: p-values of two-sided significance tests; number of asterisks: significance levels of 10%*, 5%** and 1%***).

Appendix 10 – 'GDP08-12' against different rule of law indices in developed countries

	Dependent Variable: 'GDP_{08-12}'; Sample: Developed Countries								
	(1)	(2)	(3)	(4)	(5)	(6)	(7)	(8)	(9)
Constant	-28.95 0.00***	-34.23 0.00***	-19.15 0.01***	-42.77 0.00***	-38.81 0.00***	-36.47 0.00***	-37.07 0.00***	-48.48 0.00***	-52.30 0.00***
Her. Prop. Rights & Free from Cor.	0.19 0.03**	0.30 0.00***	0.07 0.45	0.39 0.05**	0.39 0.06*	0.28 0.02**	0.27 0.02**	0.41 0.00***	0.34 0.00***
Financial Vulnerabilities	-5.73 0.00***								
Increase (Priv. Cred. / GDP)		-0.18 0.00***							
Current Acc. Balance / GDP			0.73 0.00***						
Economic Development				-2.43 0.46					
GDP per Capita					-0.16 0.52				
International Linkages						-0.11 0.92			
Trade / GDP							0.01 0.37		
Industrial Orientation								6.16 0.01***	
Manuf. Exp. / Total Exp.									0.21 0.00***
N	32	32	32	32	32	32	32	32	32
R^{2*}	0.61	0.53	0.53	0.18	0.17	0.14	0.15	0.37	0.34

Appendix 10a: Multivariate regressions of 'GDP_{08-12}' against Heritage 'property rights and corruption' and one additional control variable in developed countries (second row: p-values of two-sided significance tests; number of asterisks: significance levels of 10%*, 5%** and 1%***).

	Dependent Variable: 'GDP$_{08-12}$'; Sample: Developed Countries								
	(1)	(2)	(3)	(4)	(5)	(6)	(7)	(8)	(9)
Constant	-32.46 0.01**	-40.25 0.00***	-13.64 0.24	-40.71 0.03**	-39.84 0.03**	-40.87 0.01**	-41.20 0.01**	-59.39 0.00***	-61.44 0.00***
Fras. Leg. Syst. & Prop. Rights	2.37 0.14	3.75 0.03**	-0.03 0.98	3.32 0.19	3.10 0.27	3.34 0.09*	3.20 0.10	5.50 0.01**	4.57 0.02**
Financial Vulnerabilities	-6.02 0.00***								
Increase (Priv. Cred. / GDP)		-0.17 0.00***							
Current Acc. Balance / GDP			0.79 0.00***						
Economic Development				0.04 0.99					
GDP per Capita					0.03 0.91				
International Linkages						0.01 0.99			
Trade / GDP							0.01 0.33		
Industrial Orientation								5.66 0.02**	
Manuf. Exp. / Total Exp.									0.20 0.01**
N	32	32	32	32	32	32	32	32	32
R^{2*}	0.56	0.42	0.52	0.04	0.04	0.04	0.05	0.23	0.23

Appendix 10b: Multivariate regressions of 'GDP$_{08-12}$' against Fraser 'legal system and property rights' and one additional control variable in developed countries (second row: p-values of two-sided significance tests; number of asterisks: significance levels of 10%*, 5%** and 1%***).

	Dependent Variable: 'GDP$_{08\text{-}12}$'; Sample: Developed Countries								
	(1)	(2)	(3)	(4)	(5)	(6)	(7)	(8)	(9)
Constant	-20.24 0.00***	-21.35 0.00***	-14.59 0.00***	-25.51 0.00***	-22.63 0.00***	-24.16 0.00***	-25.37 0.00***	-30.88 0.00***	-37.62 0.00***
WGI Rule of Law & Cor.	4.23 0.07*	7.08 0.01***	0.48 0.84	8.52 0.05**	9.26 0.07*	6.41 0.04**	6.23 0.04**	9.75 0.00***	8.05 0.00***
Financial Vulnerabilities	-5.85 0.00***								
Increase (Priv. Cred. / GDP)		-0.18 0.00***							
Current Acc. Balance / GDP			0.77 0.00***						
Economic Development				-1.70 0.54					
GDP per Capita					-0.15 0.53				
International Linkages						0.01 1.00			
Trade / GDP							0.01 0.32		
Industrial Orientation								5.91 0.01**	
Manuf. Exp. / Total Exp.									0.20 0.01***
N	32	32	32	32	32	32	32	32	32
R^{2*}	0.58	0.48	0.52	0.11	0.11	0.09	0.11	0.30	0.29

Appendix 10c: Multivariate regressions of 'GDP$_{08\text{-}12}$' against WGI 'rule of law and control of corruption' and one additional control variable in developed countries (second row: p-values of two-sided significance tests; number of asterisks: significance levels of 10%*, 5%** and 1%***).

	Dependent Variable: 'GDP$_{08-12}$'; Sample: Developed Countries								
	(1)	(2)	(3)	(4)	(5)	(6)	(7)	(8)	(9)
Constant	-33.21 0.00***	-41.78 0.00***	-17.02 0.05**	-50.16 0.00***	-47.43 0.00***	-43.35 0.00***	-43.59 0.00***	-58.43 0.00***	-61.87 0.00***
GCI Public Institutions	3.74 0.03**	6.00 0.00***	0.61 0.72	7.24 0.03**	7.21 0.04**	5.58 0.02**	5.37 0.02**	8.15 0.00***	6.98 0.00***
Financial Vulnerabilities	-5.81 0.00***								
Increase (Priv. Cred. / GDP)		-0.18 0.00***							
Current Acc. Balance / GDP			0.76 0.00***						
Economic Development				-1.71 0.53					
GDP per Capita					-0.11 0.89				
International Linkages						-0.12 0.92			
Trade / GDP							0.01 0.38		
Industrial Orientation								5.84 0.02**	
Manuf. Exp. / Total Exp.									0.21 0.01**
N	32	32	32	32	32	32	32	32	32
R^{2*}	0.59	0.49	0.52	0.13	0.12	0.11	0.12	0.32	0.31

Appendix 10d: Multivariate regressions of 'GDP$_{08-12}$' against GCI 'public institutions' and one additional control variable in developed countries (second row: p-values of two-sided significance tests; number of asterisks: significance levels of 10%*, 5%** and 1%***).

Appendix 11 - Correlations amongst business regulation indices

	HF Business Freedom	Fraser Business Regulation	WGI Regulatory Quality	GCI Competition	Doing Business Summary Index
Heritage Business Freedom	1	**0.74**	**0.83**	**0.75**	**0.91**
Fraser Business Regulation	**0.74**	1	**0.68**	**0.67**	**0.75**
WGI Regulatory Quality	**0.83**	**0.68**	1	**0.86**	**0.90**
GCI Competition	**0.75**	**0.67**	**0.86**	1	**0.86**
Doing Business Summary Index	**0.91**	**0.74**	**0.90**	**0.86**	1

Appendix 11: Correlations amongst business regulation indices within the entire sample (all correlations are significant at conventional significance levels).

Appendix 12 – Scatterplots of 'GDP08-12' against different business regulation indices

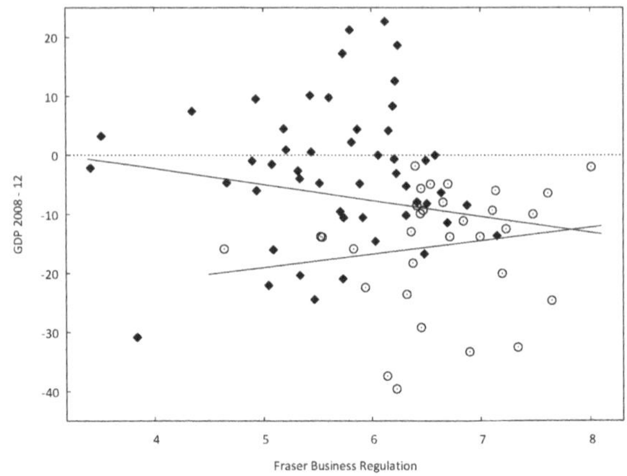

Appendix 12a: Scatterplot of '$GDP_{08\text{-}12}$' against Fraser 'business regulation' (black dots: less developed countries; white circles: developed countries; downward-sloping line: fitted values for the entire sample; upward-sloping line: fitted values for the sub-sample of developed countries).

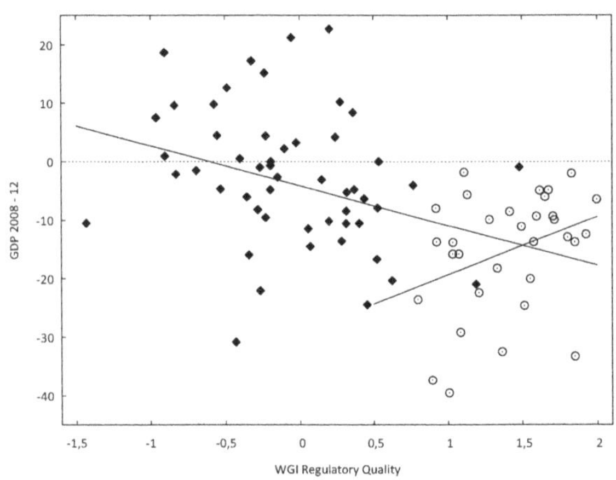

Appendix 12b: Scatterplot of '$GDP_{08\text{-}12}$' against WGI 'regulatory quality' (black dots: less developed countries; white circles: developed countries; downward-sloping line: fitted values for the entire sample; upward-sloping line: fitted values for the sub-sample of developed countries).

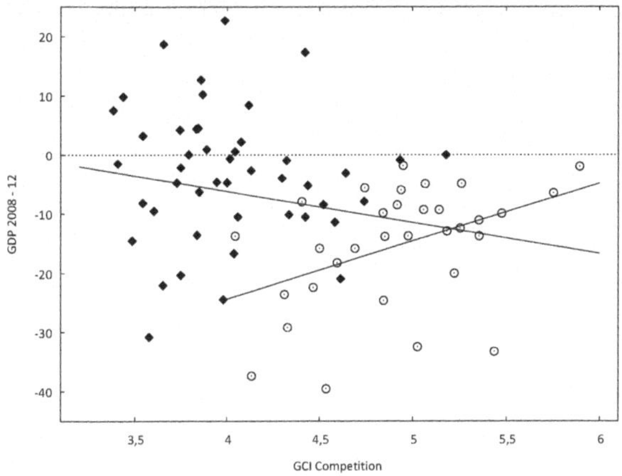

Appendix 12c: Scatterplot of 'GDP_{08-12}' against GCI 'competition' (black dots: less developed countries; white circles: developed countries; downward-sloping line: fitted values for the entire sample; upward-sloping line: fitted values for the sub-sample of developed countries).

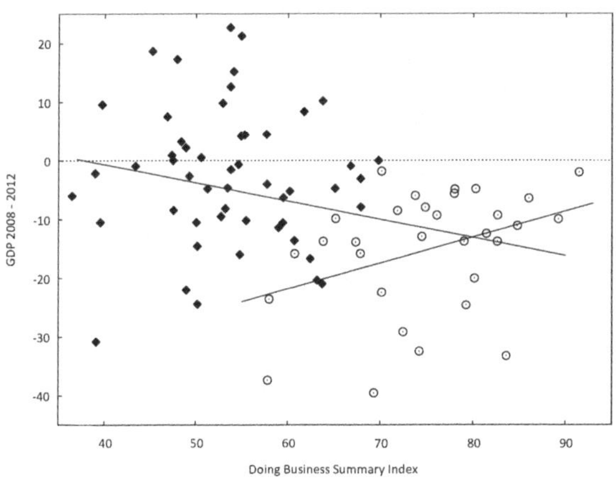

Appendix 12d: Scatterplot of 'GDP_{08-12}' against the 'doing business summary' Index (black dots: less developed countries; white circles: developed countries; downward-sloping line: fitted values for the entire sample; upward-sloping line: fitted values for the sub-sample of developed countries).

Appendix 13 – '$GDP_{08\text{-}09}$' against different business regulation indices in the entire sample

	Dependent Variable: 'GDP_{08-09}'; Sample: All Countries										
	(1)	(2)	(3)	(4)	(5)	(6)	(7)	(8)	(9)	(10)	(11)
Constant	5.22	4.55	8.83	4.24	-0.45	5.04	5.85	4.74	9.04	4.38	0.91
	0.37	0.41	0.16	0.58	0.95	0.42	0.33	0.43	0.11	0.57	0.89
Fraser Business	-1.88	-1.55	-2.37	-1.72	-0.58	-1.85	-1.72	-1.80	-1.82	-0.29	-1.17
Regulation	0.05**	0.09*	0.02**	0.18	0.65	0.07*	0.10	0.07*	0.06*	0.82	0.25
Financial	-3.04									-3.14	-3.09
Vulnerabilities	0.00***									0.00***	0.00***
Increase (Priv.		-0.12									
Cred. / GDP)		0.01**									
Current Acc.			0.22								
Balance / GDP			0.02**								
Economic				-0.75						-1.38	
Development				0.41						0.07*	
GDP					-0.13						
per Capita					0.00***						
International						-0.87				-1.27	-1.05
Linkages						0.18				0.03**	0.07*
Trade /							-0.02				
GDP							0.14				
Industrial								-2.17		-2.36	-2.24
Orientation								0.00***		0.00***	0.00***
Manuf. Exp. /									0.09		
Total Exp.									0.00***		
N	82	82	82	82	82	82	82	82	82	82	82
R^{2*}	0.24	0.23	0.13	0.06	0.13	0.07	0.07	0.15	0.15	0.37	0.35

Appendix 13a: Multivariate regressions of '$GDP_{08\text{-}09}$' against Fraser 'business regulation' and one additional control variable in the entire sample (second row: p-values of two-sided significance tests; number of asterisks: significance levels of 10%*, 5%** and 1%***).

	Dependent Variable: 'GDP08-09'; Sample: All Countries										
	(1)	(2)	(3)	(4)	(5)	(6)	(7)	(8)	(9)	(10)	(11)
Constant	-3.96	-3.06	-2.91	-2.90	-4.17	-3.82	-3.16	-4.01	-1.15	-3.95	-4.34
	0.00***	0.00***	0.00***	0.00***	0.00***	0.00***	0.00***	0.00***	0.37	0.00***	0.00***
WGI Regulatory	-3.89	-3.42	-4.58	-6.01	-5.27	-4.16	-4.13	-3.80	3.68	-3.91	-3.14
Quality	0.00***	0.00***	0.00***	0.00***	0.00***	0.00***	0.00***	0.00***	0.00***	0.01***	0.00***
Financial	-2.85									-2.84	-2.92
Vulnerabilities	0.00***									0.00***	0.00***
Increase (Priv.		-0.10									
Cred. / GDP)		0.02**									
Current Acc.			0.23								
Balance / GDP			0.01***								
Economic				2.08						0.80	
Development				0.07*						0.43	
GDP					0.05						
per Capita					0.48						
International						-0.47				-0.52	-0.68
Linkages						0.42				0.34	0.15
Trade /							-0.01				
GDP							0.47				
Industrial								-1.48		-1.45	-1.64
Orientation								0.01***		0.01**	0.00***
Manuf. Exp. /									-0.06		
Total Exp.									0.01***		
N	84	84	84	84	84	84	84	84	84	84	84
R^{2*}	0.40	0.36	0.32	0.28	0.25	0.25	0.25	0.28	0.28	0.44	0.44

Appendix 13b: Multivariate regressions of 'GDP_{08-09}' against WGI 'regulatory quality' and one additional control variable in the entire sample (second row: p-values of two-sided significance tests; number of asterisks: significance levels of 10%*, 5%** and 1%***).

	Dependent Variable: 'GDP$_{08-09}$'; Sample: All Countries										
	(1)	(2)	(3)	(4)	(5)	(6)	(7)	(8)	(9)	(10)	(11)
Constant	10.25 0.03**	8.27 0.06*	15.84 0.01***	11.56 0.13	1.74 0.80	8.32 0.11	8.84 0.09*	7.27 0.14	9.54 0.05**	1.89 0.82	5.34 0.29
GCI Competition	-3.81 0.00***	-3.05 0.00***	-4.90 0.00***	-4.11 0.02**	-1.47 0.39	-3.37 0.00***	-3.25 0.01***	-3.11 0.01***	-2.96 0.01***	-1.88 0.33	-2.68 0.02**
Financial Vulnerabilities	-3.18 0.00***									-3.18 0.00***	-3.19 0.00***
Increase (Priv. Cred. / GDP)		-0.11 0.01**									
Current Acc. Balance / GDP			0.31 0.00***								
Economic Development				0.34 0.75						-0.59 0.57	
GDP per Capita					-0.10 0.04**						
International Linkages						-0.62 0.34				-0.93 0.10	-0.76 0.16
Trade / GDP							-0.01 0.32				
Industrial Orientation								-1.70 0.01***		-1.93 0.00***	-1.80 0.00***
Manuf. Exp. / Total Exp.									-0.06 0.02**		
N	78	78	78	78	78	78	78	78	78	78	78
R^{2*}	0.31	0.26	0.23	0.09	0.12	0.09	0.09	0.14	0.13	0.36	0.37

Appendix 13c: Multivariate regressions of 'GDP$_{08-09}$' against GCI 'competition' and one additional control variable in the entire sample (second row: p-values of two-sided significance tests; number of asterisks: significance levels of 10%*, 5%** and 1%***).

	Dependent Variable: 'GDP08-09'; Sample: All Countries										
	(1)	(2)	(3)	(4)	(5)	(6)	(7)	(8)	(9)	(10)	(11)
Constant	8.24 0.02**	7.19 0.03**	12.18 0.00***	13.63 0.03**	6.83 0.26	8.42 0.03**	9.08 0.02**	7.15 0.06*	9.93 0.00***	6.28 0.32	5.38 0.13
Doing Business Summary	-0.23 0.00***	-0.19 0.00***	-0.28 0.00***	-0.32 0.00***	-0.20 0.09*	-0.23 0.00***	-0.23 0.00***	-0.21 0.00***	-0.20 0.00***	-0.20 0.05*	-0.18 0.00***
Financial Vulnerabilities	-3.09 0.00***									-3.11 0.00***	-3.12 0.00***
Increase (Priv. Cred. / GDP)		-0.11 0.02**									
Current Acc. Balance / GDP			0.27 0.00***								
Economic Development				1.37 0.25						0.24 0.82	
GDP per Capita					-0.04 0.52						
International Linkages						-0.54 0.41				-0.66 0.23	-0.71 0.14
Trade / GDP							-0.01 0.41				
Industrial Orientation								-1.80 0.00***		-1.83 0.00***	-1.88 0.00***
Manuf. Exp. / Total Exp.									-0.08 0.01***		
N	83	83	83	83	83	83	83	83	83	83	83
R^{2*}	0.36	0.32	0.28	0.19	0.18	0.18	0.18	0.23	0.23	0.41	0.42

Appendix 13d: Multivariate regressions of '$GDP_{08\text{-}09}$' against the 'doing business summary' index and one additional control variable in the entire sample (second row: p-values of two-sided significance tests; number of asterisks: significance levels of 10%*, 5%** and 1%***).

Appendix 14 – 'GDP08-12' against different business regulation indices in the entire sample

	Dependent Variable: 'GDP$_{08-12}$'; Sample: All Countries										
	(1)	(2)	(3)	(4)	(5)	(6)	(7)	(8)	(9)	(10)	(11)
Constant	9.90 0.07*	7.89 0.13	18.60 0.00***	15.16 0.09*	2.18 0.81	12.69 0.04**	13.66 0.04**	10.01 0.10	15.43 0.01**	-0.45 0.95	5.67 0.29
Heritage Business Freedom	-0.25 0.00***	-0.18 0.01***	-0.34 0.00***	-0.32 0.01***	-0.09 0.55	-0.29 0.00***	-0.28 0.00***	-0.25 0.00***	-0.24 0.00***	-0.10 0.30	-0.19 0.01***
Financial Vulnerabilities	-7.16 0.00***									-7.39 0.00***	-7.26 0.00***
Increase (Priv. Cred. / GDP)		-0.27 0.00***									
Current Acc. Balance / GDP			0.66 0.00***								
Economic Development				0.59 0.74						-1.76 0.20	
GDP per Capita					-0.21 0.05*						
International Linkages						-0.70 0.62				-1.20 0.11	-0.97 0.19
Trade / GDP							-0.01 0.54				
Industrial Orientation								-3.69 0.00***		-4.12 0.00***	-3.87 0.00***
Manuf. Exp. / Total Exp.									-0.13 0.02**		
N	84	84	84	84	84	84	84	84	84	84	84
R^{2*}	0.43	0.37	0.32	0.11	0.14	0.07	0.11	0.19	0.16	0.51	0.35

Appendix 14a: Multivariate regressions of 'GDP$_{08-12}$' against Heritage 'business freedom' and one additional control variable in the entire sample (second row: p-values of two-sided significance tests; number of asterisks: significance levels of 10%*, 5%** and 1%***).

	Dependent Variable: 'GDP$_{08-12}$'; Sample: All Countries										
	(1)	(2)	(3)	(4)	(5)	(6)	(7)	(8)	(9)	(10)	(11)
Constant	4.70 0.58	3.17 0.69	14.46 0.10	1.20 0.91	-7.46 0.48	6.82 0.48	7.42 0.43	4.57 0.62	12.20 0.17	-14.52 0.17	-1.91 0.84
Fraser Business Regulation	-2.06 0.13	-1.27 0.31	-3.37 0.02**	-1.48 0.42	0.75 0.69	-2.42 0.12	-2.20 0.17	-2.04 0.18	-2.16 0.15	1.13 0.51	-0.97 0.53
Financial Vulnerabilities	-7.29 0.00***									-7.50 0.00***	-7.37 0.00***
Increase (Priv. Cred. / GDP)		-0.28 0.00***									
Current Acc. Balance / GDP			0.64 0.00***								
Economic Development				-2.15 0.14						-3.29 0.00***	
GDP per Capita					-0.28 0.00***						
International Linkages						-0.84 0.54				-1.74 0.07*	-1.23 0.22
Trade / GDP							-0.02 0.42				
Industrial Orientation								-4.14 0.00***		-4.54 0.00***	-4.27 0.00***
Manuf. Exp. / Total Exp.									-0.15 0.01***		
N	82	82	82	82	82	82	82	82	82	82	82
R^{2*}	0.36	0.33	0.21	0.03	0.14	0.02	0.02	0.12	0.10	0.52	0.47

Appendix 14b: Multivariate regressions of 'GDP$_{08-12}$' against Fraser 'business regulation' and one additional control variable in the entire sample (second row: p-values of two-sided significance tests; number of asterisks: significance levels of 10%*, 5%** and 1%***).

	Dependent Variable: 'GDP$_{08-12}$'; Sample: All Countries										
	(1)	(2)	(3)	(4)	(5)	(6)	(7)	(8)	(9)	(10)	(11)
Constant	-4.61 0.00***	-2.39 0.08*	-1.64 0.25	-2.99 0.07*	-4.01 0.03**	-4.13 0.01***	-4.03 0.09*	-4.62 0.00***	-0.06 0.98	-5.29 0.00***	-7.53 0.00***
WGI Regulatory Quality	-5.82 0.00***	-4.66 0.00***	-7.63 0.00***	-9.07 0.00***	-6.55 0.03**	-6.79 0.00***	-6.79 0.00***	-5.82 0.00***	-5.86 0.00***	-4.47 0.03**	
Financial Vulnerabilities	-6.93 0.00***									-7.07 0.00***	-7.55 0.00***
Increase (Priv. Cred. / GDP)		-0.25 0.00***									
Current Acc. Balance / GDP			0.68 0.00***								
Economic Development				2.74 0.15						-0.09 0.95	-2.83 0.00***
GDP per Capita					-0.01 0.91						
International Linkages						-0.08 0.95				-0.55 0.55	-1.47 0.03**
Trade / GDP							-0.00 0.96				
Industrial Orientation								-2.97 0.01***		-3.30 0.00***	-4.42 0.00***
Manuf. Exp. / Total Exp.									-0.10 0.07*		
N	84	84	84	84	84	84	84	84	84	84	84
R^{2*}	0.50	0.42	0.42	0.22	0.19	0.19	0.19	0.25	0.23	0.54	0.51

Appendix 14c: Multivariate regressions of 'GDP$_{08-12}$' against WGI 'regulatory quality' and one additional control variable in the entire sample (second row: p-values of two-sided significance tests; number of asterisks: significance levels of 10%*, 5%** and 1%***).

	Dependent Variable: 'GDP08-12'; Sample: All Countries										
	(1)	(2)	(3)	(4)	(5)	(6)	(7)	(8)	(9)	(10)	(11)
Constant	15.38 0.04**	10.70 0.13	30.02 0.00***	11.47 0.39	-7.54 0.54	13.82 0.15	13.97 0.14	9.48 0.30	14.08 0.13	-5.13 0.64	8.26 0.31
GCI Competition	-5.40 0.00***	-3.59 0.02**	-8.25 0.00***	-4.49 0.14	0.93 0.76	-5.03 0.02**	-4.90 0.02**	-4.01 0.05*	-4.05 0.05*	-0.66 0.79	-3.74 0.03**
Financial Vulnerabilities	-7.38 0.00***									-7.37 0.00***	-7.41 0.00***
Increase (Priv. Cred. / GDP)		-0.27 0.00***									
Current Acc. Balance / GDP			0.80 0.00***								
Economic Development				-0.70 0.69						-2.30 0.10	
GDP per Capita					-0.27 0.00***						
International Linkages						-0.35 0.80				-1.27 0.16	-0.61 0.48
Trade / GDP							-0.01 0.75				
Industrial Orientation								-3.31 0.01***		-3.95 0.00***	-3.43 0.00***
Manuf. Exp. / Total Exp.									-0.10 0.08*		
N	78	78	78	78	78	78	78	78	78	78	78
R^{2*}	0.44	0.37	0.36	0.05	0.13	0.05	0.05	0.12	0.08	0.36	0.50

Appendix 14d: Multivariate regressions of 'GDP_{08-12}' against GCI 'competition' and one additional control variable in the entire sample (second row: p-values of two-sided significance tests; number of asterisks: significance levels of 10%*, 5%** and 1%***).

	Dependent Variable: 'GDP$_{08-12}$'; Sample: All Countries										
	(1)	(2)	(3)	(4)	(5)	(6)	(7)	(8)	(9)	(10)	(11)
Constant	9.75	7.13	19.98	13.24	-1.61	11.22	11.72	7.69	13.31	-3.18	4.65
	0.07*	0.17	0.00***	0.20	0.87	0.08*	0.08*	0.23	0.04**	0.69	0.38
Doing Business	-0.28	-0.19	-0.41	-0.33	-0.03	-0.30	-0.30	-0.24	-0.23	-0.07	-0.20
Summary	0.00***	0.01**	0.00***	0.04**	0.88	0.00***	0.00***	0.02**	0.03**	0.58	0.01**
Financial	-7.30									-7.46	-7.36
Vulnerabilities	0.00***									0.00***	0.00***
Increase (Priv.		-0.27									
Cred. / GDP)		0.00***									
Current Acc.			0.71								
Balance / GDP			0.00***								
Economic				0.46						-2.07	
Development				0.82						0.18	
GDP					-0.25						
per Capita					0.03**						
International						-0.41				-1.21	-0.77
Linkages						0.77				0.14	0.33
Trade /							-0.01				
GDP							0.69				
Industrial								-3.77		-4.26	-3.90
Orientation								0.00***		0.00***	0.00***
Manuf. Exp. /									-0.15		
Total Exp.									0.01**		
N	83	83	83	83	83	83	83	83	83	83	83
R^{2*}	0.36	0.36	0.32	0.08	0.13	0.08	0.08	0.17	0.15	0.51	0.50

Appendix 14d: Multivariate regressions of 'GDP$_{08-12}$' against the 'doing business summary' index and one additional control variable in the entire sample (second row: p-values of two-sided significance tests; number of asterisks: significance levels of 10%*, 5%** and 1%***).

Appendix 15 – 'GDP$_{10-12}$' against different business regulation indices in developed countries

	Dependent Variable: 'GDP$_{10-12}$'; Sample: Developed Countries								
	(1)	(2)	(3)	(4)	(5)	(6)	(7)	(8)	(9)
Constant	-25.87 0.00***	-29.73 0.00***	-10.35 0.13	-31.07 0.01***	-28.07 0.02**	-25.35 0.02**	-24.47 0.02**	-49.91 0.00***	-51.38 0.00***
Fraser Business Regulation	3.15 0.01***	4.06 0.00***	0.86 0.40	3.98 0.02**	3.53 0.04**	2.97 0.07*	2.56 0.08*	6.41 0.00***	5.26 0.00***
Financial Vulnerabilities	-3.94 0.00***								
Increase (Priv. Cred. / GDP)		-0.13 0.00***							
Current Acc. Balance / GDP			0.51 0.00***						
Economic Development				-0.94 0.48					
GDP per Capita					-0.02 0.78				
International Linkages						0.40 0.63			
Trade / GDP							0.02 0.11		
Industrial Orientation								5.20 0.01**	
Manuf. Exp. / Total Exp.									0.20 0.01***
N	32	32	32	32	32	32	32	32	32
R^{2*}	0.50	0.46	0.49	0.05	0.04	0.05	0.08	0.34	0.40

Appendix 15a: Multivariate regressions of 'GDP$_{10-12}$' against Fraser 'business regulation' and one additional control variable in developed countries (second row: p-values of two-sided significance tests; number of asterisks: significance levels of 10%*, 5%** and 1%***).

	Dependent Variable: 'GDP$_{10-12}$'; Sample: Developed Countries								
	(1)	(2)	(3)	(4)	(5)	(6)	(7)	(8)	(9)
Constant	-12.62 0.02**	-14.32 0.01**	-6.59 0.19	-21.22 0.01***	-17.49 0.01***	-16.51 0.01***	-16.93 0.01***	-26.85 0.00***	-30.59 0.00***
WGI Regulatory Quality	5.38 0.12	8.00 0.02**	1.35 0.69	12.62 0.02**	12.07 0.02**	7.72 0.05**	6.88 0.08*	13.77 0.00***	10.57 0.00***
Financial Vulnerabilities	-3.63 0.00***								
Increase (Priv. Cred. / GDP)		-0.12 0.00***							
Current Acc. Balance / GDP			0.51 0.00***						
Economic Development				-2.34 0.08*					
GDP per Capita					-0.14 0.14				
International Linkages						0.23 0.79			
Trade / GDP							0.01 0.17		
Industrial Orientation								5.19 0.00***	
Manuf. Exp. / Total Exp.									0.18 0.00***
N	32	32	32	32	32	32	32	32	32
R^{2*}	0.48	0.46	0.49	0.17	0.15	0.10	0.13	0.41	0.42

Appendix 15b: Multivariate regressions of 'GDP$_{10-12}$' against WGI 'regulatory quality' and one additional control variable in developed countries (second row: p-values of two-sided significance tests; number of asterisks: significance levels of 10%*, 5%** and 1%***).

	Dependent Variable: 'GDP$_{10-12}$'; Sample: Developed Countries								
	(1)	(2)	(3)	(4)	(5)	(6)	(7)	(8)	(9)
Constant	-32.88 0.04**	-39.00 0.02**	-21.61 0.16	-53.89 0.00***	-50.90 0.00***	-51.76 0.00***	-47.10 0.01***	-62.54 0.00***	-58.92 0.00***
GCI Competition	5.64 0.08*	7.23 0.02**	3.41 0.26	10.07 0.00***	9.76 0.01***	9.39 0.01***	8.35 0.02**	11.23 0.00***	9.07 0.00***
Financial Vulnerabilities	-3.25 0.00***								
Increase (Priv. Cred. / GDP)		-0.10 0.00***							
Current Acc. Balance / GDP			0.45 0.00***						
Economic Development				-1.44 0.18					
GDP per Capita					-0.07 0.33				
International Linkages						-0.46 0.53			
Trade / GDP							0.00 0.69		
Industrial Orientation								4.43 0.00***	
Manuf. Exp. / Total Exp.									0.16 0.00***
N	32	32	32	32	32	32	32	32	32
R^{2*}	0.52	0.51	0.52	0.28	0.26	0.25	0.24	0.51	0.49

Appendix 15c: Multivariate regressions of 'GDP$_{10-12}$' against GCI 'competition' and one additional control variable in developed countries (second row: p-values of two-sided significance tests; number of asterisks: significance levels of 10%*, 5%** and 1%***).

	Dependent Variable: 'GDP10-12'; Sample: Developed Countries								
	(1)	(2)	(3)	(4)	(5)	(6)	(7)	(8)	(9)
Constant	-30.01 0.01**	-34.30 0.01***	-20.98 0.06*	-45.46 0.00***	-39.41 0.01***	-36.57 0.01***	-36.00 0.01***	-56.08 0.00***	-58.99 0.00***
Doing Business Summary	0.34 0.03**	0.42 0.01***	0.22 0.13	0.56 0.01***	0.50 0.01**	0.42 0.02**	0.39 0.02**	0.65 0.00***	0.56 0.00***
Financial Vulnerabilities	-3.51 0.00***								
Increase (Priv. Cred. / GDP)		-0.12 0.00***							
Current Acc. Balance / GDP			0.44 0.00***						
Economic Development				-1.99 0.15					
GDP per Capita					-0.08 0.35				
International Linkages						0.21 0.74			
Trade / GDP							0.01 0.07*		
Industrial Orientation								5.29 0.00***	
Manuf. Exp. / Total Exp.									0.21 0.00***
N	31	31	31	31	31	31	31	31	31
R^{2*}	0.58	0.58	0.54	0.28	0.24	0.21	0.24	0.54	0.57

Appendix 15d: Multivariate regressions of 'GDP_{10-12}' against the 'doing business summary' index and one additional control variable in developed countries (second row: p-values of two-sided significance tests; number of asterisks: significance levels of 10%*, 5%** and 1%***).

Appendix 16 – '$GDP_{08\text{-}12}$' against different business regulation indices in developed countries

	Dependent Variable: '$GDP_{08\text{-}12}$'; Sample: Developed Countries								
	(1)	(2)	(3)	(4)	(5)	(6)	(7)	(8)	(9)
Constant	-32.77 0.01**	-42.41 0.00***	-16.89 0.16	-41.59 0.03**	-40.29 0.02**	-42.15 0.02**	-43.30 0.01**	-58.08 0.00***	-55.88 0.00***
Heritage Business Freedom	0.22 0.14	0.36 0.02**	0.04 0.80	0.31 0.17	0.28 0.23	0.32 0.10*	0.31 0.10*	0.48 0.01**	0.37 0.04**
Financial Vulnerabilities	-6.02 0.00***								
Increase (Priv. Cred. / GDP)		-0.18 0.00***							
Current Acc. Balance / GDP			0.77 0.00***						
Economic Development				0.15 0.96					
GDP per Capita					0.04 0.81				
International Linkages						0.13 0.90			
Trade / GDP							0.02 0.20		
Industrial Orientation								5.10 0.04**	
Manuf. Exp. / Total Exp.									0.17 0.04**
N	32	32	32	32	32	32	32	32	32
R^{2*}	0.56	0.42	0.52	0.04	0.04	0.04	0.05	0.20	0.18

Appendix 16a: Multivariate regressions of '$GDP_{08\text{-}12}$' against Heritage 'business freedom' and one additional control variable in developed countries (second row: p-values of two-sided significance tests; number of asterisks: significance levels of 10%*, 5%** and 1%***).

	Dependent Variable: 'GDP08-12'; Sample: Developed Countries								
	(1)	(2)	(3)	(4)	(5)	(6)	(7)	(8)	(9)
Constant	-28.04 0.01**	-33.60 0.01***	-2.95 0.74	-23.97 0.17	-25.82 0.10	-30.75 0.04**	-28.17 0.04**	-52.34 0.01**	-53.58 0.00***
Fraser Business Regulation	2.07 0.19	3.32 0.05*	-1.64 0.26	1.09 0.70	0.77 0.78	2.33 0.28	1.72 0.39	5.32 0.07*	4.18 0.06*
Financial Vulnerabilities	-6.25 0.00***								
Increase (Priv. Cred. / GDP)		-0.18 0.00***							
Current Acc. Balance / GDP			0.82 0.00***						
Economic Development				1.60 0.55					
GDP per Capita					0.14 0.41				
International Linkages						-0.08 0.95			
Trade / GDP							0.01 0.38		
Industrial Orientation								5.07 0.09*	
Manuf. Exp. / Total Exp.									0.19 0.04**
N	32	32	32	32	32	32	32	32	32
R^{2*}	0.53	0.34	0.53	-0.02	-0.01	-0.04	-0.03	0.10	0.12

Appendix 16b: Multivariate regressions of 'GDP_{08-12}' against Fraser 'business regulation' and one additional control variable in developed countries (second row: p-values of two-sided significance tests; number of asterisks: significance levels of 10%*, 5%** and 1%***).

	Dependent Variable: 'GDP$_{08-12}$'; Sample: Developed Countries								
	(1)	(2)	(3)	(4)	(5)	(6)	(7)	(8)	(9)
Constant	-22.23 0.00***	-25.64 0.00***	-13.11 0.05*	-29.83 0.00***	-29.30 0.00***	-30.63 0.00***	-29.31 0.00***	-40.80 0.00***	-43.75 0.00***
WGI Regulatory Quality	5.56 0.20	9.85 0.02**	-0.55 0.91	10.49 0.09*	9.70 0.12	10.97 0.05**	9.58 0.09*	16.57 0.00***	12.60 0.01**
Financial Vulnerabilities	-5.92 0.00***								
Increase (Priv. Cred. / GDP)		-0.17 0.01***							
Current Acc. Balance / GDP			0.79 0.00***						
Economic Development				-0.28 0.91					
GDP per Capita					0.01 0.96				
International Linkages						-0.64 0.61			
Trade / GDP							0.00 0.74		
Industrial Orientation								6.03 0.01**	
Manuf. Exp. / Total Exp.									0.19 0.01***
N	32	32	32	32	32	32	32	32	32
R^{2*}	0.53	0.34	0.53	-0.02	-0.01	-0.04	-0.03	0.10	0.12

Appendix 16c: Multivariate regressions of 'GDP$_{08-12}$' against WGI 'regulatory quality' and one additional control variable in developed countries (second row: p-values of two-sided significance tests; number of asterisks: significance levels of 10%*, 5%** and 1%***).

	Dependent Variable: 'GDP$_{08-12}$'; Sample: Developed Countries								
	(1)	(2)	(3)	(4)	(5)	(6)	(7)	(8)	(9)
Constant	-36.59 0.05**	-50.18 0.01***	-17.90 0.36	-62.43 0.00***	-62.02 0.00	-74.52 0.00***	-66.35 0.00***	-79.59 0.00***	-74.55 0.00***
GCI Competition	4.50 0.22	7.72 0.03**	0.80 0.84	9.51 0.02**	9.17 0.02**	12.07 0.01***	10.55 0.02**	12.68 0.00***	10.21 0.01***
Financial Vulnerabilities	-5.69 0.00***								
Increase (Priv. Cred. / GDP)		-0.15 0.02**							
Current Acc. Balance / GDP			0.76 0.00***						
Economic Development				0.28 0.90					
GDP per Capita					0.04 0.78				
International Linkages						-1.44 0.19			
Trade / GDP							-0.01 0.50		
Industrial Orientation								4.98 0.01**	
Manuf. Exp. / Total Exp.									0.16 0.02**
N	32	32	32	32	32	32	32	32	32
R^{2*}	0.55	0.40	0.52	0.13	0.13	0.16	0.13	0.29	0.26

Appendix 16d: Multivariate regressions of 'GDP$_{08-12}$' against GCI 'competition' and one additional control variable in developed countries (second row: p-values of two-sided significance tests; number of asterisks: significance levels of 10%*, 5%** and 1%***).

	Dependent Variable: 'GDP$_{08-12}$'; Sample: Developed Countries								
	(1)	(2)	(3)	(4)	(5)	(6)	(7)	(8)	(9)
Constant	-35.96 0.01***	-44.01 0.00***	-20.38 0.14	-47.73 0.00***	-46.92 0.00***	-50.02 0.00***	-47.67 0.00***	-69.44 0.00***	-72.36 0.00***
Doing Business Summary	0.29 0.09*	0.43 0.01***	0.09 0.64	0.43 0.05*	0.39 0.05*	0.46 0.02**	0.42 0.03**	0.69 0.00***	0.58 0.00***
Financial Vulnerabilities	-5.89 0.00***								
Increase (Priv. Cred. / GDP)		-0.17 0.01***							
Current Acc. Balance / GDP			0.76 0.00***						
Economic Development				0.13 0.96					
GDP per Capita					0.05 0.74				
International Linkages						-0.47 0.63			
Trade / GDP							0.01 0.58		
Industrial Orientation								5.98 0.01**	
Manuf. Exp. / Total Exp.									0.23 0.00***
N	31	31	31	31	31	31	31	31	31
R^{2*}	0.57	0.42	0.52	0.07	0.08	0.08	0.08	0.28	0.28

Appendix 16e: Multivariate regressions of 'GDP$_{08-12}$' against the 'doing business summary' index and one additional control variable in developed countries (second row: p-values of two-sided significance tests; number of asterisks: significance levels of 10%*, 5%** and 1%***).

Appendix 17 – Correlations amongst labor regulation variables

	Heritage Labor Freedom	Fraser Labor Regulation	GCI Labor Flexibility	FRDB Gross Replacement Rate	OECD Net Replacement Rate
Heritage Labor Freedom	1	**0.84**	**0.69**	0.12	0.19
Fraser Labor Regulation	**0.84**	1	**0.81**	-0.02	0.10
GCI Labor Flexibility	**0.69**	**0.81**	1	-0.18	0.09
FRDB Gross Replacement Rate	0.12	-0.02	-0.18	1	**0.49**
OECD Net Replacement Rate	0.19	0.10	0.09	**0.49**	1

Appendix 17: Correlations amongst labor regulation indices within the entire sample (significant correlations at conventional significance levels are bold).

Appendix 18 – Scatterplots of '$GDP_{08\text{-}12}$' against different labor regulation variables

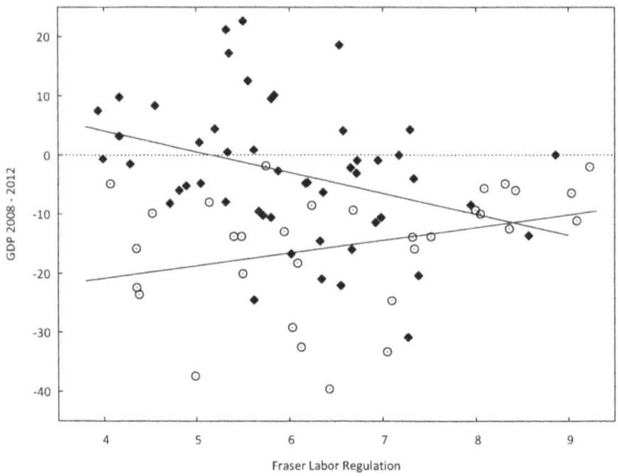

Appendix 18a: Scatterplot of '$GDP_{08\text{-}12}$' against Fraser 'labor regulation' (black dots: less developed countries; white circles: developed countries; downward-sloping line: fitted values for the sub-sample of emerging and developing countries; upward-sloping line: fitted values for the sub-sample of developed countries).

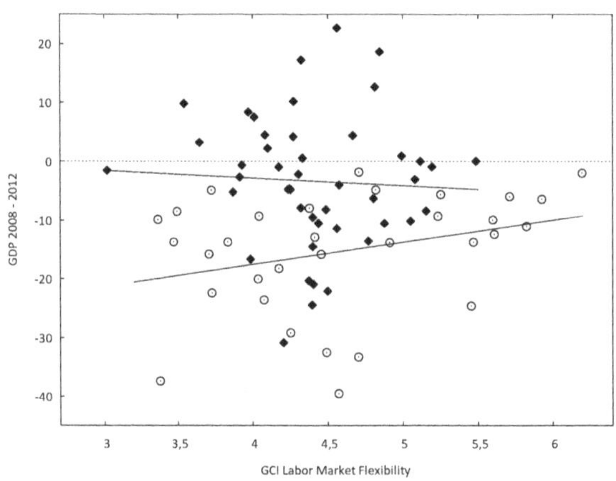

Appendix 18b: Scatterplot of '$GDP_{08\text{-}12}$' against GCI 'labor flexibility' (black dots: less developed countries; white circles: developed countries; downward-sloping line: fitted values for the sub-sample of emerging and developing countries; upward-sloping line: fitted values for the sub-sample of developed countries).

Appendix 19 - 'GDP$_{10-12}$' against different labor regulation indices in developed countries

	Dependent Variable: 'GDP$_{10-12}$'; Sample: Developed Countries								
	(1)	(2)	(3)	(4)	(5)	(6)	(7)	(8)	(9)
Constant	-13.39 0.01***	-14.06 0.01***	-10.98 0.01**	-18.02 0.01***	-17.76 0.01***	-17.17 0.01***	-17.45 0.01***	-24.11 0.00***	-30.02 0.00***
Fraser Labor Regulation	1.27 0.05*	1.65 0.02**	0.95 0.09*	1.96 0.03**	1.84 0.04**	1.75 0.03**	1.56 0.06*	2.58 0.00***	2.26 0.00***
Financial Vulnerabilities	-3.64 0.00***								
Increase (Priv. Cred. / GDP)		-0.12 0.00***							
Current Acc. Balance / GDP			0.49 0.00***						
Economic Development				-0.57 0.63					
GDP per Capita					-0.00 0.99				
International Linkages						0.28 0.70			
Trade / GDP							0.01 0.15		
Industrial Orientation								4.14 0.01***	
Manuf. Exp. / Total Exp.									0.17 0.00***
N	32	32	32	32	32	32	32	32	32
R^{2*}	0.48	0.43	0.52	0.11	0.10	0.10	0.12	0.33	0.39

Appendix 19a: Multivariate regressions of 'GDP$_{10-12}$' against Fraser 'labor regulation' and one additional control variable in developed countries (second row: p-values of two-sided significance tests; number of asterisks: significance levels of 10%*, 5%** and 1%***).

	Dependent Variable: 'GDP$_{10-12}$'; Sample: Developed Countries								
	(1)	(2)	(3)	(4)	(5)	(6)	(7)	(8)	(9)
Constant	-18.63 0.01***	-19.74 0.01***	-13.19 0.02**	-22.42 0.01**	-21.73 0.02**	-20.98 0.02**	-20.77 0.02**	-29.40 0.00***	-35.51 0.00***
GCI Labor Flexibility	2.96 0.02**	3.64 0.01**	1.84 0.10*	3.80 0.04**	3.46 0.05*	3.33 0.06*	2.97 0.08*	4.85 0.01***	4.37 0.00***
Financial Vulnerabilities	-3.78 0.00***								
Increase (Priv. Cred. / GDP)		-0.12 0.00***							
Current Acc. Balance / GDP			0.49 0.00***						
Economic Development				-0.70 0.57					
GDP per Capita					0.01 0.95				
International Linkages						0.24 0.75			
Trade / GDP							0.01 0.18		
Industrial Orientation								4.14 0.01**	
Manuf. Exp. / Total Exp.									0.18 0.00***
N	32	32	32	32	32	32	32	32	32
R^{2*}	0.53	0.49	0.53	0.11	0.11	0.11	0.13	0.33	0.41

Appendix 19b: Multivariate regressions of 'GDP$_{10-12}$' against GCI 'labor flexibility' and one additional control variable in developed countries (second row: p-values of two-sided significance tests; number of asterisks: significance levels of 10%*, 5%** and 1%***).

Appendix 20 - 'GDP_{08-12}' against different labor regulation indices in developed countries

	Dependent Variable: 'GDP_{08-12}'; Sample: Developed Countries								
	(1)	(2)	(3)	(4)	(5)	(6)	(7)	(8)	(9)
Constant	-24.30 0.00***	-26.27 0.00***	-21.53 0.00***	-31.09 0.00***	-32.76 0.00***	-31.93 0.00***	-31.75 0.00***	-40.57 0.00***	-48.26 0.00***
Heritage Labor Freedom	0.14 0.05**	0.21 0.00***	0.11 0.19	0.22 0.02**	0.21 0.02**	0.24 0.01***	0.23 0.01**	0.34 0.00***	0.31 0.00***
Financial Vulnerabilities	-5.83 0.00***								
Increase (Priv. Cred. / GDP)		-0.16 0.02**							
Current Acc. Balance / GDP			0.73 0.00***						
Economic Development				0.56 0.80					
GDP per Capita					0.08 0.60				
International Linkages						-0.32 0.75			
Trade / GDP							0.01 0.50		
Industrial Orientation								5.44 0.00***	
Manuf. Exp. / Total Exp.									0.21 0.00***
N	32	32	32	32	32	32	32	32	32
R^{2*}	0.57	0.41	0.55	0.09	0.10	0.09	0.10	0.28	0.30

Appendix 20a: Multivariate regressions of 'GDP_{08-12}' against Heritage 'labor freedom' and one additional control variable in developed countries (second row: p-values of two-sided significance tests; number of asterisks: significance levels of 10%*, 5%** and 1%***).

	Dependent Variable: 'GDP08–12'; Sample: Developed Countries								
	(1)	(2)	(3)	(4)	(5)	(6)	(7)	(8)	(9)
Constant	-22.37 0.00***	-24.31 0.00***	-19.12 0.00***	-28.93 0.00***	-31.58 0.00***	-30.48 0.00***	-29.38 0.00***	-36.70 0.00***	-42.30 0.00***
Fraser Labor Regulation	1.21 0.13	1.89 0.02**	0.78 0.35	1.92 0.06*	1.85 0.07*	2.31 0.02**	2.06 0.04**	2.99 0.00***	2.58 0.01***
Financial Vulnerabilities	-5.96 0.00***								
Increase (Priv. Cred. / GDP)		-0.16 0.01***							
Current Acc. Balance / GDP			0.75 0.00***						
Economic Development				1.07 0.63					
GDP per Capita					0.11 0.48				
International Linkages						-0.51 0.63			
Trade / GDP							0.00 0.74		
Industrial Orientation								4.69 0.02**	
Manuf. Exp. / Total Exp.									0.18 0.01**
N	32	32	32	32	32	32	32	32	32
R^{2*}	0.55	0.37	0.53	0.06	0.07	0.05	0.04	0.19	0.20

Appendix 20b: Multivariate regressions of 'GDP_{08-12}' against Fraser 'labor regulation' and one additional control variable in developed countries (second row: p-values of two-sided significance tests; number of asterisks: significance levels of 10%*, 5%** and 1%***).

	Dependent Variable: 'GDP08–12'; Sample: Developed Countries								
	(1)	(2)	(3)	(4)	(5)	(6)	(7)	(8)	(9)
Constant	-27.77 0.00***	-29.97 0.00***	-19.49 0.01***	-31.42 0.00***	-34.50 0.00***	-33.96 0.00***	-32.29 0.00***	-41.20 0.00***	-46.94 0.00***
GCI Labor Flexibility	2.91 0.05*	3.97 0.01**	1.21 0.39	3.29 0.11	3.22 0.09*	4.07 0.05**	3.57 0.07*	5.27 0.00***	4.67 0.00***
Financial Vulnerabilities	-6.08 0.00***								
Increase (Priv. Cred. / GDP)		-0.17 0.00***							
Current Acc. Balance / GDP			0.75 0.00***						
Economic Development				1.05 0.66					
GDP per Capita					0.12 0.45				
International Linkages						-0.50 0.65			
Trade / GDP							0.00 0.73		
Industrial Orientation								4.58 0.05**	
Manuf. Exp. / Total Exp.									0.18 0.02**
N	32	32	32	32	32	32	32	32	32
R^{2*}	0.57	0.39	0.53	0.04	0.06	0.04	0.03	0.17	0.19

Appendix 20c: Multivariate regressions of 'GDP_{08-12}' against GCI 'labor flexibility' and one additional control variable in the developed countries (second row: p-values of two-sided significance tests; number of asterisks: significance levels of 10%*, 5%** and 1%***).

Appendix 21 – 'GDP$_{08\text{-}09}$' and 'GDP$_{10\text{-}12}$' against gross replacement rates in the entire sample

	Dependent Variable: 'GDP$_{08\text{-}09}$'; Sample: All Countries										
	(1)	(2)	(3)	(4)	(5)	(6)	(7)	(8)	(9)	(10)	(11)
Constant	-4.65	-3.33	-3.40	-4.16	-3.35	-4.00	-1.71	-4.66	-0.60	-6.25	-5.15
	0.00***	0.00***	0.00***	0.00***	0.00***	0.00***	0.18	0.00***	0.67	0.00***	0.00***
Gross Replace-	-11.15	-6.50	-14.52	-13.26	-5.02	-14.69	-14.13	-10.07	-9.64	-0.29	-8.19
ment Rates	0.01***	0.10*	0.00***	0.01**	0.32	0.00***	0.00***	0.01***	0.01***	0.95	0.05**
Financial	-3.34									-3.85	-3.24
Vulnerabilities	0.01**									0.01***	0.01**
Increase (Priv.		-0.18									
Cred. / GDP)		0.00***									
Current Acc.			0.22								
Balance / GDP			0.08*								
Economic				-0.23						-2.02	
Development				0.83						0.00***	
GDP					-0.11						
per Capita					0.02**						
International						-1.48				-1.36	-1.47
Linkages						0.01***				0.00***	0.01***
Trade /							-0.03				
GDP							0.01***				
Industrial								-2.16		-2.08	-1.97
Orientation								0.00***		0.00***	0.00***
Manuf. Exp. /									-0.09		
Total Exp.									0.00***		
N	71	71	71	71	71	71	71	71	71	71	71
R^{2*}	0.27	0.28	0.15	0.08	0.13	0.13	0.13	0.16	0.15	0.40	0.37

Appendix 21a: Multivariate regressions of 'GDP$_{08\text{-}09}$' against 'gross replacement rates' and one additional control variable in the entire sample (second row: p-values of two-sided significance tests; number of asterisks: significance levels of 10%*, 5%** and 1%***).

	Dependent Variable: 'GDP$_{10-12}$'; Sample: All Countries										
	(1)	(2)	(3)	(4)	(5)	(6)	(7)	(8)	(9)	(10)	(11)
Constant	0.43	2.11	2.55	1.91	1.18	1.24	1.77	0.80	2.30	-0.32	-2.05
	0.65	0.02**	0.00***	0.10	0.29	0.24	0.25	0.41	0.29	0.74	0.00***
Gross Replace-	-15.30	-9.83	-20.08	-24.24	-19.75	-19.35	-19.18	-16.38	-17.79	-10.17	
ment Rates	0.00***	0.00***	0.00***	0.00***	0.00***	0.00***	0.00***	0.00***	0.00***	0.02**	
Financial	-4.42									-4.57	-4.77
Vulnerabilities	0.00***									0.00***	0.00***
Increase (Priv.		-0.22									
Cred. / GDP)		0.00***									
Current Acc.			0.45								
Balance / GDP			0.00***								
Economic				1.44						-0.73	-1.32
Development				0.26						0.39	0.04**
GDP					0.01						
per Capita					0.90						
International						-0.42					
Linkages						0.60					
Trade /							-0.01				
GDP							0.64				
Industrial								-1.50		-1.31	-1.99
Orientation								0.03**		0.02**	0.00***
Manuf. Exp. /									-0.03		
Total Exp.									0.48		
N	71	71	71	71	71	71	71	71	71	71	71
R^{2*}	0.45	0.44	0.43	0.17	0.15	0.15	0.15	0.18	0.16	0.47	0.44

Appendix 21b: Multivariate regressions of 'GDP$_{10-12}$' against 'gross replacement rates' and one additional control variable in the entire sample (second row: p-values of two-sided significance tests; number of asterisks: significance levels of 10%*, 5%** and 1%***).

Appendix 22 – 'GDP$_{08-12}$', 'GDP$_{08-09}$' and 'GDP$_{10-12}$' against gross replacement rates in less developed countries

	Dependent Variable: 'GDP$_{08-12}$'; Sample: Emerging and Developing Countries								
	(1)	(2)	(3)	(4)	(5)	(6)	(7)	(8)	(9)
Constant	0.09 0.96	2.53 0.14	2.98 0.07*	9.03 0.00***	2.95 0.19	0.56 0.75	9.20 0.00***	-0.47 0.76	7.10 0.03**
Gross Replacement Rates	-47.95 0.01***	-40.30 0.02**	-51.83 0.00***	-65.08 0.00***	-55.37 0.01***	-59.25 0.00***	-56.75 0.00***	-50.41 0.00***	-50.17 0.00***
Financial Vulnerabilities	-6.05 0.01***								
Increase (Priv. Cred. / GDP)		-0.40 0.00***							
Current Acc. Balance / GDP			0.53 0.00***						
Economic Development				13.09 0.00***					
GDP per Capita					-0.44 0.35				
International Linkages						-5.94 0.00***			
Trade / GDP							-0.10 0.00***		
Industrial Orientation								-4.32 0.00***	
Manuf. Exp. / Total Exp.									-0.17 0.01**
N	43	43	43	43	43	43	43	43	43
R^{2*}	0.45	0.46	0.36	0.38	0.24	0.31	0.34	0.37	0.33

Appendix 22a: Multivariate regressions of 'GDP$_{08-12}$' against 'gross replacement rates' and one additional control variable in emerging and developing countries (second row: p-values of two-sided significance tests; number of asterisks: significance levels of 10%*, 5%** and 1%***).

	Dependent Variable: 'GDP08–09'; Sample: Emerging and Developing Countries								
	(1)	(2)	(3)	(4)	(5)	(6)	(7)	(8)	(9)
Constant	-1.85 0.06*	-0.94 0.34	-1.01 0.27	0.91 0.52	0.26 0.81	-1.71 0.07*	1.60 0.32	-2.24 0.02**	1.35 0.40
Gross Replacement Rates	-24.26 0.04**	-20.34 0.05*	-26.82 0.04**	-30.15 0.01***	-21.10 0.15	-28.15 0.02**	-27.17 0.02**	-23.98 0.03**	-23.40 0.04**
Financial Vulnerabilities	-2.12 0.06*								
Increase (Priv. Cred. / GDP)		-0.16 0.01**							
Current Acc. Balance / GDP			0.13 0.23						
Economic Development				3.94 0.05*					
GDP per Capita					-0.51 0.07*				
International Linkages						-2.25 0.05*			
Trade / GDP							-0.04 0.02**		
Industrial Orientation								-1.93 0.01***	
Manuf. Exp. / Total Exp.									-0.08 0.02**
N	43	43	43	43	43	43	43	43	43
R^{2*}	0.26	0.30	0.19	0.21	0.23	0.20	0.22	0.26	0.25

Appendix 22b: Multivariate regressions of 'GDP_{08-09}' against 'gross replacement rates' and one additional control variable in emerging and developing countries (second row: p-values of two-sided significance tests; number of asterisks: significance levels of 10%*, 5%** and 1%***).

	Dependent Variable: 'GDP$_{10-12}$'; Sample: Emerging and Developing Countries								
	(1)	(2)	(3)	(4)	(5)	(6)	(7)	(8)	(9)
Constant	1.88 0.10	3.45 0.00***	3.93 0.00***	8.36 0.00***	2.55 0.10	2.21 0.07*	7.69 0.00***	1.75 0.12	5.65 0.01**
Gross Replacement Rates	-25.88 0.01**	-22.21 0.06*	-27.18 0.01***	-37.47 0.00***	-37.23 0.00***	-33.46 0.00***	-31.94 0.00***	-28.93 0.00***	-29.37 0.00***
Financial Vulnerabilities	-4.03 0.00***								
Increase (Priv. Cred. / GDP)		-0.24 0.00***							
Current Acc. Balance / GDP			0.42 0.00***						
Economic Development				9.63 0.00***					
GDP per Capita					0.10 0.75				
International Linkages						-3.86 0.02**			
Trade / GDP							-0.06 0.03**		
Industrial Orientation								-2.37 0.01***	
Manuf. Exp. / Total Exp.									-0.09 0.06*
N	43	43	43	43	43	43	43	43	43
R^{2*}	0.42	0.38	0.38	0.39	0.17	0.26	0.28	0.28	0.24

Appendix 22c: Multivariate regressions of 'GDP$_{10-12}$' against 'gross replacement rates' and one additional control variable in emerging and developing countries (second row: p-values of two-sided significance tests; number of asterisks: significance levels of 10%*, 5%** and 1%***).

Appendix 23 – 'GDP_{08-09}' against gross replacement rates in developed countries

	Dependent Variable: 'GDP_{08-09}'; Sample: Developed Countries								
	(1)	(2)	(3)	(4)	(5)	(6)	(7)	(8)	(9)
Constant	-13.89 0.00***	-11.84 0.00***	-12.82 0.00***	-14.30 0.00***	-17.43 0.00***	-13.04 0.00***	-13.41 0.00***	-13.61 0.00***	-16.00 0.01***
Gross Replacement Rate	12.83 0.01**	14.66 0.02**	9.95 0.05**	6.17 0.17	5.38 0.26	9.67 0.12	10.49 0.11	10.21 0.09*	10.43 0.08*
Financial Vulnerabilities	-4.46 0.00***								
Increase (Priv. Cred. / GDP)		-0.15 0.00***							
Current Acc. Balance / GDP			0.37 0.01**						
Economic Development				2.33 0.26					
GDP per Capita					0.15 0.26				
International Linkages						-0.29 0.69			
Trade / GDP							0.00 0.93		
Industrial Orientation								0.93 0.60	
Manuf. Exp. / Total Exp.									0.05 0.44
N	28	28	28	28	28	28	28	28	28
R^{2*}	0.50	0.33	0.31	0.10	0.08	0.00	0.00	0.01	0.02

Appendix 23: Multivariate regressions of 'GDP_{08-09}' against 'gross replacement rates' and one additional control variable in developed countries (second row: p-values of two-sided significance tests; number of asterisks: significance levels of 10%*, 5%** and 1%***).

Appendix 24 – Construction of a summary index based on data from the Banking Regulation and Supervision Database

The data for the index construction is taken from the 2007 survey (3rd wave) on bank regulation provided by the Bank Regulation and Supervision Database (Barth et al., 2013). Overall, I use one raw measure and five indices from the database. For the five indices I use the 'Average Scaled Indices'. I rescale each index to take values between 0 and 1. Values of 0 indicate the strictest regulation (or the maximum government involvement) within the sample and values of 1 indicate the least strict regulation (or the minimum government involvement) within the sample. After rescaling each of the six original measure, I calculate simple averages. High values of the newly constructed index indicate little government involvement (high financial freedom) and low values indicate high government involvement (little financial freedom).

First, the raw measure is labelled 'Government Banks' (index IX.IV). It measures the fraction of the banking system's assets that are in banks which are 50 % or more government-owned. I rescale this measure to take values of 1 when none of a countries assets are in government-owned banks (lowest government involvement in a variety of counties) and 0 when 75.2 % of a country's assets are in government-owned banks (highest government involvement in Belarus).

Second, I use the index labelled 'Entry into Banking Requirements' (index III.II). The original index can take values between 0 and 8, high values indicating more entry restrictions. I rescale this index to take values of 1 when the original index is 3 (least stringent entry restrictions in Cyprus and Israel) and values of 0 when the original index is 8 (most stringent entry restrictions in a variety of countries).

Third, I use the index labelled 'Overall Restrictions on Banking Activities (index I.IV). The original index can take values between 3 and 12, high values indicating more activity restrictions. I rescale this index to take values of 1 when the original index is 3 (lowest activity restrictions in Hong Kong and the UK) and 0 when the original index is 12 (strictest activity restrictions in Dominican Republic, Indonesia and Ethiopia).

Fourth, I use the index labelled 'Private Monitoring' (index VII.VI). The original index can take values between 0 and 12, high values indicating strong incentives for private monitoring, for example in terms of obligatory transparency obligations for banks or obligatory external auditing. I rescale this index to take values of 1 when the original index is 4 (lowest incentives for private monitoring in Ghana and Uganda) and 0 when the original index is 11 (highest incentives for private monitoring in China, Korea and the Netherlands).

Fifth, I use the index labelled 'Official Supervisory Power' (index V.I). The original index can take values between 0 and 16, high values indicating strong supervisory powers for public agencies. I rescale this index to take values of 1 when the original variable is 5 (lowest supervisory powers in Botswana) and 0 when the original variable is 16 (strongest supervisory powers in Indonesia).

Sixth and finally, I use the index labelled 'Capital Regulatory Index' (index IV.III). The original index can take values between 0 and 10, high values indicating strict capital requirements. I rescale this index to take values of 1 when the original variable is 1 (lowest stringency of capital regulations in Cameroon) and 0 when the original variable is 10 (highest stringency of capital regulations in Hungary).

Appendix 25 – Correlations amongst financial regulation variables

	Fraser Credit Market Regulation	BRS Summary Index	Heritage Financial Freedom
Fraser Credit Market Regulation	1	**0.53**	**0.67**
BRS Summary Index	**0.53**	1	**0.48**
Heritage Financial Freedom	**0.67**	**0.48**	1

Appendix 25: Correlations amongst financial regulation indices within the entire sample (all correlations are significant at conventional significance levels).

Appendix 26 – Scatterplots of 'GDP_{08-12}' against different financial regulation variables

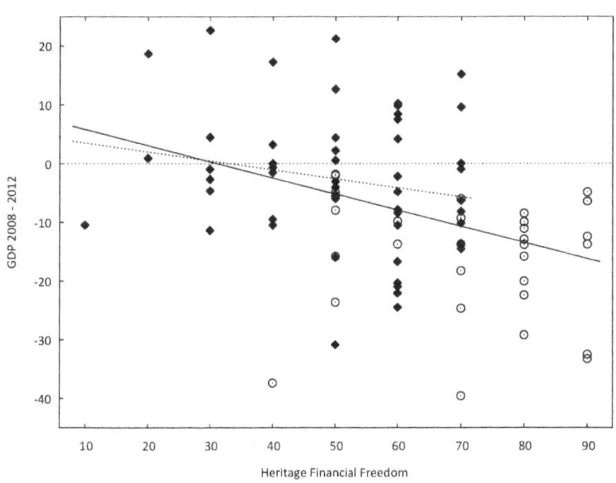

Appendix 26a: Scatterplot of 'GDP_{08-12}' against Heritage 'financial freedom' (black dots: less developed countries; white circles: developed countries; dotted line: fitted values for sub-sample of emerging and developing countries; continuous line: fitted values for the entire sample).

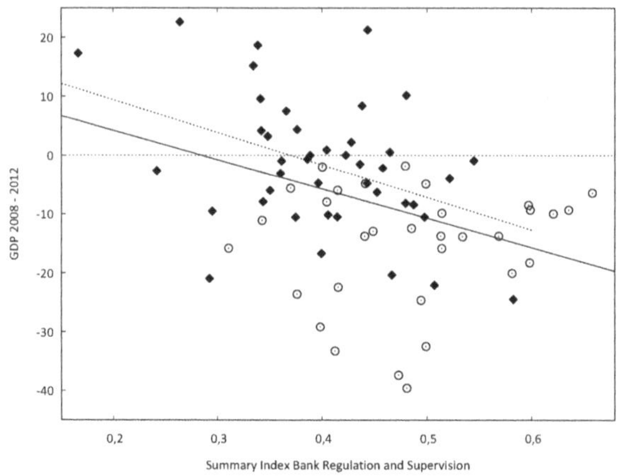

Appendix 26b: Scatterplot of 'GDP_{08-12}' against the 'bank regulation and supervision summary' index (black dots: less developed countries; white circles: developed countries; dotted line: fitted values for sub-sample of emerging and developing countries; continuous line: fitted values for the entire sample).

Appendix 27 – 'GDP$_{08\text{-}12}$' against different financial regulation indices in the entire sample

	Dependent Variable: 'GDP$_{08\text{-}12}$'; Sample: All Countries								
	(1)	(2)	(3)	(4)	(5)	(6)	(7)	(8)	(9)
Constant	4.18 0.33	4.08 0.33	8.78 0.05**	7.41 0.17	5.69 0.25	8.21 0.08*	9.39 0.06*	9.29 0.04**	15.99 0.01***
Heritage Financial Freedom	-0.20 0.00***	-0.15 0.04**	-0.25 0.00***	-0.26 0.00***	-0.17 0.07*	-0.27 0.00***	-0.26 0.00***	-0.29 0.00***	-0.27 0.00***
Financial Vulnerabilities	6.85 0.00***								
Increase (Priv. Cred. / GDP)		-0.26 0.00***							
Current Acc. Balance / GDP			0.54 0.00***						
Economic Development				-0.77 0.56					
GDP per Capita					-0.18 0.02**				
International Linkages						-0.56 0.59			
Trade / GDP							-0.02 0.43		
Industrial Orientation								-4.67 0.00***	
Manuf. Exp. / Total Exp.									-0.17 0.00***
N	84	84	84	84	84	84	84	84	84
R^{2*}	0.42	0.37	0.27	0.13	0.18	0.13	0.13	0.27	0.23

Appendix 27a: Multivariate regressions of 'GDP$_{08\text{-}12}$' against Heritage 'financial freedom' and one additional control variable in the entire sample (second row: p-values of two-sided significance tests; number of asterisks: significance levels of 10%*, 5%** and 1%***).

	Dependent Variable: 'GDP08–12'; Sample: All Countries								
	(1)	(2)	(3)	(4)	(5)	(6)	(7)	(8)	(9)
Constant	10.16 0.03**	13.27 0.01**	15.30 0.01**	11.78 0.08*	10.15 0.13	13.55 0.04**	14.42 0.03**	13.09 0.02**	19.08 0.00***
BRS Summary Index	-41.64 0.00***	-40.64 0.00***	-49.00 0.00***	-43.82 0.00***	-31.30 0.05*	-48.39 0.00***	-47.78 0.00***	-47.15 0.00***	-46.04 0.00***
Financial Vulnerabilities	-8.04 0.00***								
Increase (Priv. Cred. / GDP)		-0.27 0.00***							
Current Acc. Balance / GDP			0.58 0.00***						
Economic Development				-2.17 0.10					
GDP per Capita					-0.22 0.00***				
International Linkages						-0.61 0.66			
Trade / GDP							-0.01 0.60		
Industrial Orientation								-3.58 0.00***	
Manuf. Exp. / Total Exp.									-0.14 0.01**
N	74	74	74	74	74	74	74	74	74
R^{2*}	0.50	0.44	0.28	0.14	0.21	0.12	0.12	0.19	0.19

Appendix 27b: Multivariate regressions of '$GDP_{08\text{-}12}$' against the 'bank regulation and supervision summary' index and one additional control variable in the entire sample (second row: p-values of two-sided significance tests; number of asterisks: significance levels of 10%*, 5%** and 1%***).

Appendix 28 – 'GDP$_{08-09}$' against different financial regulation indices in the entire sample

	Dependent Variable: 'GDP$_{08-09}$'; Sample: All Countries								
	(1)	(2)	(3)	(4)	(5)	(6)	(7)	(8)	(9)
Constant	2.44 0.25	2.39 0.28	4.27 0.06*	3.81 0.20	2.79 0.29	3.73 0.10*	5.06 0.04**	4.61 0.04**	8.94 0.00***
Heritage Financial Freedom	-0.14 0.00***	-0.12 0.00***	-0.17 0.00***	-0.17 0.00***	-0.12 0.03**	-0.16 0.00***	-0.16 0.00***	-0.18 0.00***	-0.17 0.00***
Financial Vulnerabilities	-2.76 0.00***								
Increase (Priv. Cred. / GDP)		-0.11 0.02**							
Current Acc. Balance / GDP			0.15 0.10						
Economic Development				-0.27 0.74					
GDP per Capita					-0.09 0.04**				
International Linkages						-0.77 0.15			
Trade / GDP							-0.02 0.11		
Industrial Orientation								-2.58 0.00***	
Manuf. Exp. / Total Exp.									-0.11 0.00***
N	84	84	84	84	84	84	84	84	84
R^{2*}	0.30	0.28	0.19	0.16	0.20	0.17	0.18	0.29	0.29

Appendix 28a: Multivariate regressions of 'GDP$_{08-09}$' against Heritage 'financial freedom' and one additional control variable in the entire sample (second row: p-values of two-sided significance tests; number of asterisks: significance levels of 10%*, 5%** and 1%***).

	Dependent Variable: 'GDP08-09'; Sample: All Countries								
	(1)	(2)	(3)	(4)	(5)	(6)	(7)	(8)	(9)
Constant	18.11 0.00***	18.82 0.00***	24.16 0.00***	22.38 0.00***	18.82 0.00***	22.80 0.00***	22.98 0.00***	20.83 0.00***	23.22 0.00***
Fraser Credit Market Regulation	-2.73 0.00***	-2.68 0.00***	-3.35 0.00***	-3.21 0.00***	-2.66 0.00***	-3.26 0.00***	-3.21 0.00***	-3.04 0.00***	-2.94 0.00***
Financial Vulnerabilities	-2.50 0.01***								
Increase (Priv. Cred. / GDP)		-0.10 0.01**							
Current Acc. Balance / GDP			0.19 0.03**						
Economic Development				-0.46 0.51					
GDP per Capita					-0.08 0.02**				
International Linkages						-0.33 0.52			
Trade / GDP							-0.01 0.43		
Industrial Orientation								-1.88 0.00***	
Manuf. Exp. / Total Exp.									-0.07 0.00***
N	82	82	82	82	82	82	82	82	82
R^{2*}	0.33	0.33	0.26	0.21	0.24	0.21	0.21	0.28	0.26

Appendix 28b: Multivariate regressions of 'GDP_{08-09}' against Fraser 'credit market regulation' and one additional control variable in the entire sample (second row: p-values of two-sided significance tests; number of asterisks: significance levels of 10%*, 5%** and 1%***).

	Dependent Variable: 'GDP$_{08-09}$'; Sample: All Countries								
	(1)	(2)	(3)	(4)	(5)	(6)	(7)	(8)	(9)
Constant	4.38 0.10	5.68 0.05**	6.40 0.05*	4.77 0.17	3.84 0.26	5.17 0.14	6.43 0.07*	5.46 0.07*	9.43 0.01***
BRS Summary Index	-24.12 0.00***	-23.56 0.00***	-27.33 0.00***	-24.32 0.00***	-17.29 0.03**	-25.50 0.00***	-24.82 0.00***	-26.06 0.00***	-25.01 0.00***
Financial Vulnerabilities	-3.40 0.00***								
Increase (Priv. Cred. / GDP)		-0.12 0.01**							
Current Acc. Balance / GDP			-0.17 0.12						
Economic Development				-1.18 0.11					
GDP per Capita					-0.12 0.00***				
International Linkages						-0.91 0.19			
Trade / GDP							-0.02 0.15		
Industrial Orientation								-2.04 0.00***	
Manuf. Exp. / Total Exp.									-0.10 0.00***
N	74	74	74	74	74	74	74	74	74
R^{2*}	0.33	0.31	0.16	0.14	0.20	0.13	0.13	0.19	0.22

Appendix 28c: Multivariate regressions of 'GDP$_{08-09}$' against the 'bank regulation and supervision summary' index and one additional control variable in the entire sample (second row: p-values of two-sided significance tests; number of asterisks: significance levels of 10%*, 5%** and 1%***).

Appendix 29 – 'GDP$_{10-12}$' against different financial regulation indices in the entire sample

	Dependent Variable: 'GDP$_{10-12}$'; Sample: All Countries								
	(1)	(2)	(3)	(4)	(5)	(6)	(7)	(8)	(9)
Constant	1.50 0.59	1.44 0.59	4.60 0.09*	3.61 0.28	2.85 0.38	4.54 0.13	4.35 0.16	4.75 0.10	7.04 0.06*
Heritage Financial Freedom	-0.06 0.15	-0.03 0.54	-0.09 0.03**	-0.10 006*	-0.06 0.35	-0.11 0.01**	-0.11 0.02**	-0.12 0.01***	-0.11 0.01**
Financial Vulnerabilities	-4.56 0.00***								
Increase (Priv. Cred. / GDP)		-0.17 0.00***							
Current Acc. Balance / GDP			0.44 0.00***						
Economic Development				-0.54 0.55					
GDP per Capita					-0.10 0.07*				
International Linkages						0.20 0.80			
Trade / GDP							0.00 0.93		
Industrial Orientation								-2.09 0.00***	
Manuf. Exp. / Total Exp.									-0.06 0.10*
N	84	84	84	84	84	84	84	84	84
R^{2*}	0.37	0.32	0.28	0.04	0.08	0.04	0.04	0.11	0.07

Appendix 29a: Multivariate regressions of 'GDP$_{10-12}$' against Heritage 'financial freedom' and one additional control variable in the entire sample (second row: p-values of two-sided significance tests; number of asterisks: significance levels of 10%*, 5%** and 1%***).

	Dependent Variable: 'GDP10-12'; Sample: All Countries								
	(1)	(2)	(3)	(4)	(5)	(6)	(7)	(8)	(9)
Constant	9.67 0.13	11.55 0.08	20.64 0.00***	17.74 0.02**	14.31 0.08*	21.73 0.00***	21.10 0.00***	17.16 0.01**	19.42 0.01***
Fraser Credit Market Regulation	-1.32 0.05*	-1.31 0.07*	-2.40 0.00***	-2.22 0.01***	-1.67 0.08*	-2.67 0.00***	-2.73 0.00***	-2.16 0.00***	-2.23 0.00***
Financial Vulnerabilities	-4.43 0.00***								
Increase (Priv. Cred. / GDP)		-0.17 0.00***							
Current Acc. Balance / GDP			0.45 0.00***						
Economic Development				-0.65 0.44					
GDP per Capita					-0.09 0.07*				
International Linkages						0.69 0.41			
Trade / GDP							0.01 0.39		
Industrial Orientation								-1.63 0.02**	
Manuf. Exp. / Total Exp.									-0.04 0.30
N	82	82	82	82	82	82	82	82	82
R^{2*}	0.38	0.34	0.33	0.08	0.10	0.08	0.08	0.11	0.08

Appendix 29b: Multivariate regressions of '$GDP_{10\text{-}12}$' against Fraser 'credit market regulation' and one additional control variable in the entire sample (second row: p-values of two-sided significance tests; number of asterisks: significance levels of 10%*, 5%** and 1%***).

	Dependent Variable: 'GDP$_{10-12}$'; Sample: All Countries								
	(1)	(2)	(3)	(4)	(5)	(6)	(7)	(8)	(9)
Constant	5.28 0.03**	7.31 0.01**	8.78 0.01***	6.68 0.09*	5.90 0.14	8.14 0.04**	7.75 0.04**	7.42 0.03**	9.33 0.01**
BRS Summary Index	-17.44 0.00***	-16.96 0.01***	-22.11 0.00***	-19.75 0.03**	-13.65 0.17	-23.33 0.01***	-23.56 0.01***	-21.61 0.01***	-21.60 0.01**
Financial Vulnerabilities	-5.22 0.00***								
Increase (Priv. Cred. / GDP)		-0.17 0.00***							
Current Acc. Balance / GDP			0.46 0.00***						
Economic Development				-1.08 0.22					
GDP per Capita					-0.11 0.02**				
International Linkages						0.28 0.76			
Trade / GDP							0.01 0.73		
Industrial Orientation								-1.51 0.05**	
Manuf. Exp. / Total Exp.									-0.04 0.28
N	74	74	74	74	74	74	74	74	74
R^{2*}	0.47	0.39	0.33	0.07	0.11	0.05	0.05	0.09	0.07

Appendix 29c: Multivariate regressions of 'GDP$_{10-12}$' against the 'bank regulation and supervision summary' index and one additional control variable in the entire sample (second row: p-values of two-sided significance tests; number of asterisks: significance levels of 10%*, 5%** and 1%***).

Appendix 30 – Correlations between financial regulation variables and control variables within the sub-sample of less developed countries

	Fraser Credit Market Regulation	BRS Summary Index	Heritage Financial Freedom
Financial Vulnerabilities	**0.34**	0.26	0.09
Increase (Priv. Cred. / GDP)	**0.28**	**0.31**	0.21
Current Acc. Balance / GDP	-0.17	-0.23	-0.19
Economic Development	-0.14	-0.16	0.02
GDP per Capita	0.24	0.22	0.18
International Linkages	**0.44**	0.19	0.15
Trade / GDP	**0.48**	0.16	0.12
Industrial Orientation	0.20	-0.06	-0.21
Manuf. Exp. / Total Exp.	0.24	-0.05	-0.23

Appendix 30: Correlations between financial regulation variables and control variables within emerging and developing countries (significant correlations at conventional significance levels are bold).

Appendix 31 – '$GDP_{08\text{-}12}$' against different financial regulation indices in less developed countries

	Dependent Variable: 'GDP_{08-12}'; Sample: Emerging and Developing Countries								
	(1)	(2)	(3)	(4)	(5)	(6)	(7)	(8)	(9)
Constant	22.75 0.05**	26.16 0.01***	34.84 0.00***	40.44 0.00***	36.09 0.00***	36.57 0.01***	35.60 0.00***	29.86 0.01***	37.52 0.00***
Fraser Credit Market Regulation	-3.08 0.02**	-3.12 0.01***	-4.20 0.00***	-4.51 0.00***	-4.08 0.00***	-4.64 0.00***	-4.05 0.01***	-3.96 0.00***	-3.90 0.00***
Financial Vulnerabilities	-6.21 0.01**								
Increase (Priv. Cred. / GDP)		-0.46 0.00***							
Current Acc. Balance / GDP			0.50 0.00***						
Economic Development				8.83 0.01**					
GDP per Capita					-0.99 0.01***				
International Linkages						-0.05 0.29			
Trade / GDP							-0.05 0.29		
Industrial Orientation								-4.52 0.00***	
Manuf. Exp. / Total Exp.									-0.18 0.00***
N	50	50	50	50	50	50	50	50	50
R^{2*}	0.34	0.43	0.28	0.21	0.23	0.16	0.16	0.31	0.27

Appendix 31a: Multivariate regressions of '$GDP_{08\text{-}12}$' against Fraser 'credit market regulation' and one additional control variable in emerging and developing countries (second row: p-values of two-sided significance tests; number of asterisks: significance levels of 10%*, 5%** and 1%***).

	Dependent Variable: 'GDP$_{08-12}$'; Sample: Emerging and Developing Countries								
	(1)	(2)	(3)	(4)	(5)	(6)	(7)	(8)	(9)
Constant	2.45 0.65	2.53 0.60	4.17 0.45	11.78 0.03**	7.57 0.18	3.37 0.52	11.35 0.05*	7.97 0.15	20.53 0.00***
Heritage Financial Freedom	-0.12 0.23	-0.05 0.55	-0.09 0.36	-0.16 0.10	-0.11 0.32	-0.13 0.19	-0.13 0.19	-0.24 0.03**	-0.25 0.01**
Financial Vulnerabilities	-7.47 0.00***								
Increase (Priv. Cred. / GDP)		-0.53 0.00***							
Current Acc. Balance / GDP			0.54 0.00***						
Economic Development				11.57 0.00***					
GDP per Capita					-1.14 0.01***				
International Linkages						-4.46 0.06*			
Trade / GDP							-0.09 0.01**		
Industrial Orientation								-5.95 0.00***	
Manuf. Exp. / Total Exp.									-0.27 0.00***
N	52	52	52	52	52	52	52	52	52
R^{2*}	0.30	0.38	0.14	0.11	0.11	0.04	0.08	0.27	0.28

Appendix 31b: Multivariate regressions of 'GDP$_{08-12}$' against Heritage 'financial freedom' and one additional control variable in emerging and developing countries (second row: p-values of two-sided significance tests; number of asterisks: significance levels of 10%*, 5%** and 1%***).

	Dependent Variable: 'GDP$_{08-12}$'; Sample: Emerging and Developing Countries								
	(1)	(2)	(3)	(4)	(5)	(6)	(7)	(8)	(9)
Constant	10.95 0.14	12.43 0.15	18.03 0.06*	22.21 0.02**	21.32 0.02**	17.89 0.07*	24.62 0.01***	20.71 0.00***	31.03 0.00***
BRS Summary Index	-36.23 0.05**	-30.48 0.14	-46.26 0.04**	-50.80 0.03**	-45.21 0.05*	-50.38 0.03**	-49.37 0.03**	-58.75 0.00***	-58.83 0.00***
Financial Vulnerabilities	-8.63 0.00***								
Increase (Priv. Cred. / GDP)		-0.49 0.00***							
Current Acc. Balance / GDP			0.39 0.03**						
Economic Development				6.96 0.17					
GDP per Capita					-1.08 0.03**				
International Linkages						-4.24 0.23			
Trade / GDP							-0.08 0.08*		
Industrial Orientation								-4.76 0.00***	
Manuf. Exp. / Total Exp.									-0.23 0.00***
N	42	42	42	42	42	42	42	42	42
R^{2*}	0.42	0.46	0.20	0.17	0.24	0.16	0.20	0.32	0.38

Appendix 31c: Multivariate regressions of 'GDP$_{08\text{-}12}$' against the 'bank regulation and supervision summary' index and one additional control variable in emerging and developing countries (second row: p-values of two-sided significance tests; number of asterisks: significance levels of 10%*, 5%** and 1%***).

Appendix 32 – '$GDP_{08\text{-}09}$' against different financial regulation indices in less developed countries

	Dependent Variable: '$GDP_{08\text{-}09}$'; Sample: Emerging and Developing Countries								
	(1)	(2)	(3)	(4)	(5)	(6)	(7)	(8)	(9)
Constant	14.40 0.01**	14.01 0.01***	18.16 0.00***	19.29 0.00***	17.03 0.00***	18.49 0.00***	17.74 0.00***	14.90 0.01***	18.31 0.00***
Fraser Credit Market Regulation	-2.10 0.00***	-1.93 0.00***	-2.48 0.00***	-2.53 0.00***	-2.06 0.00***	-2.57 0.00***	-2.31 0.00***	-2.20 0.00***	-2.17 0.00***
Financial Vulnerabilities	-1.74 0.15								
Increase (Priv. Cred. / GDP)		-0.18 0.01***							
Current Acc. Balance / GDP			0.10 0.21						
Economic Development				2.00 0.25					
GDP per Capita					-0.66 0.00***				
International Linkages						-0.22 0.88			
Trade / GDP							-0.02 0.44		
Industrial Orientation								-2.01 0.00***	
Manuf. Exp. / Total Exp.									-0.08 0.02**
N	50	50	50	50	50	50	50	50	50
R^{2*}	0.22	0.32	0.18	0.17	0.30	0.16	0.17	0.28	0.26

Appendix 32a: Multivariate regressions of '$GDP_{08\text{-}09}$' against Fraser 'credit market regulation' and one additional control variable in emerging and developing countries (second row: p-values of two-sided significance tests; number of asterisks: significance levels of 10%*, 5%** and 1%***).

	Dependent Variable: 'GDP$_{08-09}$'; Sample: Emerging and Developing Countries								
	(1)	(2)	(3)	(4)	(5)	(6)	(7)	(8)	(9)
Constant	0.30 0.92	0.12 0.96	1.03 0.72	3.29 0.26	2.80 0.29	0.52 0.84	3.86 0.23	2.58 0.35	8.92 0.00***
Heritage Financial Freedom	-0.07 0.19	-0.04 0.44	-0.07 0.21	-0.09 0.12	-0.06 0.33	-0.08 0.17	-0.07 0.17	-0.12 0.03**	-0.13 0.01***
Financial Vulnerabilities	-2.63 0.02**								
Increase (Priv. Cred. / GDP)		-0.23 0.00***							
Current Acc. Balance / GDP			0.11 0.22						
Economic Development				3.58 0.07*					
GDP per Capita					-0.71 0.00***				
International Linkages						-1.83 0.11			
Trade / GDP							-0.04 0.03**		
Industrial Orientation								-2.78 0.00***	
Manuf. Exp. / Total Exp.									-0.14 0.00***
N	52	52	52	52	52	52	52	52	52
R^{2*}	0.13	0.25	0.02	0.04	0.15	0.03	0.05	0.21	0.24

Appendix 32b: Multivariate regressions of 'GDP$_{08-09}$' against the 'bank regulation and supervision summary' index and one additional control variable in emerging and developing countries (second row: p-values of two-sided significance tests; number of asterisks: significance levels of 10%*, 5%** and 1%***).

	Dependent Variable: 'GDP_{08-09}'; Sample: Emerging and Developing Countries								
	(1)	(2)	(3)	(4)	(5)	(6)	(7)	(8)	(9)
Constant	5.84 0.18	5.47 0.18	8.37 0.08*	8.67 0.05*	8.94 0.03**	7.36 0.13	10.24 0.01**	8.53 0.03**	13.70 0.00***
BRS Summary Index	-22.21 0.03**	-18.27 0.06*	-27.19 0.02**	-26.71 0.01**	-21.27 0.05**	-25.35 0.02**	-24.78 0.02**	-28.94 0.00***	-29.14 0.00***
Financial Vulnerabilities	-2.34 0.06*								
Increase (Priv. Cred. / GDP)		-0.18 0.00***							
Current Acc. Balance / GDP			0.01 0.94						
Economic Development				1.01 0.64					
GDP per Capita					-0.66 0.01***				
International Linkages						-1.75 0.31			
Trade / GDP							-0.04 0.12		
Industrial Orientation								-2.16 0.00***	
Manuf. Exp. / Total Exp.									-0.12 0.00***
N	42	42	42	42	42	42	42	42	42
R^{2*}	0.20	0.29	0.12	0.12	0.29	0.14	0.17	0.28	0.36

Appendix 32c: Multivariate regressions of 'GDP_{08-09}' against Heritage 'financial freedom' and one additional control variable in emerging and developing countries (second row: p-values of two-sided significance tests; number of asterisks: significance levels of 10%*, 5%** and 1%***).

Appendix 33 – 'GDP$_{10-12}$' against different financial regulation indices in less developed countries

	Dependent Variable: 'GDP$_{10-12}$'; Sample: Emerging and Developing Countries								
	(1)	(2)	(3)	(4)	(5)	(6)	(7)	(8)	(9)
Constant	7.15 0.32	11..23 0.09*	15.93 0.03**	20.69 0.01***	18.44 0.02**	20.69 0.01***	17.12 0.03**	14.37 0.05**	18.67 0.01**
Fraser Credit Market Regulation	-0.86 0.29	-1.10 0.15	-1.65 0.05**	-1.92 0.04**	-1.96 0.03**	-1.92 0.04**	-1.65 0.12	-1.72 0.04**	-1.69 0.05**
Financial Vulnerabilities	-4.72 0.00***								
Increase (Priv. Cred. / GDP)		-0.29 0.00***							
Current Acc. Balance / GDP			0.43 0.00***						
Economic Development				7.27 0.01***					
GDP per Capita					-0.35 0.22				
International Linkages						7.27 0.01***			
Trade / GDP							-0.03 0.32		
Industrial Orientation								-2.53 0.00***	
Manuf. Exp. / Total Exp.									-0.10 0.01**
N	50	50	50	50	50	50	50	50	50
R^{2*}	0.32	0.33	0.28	0.15	0.08	0.15	0.07	0.17	0.14

Appendix 33a: Multivariate regressions of 'GDP$_{10-12}$' against Fraser 'credit market regulation' and one additional control variable in emerging and developing countries (second row: p-values of two-sided significance tests; number of asterisks: significance levels of 10%*, 5%** and 1%***).

	Dependent Variable: 'GDP10-12'; Sample: Emerging and Developing Countries								
	(1)	(2)	(3)	(4)	(5)	(6)	(7)	(8)	(9)
Constant	1.81 0.58	2.07 0.49	2.83 0.38	8.45 0.01**	4.55 0.19	2.52 0.44	7.35 0.03**	5.13 0.13	11.35 0.01***
Heritage Financial Freedom	-0.04 0.48	-0.01 0.91	-0.02 0.75	-0.07 0.21	-0.05 0.47	-0.05 0.40	-0.05 0.39	-0.11 0.10*	-0.11 0.08*
Financial Vulnerabilities	-5.05 0.00***								
Increase (Priv. Cred. / GDP)		-0.31 0.00***							
Current Acc. Balance / GDP			0.46 0.00***						
Economic Development				8.40 0.00***					
GDP per Capita					-0.45 0.14				
International Linkages						-2.79 0.12			
Trade / GDP							-0.01 0.06*		
Industrial Orientation								-3.20 0.00***	
Manuf. Exp. / Total Exp.									-0.14 0.00***
N	52	52	52	52	52	52	52	52	52
R^{2*}	0.32	0.31	0.23	0.12	0.02	0.02	0.05	0.17	0.15

Appendix 33b: Multivariate regressions of 'GDP10-12' against the 'bank regulation and supervision summary' index and one additional control variable in emerging and developing countries (second row: p-values of two-sided significance tests; number of asterisks: significance levels of 10%*, 5%** and 1%***).

Dependent Variable: 'GDP10-12'; Sample: Emerging and Developing Countries									
	(1)	(2)	(3)	(4)	(5)	(6)	(7)	(8)	(9)
Constant	4.46 0.27	6.50 0.23	9.19 0.09*	13.37 0.02**	12.13 0.03**	10.15 0.09*	14.17 0.01**	11.89 0.01***	17.01 0.00***
BRS Summary Index	-13.08 0.21	-11.47 0.39	-18.14 0.18	-23.58 0.10	-23.34 0.11	-24.65 0.10*	-24.28 0.09*	-29.60 0.01**	-29.47 0.02**
Financial Vulnerabilities	-6.62 0.00***								
Increase (Priv. Cred. / GDP)		-0.32 0.00***							
Current Acc. Balance / GDP			0.41 0.00***						
Economic Development				6.40 0.06*					
GDP per Capita					-0.47 0.16				
International Linkages						-2.64 0.27			
Trade / GDP							-0.05 0.16		
Industrial Orientation								-2.60 0.00***	
Manuf. Exp. / Total Exp.									-0.12 0.01**
N	42	42	42	42	42	42	42	42	42
R^{2*}	0.47	0.40	0.27	0.14	0.11	0.09	0.11	0.20	0.20

Appendix 33c: Multivariate regressions of 'GDP_{10-12}' against Heritage 'financial freedom' and one additional control variable in emerging and developing countries (second row: p-values of two-sided significance tests; number of asterisks: significance levels of 10%*, 5%** and 1%***).

Appendix 34 – Correlations amongst government size variables

	Fraser Size of Government	Fraser Government Consumption	Heritage Government Spending
Fraser Size of Government	1	**0.76**	**0.74**
Fraser Government Consumption	**0.76**	1	**0.75**
Heritage Government Spending	**0.74**	**0.75**	1

Appendix 34: Correlations amongst government size indices within the entire sample (all correlations are significant at conventional significance levels).

Appendix 35 – Scatterplots of 'GDP$_{08-12}$' against different government size indices

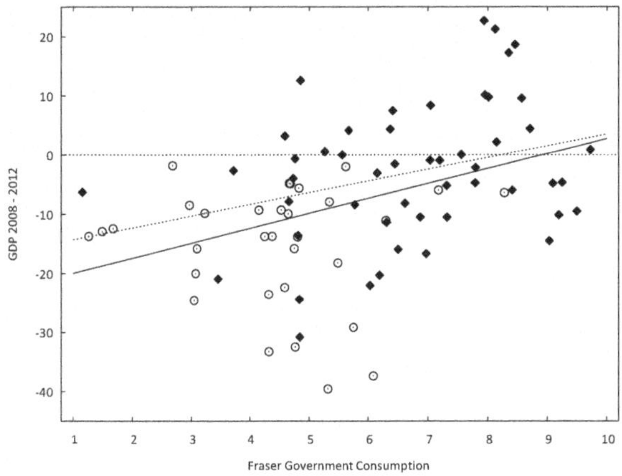

Appendix 35a: Scatterplot of 'GDP$_{08-12}$' against Fraser 'government consumption' (black dots: less developed countries; white circles: developed countries; dotted line: fitted values for sub-sample of emerging and developing countries; continuous line: fitted values for the entire sample).

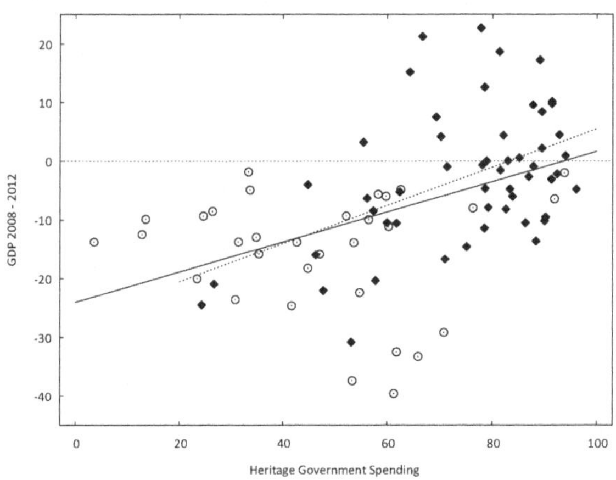

Appendix 35b: Scatterplot of 'GDP$_{08-12}$' against Heritage 'government spending' (black dots: less developed countries; white circles: developed countries; dotted line: fitted values for sub-sample of emerging and developing countries; continuous line: fitted values for the entire sample).

Appendix 36 – '$GDP_{08\text{-}12}$' against different government size indices in the entire sample

	Dependent Variable: 'GDP_{08-12}'; Sample: All Countries								
	(1)	(2)	(3)	(4)	(5)	(6)	(7)	(8)	(9)
Constant	-20.33 0.00***	-14.18 0.00***	-22.80 0.00***	-21.92 0.00***	-14.82 0.00***	-22.59 0.00***	-19.76 0.00***	-19.97 0.00***	-15.58 0.00***
Fraser Gov. Consumption	2.15 0.00***	1.59 0.00***	2.92 0.00***	2.43 0.00***	1.67 0.02**	2.54 0.00***	2.48 0.00***	2.09 0.00***	2.13 0.00***
Financial Vulnerabilities	-6.96 0.00***								
Increase (Priv. Cred. / GDP)		-0.25 0.00***							
Current Acc. Balance / GDP			0.69 0.00***						
Economic Development				-0.42 0.76					
GDP per Capita					-0.16 0.03**				
International Linkages						-1.53 0.20			
Trade / GDP							-0.03 0.17		
Industrial Orientation								-3.26 0.00***	
Manuf. Exp. / Total Exp.									-0.10 0.06*
N	82	82	82	82	82	82	82	82	82
R^{2*}	0.46	0.38	0.38	0.15	0.18	0.16	0.16	0.21	0.28

Appendix 36a: Multivariate regressions of '$GDP_{08\text{-}12}$' against Fraser 'government consumption' and one additional control variable in the entire sample (second row: p-values of two-sided significance tests; number of asterisks: significance levels of 10%*, 5%** and 1%***).

	Dependent Variable: 'GDP$_{08-12}$'; Sample: All Countries								
	(1)	(2)	(3)	(4)	(5)	(6)	(7)	(8)	(9)
Constant	-20.16 0.00***	-15.58 0.00***	-21.45 0.00***	-23.77 0.00***	-18.31 0.00***	-24.86 0.00***	-20.96 0.00***	-21.46 0.00***	-17.12 0.00***
Heritage Gov. Spending	0.20 0.00***	0.17 0.00***	0.24 0.00***	0.25 0.00***	0.20 0.00***	0.27 0.00***	0.26 0.00***	0.22 0.00***	0.22 0.00***
Financial Vulnerabilities	-6.60 0.00***								
Increase (Priv. Cred. / GDP)		-0.25 0.00***							
Current Acc. Balance / GDP			0.54 0.00***						
Economic Development				-0.21 0.89					
GDP per Capita					-0.11 0.18				
International Linkages						-2.28 0.03**			
Trade / GDP							-0.04 0.02**		
Industrial Orientation								-2.76 0.01**	
Manuf. Exp. / Total Exp.									-0.10 0.05*
N	84	84	84	84	84	84	84	84	84
R^{2*}	0.46	0.41	0.34	0.20	0.21	0.23	0.23	0.24	0.23

Appendix 36b: Multivariate regressions of 'GDP$_{08-12}$' against Heritage 'government spending' and one additional control variable in the entire sample (second row: p-values of two-sided significance tests; number of asterisks: significance levels of 10%*, 5%** and 1%***).

Appendix 37 – 'GDP$_{08-09}$' against different government size indices in the entire sample

	Dependent Variable: 'GDP$_{08-09}$'; Sample: All Countries										
	(1)	(2)	(3)	(4)	(5)	(6)	(7)	(8)	(9)	(10)	(11)
Constant	-13.63 0.00***	-11.21 0.00***	-15.07 0.00***	-13.37 0.00***	-7.94 0.02**	-16.34 0.00***	-13.22 0.00***	-12.10 0.00***	-7.77 0.03**	-9.81 0.00***	-11.93 0.00***
Fraser Size of Government	1.12 0.00***	0.97 0.01**	1.43 0.00***	1.08 0.01***	0.60 0.17	1.52 0.00***	1.47 0.00***	0.89 0.03**	0.83 0.06*	0.55 0.13	0.86 0.01**
Financial Vulnerabilities	-3.04 0.00***									-3.10 0.00***	-3.07 0.00***
Increase (Priv. Cred. / GDP)		-0.12 0.01***									
Current Acc. Balance / GDP			0.21 0.05*								
Economic Development				-1.14 0.08*						-1.31 0.03**	
GDP per Capita					-0.13 0.00***						
International Linkages						-1.65 0.00***				-1.45 0.00***	-1.52 0.00***
Trade / GDP							-0.03 0.00***				
Industrial Orientation								-2.09 0.00***		-2.21 0.00***	-2.10 0.00***
Manuf. Exp. / Total Exp.									-0.09 0.00***		
N	82	82	82	82	82	82	82	82	82	82	82
R^{2*}	0.23	0.23	0.10	0.06	0.14	0.09	0.10	0.12	0.12	0.38	0.35

Appendix 37a: Multivariate regressions of 'GDP$_{08-09}$' against Fraser 'size of government' and one additional control variable in the entire sample (second row: p-values of two-sided significance tests; number of asterisks: significance levels of 10%*, 5%** and 1%***).

	Dependent Variable: 'GDP$_{08-09}$'; Sample: All Countries										
	(1)	(2)	(3)	(4)	(5)	(6)	(7)	(8)	(9)	(10)	(11)
Constant	-13.71 0.00***	-11.20 0.00***	-14.71 0.00***	-14.44 0.00***	-10.68 0.00***	-14.68 0.00***	-12.17 0.00***	-13.26 0.00***	-10.03 0.00***	-11.36 0.00***	-5.91 0.00***
Fraser Gov. Consumption	1.29 0.00***	1.07 0.00***	1.59 0.00***	1.42 0.00***	1.01 0.01***	1.46 0.00***	1.40 0.00***	1.22 0.00***	1.19 0.00***	0.89 0.01***	
Financial Vulnerabilities	-2.88 0.00***									-2.97 0.00***	-3.26 0.00***
Increase (Priv. Cred. / GDP)		-0.10 0.02**									
Current Acc. Balance / GDP			0.24 0.02**								
Economic Development				-0.13 0.87						-0.63 0.32	-1.61 0.01***
GDP per Capita					-0.08 0.04**						
International Linkages						-1.39 0.01***				-1.38 0.00***	-1.33 0.00***
Trade / GDP							-0.02 0.00***				
Industrial Orientation								-1.73 0.01***		-1.91 0.00***	-2.42 0.00***
Manuf. Exp. / Total Exp.									-0.07 0.01***		
N	82	82	82	82	82	82	82	82	82	82	82
R^{2*}	0.33	0.28	0.25	0.16	0.19	0.20	0.20	0.22	0.20	0.38	0.37

Appendix 37b: Multivariate regressions of 'GDP$_{08-09}$' against Fraser 'government consumption' and one additional control variable in the entire sample (second row: p-values of two-sided significance tests; number of asterisks: significance levels of 10%*, 5%** and 1%***).

	Dependent Variable: 'GDP$_{08-09}$'; Sample: All Countries										
	(1)	(2)	(3)	(4)	(5)	(6)	(7)	(8)	(9)	(10)	(11)
Constant	2.44 0.25	2.39 0.28	4.27 0.06*	3.81 0.20	2.79 0.29	3.73 0.10*	5.06 0.04**	4.61 0.04**	9.84 0.00***	1.34 0.60	-5.91 0.00***
Heritage Gov. Spending	-0.14 0.00***	-0.12 0.00***	-0.17 0.00***	-0.17 0.00***	-0.12 0.03**	-0.16 0.00***	-0.16 0.00***	-0.18 0.00***	-0.17 0.00***	-0.12 0.01***	
Financial Vulnerabilities	-2.76 0.00***									-2.82 0.00***	-3.26 0.00***
Increase (Priv. Cred. / GDP)		-0.11 0.02**									
Current Acc. Balance / GDP			0.15 0.10								
Economic Development				-0.27 0.74						-0.61 0.34	-1.61 0.01***
GDP per Capita					-0.09 0.04**						
International Linkages						-0.77 0.15				-0.91 0.14	-1.33 0.00***
Trade / GDP							-0.02 0.11				
Industrial Orientation								-2.58 0.00***		-2.53 0.00***	-2.42 0.00***
Manuf. Exp. / Total Exp.									-0.11 0.00***		
N	84	84	84	84	84	84	84	84	84	84	84
R^{2*}	0.30	0.28	0.19	0.16	0.20	0.17	0.18	0.29	0.29	0.43	0.37

Appendix 37c: Multivariate regressions of 'GDP$_{08-09}$' against Heritage 'government spending' and one additional control variable in the entire sample (second row: p-values of two-sided significance tests; number of asterisks: significance levels of 10%*, 5%** and 1%***).

Appendix 38 – 'GDP_{10-12}' against different government size indices in the entire sample

	Dependent Variable: 'GDP_{10-12}'; Sample: All Countries										
	(1)	(2)	(3)	(4)	(5)	(6)	(7)	(8)	(9)	(10)	(11)
Constant	-10.93 0.00***	-7.66 0.02**	-13.16 0.00***	-11.76 0.00***	-7.55 0.10*	-13.40 0.00***	-12.49 0.00***	-10.86 0.00***	-10.00 0.03**	-6.84 0.03**	-8.60 0.00***
Fraser Size of Government	1.33 0.00***	1.14 0.01**	1.88 0.00***	1.46 0.01**	1.08 0.08*	1.70 0.00***	1.69 0.00***	1.32 0.01**	1.44 0.01***	0.72 0.12	0.98 0.03**
Financial Vulnerabilities	-4.60 0.00***									-4.66 0.00***	-4.64 0.00***
Increase (Priv. Cred. / GDP)		-0.17 0.00***									
Current Acc. Balance / GDP			0.48 0.00***								
Economic Development				-0.88 0.31						-1.13 0.09*	
GDP per Capita					-0.10 0.03**						
International Linkages						-0.48 0.57					
Trade / GDP							-0.01 0.53				
Industrial Orientation								-1.55 0.04**		-1.76 0.00***	-1.67 0.00***
Manuf. Exp. / Total Exp.									-0.04 0.36		
N	82	82	82	82	82	82	82	82	82	82	82
R^{2*}	0.40	0.35	0.34	0.06	0.10	0.05	0.05	0.09	0.06	0.45	0.43

Appendix 38a: Multivariate regressions of 'GDP_{10-12}' against Fraser 'size of government' and one additional control variable in the entire sample (second row: p-values of two-sided significance tests; number of asterisks: significance levels of 10%*, 5%** and 1%***).

	Dependent Variable: 'GDP10-12'; Sample: All Countries										
	(1)	(2)	(3)	(4)	(5)	(6)	(7)	(8)	(9)	(10)	(11)
Constant	-7.33 0.00***	-3.23 0.09*	-8.96 0.00***	-8.29 0.00***	-4.66 0.15	-8.77 0.00***	-8.49 0.00***	-7.60 0.00***	-6.69 0.05**	-4.59 0.01**	-6.04 0.00***
Fraser Gov. Consumption	0.91 0.01***	0.53 0.09*	1.44 0.00***	1.07 0.00**	0.69 0.12	1.15 0.00***	1.15 0.00***	0.95 0.01**	1.03 0.01***	0.44 0.17	0.69 0.04**
Financial Vulnerabilities	-4.55 0.00***									-4.65 0.00***	-4.60 0.00***
Increase (Priv. Cred. / GDP)		-0.17 0.00***									
Current Acc. Balance / GDP			0.50 0.00***								
Economic Development				-0.33 0.71						-0.95 0.14	
GDP per Capita					-0.08 0.09*						
International Linkages						-0.18 0.84					
Trade / GDP							-0.00 0.85				
Industrial Orientation								-1.48 0.04**		-1.76 0.00***	-1.62 0.00***
Manuf. Exp. / Total Exp.									-0.03 0.41		
N	82	82	82	82	82	82	82	82	82	82	82
R^{2*}	0.41	0.33	0.38	0.07	0.09	0.07	0.06	0.10	0.07	0.44	0.44

Appendix 38b: Multivariate regressions of '$GDP_{10\text{-}12}$' against Fraser 'government consumption' and one additional control variable in the entire sample (second row: p-values of two-sided significance tests; number of asterisks: significance levels of 10%*, 5%** and 1%***).

Dependent Variable: 'GDP_{10-12}'; Sample: All Countries											
	(1)	(2)	(3)	(4)	(5)	(6)	(7)	(8)	(9)	(10)	(11)
Constant	-9.40	-6.73	-9.82	-12.29	-11.31	-12.11	-11.17	-11.01	-10.86	-7.51	-2.05
	0.00***	0.00***	0.00***	0.00***	0.00***	0.00***	0.00***	0.00***	0.00***	0.00***	0.00***
Heritage Gov. Spending	0.11	0.10	0.14	0.16	0.15	0.16	0.15	0.14	0.15	0.08	
	0.00***	0.00***	0.00***	0.00***	0.00***	0.00***	0.00***	0.00***	0.00***	0.01***	
Financial Vulnerabilities	-4.22									-4.36	-4.77
	0.00***									0.00***	0.00***
Increase (Priv. Cred. / GDP)		-0.15									
		0.00***									
Current Acc. Balance / GDP			0.43								
			0.00***								
Economic Development				0.33						-0.44	-1.32
				0.74						0.54	0.04**
GDP per Capita					-0.01						
					0.85						
International Linkages						-0.65					
						0.39					
Trade / GDP							-0.01				
							0.46				
Industrial Orientation								-0.92		-1.34	-1.99
								0.17		0.01**	0.00***
Manuf. Exp. / Total Exp.									-0.02		
									0.68		
N	84	84	84	84	84	84	84	84	84	84	84
R^{2*}	0.46	0.39	0.41	0.18	0.18	0.19	0.18	0.19	0.18	0.48	0.44

Appendix 38c: Multivariate regressions of 'GDP_{10-12}' against Heritage 'government spending' and one additional control variable in the entire sample (second row: p-values of two-sided significance tests; number of asterisks: significance levels of 10%*, 5%** and 1%***).

Appendix 39 – 'GDP$_{08-12}$' against different government size indices in less developed countries

	Dependent Variable: 'GDP$_{08-12}$'; Sample: Emerging and Developing Countries								
	(1)	(2)	(3)	(4)	(5)	(6)	(7)	(8)	(9)
Constant	-14.90 0.06*	-9.78 0.14	-17.24 0.04**	-14.26 0.12	-5.88 0.53	-17.30 0.06*	-7.94 0.41	-15.14 0.12	-5.10 0.63
Fraser Size of Government	1.60 0.13	1.36 0.13	2.35 0.04**	2.55 0.05*	1.12 0.34	1.96 0.13	1.85 0.13	1.57 0.24	1.49 0.30
Financial Vulnerabilities	-7.24 0.00***								
Increase (Priv. Cred. / GDP)		-0.51 0.00***							
Current Acc. Balance / GDP			0.61 0.00***						
Economic Development				11.97 0.01***					
GDP per Capita					-1.17 0.00***				
International Linkages						-4.76 0.06*			
Trade / GDP							-0.10 0.02**		
Industrial Orientation								-5.08 0.00***	
Manuf. Exp. / Total Exp.									-0.21 0.00***
N	50	50	50	50	50	50	50	50	50
R^{2*}	0.30	0.38	0.20	0.12	0.12	0.05	0.11	0.22	0.19

Appendix 39a: Multivariate regressions of 'GDP$_{08-12}$' against Fraser 'size of government' and one additional control variable in emerging and developing countries (second row: p-values of two-sided significance tests; number of asterisks: significance levels of 10%*, 5%** and 1%***).

	Dependent Variable: 'GDP$_{08-12}$'; Sample: Emerging and Developing Countries								
	(1)	(2)	(3)	(4)	(5)	(6)	(7)	(8)	(9)
Constant	-16.99 0.00***	-9.00 0.06*	-16.50 0.00***	-12.33 0.03**	-6.73 0.36	-15.75 0.01***	-6.86 0.28	-13.94 0.01**	-4.52 0.49
Fraser Gov. Consumption	1.98 0.01**	1.29 0.07*	2.37 0.00***	2.51 0.00***	1.21 0.18	1.82 0.03**	1.63 0.04**	1.47 0.06*	1.38 0.10
Financial Vulnerabilities	-7.42 0.00***								
Increase (Priv. Cred. / GDP)		-0.49 0.00***							
Current Acc. Balance / GDP			0.65 0.00***						
Economic Development				13.54 0.00***					
GDP per Capita					-1.03 0.02**				
International Linkages						-4.19 0.07*			
Trade / GDP							-0.09 0.03**		
Industrial Orientation								-4.82 0.00***	
Manuf. Exp. / Total Exp.									-0.20 0.00***
N	50	50	50	50	50	50	50	50	50
R^{2*}	0.37	0.40	0.28	0.20	0.14	0.09	0.13	0.25	0.21

Appendix 39b: Multivariate regressions of 'GDP$_{08-12}$' against Fraser 'government consumption' and one additional control variable in emerging and developing countries (second row: p-values of two-sided significance tests; number of asterisks: significance levels of 10%*, 5%** and 1%***).

	Dependent Variable: 'GDP$_{08-12}$'; Sample: Emerging and Developing Countries								
	(1)	(2)	(3)	(4)	(5)	(6)	(7)	(8)	(9)
Constant	-20.44 0.00***	-13.74 0.01**	-20.99 0.00***	-19.94 0.00***	-21.49 0.04**	-26.00 0.00***	-18.92 0.01**	-23.71 0.00***	-15.43 0.03**
Heritage Gov. Spending	0.23 0.00***	0.18 0.01***	0.26 0.00***	0.30 0.00***	0.28 0.01**	0.31 0.00***	0.29 0.00***	0.27 0.00***	0.27 0.00***
Financial Vulnerabilities	-6.25 0.01***								
Increase (Priv. Cred. / GDP)		-0.45 0.00***							
Current Acc. Balance / GDP			0.41 0.00***						
Economic Development				9.10 0.03**					
GDP per Capita					-0.43 0.41				
International Linkages						-3.12 0.11			
Trade / GDP							-0.07 0.03**		
Industrial Orientation								-4.27 0.00***	
Manuf. Exp. / Total Exp.									-0.19 0.00***
N	52	52	52	52	52	52	52	52	52
R^{2*}	0.39	0.44	0.27	0.26	0.20	0.21	0.23	0.33	0.33

Appendix 39c: Multivariate regressions of 'GDP$_{08-12}$' against Heritage 'government spending' and one additional control variable in emerging and developing countries (second row: p-values of two-sided significance tests; number of asterisks: significance levels of 10%*, 5%** and 1%***).

Appendix 40 –'$GDP_{08\text{-}09}$' against different government size indices in less developed countries

	Dependent Variable: '$GDP_{08\text{-}09}$'; Sample: Emerging and Developing Countries								
	(1)	(2)	(3)	(4)	(5)	(6)	(7)	(8)	(9)
Constant	-8.05 0.06*	-5.74 0.11	-8.88 0.05*	-8.00 0.08*	-1.06 0.80	-8.86 0.04**	-4.41 0.29	-7.86 0.10	-3.06 0.54
Fraser Size of Government	0.63 0.28	0.49 0.32	0.86 0.16	0.93 0.16	0.15 0.77	0.73 0.22	0.69 0.22	0.56 0.39	0.51 0.45
Financial Vulnerabilities	-2.50 0.04								
Increase (Priv. Cred. / GDP)		-0.21 0.00***							
Current Acc. Balance / GDP			0.16 0.07*						
Economic Development				3.52 0.11					
GDP per Capita					-0.79 0.00***				
International Linkages						-2.27 0.08*			
Trade / GDP							-0.05 0.02**		
Industrial Orientation								-2.37 0.00***	
Manuf. Exp. / Total Exp.									-0.10 0.01***
N	52	52	52	52	52	52	52	52	52
R^{2*}	0.12	0.23	0.03	0.02	0.18	0.02	0.07	0.16	0.14

Appendix 40a: Multivariate regressions of '$GDP_{08\text{-}09}$' against Fraser 'size of government' and one additional control variable in emerging and developing countries (second row: p-values of two-sided significance tests; number of asterisks: significance levels of 10%*, 5%** and 1%***).

	Dependent Variable: 'GDP$_{08-09}$'; Sample: Emerging and Developing Countries								
	(1)	(2)	(3)	(4)	(5)	(6)	(7)	(8)	(9)
Constant	-11.63 0.00***	-8.49 0.00***	-11.44 0.00***	-10.04 0.00***	-5.14 0.25	-11.14 0.00***	-7.21 0.04**	-10.34 0.00***	-6.15 0.10*
Fraser Gov Consumption	1.18 0.01***	0.91 0.02**	1.29 0.01***	1.36 0.00***	0.68 0.19	1.11 0.01**	1.03 0.01**	0.96 0.02**	0.92 0.04**
Financial Vulnerabilities	-2.58 0.01***								
Increase (Priv. Cred. / GDP)		-0.19 0.00***							
Current Acc. Balance / GDP			0.18 0.01***						
Economic Development				4.59 0.03**					
GDP per Capita					-0.67 0.01***				
International Linkages						-1.87 0.09*			
Trade / GDP							-0.04 0.03**		
Industrial Orientation								-2.14 0.01***	
Manuf. Exp. / Total Exp.									-0.09 0.02**
N	50	50	50	50	50	50	50	50	50
R^{2*}	0.23	0.29	0.15	0.15	0.22	0.12	0.14	0.23	0.20

Appendix 40b: Multivariate regressions of 'GDP$_{08-09}$' against Fraser 'government consumption' and one additional control variable in emerging and developing countries (second row: p-values of two-sided significance tests; number of asterisks: significance levels of 10%*, 5%** and 1%***).

	Dependent Variable: 'GDP$_{08-09}$'; Sample: Emerging and Developing Countries								
	(1)	(2)	(3)	(4)	(5)	(6)	(7)	(8)	(9)
Constant	-9.74 0.02**	-5.83 0.11	-11.14 0.01**	-10.04 0.02**	-3.99 0.51	-11.60 0.00***	-8.33 0.03**	-10.47 0.00***	-5.98 0.16
Heritage Gov. Spending	0.09 0.08*	0.05 0.24	0.11 0.03**	0.11 0.02**	0.05 0.46	0.11 0.01**	0.10 0.02**	0.09 0.03**	0.09 0.05**
Financial Vulnerabilities	-2.22 0.07*								
Increase (Priv. Cred. / GDP)		-0.21 0.00***							
Current Acc. Balance / GDP			0.06 0.53						
Economic Development				2.62 0.26					
GDP per Capita					-0.62 0.03*				
International Linkages						-1.46 0.18			
Trade / GDP							-0.03 0.06*		
Industrial Orientation								-2.07 0.00***	
Manuf. Exp. / Total Exp.									-0.10 0.01***
N	52	52	52	52	52	52	52	52	52
R^{2*}	0.15	0.26	0.07	0.09	0.15	0.08	0.10	0.18	0.20

Appendix 40c: Multivariate regressions of 'GDP$_{08-09}$' against Heritage 'government spending' and one additional control variable in emerging and developing countries (second row: p-values of two-sided significance tests; number of asterisks: significance levels of 10%*, 5%** and 1%***).

Appendix 41 –'GDP_{10-12}' against different government size indices in less developed countries

	Dependent Variable: 'GDP_{10-12}'; Sample: Emerging and Developing Countries								
	(1)	(2)	(3)	(4)	(5)	(6)	(7)	(8)	(9)
Constant	-7.83 0.12	-4.93 0.32	-9.40 0.08*	-7.19 0.25	-5.73 0.40	-9.49 0.14	-4.44 0.51	-9.49 0.14	-3.12 0.64
Fraser Size of Government	1.08 0.12	0.97 0.15	1.62 0.03**	1.76 0.05**	1.08 0.22	1.34 0.14	1.28 0.14	1.34 0.14	1.10 0.24
Financial Vulnerabilities	-4.93 0.00***								
Increase (Priv. Cred. / GDP)		-0.31 0.00***							
Current Acc. Balance / GDP			0.48 0.00***						
Economic Development				8.95 0.00***					
GDP per Capita					-0.39 0.18				
International Linkages						-2.64 0.14			
Trade / GDP							-0.05 0.08*		
Industrial Orientation								-2.64 0.14	
Manuf. Exp. / Total Exp.									-0.11 0.01***
N	50	50	50	50	50	50	50	50	50
R^{2*}	0.33	0.33	0.29	0.16	0.04	0.04	0.07	0.04	0.12

Appendix 41a: Multivariate regressions of 'GDP_{10-12}' against Fraser 'size of government' and one additional control variable in emerging and developing countries (second row: p-values of two-sided significance tests; number of asterisks: significance levels of 10%*, 5%** and 1%***).

	Dependent Variable: 'GDP10-12'; Sample: Emerging and Developing Countries								
	(1)	(2)	(3)	(4)	(5)	(6)	(7)	(8)	(9)
Constant	-5.80 0.05*	-0.75 0.83	-5.48 0.08*	-2.57 0.53	-1.80 0.70	-5.01 0.20	0.10 0.98	-4.01 0.30	1.21 0.77
Fraser Gov. Consumption	0.83 0.07*	0.39 0.42	1.12 0.02**	1.19 0.04**	0.54 0.37	0.73 0.20	0.63 0.26	0.54 0.32	0.50 0.38
Financial Vulnerabilities	-5.06 0.00***								
Increase (Priv. Cred. / GDP)		-0.31 0.00***							
Current Acc. Balance / GDP			0.50 0.00***						
Economic Development				9.42 0.00***					
GDP per Capita					-0.38 0.23				
International Linkages						-2.47 0.17			
Trade / GDP							-0.05 0.10*		
Industrial Orientation								-2.70 0.00***	
Manuf. Exp. / Total Exp.									-0.11 0.01***
N	50	50	50	50	50	50	50	50	50
R^{2*}	0.34	0.31	0.30	0.17	0.02	0.03	0.05	0.14	0.11

Appendix 41b: Multivariate regressions of '$GDP_{10\text{-}12}$' against Fraser 'government consumption' and one additional control variable in emerging and developing countries (second row: p-values of two-sided significance tests; number of asterisks: significance levels of 10%*, 5%** and 1%***).

	Dependent Variable: 'GDP10-12'; Sample: Emerging and Developing Countries								
	(1)	(2)	(3)	(4)	(5)	(6)	(7)	(8)	(9)
Constant	-12.06 0.00***	-9.27 0.01**	-11.11 0.00***	-11.16 0.00***	-19.49 0.00***	-15.87 0.00***	-12.08 0.02**	-14.76 0.00***	-11.08 0.01**
Heritage Gov. Spending	0.16 0.00***	0.14 0.00***	0.17 0.00***	0.20 0.00***	0.25 0.00***	0.21 0.00***	0.20 0.00***	0.19 0.00***	0.20 0.00***
Financial Vulnerabilities	-4.15 0.00***								
Increase (Priv. Cred. / GDP)		-0.24 0.00***							
Current Acc. Balance / GDP			0.36 0.00***						
Economic Development				6.76 0.01***					
GDP per Capita					0.23 0.49				
International Linkages						-1.72 0.26			
Trade / GDP							-0.04 0.14		
Industrial Orientation								-2.16 0.00***	
Manuf. Exp. / Total Exp.									-0.09 0.02**
N	52	52	52	52	52	52	52	52	52
R^{2*}	0.43	0.40	0.37	0.31	0.23	0.24	0.25	0.31	0.29

Appendix 41c: Multivariate regressions of '$GDP_{10\text{-}12}$' against Heritage 'government spending' and one additional control variable in emerging and developing countries (second row: p-values of two-sided significance tests; number of asterisks: significance levels of 10%*, 5%** and 1%***).

Appendix 42 - Correlations between exchange rate regime dummies and control variables in developed countries

	Float	Peg
Financial Vulnerabilities	-0.19	0.03
Increase (Priv. Cred. / GDP)	-0.01	-0.04
Current Acc. Balance / GDP	0.24	-0.11
Economic Development	0.32	-0.17
GDP per Capita	0.22	-0.12
International Linkages	-0.16	0.13
Trade / GDP	-0.13	0.10
Industrial Orientation	-0.15	0.13
Manuf. Exp. / Total Exp.	-0.12	0.15

Appendix 42: Correlations between financial regulation variables and control variables within emerging and developing countries (all correlations are insignificant at conventional significance levels).

Appendix 43 – '$GDP_{08\text{-}09}$' and '$GDP_{10\text{-}12}$' against the 'peg' dummy in the entire sample

	Dependent Variable: '$GDP_{08\text{-}09}$'; Sample: All Countries								
	(1)	(2)	(3)	(4)	(5)	(6)	(7)	(8)	(9)
Constant	-4.71 0.00***	-3.36 0.00***	-4.09 0.00***	-4.60 0.00***	-2.97 0.00***	-4.55 0.00***	-2.98 0.02**	-4.72 0.00***	-0.92 0.53
Peg	-5.02 0.00***	-4.94 0.00***	-5.75 0.00***	-5.49 0.00***	-4.19 0.03**	-5.69 0.00***	-5.56 0.00***	-5.00 0.01***	-4.71 0.01***
Financial Vulnerabilities	-2.92 0.00***								
Increase (Priv. Cred. / GDP)		-0.12 0.00***							
Current Acc. Balance / GDP			0.15 0.14						
Economic Development				-1.02 0.10					
GDP per Capita					-0.11 0.00***				
International Linkages						-0.85 0.11			
Trade / GDP							-0.02 0.07*		
Industrial Orientation								-1.90 0.00***	
Manuf. Exp. / Total Exp.									-0.09 0.00***
N	84	84	84	84	84	84	84	84	84
R^{2*}	0.27	0.29	0.14	0.13	0.19	0.12	0.13	0.17	0.18

Appendix 43a: Multivariate regressions of '$GDP_{08\text{-}09}$' against the 'peg' dummy and one additional control variable in the entire sample (second row: p-values of two-sided significance tests; number of asterisks: significance levels of 10%*, 5%** and 1%***).

	Dependent Variable: 'GDP$_{10-12}$'; Sample: All Countries								
	(1)	(2)	(3)	(4)	(5)	(6)	(7)	(8)	(9)
Constant	-0.72 0.31	1.15 0.14	0.73 0.32	-0.42 0.62	-0.64 0.55	-0.29 0.74	-0.83 0.56	-0.52 0.53	0.75 0.70
Peg	-5.58 0.00***	-5.64 0.00***	-6.23 0.00***	-6.83 0.00***	-5.94 0.01***	-7.37 0.00***	-7.35 0.00***	-6.43 0.00***	-6.76 0.00***
Financial Vulnerabilities	-4.40 0.00***								
Increase (Priv. Cred. / GDP)		-0.16 0.00***							
Current Acc. Balance / GDP			0.42 0.00***						
Economic Development				-0.59 0.46					
GDP per Capita					-0.07 0.05*				
International Linkages						-0.43 0.57			
Trade / GDP							0.01 0.66		
Industrial Orientation								-1.32 0.07*	
Manuf. Exp. / Total Exp.									-0.03 0.49
N	84	84	84	84	84	84	84	84	84
R^{2*}	0.45	0.41	0.36	0.14	0.16	0.14	0.16	0.16	0.21

Appendix 43b: Multivariate regressions of 'GDP$_{10-12}$' against the 'peg' dummy and one additional control variable in the entire sample (second row: p-values of two-sided significance tests; number of asterisks: significance levels of 10%*, 5%** and 1%***).

Appendix 44 – '$GDP_{08\text{-}12}$', '$GDP_{08\text{-}09}$' and '$GDP_{10\text{-}12}$' against the 'float' dummy in the entire sample

	Dependent Variable: 'GDP_{08-12}'; Sample: All Countries								
	(1)	(2)	(3)	(4)	(5)	(6)	(7)	(8)	(9)
Constant	-9.59 0.00***	-7.08 0.00***	-8.60 0.00***	-10.80 0.00***	-6.10 0.01***	-10.55 0.00***	-8.33 0.01***	-10.12 0.00***	-3.10 0.43
Float	4.12 0.06*	5.66 0.01**	5.57 0.03**	6.54 0.02**	5.95 0.02**	6.04 0.03**	5.88 0.04**	5.18 0.05**	5.23 0.05*
Financial Vulnerabilities	-7.22 0.00***								
Increase (Priv. Cred. / GDP)		-0.29 0.00***							
Current Acc. Balance / GDP			0.56 0.00***						
Economic Development				-2.94 0.01*					
GDP per Capita					-0.26 0.00***				
International Linkages						-0.98 0.37			
Trade / GDP							-0.02 0.26		
Industrial Orientation								-4.04 0.00***	
Manuf. Exp. / Total Exp.									-0.16 0.01***
N	84	84	84	84	84	84	84	84	84
R^{2*}	0.36	0.38	0.19	0.10	0.19	0.05	0.05	0.14	0.11

Appendix 44a: Multivariate regressions of '$GDP_{08\text{-}12}$' against the 'float' dummy and one additional control variable in the entire sample (second row: p-values of two-sided significance tests; number of asterisks: significance levels of 10%*, 5%** and 1%***).

	Dependent Variable: 'GDP_{08-09}'; Sample: All Countries								
	(1)	(2)	(3)	(4)	(5)	(6)	(7)	(8)	(9)
Constant	-6.56 0.00***	-5.18 0.00***	-6.21 0.00***	-6.90 0.00***	4.22 0.00***	-6.66 0.00***	-4.40 0.01***	-6.51 0.00***	-1.66 0.40
Float	0.90 0.51	1.56 0.27	1.64 0.28	1.99 0.20	1.65 0.26	1.50 0.34	1.39 0.37	1.20 0.43	1.12 0.46
Financial Vulnerabilities	-3.19 0.00***								
Increase (Priv. Cred. / GDP)		-0.13 0.00***							
Current Acc. Balance / GDP			0.17 0.09*						
Economic Development				-1.64 0.01***					
GDP per Capita					-0.15 0.00***				
International Linkages						-1.21 0.03**			
Trade / GDP							-0.02 0.02**		
Industrial Orientation								-2.34 0.00***	
Manuf. Exp. / Total Exp.									-0.11 0.00***
N	84	84	84	84	84	84	84	84	84
R^{2*}	0.19	0.21	0.04	0.05	0.15	0.02	0.03	0.10	0.12

Appendix 44b: Multivariate regressions of 'GDP_{08-09}' against the 'float' dummy and one additional control variable in the entire sample (second row: p-values of two-sided significance tests; number of asterisks: significance levels of 10%*, 5%** and 1%***).

	Dependent Variable: 'GDP$_{10-12}$'; Sample: All Countries								
	(1)	(2)	(3)	(4)	(5)	(6)	(7)	(8)	(9)
Constant	-3.80 0.00***	-2.31 0.03**	-2.86 0.00***	-4.54 0.00***	-2.36 0.07*	-4.53 0.00***	-4.66 0.02**	-4.25 0.00***	-2.22 0.39
Float	3.50 0.01***	4.48 0.00***	4.28 0.00***	4.98 0.00***	4.71 0.00***	4.96 0.00***	4.93 0.01***	4.41 0.01***	4.56 0.01***
Financial Vulnerabilities	-4.50 0.00***								
Increase (Priv. Cred. / GDP)		-0.18 0.00***							
Current Acc. Balance / GDP			0.44 0.00***						
Economic Development				-1.40 0.06*					
GDP per Capita					-0.12 0.00***				
International Linkages						0.22 0.76			
Trade / GDP							0.00 0.90		
Industrial Orientation								-1.66 0.03**	
Manuf. Exp. / Total Exp.									-0.05 0.22
N	84	84	84	84	84	84	84	84	84
R^{2*}	0.40	0.40	0.31	0.11	0.16	0.08	0.08	0.12	0.10

Appendix 44c: Multivariate regressions of 'GDP$_{10-12}$' against the 'float' dummy and one additional control variable in the entire sample (second row: p-values of two-sided significance tests; number of asterisks: significance levels of 10%*, 5%** and 1%***).

Appendix 45 –'GDP_{08-12}', 'GDP_{08-09}' and 'GDP_{10-12}' against the 'float' dummy in developed countries

	Dependent Variable: 'GDP_{08-12}'; Sample: Developed Countries								
	(1)	(2)	(3)	(4)	(5)	(6)	(7)	(8)	(9)
Constant	-17.21 0.00***	-15.59 0.00***	-16.52 0.00***	-19.55 0.00***	-22.51 0.00***	-19.47 0.00***	-22.24 0.00***	-20.96 0.00***	-29.38 0.00***
Float	6.81 0.00***	9.30 0.00***	6.10 0.01***	9.01 0.01***	8.77 0.01***	9.81 0.00***	10.00 0.00***	10.42 0.00***	10.34 0.00***
Financial Vulnerabilities	-5.74 0.00***								
Increase (Priv. Cred. / GDP)		-0.17 0.00***							
Current Acc. Balance / GDP			0.71 0.00***						
Economic Development				0.60 0.77					
GDP per Capita					0.10 0.47				
International Linkages						0.85 0.36			
Trade / GDP							0.03 0.03**		
Industrial Orientation								3.85 0.05**	
Manuf. Exp. / Total Exp.									0.18 0.03**
N	32	32	32	32	32	32	32	32	32
R^{2*}	0.63	0.50	0.61	0.16	0.18	0.17	0.21	0.26	0.31

Appendix 45a: Multivariate regressions of 'GDP_{08-12}' against the 'float' dummy and one additional control variable in developed countries (second row: p-values of two-sided significance tests; number of asterisks: significance levels of 10%*, 5%** and 1%***).

	Dependent Variable: 'GDP$_{08-09}$'; Sample: Developed Countries								
	(1)	(2)	(3)	(4)	(5)	(6)	(7)	(8)	(9)
Constant	-11.41 0.00***	-10.93 0.00***	-11.22 0.00***	-13.09 0.00***	-15.55 0.00***	-12.20 0.00***	-12.23 0.00***	-12.84 0.00***	-14.25 0.00***
Float	3.33 0.05*	4.50 0.02**	3.16 0.04**	3.74 0.05*	3.92 0.03**	4.40 0.03**	4.53 0.03**	4.84 0.02**	4.72 0.02**
Financial Vulnerabilities	-2.69 0.02**								
Increase (Priv. Cred. / GDP)		-0.06 0.02**							
Current Acc. Balance / GDP			0.30 0.05**						
Economic Development				1.21 0.39					
GDP per Capita					0.09 0.33				
International Linkages						-0.32 0.53			
Trade / GDP							-0.00 0.93		
Industrial Orientation								1.11 0.25	
Manuf. Exp. / Total Exp.									0.03 0.43
N	32	32	32	32	32	32	32	32	32
R^{2*}	0.33	0.20	0.27	0.11	0.12	0.07	0.08	0.09	0.20

Appendix 45b: Multivariate regressions of 'GDP$_{08-09}$' against the 'float' dummy and one additional control variable in developed countries (second row: p-values of two-sided significance tests; number of asterisks: significance levels of 10%*, 5%** and 1%***).

	Dependent Variable: 'GDP_{10-12}'; Sample: Developed Countries								
	(1)	(2)	(3)	(4)	(5)	(6)	(7)	(8)	(9)
Constant	-6.73 0.00***	-5.41 0.00***	-6.15 0.00***	-7.59 0.00***	-8.37 0.02**	-8.43 0.00***	-11.48 0.00***	-9.46 0.00***	-17.40 0.00***
Float	4.12 0.01**	5.69 0.00***	3.49 0.02**	6.18 0.01**	5.70 0.02**	6.36 0.01***	6.44 0.01***	6.61 0.01***	6.63 0.00***
Financial Vulnerabilities	-6.65 0.00***								
Increase (Priv. Cred. / GDP)		-0.12 0.00***							
Current Acc. Balance / GDP			0.49 0.00***						
Economic Development				-0.59 0.62					
GDP per Capita					0.01 0.89				
International Linkages						1.25 0.06*			
Trade / GDP							0.03 0.00***		
Industrial Orientation								3.19 0.03**	
Manuf. Exp. / Total Exp.									0.16 0.01**
N	32	32	32	32	32	32	32	32	32
R^{2*}	0.49	0.47	0.54	0.11	0.11	0.17	0.23	0.25	0.37

Appendix 45c: Multivariate regressions of 'GDP_{10-12}' against the 'float' dummy and one additional control variable in developed countries (second row: p-values of two-sided significance tests; number of asterisks: significance levels of 10%*, 5%** and 1%***).

Appendix 46 –'$GDP_{08\text{-}12}$', '$GDP_{08\text{-}09}$' and '$GDP_{10\text{-}12}$' against the 'peg' dummy in developed countries

	Dependent Variable: '$GDP_{08\text{-}12}$'; Sample: Developed Countries								
	(1)	(2)	(3)	(4)	(5)	(6)	(7)	(8)	(9)
Constant	-11.27 0.00***	-8.19 0.00***	-11.48 0.00***	-13.61 0.00***	-17.38 0.02**	-12.02 0.00***	-14.30 0.00***	-12.92 0.00***	-21.24 0.00***
Peg	-6.21 0.01**	-7.03 0.02**	-4.96 0.04*	-6.09 0.11	-6.12 0.10	-6.85 0.06*	-6.98 0.05*	-7.35 0.04**	-7.72 0.02**
Financial Vulnerabilities	-6.20 0.00***								
Increase (Priv. Cred. / GDP)		-0.17 0.00***							
Current Acc. Balance / GDP			0.75 0.00***						
Economic Development				1.45 0.52					
GDP per Capita					0.14 0.37				
International Linkages						0.64 0.55			
Trade / GDP							0.02 0.09*		
Industrial Orientation								3.48 0.07*	
Manuf. Exp. / Total Exp.									0.18 0.03**
N	32	32	32	32	32	32	32	32	32
R^{2*}	0.61	0.41	0.58	0.26	0.09	0.06	0.08	0.13	0.20

Appendix 46a: Multivariate regressions of '$GDP_{08\text{-}12}$' against the 'peg' dummy and one additional control variable in developed countries (second row: p-values of two-sided significance tests; number of asterisks: significance levels of 10%*, 5%** and 1%***).

	Dependent Variable: 'GDP$_{08-09}$'; Sample: Developed Countries								
	(1)	(2)	(3)	(4)	(5)	(6)	(7)	(8)	(9)
Constant	-8.93 0.00***	-7.80 0.00***	-9.05 0.00***	-11.05 0.00***	-13.76 0.01***	-9.30 0.00***	-9.00 0.00***	-9.51 0.00***	-10.84 0.00***
Peg	-2.17 0.26	-2.53 0.24	-1.65 0.41	-1.79 0.45	-1.96 0.40	-2.18 0.34	-2.31 0.31	-2.55 0.27	-2.55 0.27
Financial Vulnerabilities	-2.93 0.02**								
Increase (Priv. Cred. / GDP)		-0.07 0.04**							
Current Acc. Balance / GDP			0.33 0.04**						
Economic Development				1.62 0.29					
GDP per Capita					0.11 0.28				
International Linkages						-0.45 0.42			
Trade / GDP							-0.00 0.70		
Industrial Orientation								0.87 0.38	
Manuf. Exp. / Total Exp.									0.03 0.46
N	32	32	32	32	32	32	32	32	32
R^{2*}	0.29	0.11	0.23	0.04	0.05	-0.02	-0.03	-0.02	-0.02

Appendix 46b: Multivariate regressions of 'GDP$_{08-09}$' against the 'peg' dummy and one additional control variable in developed countries (second row: p-values of two-sided significance tests; number of asterisks: significance levels of 10%*, 5%** and 1%***).

	Dependent Variable: 'GDP$_{10-12}$'; Sample: Developed Countries								
	(1)	(2)	(3)	(4)	(5)	(6)	(7)	(8)	(9)
Constant	-2.75 0.00***	-0.48 0.64	-2.86 0.00***	-3.17 0.12	-4.60 0.21	-3.22 0.03**	-6.04 0.00***	-4.01 0.01**	-11.91 0.00***
Peg	-4.52 0.02**	-5.07 0.01**	-3.65 0.03**	-4.79 0.06*	-4.64 0.07*	-5.22 0.04**	-5.24 0.04**	-5.42 0.03**	-5.82 0.01**
Financial Vulnerabilities	-3.92 0.00***								
Increase (Priv. Cred. / GDP)		-0.12 0.00***							
Current Acc. Balance / GDP			0.51 0.00***						
Economic Development				-0.06 0.95					
GDP per Capita					0.03 0.68				
International Linkages						1.15 0.13			
Trade / GDP							0.03 0.01***		
Industrial Orientation								3.02 0.03**	
Manuf. Exp. / Total Exp.									0.17 0.01**
N	32	32	32	32	32	32	32	32	32
R^{2*}	0.51	0.44	0.55	0.05	0.06	0.11	0.17	0.19	0.33

Appendix 46c: Multivariate regressions of 'GDP$_{10-12}$' against the 'peg' dummy and one additional control variable in developed countries (second row: p-values of two-sided significance tests; number of asterisks: significance levels of 10%*, 5%** and 1%***).

Appendix 47 –Correlations amongst significant institutional variables based on Heritage data for the entire sample

	Heritage Property Rights & Freedom from Corruption	Heritage Business Freedom	Gross Replacement Rates	Heritage Financial Freedom	Heritage Government Spending	Pegs
Heritage Property Rights & Freedom from Corruption	1	**0.82**	**0.59**	**0.56**	**-0.55**	**0.32**
Heritage Business Freedom	**0.82**	1	**0.52**	**0.51**	**-0.44**	**0.34**
Gross Replacement Rates	**0.59**	**0.52**	1	**0.34**	**-0.72**	**0.54**
Heritage Financial Freedom	**0.56**	**0.51**	**0.34**	1	**-0.33**	**0.32**
Heritage Government Spending	**-0.55**	**-0.44**	**-0.72**	**-0.33**	1	**-0.37**
Pegs	**0.32**	**0.34**	**0.54**	**0.32**	**-0.37**	1

Appendix 47: Correlations amongst significant institutional variables based on Heritage data for the entire sample (significant correlations at conventional significance levels are bold).

Appendix 48 – 'GDP08-09' and 'GDP10-12' against the composite index 'developed economic institutions' based on Fraser data in the entire sample

	Dependent Variable: 'GDP08-09'; Sample: All Countries									
	(1)	(2)	(3)	(4)	(5)	(6)	(7)	(8)	(9)	(10)
Constant	14.22	12.33	8.06	8.36	8.82	8.00	13.51	12.31	14.71	14.56
	0.00***	0.00***	0.13	0.11	0.01***	0.01**	0.00***	0.00***	0.01***	0.01***
Fras. Developed	-3.23	-2.79	-2.25	-2.22	-2.37	-2.15	-2.24	-2.04	-2.48	-2.52
Econ. Institutions	0.00***	0.00***	0.01***	0.01***	0.00***	0.00***	0.00***	0.00***	0.01***	0.01***
Peg		-3.60		-2.10		-2.30		-1.82		-2.21
		0.02**		0.17		0.11		0.21		0.15
Financial			-2.75	-2.62	-2.73	-2.61				
Vulnerabilities			0.00***	0.00***	0.00***	0.00***				
Industrial			1.69	-1.49	-1.66	-1.49				
Orientation			0.00***	0.02**	0.00***	0.01***				
Economic			0.09	0.29						
Development			0.92	0.74						
International			-0.85	-0.68						
Linkages			0.06*	0.17						
Increase (Priv.							-0.07	-0.07	-0.08	-0.08
Cred. / GDP)							0.10	0.08*	0.09*	0.05*
Current Acc.							0.20	0.17	0.18	0.14
Balance / GDP							0.08*	0.12	0.08*	0.18
Man. Exp. /							-0.09	-0.08	-0.09	-0.08
Total Exp.							0.00***	0.00***	0.00***	0.00***
GDP									0.02	0.05
per Capita									0.65	0.36
N	82	82	82	82	82	82	82	82	82	82
R^{2*}	0.25	0.28	0.43	0.43	0.43	0.44	0.43	0.44	0.43	0.43

Appendix 48a: Multivariate regressions of 'GDP08-09' against Fraser 'developed economic institutions', the 'peg' dummy and different sets of control variables in the entire sample (second row: p-values of two-sided significance tests; number of asterisks: significance levels of 10%*, 5%** and 1%***; heteroscedasticity in regressions 3, 5, 6, 7, 8 and 9; residuals in regressions 1 to 10 are not normally-distributed).

	Dependent Variable: 'GDP10-12'; Sample: All Countries									
	(1)	(2)	(3)	(4)	(5)	(6)	(7)	(8)	(9)	(10)
Constant	12.23	9.05	0.40	0.15	5.06	3.51	12.65	10.27	8.62	8.39
	0.00***	0.04**	0.93	0.97	0.19	0.34	0.00***	0.00***	0.06*	0.06*
Fras. Developed	-2.26	-1.52	-0.38	-0.18	-1.12	-0.71	-1.33	-3.62	-0.49	-0.55
Econ. Institutions	0.00***	0.03**	0.56	0.78	0.05**	0.19	0.02**	0.07*	0.51	0.46
Peg		-6.04		-4.17		-4.36		-3.62		-3.29
		0.01**		0.04**		0.03**		0.07*		0.09*
Financial			-4.67	-4.43	-4.54	-4.33				
Vulnerabilities			0.00***	0.00***	0.00***	0.00***				
Industrial			-1.88	-1.51	-1.65	-1-33				
Orientation			0.00***	0.00***	0.00***	0.01***				
Economic			-1.11	-0.82						
Development			0.15	0.22						
Increase (Priv.							-0.10	-0.10	-0.08	-0.09
Cred. / GDP)							0.02**	0.01***	0.07*	0.02**
Current Acc.							0.40	0.36	0.45	0.39
Balance / GDP							0.01***	0.00***	0.00***	0.00***
Man. Exp. /							-0.09	-0.07	-0.09	-0.07
Total Exp.							0.00***	0.02**	0.00***	0.02**
GDP									-0.08	-0.04
per Capita									0.17	0.40
N	82	82	82	82	82	82	82	82	82	82
R^{2*}	0.09	0.18	0.44	0.47	0.43	0.48	0.49	0.52	0.49	0.51

Appendix 48b: Multivariate regressions of 'GDP_{10-12}' against Fraser 'developed economic institutions', the 'peg' dummy and different sets of control variables in the entire sample (second row: p-values of two-sided significance tests; number of asterisks: significance levels of 10%*, 5%** and 1%***; misspecifications in regressions 3 and 5; heteroscedasticity in regression 8; residuals in regressions 3 to 10 are not normally-distributed).

Appendix 49 – 'GDP_{08-12}', 'GDP_{08-09}' and 'GDP_{10-12}' against the composite index 'developed economic institutions' based on Heritage data in the entire sample

	Dependent Variable: 'GDP_{08-12}'; Sample: All Countries									
	(1)	(2)	(3)	(4)	(5)	(6)	(7)	(8)	(9)	(10)
Constant	12.26	9.28	7.17	5.75	6.35	4.88	16.36	13.87	17.32	15.63
	0.00***	0.02**	0.17	0.26	0.06*	0.16	0.00***	0.00***	0.01***	0.02**
Her. Developed	-0.37	-0.28	-0.27	-0.23	-0.26	-0.21	-0.21	-0.16	-0.24	-0.21
Econ. Institutions	0.00***	0.00***	0.00***	0.02**	0.00***	0.00***	0.00***	0.01***	0.11	0.14
Peg		-8.24		-4.73		-5.06		-4.42		-4.55
		0.01**		0.10*		0.06*		0.10		0.08*
Financial			-6.89	-6.69	-6.92	-6.71				
Vulnerabilities			0.00***	0.00***	0.00***	0.00***				
Industrial			-3.51	-3.17	-3.56	-3.20				
Orientation			0.00***	0.00***	0.00***	0.00***				
Economic			0.46	0.39						
Development			0.75	0.75						
International			-0.97	-0.66						
Linkages			0.20	0.44						
Increase (Priv.							-0.17	-0.18	-0.18	-0.19
Cred. / GDP)							0.02**	0.01***	0.02**	0.01***
Current Acc.							0.52	0.46	0.50	0.43
Balance / GDP							0.00***	0.00***	0.00***	0.01***
Man. Exp. /							-0.20	-0.18	-0.20	-0.18
Total Exp.							0.00***	0.00***	0.00***	0.00***
GDP									0.03	0.06
per Capita									0.84	0.67
N	84	84	84	84	84	84	84	84	84	84
R^{2*}	0.21	0.26	0.55	0.57	0.56	0.58	0.57	0.58	0.57	0.58

Appendix 49a: Multivariate regressions of 'GDP_{08-12}' against Heritage 'developed economic institutions', the 'peg' dummy and different sets of control variables in the entire sample (second row: p-values of two-sided significance tests; number of asterisks: significance levels of 10%*, 5%** and 1%***; misspecification in regression 2; residuals in regressions 1 to 7 and 9 are not normally-distributed).

	Dependent Variable: 'GDP$_{08-09}$'; Sample: All Countries									
	(1)	(2)	(3)	(4)	(5)	(6)	(7)	(8)	(9)	(10)
Constant	5.85	4.70	4.93	4.56	3.14	2.65	7.55	6.71	11.52	10.85
	0.00***	0.01**	0.14	0.15	0.11	0.16	0.00***	0.00***	0.00***	0.00***
Her. Developed	-0.22	-0.18	-0.20	-0.19	-0.17	-0.15	-0.13	-0.12	-0.24	-0.23
Econ. Institutions	0.00***	0.00***	0.00***	0.00***	0.00***	0.00***	0.00***	0.00***	0.01***	0.01***
Peg		-3.20		-1.24		-1.69		-1.49		-1.80
		0.05*		0.40		0.24		0.31		0.24
Financial			-2.77	-2.72	-2.85	-2.78				
Vulnerabilities			0.00***	0.00***	0.00***	0.00***				
Industrial			-1.76	-1.67	-1.87	-1.74				
Orientation			0.00***	0.00***	0.00***	0.00***				
Economic			0.82	0.80						
Development			0.40	0.39						
International			-0.95	-0.87						
Linkages			0.06*	0.11						
Increase (Priv.							-0.09	-0.09	-0.11	-0.12
Cred. / GDP)							0.05*	0.04**	0.01**	0.01***
Current Acc.							0.15	0.14	0.08	0.05
Balance / GDP							0.17	0.23	0.42	0.62
Man. Exp. /							-0.11	-0.10	-0.11	-0.10
Total Exp.							0.00***	0.00***	0.00***	0.09*
GDP									0.12	0.13
per Capita									0.13	0.09*
N	84	84	84	84	84	84	84	84	84	84
R^{2*}	0.23	0.25	0.44	0.43	0.42	0.43	0.42	0.42	0.43	0.44

Appendix 49b: Multivariate regressions of 'GDP$_{08-09}$' against Heritage 'developed economic institutions', the 'peg' dummy and different sets of control variables in the entire sample (second row: p-values of two-sided significance tests; number of asterisks: significance levels of 10%*, 5%** and %***; heteroscedasticity in regressions 5, 7 and 8; residuals in regressions 1 to 10 are not normally-distributed).

	Dependent Variable: 'GDP10-12'; Sample: All Countries									
	(1)	(2)	(3)	(4)	(5)	(6)	(7)	(8)	(9)	(10)
Constant	6.53 0.01***	4.48 0.08*	2.00 0.51	0.56 0.87	3.11 0.15	1.98 0.39	8.91 0.00***	6.96 0.01***	5.48 0.21	4.27 0.35
Her. Developed Econ. Institutions	-0.16 0.00***	-0.10 0.04**	-0.08 0.16	-0.03 0.62	-0.10 0.01***	-0.06 0.16	-0.08 0.01**	-0.04 0.22	0.01 0.89	0.03 0.75
Peg		-5.66 0.02**		-3.94 0.08*		-3.90 0.08*		-3.46 0.11		-3.25 0.11
Financial Vulnerabilities			-4.59 0.00***	-4.43 0.00***	-4.54 0.00***	-4.37 0.00***				
Industrial Orientation			-1.74 0.00***	-1.47 0.00***	-1.67 0.00***	-1.39 0.01***				
Economic Development			-0.42 0.65	-0.53 0.53						
Increase (Priv. Cred. / GDP)							-0.10 0.01***	-0.10 0.00***	-0.08 0.08*	-0.09 0.03**
Current Acc. Balance / GDP							0.39 0.00***	0.35 0.00***	0.46 0.00***	0.41 0.00***
Man. Exp. / Total Exp.							-0.09 0.00***	-0.08 0.01**	-0.09 0.00***	-0.08 0.01**
GDP per Capita									-0.11 0.32	-0.09 0.35
N	84	84	84	84	84	84	84	84	84	84
R^{2*}	0.10	0.17	0.44	0.47	0.45	0.48	0.49	0.51	0.49	0.51

Appendix 49c: Multivariate regressions of 'GDP_{10-12}' against Heritage 'developed economic institutions', the 'peg' dummy and different sets of control variables in the entire sample (second row: p-values of two-sided significance tests; number of asterisks: significance levels of 10%*, 5%** and 1%***; misspecifications in regressions 2, 3 and 5; heteroscedasticity in regressions 2, 6, 8, 9 and 10; residuals in regressions 1, 3, 4, 5, 6, 7, 9 and10 are not normally-distributed).

Appendix 50 – Correlations amongst significant institutional variables based on Heritage and GCI data in developed countries

	Heritage Property Rights & Freedom from Corruption	Heritage Business Freedom	Heritage Labor Freedom	Floating Exchange Rates
Heritage Property Rights & Freedom from Corruption	1	**0.77**	**0.39**	0.33
Heritage Business Freedom	**0.77**	1	**0.45**	0.28
Heritage Labor Freedom	**0.39**	**0.45**	1	**0.43**
Floating Exchange Rates	0.33	0.28	**0.43**	1

Appendix 50a: Correlations amongst significant institutional variables based on Heritage data in developed countries (significant correlations at conventional significance levels are bold).

	GCI Public Institutions	GCI Competition	GCI Labor Flexibility	Floating Exchange Rates
GCI Public Institutions	1	**0.71**	**0.41**	0.23
GCI Competition	**0.71**	1	**0.67**	0.29
GCI Labor Flexibility	**0.41**	**0.67**	1	**0.56**
Floating Exchange Rates	0.23	0.29	**0.56**	1

Appendix 50b: Correlations amongst significant institutional variables based on GCI data in developed countries (significant correlations at conventional significance levels are bold).

Appendix 51 – '$GDP_{10\text{-}12}$' against the composite index 'open access economic institutions' based on Heritage and GCI data in developed countries

	Dependent Variable: '$GDP_{10\text{-}12}$'; Sample: Developed Countries									
	(1)	(2)	(3)	(4)	(5)	(6)	(7)	(8)	(9)	(10)
Constant	-28.61 0.00***	-25.34 0.00***	-21.70 0.01***	-19.46 0.02**	-26.22 0.00***	-23.10 0.00***	-14.22 0.04**	-11.54 0.09*	-20.41 0.00***	-17.74 0.00***
Her. Open Access Econ. Institutions	0.30 0.01***	0.24 0.03**	0.22 0.02**	0.18 0.07*	0.30 0.00***	0.25 0.01***	0.12 0.15	0.07 0.39	0.22 0.00***	0.17 0.02**
Float		3.28 0.15		2.43 0.09*		3.15 0.02**		2.90 0.05*		3.02 0.02**
Financial Vulnerabilities			-3.46 0.00***	-3.37 0.00***						
Increase (Priv. Cred. / GDP)					-0.12 0.00***	-0.12 0.00***			-0.08 0.02**	-0.09 0.01**
Current Acc. Balance / GDP							0.46 0.00***	0.45 0.00***	0.21 0.09*	0.20 0.11
N	32	32	32	32	32	32	32	32	32	32
R^{2*}	0.22	0.24	0.54	0.55	0.57	0.60	0.52	0.54	0.59	0.61

Appendix 51a: Multivariate regressions of '$GDP_{10\text{-}12}$' against Heritage 'open access economic institutions', the 'float' dummy and different sets of control variables in the sub-sample of developed countries (second row: p-values of two-sided significance tests; number of asterisks: significance levels of 10%*, 5%** and 1%***; residuals are not normally-distributed in regressions 3 to 10).

Dependent Variable: 'GDP$_{10-12}$'; Sample: Developed Countries										
	(1)	(2)	(3)	(4)	(5)	(6)	(7)	(8)	(9)	(10)
Constant	-35.52 0.00***	-30.66 0.01**	-27.07 0.01***	-23.79 0.02**	-32.75 0.00***	-28.00 0.01***	-15.40 0.08*	-10.94 0.22	-24.46 0.01***	-20.00 0.04**
GCI Open Access Econ. Institutions	6.17 0.01**	4.89 0.04**	4.54 0.02**	3.66 0.07*	6.12 0.00***	4.87 0.01**	2.19 0.21	1.01 0.57	4.32 0.01**	3.14 0.13
Float		3.26 0.11		2.35 0.09*		3.19 0.01**		3.09 0.04**		3.13 0.10*
Financial Vulnerabilities			-3.49 0.00***	-3.40 0.00***						
Increase (Priv. Cred. / GDP)					-0.12 0.00***	-0.12 0.01**			-0.08 0.01**	-0.08 0.00***
Current Acc. Balance / GDP							0.47 0.00***	0.46 0.00***	0.21 0.10	0.21 0.16
N	32	32	32	32	32	32	32	32	32	32
R^{2*}	0.22	0.24	0.54	0.55	0.56	0.58	0.51	0.53	0.59	0.60

Appendix 51b: Multivariate regressions of 'GDP$_{10-12}$' against GCI 'open access economic institutions', the 'float' dummy and different sets of control variables in the sub-sample of developed countries (second row: p-values of two-sided significance tests; number of asterisks: significance levels of 10%*, 5%** and 1%***; residuals are non-normally-distributed in all regressions).

Appendix 52 –'GDP$_{08-12}$' against the composite index 'open access economic institutions' based on Fraser, Heritage and GCI data in developed countries

Dependent Variable: 'GDP$_{08-12}$'; Sample: Developed Countries										
	(1)	(2)	(3)	(4)	(5)	(6)	(7)	(8)	(9)	(10)
Constant	-43.24 0.00***	-32.74 0.01**	-32.68 0.00***	-25.26 0.02**	-40.25 0.00***	-30.08 0.00***	-17.48 0.11	-9.15 0.35	-22.51 0.06***	-14.41 0.16
Fras. Open Access Econ. Institutions	4.02 0.02**	2.05 0.26	2.63 0.08*	1.21 0.45	4.10 0.01***	2.19 0.14	0.51 0.74	-1.09 0.45	1.39 0.42	-0.18 0.90
Float		7.82 0.03**		5.90 0.02**		7.59 0.00***		6.80 0.01***		6.98 0.00***
Financial Vulnerabilities			-5.94 0.00***	-5.66 0.00***						
Increase (Priv. Cred. / GDP)					-0.17 0.00***	-0.17 0.00***			-0.07 0.26	-0.07 0.12
Current Acc. Balance / GDP							0.77 0.00***	0.74 0.00***	0.58 0.03**	0.54 0.02**
N	32	32	32	32	32	32	32	32	32	32
R^{2*}	0.09	0.18	0.57	0.62	0.42	0.52	0.52	0.60	0.53	0.62

Appendix 52a: Multivariate regressions of 'GDP$_{08-12}$' against Fraser 'open access economic institutions', the 'float' dummy and different sets of control variables in the sub-sample of developed countries (second row: p-values of two-sided significance tests; number of asterisks: significance levels of 10%*, 5%** and 1%***; misspecifications in regressions 7 to 10).

	Dependent Variable: 'GDP08-12'; Sample: Developed Countries									
	(1)	(2)	(3)	(4)	(5)	(6)	(7)	(8)	(9)	(10)
Constant	-40.57 0.00***	-40.20 0.00***	-35.34 0.00***	-30.71 0.00***	-43.25 0.00***	-37.09 0.00***	-24.53 0.02**	-19.18 0.03**	-31.35 0.00***	-26.09 0.00***
Her. Open Access Econ. Institutions	0.41 0.00***	0.29 0.04**	0.27 0.02**	0.19 0.13	0.41 0.00***	0.30 0.01***	0.14 0.29	0.04 0.76	0.25 0.04**	0.15 0.16
Float		6.39 0.07*		5.02 0.04**		6.21 0.01***		5.81 0.02**		5.94 0.01***
Financial Vulnerabilities			-5.63 0.00***	-5.44 0.00***						
Increase (Priv. Cred. / GDP)					-0.17 0.00***	-0.17 0.00***			-0.09 0.13	-0.10 0.05**
Current Acc. Balance / GDP							0.71 0.00***	0.69 0.02**	0.43 0.08*	0.41 0.07*
N	32	32	32	32	32	32	32	32	32	32
R^{2*}	0.20	0.26	0.61	0.65	0.53	0.59	0.51	0.60	0.58	0.64

Appendix 52b: Multivariate regressions of 'GDP_{08-12}' against Heritage 'open access economic institutions', the 'float' dummy and different sets of control variables in the sub-sample of developed countries (second row: p-values of two-sided significance tests; number of asterisks: significance levels of 10%*, 5%** and 1%***; misspecifications in regressions 7, 8 and 10).

	Dependent Variable: 'GDP08-12'; Sample: Developed Countries									
	(1)	(2)	(3)	(4)	(5)	(6)	(7)	(8)	(9)	(10)
Constant	-53.32 0.00***	-43.28 0.00***	-39.48 0.00***	-32.14 0.01***	-49.46 0.00***	-39.58 0.00***	-21.47 0.06*	-12.13 0.28	-30.32 0.02**	-21.05 0.08*
GCI Open Access Econ. Institutions	7.84 0.01***	5.20 0.07*	5.17 0.03**	3.20 0.19	7.77 0.00***	5.17 0.03**	1.54 0.51	-0.93 0.69	3.63 0.18	1.17 0.64
Float		6.74 0.04**		5.26 0.03**		6.64 0.00***		0.73 0.00***		6.51 0.01***
Financial Vulnerabilities			-5.72 0.00***	-5.52 0.00***						
Increase (Priv. Cred. / GDP)					-0.17 0.00***	-0.17 0.00***			-0.08 0.17	-0.08 0.09*
Current Acc. Balance / GDP							0.74 0.00***	0.73 0.00***	0.49 0.07*	0.48 0.05*
N	32	32	32	32	32	32	32	32	32	32
R^{2*}	0.17	0.23	0.60	0.64	0.49	0.56	0.53	0.60	0.55	0.62

Appendix 52c: Multivariate regressions of 'GDP_{08-12}' against GCI 'open access economic institutions', the 'float' dummy and different sets of control variables in the sub-sample of developed countries (second row: p-values of two-sided significance tests; number of asterisks: significance levels of 10%*, 5%** and 1%***; residuals are not normally-distributed in regression 1; misspecifications in regressions 7 to 10).

Appendix 53 – '$GDP_{10\text{-}12}$' against the composite index 'open access economic institutions' based on Heritage and GCI data in developed countries without Greece

	Dependent Variable: '$GDP_{10\text{-}12}$'; Sample: Developed Countries									
	(1)	(2)	(3)	(4)	(5)	(6)	(7)	(8)	(9)	(10)
Constant	-23.63	-19.49	-17.80	-15.29	-21.84	-17.89	-10.55	-7.32	-16.99	-13.68
	0.01***	0.02**	0.00***	0.01***	0.00***	0.00***	0.09*	0.23	0.00***	0.02**
Fras. Open Access	2.69	1.90	1.92	1.44	2.79	2.04	0.90	0.28	2.04	1.39
Econ. Institutions	0.02**	0.11	0.00***	0.07*	0.00***	0.01***	0.29	0.76	0.01**	0.08*
Float		3.20		2.07		3.06				2.90
		0.11		0.13		0.02**				0.02**
Financial			-3.49	-3.39				2.70		
Vulnerabilities			0.00***	0.00***				0.07*		
Increase (Priv.					-0.12	-0.12			-0.09	-0.09
Cred. / GDP)					0.00***	0.00***			0.01***	0.00***
Current Acc.							0.42	0.41	0.17	0.16
Balance / GDP							0.00***	0.00***	0.09*	0.12
N	31	31	31	31	31	31	31	31	31	31
R^{2*}	0.13	0.17	0.65	0.67	0.65	0.70	0.54	0.57	0.68	0.72

Appendix 53a: Multivariate regressions of '$GDP_{10\text{-}12}$' against Fraser 'open access economic institutions', the 'float' dummy and different sets of control variables in the sub-sample of developed countries excluding Greece (second row: p-values of two-sided significance tests; number of asterisks: significance levels of 10%*, 5%** and 1%***; residuals are not normally-distributed in regression 6).

	Dependent Variable: '$GDP_{10\text{-}12}$'; Sample: Developed Countries									
	(1)	(2)	(3)	(4)	(5)	(6)	(7)	(8)	(9)	(10)
Constant	-21.52	-18.56	-14.83	-12.84	-19.51	-16.67	-9.24	-6.77	-15.86	-13.37
	0.00***	0.00***	0.00***	0.01*	0.00***	0.00***	0.09*	0.21	0.00***	0.00***
Her. Open Access	0.22	0.16	0.14	0.10	0.22	0.17	0.06	0.02	0.17	0.12
Econ. Institutions	0.01**	0.06*	0.01**	0.14	0.00***	0.00***	0.35	0.81	0.00***	0.04**
Float		3.06		2.22		2.94		2.74		2.86
		0.15		0.12		0.00***		0.07*		0.02**
Financial			-3.42	-3.33						
Vulnerabilities			0.00***	0.00***						
Increase (Priv.					-0.12	-0.12			-0.09	-0.09
Cred. / GDP)					0.00***	0.00***			0.01***	0.00***
Current Acc.							0.42	0.41	0.14	0.13
Balance / GDP							0.00***	0.00***	0.16	0.18
N	31	31	31	31	31	31	31	31	31	31
R^{2*}	0.16	0.19	0.64	0.66	0.68	0.72	0.54	0.57	0.69	0.73

Appendix 53a: Multivariate regressions of '$GDP_{10\text{-}12}$' against Heritage 'open access economic institutions', the 'float' dummy and different sets of control variables in the sub-sample of developed countries excluding Greece (second row: p-values of two-sided significance tests; number of asterisks: significance levels of 10%*, 5%** and 1%***).

	Dependent Variable: 'GDP$_{10-12}$'; Sample: Developed Countries									
	(1)	(2)	(3)	(4)	(5)	(6)	(7)	(8)	(9)	(10)
Constant	-26.51 0.00***	-22.07 0.01**	-18.44 0.00***	-15.50 0.01***	-24.14 0.00***	-19.80 0.00***	-9.12 0.14	-4.98 0.46	-18.93 0.00***	-14.79 0.02**
GCI Open Access Econ. Institutions	4.44 0.01**	3.27 0.08*	2.88 0.00***	2.09 0.10	4.45 0.00***	3.31 0.00***	1.00 0.43	-0.10 0.94	3.32 0.01***	2.22 0.08*
Float		3.04 0.13		2.15 0.12		2.98 0.02**		2.91 0.06*		2.95 0.02*
Financial Vulnerabilities			-3.43 0.00***	-3.35 0.00***						
Increase (Priv. Cred. / GDP)					-0.12 0.00***	-0.12 0.00***			-0.09 0.01***	-0.09 0.00***
Current Acc. Balance / GDP							0.43 0.00***	0.42 0.00***	0.14 0.17	0.14 0.17
N	31	31	31	31	31	31	31	31	31	31
R^{2*}	0.15	0.18	0.65	0.66	0.66	0.71	0.53	0.57	0.67	0.72

Appendix 53c: Multivariate regressions of 'GDP$_{10-12}$' against GCI 'open access economic institutions', the 'float' dummy and different sets of control variables in the sub-sample of developed countries excluding Greece (second row: p-values of two-sided significance tests; number of asterisks: significance levels of 10%*, 5%** and 1%***).

Appendix 54 – Correlations amongst significant institutional variables based on Heritage data in emerging and developing countries

	Gross Replacement Rates	Heritage Financial Freedom	Heritage Government Spending
Gross Replacement Rates	1	-0.05	**-0.44**
Heritage Financial Freedom	-0.05	1	-0.10
Heritage Government Spending	**-0.44**	-0.10	1

Appendix 54: Correlations among significant institutional variables (mainly based on Heritage data) in the sub-sample of less developed countries (significant correlations at 5% level are bold).

Appendix 55 – 'GDP_{08-09}' against two institutional variables based on Heritage data in less developed countries

	Dependent Variable: 'GDP_{08-09}'; Sample: Emerging and Developing Countries									
	(1)	(2)	(3)	(4)	(5)	(6)	(7)	(8)	(9)	(10)
Constant	-7.96 0.08*	-6.09 0.15	-3.81 0.37	-2.93 0.46	-3.84 0.31	-7.57 0.12	2.13 0.62	4.27 0.25	3.46 0.46	3.68 0.38
Heritage Financial Freedom	-0.07 0.20	-0.06 0.22	-0.11 0.05**	-0.10 0.06*	-0.04 0.45	-0.07 0.23	-0.12 0.01**	-0.09 0.06*	-0.11 0.01**	-0.09 0.06*
Heritage Government Spending	0.11 0.01**	0.08 0.08*	0.08 0.06*	0.06 0.17	0.05 0.24	0.11 0.03**	0.07 0.09*	0.03 0.55	0.06 0.22	0.03 0.50
Financial Vulnerabilities		-2.15 0.05*		-1.57 0.10*						
Industrial Orientation			-2.46 0.00***	-2.17 0.00***						
Increase (Priv. Cred. / GDP)					-0.20 0.01***			-0.17 0.01***		-0.19 0.02**
Current Acc. Balance / GDP						0.04 0.67			0.09 0.26	-0.06 0.60
Manuf. Exp. / Total Exp.							-0.12 0.00***	-0.11 0.00***	-0.13 0.00***	-0.10 0.00***
N	52	52	52	52	52	52	52	52	52	52
R^{2*}	0.10	0.16	0.23	0.26	0.25	0.08	0.27	0.37	0.26	0.37

Appendix 55: Multivariate regressions of 'GDP_{08-09}' against Heritage 'financial freedom', Heritage 'government spending' and different sets of control variables in the sub-sample of less developed countries (second row: p-values of two-sided significance tests; number of asterisks: significance levels of 10%*, 5%** and 1%***; residuals in regressions 1, 2, 3, 4, 6, 7 and 9).

Appendix 56 – 'GDP_{08-12}' against two institutional variables based on Fraser or Heritage data in less developed countries

	Dependent Variable: 'GDP_{08-12}'; Sample: Emerging and Developing Countries									
	(1)	(2)	(3)	(4)	(5)	(6)	(7)	(8)	(9)	(10)
Constant	24.33 0.04**	5.40 0.64	19.37 0.08*	4.20 0.70	16.42 0.14	15.37 0.21	27.11 0.02**	19.22 0.06*	17.60 0.09*	16.26 0.10
Fraser Credit Market Regulation	-4.38 0.00***	-2.40 0.04**	-3.62 0.00***	-2.09 0.06*	-2.83 0.01**	-3.43 0.01***	-3.62 0.00***	-2.21 0.03**	-2.43 0.02**	-1.97 0.05*
Fraser Government Consumption	1.51 0.06*	1.72 0.02**	1.14 0.11	1.41 0.03**	1.06 0.13	1.95 0.01***	1.09 0.15	0.71 0.30	1.51 0.01**	1.07 0.08*
Financial Vulnerabilities		-6.47 0.00***		-5.57 0.00***						
Industrial Orientation			-4.23 0.00***	-3.26 0.00***						
Increase (Priv. Cred. / GDP)					-0.44 0.00***			-0.42 0.00***		-0.29 0.02**
Current Acc. Balance / GDP						0.57 0.00***			0.64 0.00***	0.36 0.02**
Manuf. Exp. / Total Exp.							-0.17 0.01***	-0.15 0.00***	-0.20 0.00***	-0.17 0.00***
N	50	50	50	50	50	50	50	50	50	50
R^{2*}	0.20	0.40	0.33	0.47	0.44	0.35	0.29	0.51	0.48	0.55

Table 56a: Multivariate regressions of 'GDP_{08-12}' against Fraser 'credit market regulation', Fraser 'government consumption' and different sets of control variables in the sub-sample of less developed countries (second row: p-values of two-sided significance tests; number of asterisks: significance levels of 10%*, 5%** and 1%***).

	Dependent Variable: 'GDP08–12'; Sample: Emerging and Developing Countries									
	(1)	(2)	(3)	(4)	(5)	(6)	(7)	(8)	(9)	(10)
Constant	-20.32 0.01**	-14.96 0.03**	-11.96 0.15	-9.11 0.20	-11.38 0.10	-16.65 0.03**	-1.44 0.87	3.32 0.66	5.41 0.55	5.77 0.46
Heritage Financial Freedom	-0.12 0.24	-0.10 0.27	-0.19 0.05**	-0.16 0.06*	-0.05 0.56	-0.08 0.39	-0.21 0.02**	-0.13 0.07*	-0.17 0.03**	-0.13 0.07*
Heritage Government Spending	0.31 0.00***	0.22 0.00***	0.24 0.00***	0.18 0.01**	0.18 0.01***	0.26 0.00***	0.24 0.00***	0.13 0.06*	0.17 0.04**	0.12 0.11
Financial Vulnerabilities		-6.14 0.00***		-5.07 0.00***						
Industrial Orientation			-4.95 0.00***	-4.02 0.00***						
Increase (Priv. Cred. / GDP)					-0.44 0.00***			-0.39 0.00***		-0.31 0.01***
Current Acc. Balance / GDP						0.38 0.00***			0.49 0.00***	0.24 0.11
Manuf. Exp. / Total Exp.							-0.23 0.00***	-0.19 0.00***	-0.26 0.00***	-0.21 0.00***
N	52	52	52	52	52	52	52	52	52	52
R^{2*}	0.21	0.39	0.38	0.49	0.43	0.26	0.39	0.55	0.48	0.56

Appendix 56b: Multivariate regressions of '$GDP_{08\text{-}12}$' against Heritage 'financial freedom', Heritage 'government spending' and different sets of control variables in the sub-sample of less developed countries (second row: p-values of two-sided significance tests; number of asterisks: significance levels of 10%*, 5%** and 1%***).

Appendix 57 – Control variables for explaining institutional quality

Throughout the regressions explaining the shape of economic institutions, I consider nine cultural and social control variables.

First, I consider two variables capturing the origin of the legal system. The use of these variables to explain the shape of institutions and of economic outcomes goes back to La Porta et al. (1997). According to their argument, countries with common law (typically countries with British legal origin) developed better economic institutions than countries with civil law (most importantly countries with French legal origin). La Porta et al (2008) provide a good review of the related arguments and empirical evidence. In their dataset,[248] the authors distinguish between French, British, German, Scandinavian and Socialist legal origin. From that dataset I consider two dummy variables.

- The first variable labeled 'British legal origin' attributes the score 1 to all countries with British legal origin and a 0 to countries with French, German, Scandinavian or Socialist legal origin. Hence, that variable distinguishes countries with the allegedly 'best' legal tradition (the British) from all other countries. In regressions explaining the quality of institutions this variable should have positive coefficients.
- The second variable labeled 'French legal origin' attributes scores of 1 to all countries with French legal origin and a 0 to countries with British, German, Scandinavian or Socialist legal origin. Hence, that variable distinguishes countries with the allegedly 'worst' legal tradition (the French) from all other countries. In regressions explaining the quality of institutions this variable should have negative coefficients.

Second, I consider two variables capturing the predominant religion in the respective country. Drawing on Weber (2016 [1920]), some authors argue that being predominantly Protestant instead of predominantly Catholic or Muslim is conducive for the development of capitalist institutions. Short summaries of the argument can be found in La Porta et al. (1999) or Borner et. al (2004). Accordingly, I use two variables capturing the religious composition of the respective countries based on data from the World Religion Database (Maoz & Henderson, 2013).[249]

- The first variable labeled 'percentage Protestants' measures the percentage of the population of the respective country that was either Protestant or Anglican in the year 2005.

[248] The data is downloadable at https://scholar.harvard.edu/shleifer/publications/economic-consequences-legal-origins.

[249] The data is downloadable at http://www.thearda.com/Archive/Files/Descriptions/WRPGLOBL.asp.

- The second variable labeled 'percentage Catholic Muslim' measures the percentage of the population of the respective country that was either Catholic or Muslim in the year 2005.

Third, I consider three variables capturing cultural heterogeneity in the respective country. The use of these variables is based on the argument that ethnic conflict within a country causes worse institutions and worse economic performance. For a short review of related papers see Alesina et al. (2003). These authors also provide the data on the three aspects of cultural heterogeneity I consider. The three measures capture "the probability that two randomly selected individuals from a population belong[.] to different groups" (Alesina et. al, 2003, pp. 158-159).[250] Fractionalization measures are based on data from different years in different countries, mainly from the 1990's. As, however, the ethnic, linguistic and religious composition of a country can be regarded as fairly stable, the time of measurement does not invalidate the variables.

- The first variable labeled 'ethnic fractionalization' differentiates groups according to racial properties. Values near 0 indicate low diversity, and values near 1 indicate high diversity.
- The second variable labeled 'linguistic fractionalization' differentiates groups according to language their mother language. Values near 0 indicate low diversity, and values near 1 indicate high diversity.
- The third variable labeled 'religious fractionalization' differentiates groups according to their religion. Values near 0 indicate low diversity, and values near 1 indicate high diversity.

Fourth, I consider a measure for economic inequalities. The use of this measures is based on the argument that social conflict is more prevalent in countries marked by economic inequalities and that it leads to inferior institutions (Rodrik, 1999).

- The variable I use is the Gini coefficient of the year 2007 from the World Development Indicators Database (indicator code: SI.POV.GINI). If there are missing values for a country, I use data from the World Income Inequality Database.[251]

Finally, I consider a measure for economic development, as a variety of authors argue that richer countries support better economic institutions. This variable, however, is highly endogenous as causality might run both ways from good institutions to high development and from high development to better institutions.

- The variable I use is the GDP per capita of the year 2007 in current USD from the World Development Indicators Database (indicator code: NY.GDP.PCAP.CD).

[250] Data is downloadable at http://www.nsd.uib.no/macrodataguide/set.html?id=16&sub=1.

[251] Data is downloadable at https://www.wider.unu.edu/database/world-income-inequality-database-wiid34.

Appendix 58 – Scatterplots of different 'developed economic institutions' indices against different political openness indices in the entire sample

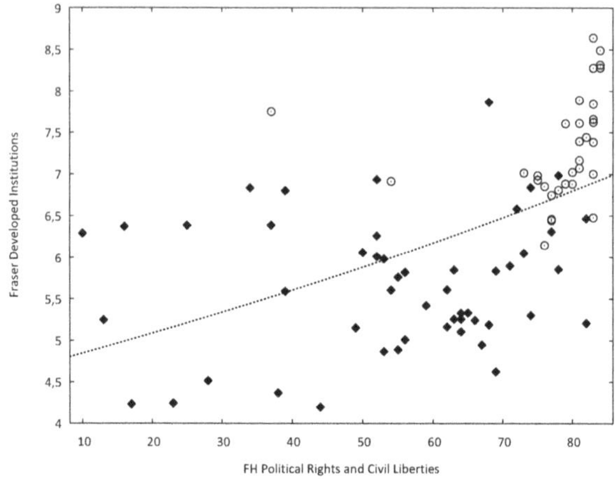

Appendix 58a: Scatterplot of Fraser 'developed economic institutions against Freedom House 'political rights and civil liberties' (black dots: less developed countries; white circles: developed countries; upward-sloping line: fitted values for the entire sample based on a log-linear model).

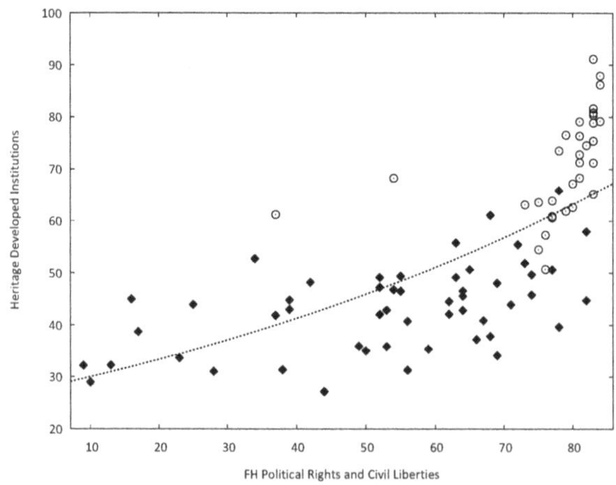

Appendix 58b: Scatterplot of Heritage 'developed economic institutions' against Freedom House 'political rights and civil liberties' (black dots: less developed countries; white circles: developed countries; upward-sloping line: fitted values for the entire sample based on a log-linear model).

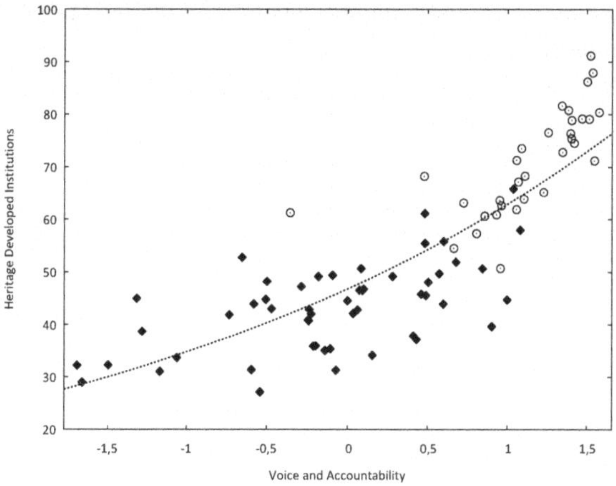

Appendix 58c: Scatterplot of Heritage 'developed economic institutions against WGI 'voice and accountability' (black dots: less developed countries; white circles: developed countries; upward-sloping line: fitted values for the entire sample based on a log-linear model).

Appendix 59 – Different 'developed economic institutions' indices against different political openness indices

	Dependent Variable: Log Fraser 'Developed Economic Institutions'; Sample: All Countries									
	(1)	(2)	(3)	(4)	(5)	(6)	(7)	(8)	(9)	(10)
Constant	1.52	1.50	1.62	1.52	1.59	1.64	1.56	1.49	1.70	1.65
	0.00***	0.00***	0.00***	0.00***	0.00***	0.00***	0.00***	0.00***	0.00***	0.00***
FH Political Rights	0.005	0.005	0.004	0.004	0.005	0.004	0.005	0.005	0.004	0.001
& Civil Liberties	0.00***	0.00***	0.00***	0.00***	0.00***	0.00***	0.00***	0.00***	0.00***	0.30
British Legal		0.06								
Origin		0.14								
French Legal			-0.13							
Origin			0.00***							
Percentage				0.17						
Protestants				0.01**						
Percentage Catho-					-0.14					
lics & Muslims					0.01**					
Ethnic						-0.18				
Fractionalization						0.02**				
Linguistic							-0.07			
Fractionalization							0.29			
Religious								0.08		
Fractionalization								0.30		
WB									-0.04	
Inequality									0.06*	
GDP										0.01
per Capita										0.00***
N	82	82	81	81	82	80	81	82	82	82
R^{2*}	0.28	0.40	0.31	0.33	0.31	0.27	0.27	0.30	0.27	0.57

Appendix 59a: Multivariate regressions of log Fraser 'developed economic institutions' against Freedom House 'political rights and civil liberties' and one additional control variable in the entire sample (second row: p-values of two-sided significance tests; number of asterisks: significance levels of 10%*, 5%** and 1%***).

	Dependent Variable: Log Heritage 'Developed Economic Institutions'; Sample: All Countries									
	(1)	(2)	(3)	(4)	(5)	(6)	(7)	(8)	(9)	(10)
Constant	3.83 0.00***	3.82 0.00***	3.87 0.00***	3.81 0.00***	3.87 0.00***	3.88 0.00***	3.87 0.00***	3.79 0.00***	4.02 0.00***	3.74 0.00***
WGI Voice & Accountability	0.30 0.00***	0.30 0.00***	0.28 0.00***	0.28 0.00***	0.29 0.00***	0.28 0.00***	0.29 0.00***	0.30 0.00***	0.28 0.00***	0.16 0.00***
British Legal Origin		0.03 0.56								
French Legal Origin			-0.08 0.05**							
Percentage Protestants				0.15 0.02**						
Percentage Catholics & Muslims					-0.08 0.17					
Ethnic Fractionalization						-0.11 0.21				
Linguistic Fractionalization							-0.10 0.21			
Religious Fractionalization								0.09 0.26		
WB Inequality									-0.005 0.03**	
GDP per Capita										0.01 0.00***
N	84	84	84	83	83	84	82	83	84	84
R^{2*}	0.69	0.68	0.70	0.70	0.70	0.70	0.69	0.69	0.70	0.80

Appendix 59b: Multivariate regressions of log Heritage 'developed economic institutions' against WGI 'voice and accountability' and one additional control variable in the entire sample (second row: p-values of two-sided significance tests; number of asterisks: significance levels of 10%*, 5%** and 1%***).

	Dependent Variable: Log Heritage 'Developed Economic Institutions'; Sample: All Countries									
	(1)	(2)	(3)	(4)	(5)	(6)	(7)	(8)	(9)	(10)
Constant	3.27 0.00***	3.25 0.00***	3.37 0.00***	3.27 0.00***	3.34 0.00***	3.41 0.00***	3.37 0.00***	3.21 0.00***	3.62 0.00***	3.46 0.00***
FH Political Rights & Civil Liberties	0.01 0.00***	0.01 0.00***	0.01 0.00***	0.01 0.00***	0.01 0.00***	0.01 0.00***	0.01 0.00***	0.01 0.00***	0.01 0.00***	0.005 0.00***
British Legal Origin		0.06 0.31								
French Legal Origin			-0.13 0.01***							
Percentage Protestants				0.29 0.00***						
Percentage Catholics & Muslims					-0.14 0.05**					
Ethnic Fractionalization						-0.23 0.02**				
Linguistic Fractionalization							-0.17 0.06*			
Religious Fractionalization								0.13 0.21		
WB Inequality									-0.01 0.00***	
GDP per Capita										0.01 0.00***
N	84	84	84	83	83	84	82	83	84	84
R^{2*}	0.51	0.51	0.55	0.55	0.54	0.53	0.52	0.51	0.56	0.79

Appendix 59c: Multivariate regressions of log Heritage 'developed economic institutions' against Freedom House 'political rights and civil liberties' and one additional control variable in the entire sample (second row: p-values of two-sided significance tests; number of asterisks: significance levels of 10%*, 5%** and 1%***).

Appendix 60 – Scatterplots of different 'open access economic institutions' indices against different political openness indices for developed countries

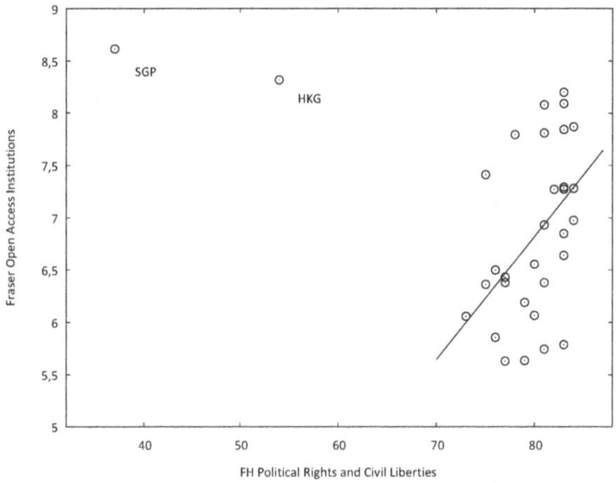

Appendix 60a: Scatterplot of Fraser 'open access economic institutions' against Freedom House 'political rights and civil liberties' in the sub-group of developed countries (upward-sloping line: fitted values for the sub-group of 30 developed countries after excluding Singapore and Hong Kong).

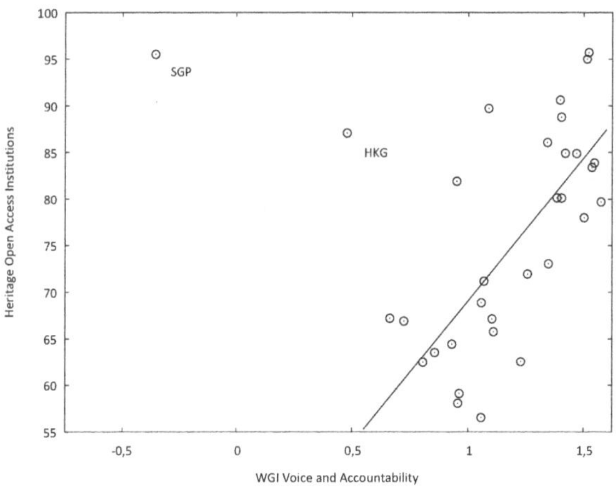

Appendix 60a: Scatterplot of Heritage 'open access economic institutions' against WGI 'voice and accountability' in the sub-group of developed countries (upward-sloping line: fitted values for the sub-group of 30 developed countries after excluding Singapore and Hong Kong).

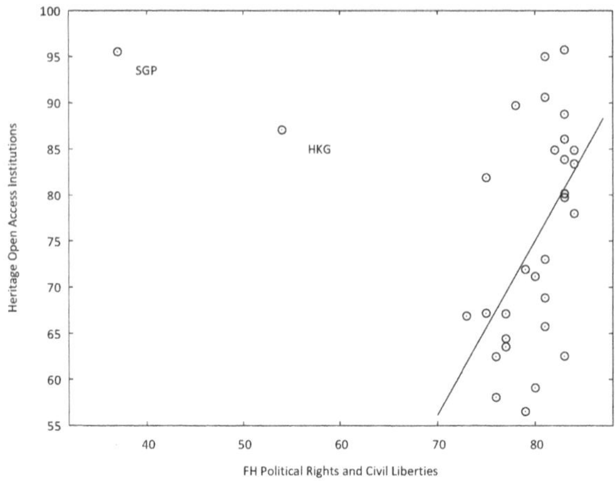

Appendix 60c: Scatterplot of Heritage 'open access economic institutions' against Freedom House 'political rights and civil liberties' in the sub-group of developed countries (upward-sloping line: fitted values for the sub-group of 30 developed countries after excluding Singapore and Hong Kong).

Appendix 61 – Different 'open access economic institutions' indices against different political openness indices in developed democracies

	Dependent Variable: Fraser 'open access economic institutions'; Sample: Developed Democracies									
	(1)	(2)	(3)	(4)	(5)	(6)	(7)	(8)	(9)	(10)
Constant	-2.58 0.38	-2.83 0.38	-1.76 0.46	3.09 0.33	-2.56 0.33	-2.77 0.38	-2.60 0.39	-4.17 0.13	-5.47 0.24	3.87 0.32
Political Rights & Civil Liberties	0.12 0.00***	0.12 0.01***	0.11 0.00***	0.04 0.30	0.12 0.00***	0.12 0.00***	0.12 0.00***	0.13 0.00***	0.14 0.01***	0.02 0.66
British Legal Origin		0.69 0.01***								
French Legal Origin			-0.91 0.00***							
Percentage Protestants				1.57 0.00***						
Percentage Catholics & Muslims					-1.10 0.00***					
Ethnic Fractionalization						0.55 0.42				
Linguistic Fractionalization							0.07 0.92			
Religious Fractionalization								1.44 0.02**		
WB Inequality									0.04 0.28	
GDP per Capita										0.03 0.01***
N	30	30	30	30	30	30	30	30	30	30
R^{2*}	0.18	0.31	0.43	0.39	0.35	0.17	0.16	0.32	0.20	0.36

Appendix 61a: Multivariate regressions of Fraser 'open access economic institutions' against Freedom House 'political rights and civil liberties' and one additional control variable in the subsample of 30 developed democracies after excluding Singapore and Hong Kong (second row: p-values of two-sided significance tests; number of asterisks: significance levels of 10%*, 5%** and 1%***).

	Dependent Variable: Heritage 'open access economic institutions'; Sample: Developed Democracies									
	(1)	(2)	(3)	(4)	(5)	(6)	(7)	(8)	(9)	(10)
Constant	38.45 0.00***	37.51 0.00***	41.52 0.00***	44.13 0.00***	42.17 0.00***	37.13 0.00***	38.87 0.00***	30.21 0.00***	11.24 0.47	45.15 0.00***
WGI Voice & Accountability	30.61 0.00***	29.10 0.00***	29.92 0.00***	23.71 0.00***	30.71 0.00***	30.88 0.00***	30.56 0.00***	31.15 0.00***	33.73 0.00***	13.84 0.27
British Legal Origin		10.41 0.00***								
French Legal Origin			-8.34 0.00***							
Percentage Protestants				11.51 0.07*						
Percentage Catholics & Muslims					-10.04 0.02**					
Ethnic Fractionalization						4.11 0.59				
Linguistic Fractionalization							1.37 0.85			
Religious Fractionalization								16.37 0.02**		
WB Inequality									0.73 0.07*	
GDP per Capita										0.36 0.08*
N	30	30	30	30	30	30	30	30	30	30
R^{2*}	0.50	0.66	0.59	0.54	0.56	0.49	0.48	0.58	0.55	0.59

Appendix 61b: Multivariate regressions of Heritage 'open access economic institutions' against WGI 'voice and accountability' and one additional control variable in the sub-sample of 30 developed democracies after excluding Singapore and Hong Kong (second row: p-values of two-sided significance tests; number of asterisks: significance levels of 10%*, 5%** and 1%***).

	Dependent Variable: Heritage 'open access economic institutions'; Sample: Developed Democracies									
	(1)	(2)	(3)	(4)	(5)	(6)	(7)	(8)	(9)	(10)
Constant	-76.28 0.07*	-80.59 0.05*	-68.55 0.06*	-9.70 0.84	-76.07 0.05**	-76.59 0.07*	-75.50 0.08*	-96.38 0.02**	-126.30 0.05**	37.68 0.37
FH Political Rights & Civil Liberties	1.89 0.00***	1.91 0.00***	1.82 0.00***	1.01 0.10*	1.94 0.00***	1.89 0.00***	1.89 0.00***	2.04 0.00***	2.23 0.00***	0.22 0.69
British Legal Origin		12.05 0.00***								
French Legal Origin			-8.52 0.01**							
Percentage Protestants				18.42 0.01**						
Percentage Catholics & Muslims					-10.71 0.05*					
Ethnic Fractionalization						0.92 0.92				
Linguistic Fractionalization							-3.97 0.63			
Religious Fractionalization								18.22 0.04**		
WB Inequality									0.73 0.19	
GDP per Capita										0.52 0.00***
N	30	30	30	30	30	30	30	30	30	30
R^{2*}	0.25	0.46	0.34	0.37	0.31	0.22	0.22	0.34	0.28	0.28

Appendix 61c: Multivariate regressions of Heritage 'open access economic institutions' against Freedom House 'political rights and civil liberties' and one additional control variable in the subsample of 30 developed democracies after excluding Singapore and Hong Kong (second row: p-values of two-sided significance tests; number of asterisks: significance levels of 10%*, 5%** and 1%***).

Appendix 62 – Heritage 'government spending' and 'financial freedom' against different political openness indices in less developed countries

	Dependent Variable: Heritage 'government spending'; Sample: Emerging and Developing Countries									
	(1)	(2)	(3)	(4)	(5)	(6)	(7)	(8)	(9)	(10)
Constant	74.02 0.00***	72.65 0.00***	68.96 0.00***	71.24 0.00***	70.36 0.00***	70.35 0.00***	68.70 0.00***	79.66 0.00***	36.53 0.00***	87.09 0.00***
WGI Voice & Accountability	-8.23 0.03**	-8.34 0.03**	-7.95 0.02**	-9.28 0.02**	-8.44 0.02**	-7.83 0.03**	-6.27 0.07*	-8.08 0.03**	-10.83 0.00***	-0.12 0.97
British Legal Origin		5.41 0.16								
French Legal Origin			8.52 0.07*							
Percentage Protestants				24.05 0.12						
Percentage Catholics & Muslims					6.65 0.30					
Ethnic Fractionalization						8.01 0.32				
Linguistic Fractionalization							14.29 0.02**			
Religious Fractionalization								-12.26 0.12		
WB Inequality									0.88 0.00***	
GDP per Capita										-2.87 0.00***
N	52	52	52	52	52	52	50	51	52	52
R^{2*}	0.09	0.10	0.14	0.11	0.09	0.09	0.15	0.10	0.31	0.31

Appendix 62a: Multivariate regressions of Heritage 'government spending' against WGI 'voice and accountability' and one additional control variable in the sub-sample of emerging and developing countries (second row: p-values of two-sided significance tests; number of asterisks: significance levels of 10%*, 5%** and 1%***).

	Dependent Variable: Heritage 'gov. spending'; Sample: Emerging and Developing Countries									
	(1)	(2)	(3)	(4)	(5)	(6)	(7)	(8)	(9)	(10)
Constant	87.51 0.00***	86.21 0.00***	82.30 0.00***	86.64 0.00***	84.33 0.00***	82.61 0.00***	78.47 0.00***	93.26 0.00***	55.74 0.00***	86.47 0.00***
FH Political Rights & Civil Liberties	-0.24 0.05*	-0.24 0.05*	-0.24 0.03**	-0.26 0.03**	-0.25 0.03**	-0.22 0.05*	-0.18 0.11	-0.24 0.06*	-0.34 0.00***	0.02 0.87
British Legal Origin		4.78 0.22								
French Legal Origin			9.25 0.06*							
Percentage Protestants				20.83 0.22						
Percentage Catholics & Muslims					7.54 0.24					
Ethnic Fractionalization						9.13 0.27				
Linguistic Fractionalization							15.41 0.01**			
Religious Fractionalization								-12.49 0.13		
WB Inequality									0.89 0.00***	
GDP per Capita										-2.93 0.00***
N	52	52	52	52	52	52	50	51	52	52
R^{2*}	0.06	0.05	0.11	0.07	0.06	0.05	0.12	0.07	0.27	0.31

Appendix 62b: Multivariate regressions of Heritage 'government spending' against Freedom House 'political rights and civil liberties' and one additional control variable in the sub-sample of emerging and developing countries (second row: p-values of two-sided significance tests; number of asterisks: significance levels of 10%*, 5%** and 1%***).

	Dependent Variable: Heritage 'fin. freedom'; Sample: Emerging and Developing Countries									
	(1)	(2)	(3)	(4)	(5)	(6)	(7)	(8)	(9)	(10)
Constant	51.73 0.00***	52.68 0.00***	49.53 0.00***	49.68 0.00***	48.84 0.00***	45.91 0.00***	49.94 0.00***	47.31 0.00***	37.20 0.00***	52.63 0.00***
WGI Voice & Accountability	7.95 0.03**	8.03 0.03**	8.07 0.03**	7.17 0.05*	7.78 0.03**	8.57 0.01**	8.34 0.02**	8.24 0.02**	6.94 0.04**	8.51 0.06*
British Legal Origin		-3.75 0.41								
French Legal Origin			3.72 0.36							
Percentage Protestants				17.76 0.10*						
Percentage Catho-lics &Muslims					5.25 0.33					
Ethnic Fractionalization						12.72 0.15				
Linguistic Fractionalization							3.90 0.56			
Religious Fractionalization								10.84 0.13		
WB Inequality									0.34 0.06*	
GDP per Capita										-0.20 0.77
N	52	52	52	52	52	52	50	51	52	52
R^{2*}	0.11	0.11	0.11	0.12	0.11	0.14	0.10	0.13	0.14	0.10

Appendix 62c: Multivariate regressions of Heritage 'financial freedom' against WGI 'voice and accountability' and one additional control variable in the sub-sample of emerging and developing countries (second row: p-values of two-sided significance tests; number of asterisks: significance levels of 10%*, 5%** and 1%***).

	Dependent Variable: Heritage 'financial freedom'; Sample: Emerging and Developing Countries									
	(1)	(2)	(3)	(4)	(5)	(6)	(7)	(8)	(9)	(10)
Constant	36.73 0.00***	37.58 0.00***	35.06 0.00***	35.92 0.00***	34.94 0.00***	30.39 0.00***	35.22 0.00***	31.34 0.00***	24.70 0.03**	36.75 0.00***
FH Political Rights & Civil Liberties	0.27 0.04**	0.26 0.05**	0.26 0.04**	0.24 0.06*	0.26 0.04**	0.28 0.02**	0.27 0.03**	0.28 0.03**	0.23 0.06*	0.26 0.08*
British Legal Origin		-3.11 0.51								
French Legal Origin			2.96 0.47							
Percentage Protestants				19.32 0.07*						
Percentage Catholics & Muslims					4.26 0.45					
Ethnic Fractionalization						11.82 0.19				
Linguistic Fractionalization							2.81 0.67			
Religious Fractionalization								11.32 0.12		
WB Inequality									0.33 0.08*	
GDP per Capita										0.04 0.94
N	52	52	52	52	52	52	50	51	52	52
R^{2*}	0.10	0.09	0.09	0.11	0.09	0.12	0.08	0.12	0.12	0.08

Appendix 62d: Multivariate regressions of Heritage 'financial freedom' against Freedom House 'political rights and civil liberties' and one additional control variable in the sub-sample of emerging and developing countries (second row: p-values of two-sided significance tests; number of asterisks: significance levels of 10%*, 5%** and 1%***).

Appendix 63 – Scatterplot of 'GDP_{08-12}' against Freedom House 'political rights and civil liberties'

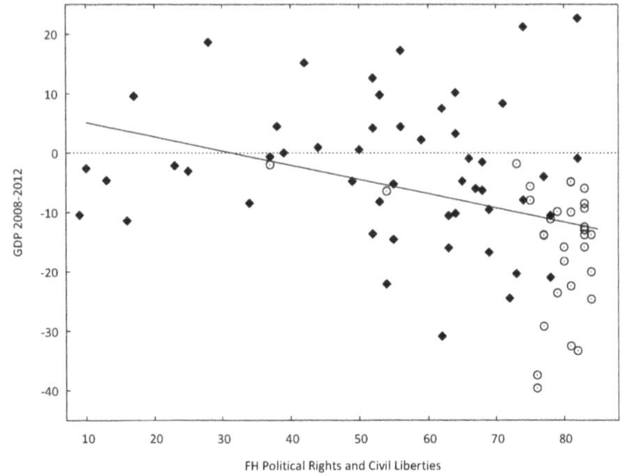

Appendix 63: Scatterplot of 'GDP_{08-12}' against Freedom House 'political rights and civil liberties' in the entire sample (black dots: less developed countries; white circles: developed countries; downward-sloping line: fitted values for the entire sample).

Appendix 64 – '$GDP_{08\text{-}12}$' against different political openness indices, different 'developed economic institutions' indices and different control variables in the entire sample

Dependent Variable: '$GDP_{08\text{-}12}$'; Sample: All Countries										
	(1)	(2)	(3)	(4)	(5)	(6)	(7)	(8)	(9)	(10)
Constant	-5.16	-5.95	-5.77	8.69	-3.76	7.79	0.73	-5.07	1.21	2.81
	0.00***	0.00***	0.00***	0.24	0.01***	0.27	0.91	0.00***	0.84	0.62
WGI Voice & Accountability	-6.36	-4.22	-4.71	-1.83	-4.45	-0.79	-2.59	-3.83	-1.79	-1.10
	0.00***	0.02**	0.00***	0.52	0.00***	0.77	0.31	0.00***	0.46	0.63
Her. Developed Econ. Institutions				-0.29		-0.24	-0.14		-0.13	-0.16
				0.05**		0.08*	0.27		0.28	0.16
Peg					-8.85	-8.09		-4.33	-4.25	-4.84
					0.01***	0.01**		0.10	0.11	0.06*
Financial Vulnerabilities		-7.08	-7.03				-6.93	-6.84	-6.75	-6.71
		0.00***	0.00***				0.00***	0.00***	0.00***	0.00***
Industrial Orientation		-3.83	-3.77				-3.61	-3.44	-3.29	-3.22
		0.00***	0.00***				0.00***	0.00***	0.00***	0.00***
Economic Development		-0.63								
		0.61								
International Linkages		-1.74	-1.77				-1.39	-1.36	-0.99	
		0.01***	0.01***				0.06*	0.09*	0.23	
N	84	84	84	84	84	84	84	84	84	84
R^{2*}	0.17	0.56	0.56	0.20	0.23	0.26	0.56	0.57	0.57	0.57

Appendix 64a: Multivariate regressions of '$GDP_{08\text{-}12}$' against WGI 'voice and accountability', Heritage 'developed economic institutions', the 'peg' dummy and different sets of control variables in the entire sample (second row: p-values of two-sided significance tests; number of asterisks: significance levels of 10%*, 5%** and 1%***; residuals in regressions 2, 3, 7, 8, 9 and 10 are not normally-distributed).

	Dependent Variable: 'GDP$_{08-12}$'; Sample: All Countries									
	(1)	(2)	(3)	(4)	(5)	(6)	(7)	(8)	(9)	(10)
Constant	7.46	1.58	3.84	26.83	4.96	22.26	12.89	2.58	11.65	12.54
	0.05*	0.72	0.31	0.00***	0.18	0.00***	0.03**	0.49	0.05*	0.03**
FH Political Rights	-0.24	-0.14	-0.18	-0.13	-0.16	-0.08	-0.13	-0.14	-0.09	-0.07
& Civil Liberties	0.00***	0.04**	0.00***	0.05*	0.01**	0.23	0.05*	0.02**	0.18	0.26
Fras. Developed				-4.16		-3.63	-1.94		-1.96	-2.27
Econ. Institutions				0.00***		0.00***	0.07*		0.06*	0.02**
Peg					-9.75	-8.19		-4.94	-4.81	-5.37
					0.00***	0.01**		0.06*	0.07*	0.03**
Financial		-7.15	-7.06				-6.70	-6.83	-6.49	-6.45
Vulnerabilities		0.00***	0.00***				0.00***	0.00***	0.00***	0.00***
Industrial		-4.00	-3.90				-3.44	-3.50	-3.04	-2.94
Orientation		0.00***	0.00***				0.00***	0.00***	0.00***	0.00***
Economic		-1.42								
Development		0.20								
International		-1.94	-2.05				-1.41	-1.52	-0.89	
Linkages		0.00***	0.00***				0.04**	0.06*	0.27	
N	84	84	84	82	84	82	82	84	82	82
R^{2*}	0.13	0.55	0.54	0.23	0.22	0.29	0.56	0.56	0.58	0.58

Appendix 64b: Multivariate regressions of 'GDP$_{08-12}$' against Freedom House 'political rights and civil liberties', Fraser 'developed economic institutions', the 'peg' dummy and different sets of control variables in the entire sample (second row: p-values of two-sided significance tests; number of asterisks: significance levels of 10%*, 5%** and 1%***; misspecification in regression 1; residuals in regressions 2, 3, 7, 8, 9 and 10 are not normally-distributed).

	Dependent Variable: 'GDP$_{08-12}$'; Sample: All Countries									
	(1)	(2)	(3)	(4)	(5)	(6)	(7)	(8)	(9)	(10)
Constant	7.46 0.05*	1.58 0.72	3.84 0.31	13.33 0.00***	4.96 0.18	10.00 0.01***	7.08 0.06*	2.58 0.49	5.61 0.14	5.46 0.14
FH Political Rights & Civil Liberties	-0.24 0.00***	-0.14 0.04**	-0.18 0.00***	-0.07 0.45	-0.16 0.01**	-0.04 0.64	-0.09 0.34	-0.14 0.02**	-0.06 0.48	-0.03 0.66
Her. Developed Econ. Institutions				-0.31 0.00***		-0.24 0.02**	-0.18 0.05*		-0.16 0.09*	-0.18 0.04**
Peg					-9.75 0.00***	-8.05 0.01**		-4.94 0.06*	-4.34 0.12	-4.91 0.07*
Financial Vulnerabilities		-7.15 0.00***	-7.06 0.00***				-6.90 0.00***	-6.83 0.00***	-6.72 0.00***	-6.69 0.00***
Industrial Orientation		-4.00 0.00***	-3.90 0.00***				-3.60 0.00***	-3.50 0.00***	-3.28 0.00***	-3.21 0.00***
Economic Development		-1.42 0.20								
International Linkages		-1.94 0.00***	-2.05 0.00***				-1.40 0.05*	-1.52 0.06*	-1.01 0.23	
N	84	84	84	84	84	84	84	84	84	84
R^{2*}	0.13	0.55	0.54	0.20	0.22	0.26	0.56	0.56	0.57	0.57

Appendix 64c: Multivariate regressions of 'GDP$_{08-12}$' against Freedom House 'political rights and civil liberties', Heritage 'developed economic institutions', the 'peg' dummy and different sets of control variables in the entire sample (second row: p-values of two-sided significance tests; number of asterisks: significance levels of 10%*, 5%** and 1%***; misspecification in regression 1; residuals in regressions 2, 3, 7, 8, 9 and 10 are not normally-distributed).

Appendix 65 – 'GDP$_{08-09}$' against different political openness indices, 'developed economic institutions' indices and different control variables in the entire sample

	Dependent Variable: 'GDP$_{08-09}$'; Sample: All Countries								
	(1)	(2)	(3)	(4)	(5)	(6)	(7)	(8)	(9)
Constant	-4.42 0.00***	-4.62 0.00***	-4.58 0.00***	8.85 0.04**	-3.90 0.00***	8.92 0.03**	0.42 0.92	-4.58 0.00***	0.77 0.85
WGI Voice & Accountability	-3.99 0.00***	-3.45 0.00***	-3.30 0.00***	-2.00 0.02**	-3.27 0.00***	-1.39 0.13	-2.47 0.01***	-3.18 0.00***	-2.28 0.02**
Fras. Developed Econ. Institutions				-2.25 0.00***		-2.19 0.00***	-0.88 0.19		-0.92 0.18
Peg					-3.33 0.06*	-2.96 0.08*		-0.61 0.69	-0.73 0.63
Financial Vulnerabilities		-2.88 0.00***	-2.89 0.00***				-2.72 0.00***	-2.87 0.00***	-2.69 0.00***
Industrial Orientation		-1.95 0.00***	-1.97 0.00***				-1.79 0.00***	-1.92 0.00***	-1.73 0.00***
Economic Development		0.19 0.80							
International Linkages		-1.55 0.00***	-1.54 0.00***				-1.28 0.19	-1.48 0.00***	-1.20 0.01**
N	84	82	84	82	84	82	82	84	84
R^{2*}	0.21	0.46	0.46	0.27	0.23	0.29	0.47	0.46	0.47

Appendix 65a: Multivariate regressions of 'GDP$_{08-09}$' against WGI 'voice and accountability', Fraser 'developed economic institutions', the 'peg' dummy and different sets of control variables in the entire sample (second row: p-values of two-sided significance tests; number of asterisks: significance levels of 10%*, 5%** and 1%***; residuals in regressions 1 to 9 are not normally-distributed).

	Dependent Variable: '$GDP_{08–09}$; Sample: All Countries								
	(1)	(2)	(3)	(4)	(5)	(6)	(7)	(8)	(9)
Constant	-4.42 0.00***	-4.62 0.00***	-4.58 0.00***	2.45 0.48	-3.90 0.00***	2.12 0.53	-2.49 0.45	-4.58 0.00***	-2.42 0.46
WGI Voice & Accountability	-3.99 0.00***	-3.45 0.00***	-3.30 0.00***	-1.74 0.21	-3.27 0.00***	-1.37 0.33	-2.59 0.06*	-3.18 0.00***	-2.48 0.08*
Her. Developed Econ Institutions				-0.14 0.04**		-0.13 0.06*	-0.05 0.49		-0.05 0.50
Peg					-3.33 0.06*	-2.93 0.08*		-0.61 0.69	-0.58 0.70
Financial Vulnerabilities		-2.88 0.00***	-2.89 0.00***				-2.86 0.00***	-2.87 0.00***	-2.84 0.00***
Industrial Orientation		-1.95 0.00***	-1.97 0.00***				-1.91 0.00***	-1.92 0.00***	-1.87 0.00***
Economic Development		0.19 0.80							
International Linkages		-1.55 0.00***	-1.54 0.00***				-1.41 0.01***	-1.48 0.00***	-1.36 0.01**
N	84	84	84	84	84	84	84	84	84
R^{2*}	0.21	0.46	0.46	0.23	0.23	0.25	0.46	0.46	0.45

Appendix 65b: Multivariate regressions of 'GDP_{08-09}' against WGI 'voice and accountability', Heritage 'developed economic institutions', the 'peg' dummy and different sets of control variables in the entire sample (second row: p-values of two-sided significance tests; number of asterisks: significance levels of 10%*, 5%** and 1%***; residuals in regressions 1 to 9 are not normally-distributed).

	Dependent Variable: 'GDP08-09; Sample: All Countries								
	(1)	(2)	(3)	(4)	(5)	(6)	(7)	(8)	(9)
Constant	4.21 0.05**	2.42 0.31	2.92 0.15	14.69 0.00***	3.14 0.11	13.09 0.00***	7.55 0.02**	2.71 0.17	7.36 0.02**
FH Political Rights & Civil Liberties	-0.16 0.00***	-0.13 0.00***	-0.14 0.00***	-0.09 0.01***	-0.13 0.00***	-0.07 0.03**	-0.11 0.00***	-0.13 0.00***	-0.10 0.01***
Fras. Developed Econ. Institutions				-2.40 0.00***		-2.21 0.00***	-1.10 0.06*		-1.10 0.06*
Peg					-3.81 0.03**	-2.87 0.08*		-0.82 0.58	-0.74 0.62
Financial Vulnerabilities		-2.90 0.00***	-2.88 0.00***				-2.66 0.00***	-2.84 0.00***	-2.63 0.00***
Industrial Orientation		-2.05 0.00***	-2.02 0.00***				-1.77 0.00***	-1.96 0.00***	-1.70 0.00***
Economic Development		-0.31 0.63							
International Linkages		-1.75 0.00***	-1.78 0.00***				-1.41 0.00***	-1.69 0.00***	-1.33 0.01***
N	84	84	84	82	84	82	82	84	82
R^{2*}	0.19	0.46	0.47	0.28	0.22	0.30	0.49	0.46	0.48

Appendix 65c: Multivariate regressions of '$GDP_{08\text{-}09}$' against Freedom House 'political rights and civil liberties', Fraser 'developed economic institutions', the 'peg' dummy and different sets of control variables in the entire sample (second row: p-values of two-sided significance tests; number of asterisks: significance levels of 10%*, 5%** and 1%***; misspecification in regression 3; residuals in regressions 1, 2, 4, 5, 6, 7, 8 and 9 are not normally-distributed).

	Dependent Variable: 'GDP08-09; Sample: All Countries								
	(1)	(2)	(3)	(4)	(5)	(6)	(7)	(8)	(9)
Constant	4.21 0.05**	2.42 0.31	2.92 0.15	7.03 0.00***	3.14 0.11	5.32 0.00***	4.16 0.04**	2.71 0.17	3.97 0.04**
FH Political Rights & Civil Liberties	-0.16 0.00***	-0.13 0.00***	-0.14 0.00***	-0.07 0.10*	-0.13 0.00***	-0.07 0.15	-0.10 0.03**	-0.13 0.00***	-0.10 0.04**
Her. Developed Econ. Institutions				-0.15 0.00***		-0.13 0.01**	-0.07 0.17		-0.07 0.19
Peg					-3.81 0.03**	-2.90 0.08*		-0.82 0.58	-0.57 0.70
Financial Vulnerabilities		-2.90 0.00***	-2.88 0.00***				-2.82 0.00***	-2.84 0.00***	-2.79 0.00***
Industrial Orientation		-2.05 0.00***	-2.02 0.00***				-1.91 0.00***	-1.96 0.00***	-1.86 0.00***
Economic Development		-0.31 0.63							
International Linkages		-1.75 0.00***	-1.78 0.00***				-1.53 0.00***	-1.69 0.00***	-1.48 0.01***
N	84	84	84	84	84	84	84	84	84
R^{2*}	0.19	0.46	0.47	0.24	0.22	0.26	0.47	0.46	0.46

Appendix 65d: Multivariate regressions of 'GDP_{08-09}' against Freedom House 'political rights and civil liberties', Heritage 'developed economic institutions', the 'peg' dummy and different sets of control variables in the entire sample (second row: p-values of two-sided significance tests; number of asterisks: significance levels of 10%*, 5%** and 1%***; misspecification in regression 3; residuals in regressions 1, 2, 4, 5, 6, 7, 8 and 9 are not normally-distributed).

Appendix 66 – 'GDP$_{10\text{-}12}$' against different political openness indices, 'developed economic institutions' indices and different control variables in the entire sample

	Dependent Variable: 'GDP$_{10-12}$'; Sample: All Countries								
	(1)	(2)	(3)	(4)	(5)	(6)	(7)	(8)	(9)
Constant	-1.05	-1.67	-1.44	7.30	-0.10	7.44	0.67	-0.77	1.46
	0.23	0.03**	0.05*	0.27	0.91	0.23	0.89	0.28	0.75
WGI Voice &	-2.67	-1.02	-1.62	-1.83	-1.38	-0.66	-1.63	-0.84	-0.81
Accountability	0.00***	0.34	0.05*	0.21	0.13	0.62	0.17	0.30	0.47
Fras. Developed				-1.36		-1.24	-0.32		-0.35
Econ. Institutions				0.21		0.23	0.68		0.64
Peg					-6.02	-5.74		-4.05	-3.97
					0.01***	0.01**		0.04**	0.05**
Financial		-4.66	-4.59				-4.50	-4.41	-4.33
Vulnerabilities		0.00***	0.00***				0.00***	0.00***	0.00***
Industrial		-1.85	-1.76				-1.68	-1.45	-1.37
Orientation		0.00***	0.00***				0.00***	0.01***	0.01***
Economic		-0.79							
Development		0.32							
N	84	82	84	82	84	82	82	84	82
R^{2*}	0.07	0.44	0.44	0.10	0.15	0.17	0.44	0.47	0.47

Appendix 66a: Multivariate regressions of 'GDP$_{10\text{-}12}$' against WGI 'voice and accountability', Fraser 'developed economic institutions', the 'peg' dummy and different sets of control variables in the entire sample (second row: p-values of two-sided significance tests; number of asterisks: significance levels of 10%*, 5%** and 1%***).

	Dependent Variable: 'GDP10–12; Sample: All Countries								
	(1)	(2)	(3)	(4)	(5)	(6)	(7)	(8)	(9)
Constant	-1.05 0.23	-1.67 0.03**	-1.44 0.05*	5.49 0.27	-0.10 0.91	4.86 0.31	2.25 0.55	-0.77 0.28	2.10 0.57
WGI Voice & Accountability	-2.67 0.00***	-1.02 0.34	-1.62 0.05*	-0.53 0.79	-1.38 0.13	0.20 0.91	-0.44 0.79	-0.84 0.30	0.06 0.97
Fras. Developed Econ. Institutions				-0.14 0.17		-0.10 0.29	-0.08 0.31		-0.06 0.44
Peg					-6.02 0.01***	-5.70 0.02**		-4.05 0.04**	-3.91 0.06*
Financial Vulnerabilities		-4.66 0.00***	-4.59 0.00***				-4.55 0.00***	-4.41 0.00***	-4.37 0.00***
Industrial Orientation		-1.85 0.00***	-1.76 0.00***				-1.67 0.00***	-1.45 0.01***	-1.39 0.01***
Economic Development		-0.79 0.32							
N	84	82	84	84	84	84	84	84	84
R^{2*}	0.07	0.44	0.44	0.09	0.15	0.16	0.44	0.47	0.47

Appendix 66b: Multivariate regressions of 'GDP10-12' against WGI 'voice and accountability', Heritage 'developed economic institutions', the 'peg' dummy and different sets of control variables in the entire sample (second row: p-values of two-sided significance tests; number of asterisks: significance levels of 10%*, 5%** and 1%***).

	Dependent Variable: 'GDP10–12; Sample: All Countries								
	(1)	(2)	(3)	(4)	(5)	(6)	(7)	(8)	(9)
Constant	3.74 0.13	-0.73 0.79	1.01 0.68	12.52 0.00***	2.09 0.38	9.26 0.03**	5.30 0.16	0.13 0.96	3.63 0.33
FH Political Rights & Civil Liberties	-0.09 0.02**	-0.02 0.62	-0.05 0.19	-0.06 0.28	-0.04 0.29	-0.02 0.69	-0.04 0.39	-0.02 0.62	-0.01 0.77
Fras. Developed Econ. Institutions				-1.74 0.06*		-1.37 0.13	-0.77 0.23		-0.61 0.33
Peg					-6.45 0.01***	-5.84 0.01**		-4.42 0.02**	-4.23 0.04**
Financial Vulnerabilities		-4.71 0.00***	-4.64 0.00***				-4.50 0.00***	-4.43 0.00***	-4.32 0.00***
Industrial Orientation		-1.93 0.00***	-1.85 0.00***				-1.66 0.00***	-1.48 0.00***	-1.34 0.01***
Economic Development		-1.12 0.12							
N	84	84	84	82	84	82	82	84	82
R^{2*}	0.04	0.44	0.43	0.09	0.14	0.17	0.43	0.47	0.47

Appendix 66c: Multivariate regressions of 'GDP10-12' against Freedom House 'political rights and civil liberties', Fraser 'developed economic institutions', the 'peg' dummy and different sets of control variables in the entire sample (second row: p-values of two-sided significance tests; number of asterisks: significance levels of 10%*, 5%** and 1%***).

	Dependent Variable: 'GDP10-12; Sample: All Countries								
	(1)	(2)	(3)	(4)	(5)	(6)	(7)	(8)	(9)
Constant	3.74	-0.73	1.01	6.65	2.09	4.29	3.03	0.13	1.67
	0.13	0.79	0.68	0.01***	0.38	0.09*	0.21	0.96	0.50
FH Political Rights & Civil Liberties	-0.09	-0.02	-0.05	-0.01	-0.04	0.01	0.01	-0.02	0.02
	0.02**	0.62	0.19	0.90	0.29	0.85	0.92	0.62	0.71
Her. Developed Econ. Institutions				-0.15		-0.11	-0.10		-0.07
				0.03**		0.15	0.06*		0.21
Peg					-6.45	-5.71		-4.42	-3.98
					0.01***	0.02**		0.02**	0.07*
Financial Vulnerabilities		-4.71	-4.64				-4.54	-4.43	-4.38
		0.00***	0.00***				0.00***	0.00***	0.00***
Industrial Orientation		-1.93	-1.85				-1.67	-1.48	-1.38
		0.00***	0.00***				0.00***	0.00***	0.01***
Economic Development		-1.12							
		0.12							
N	84	84	84	84	84	84	84	84	84
R^{2*}	0.04	0.44	0.43	0.09	0.14	0.16	0.44	0.47	0.47

Appendix 66d: Multivariate regressions of '$GDP_{10\text{-}12}$' against Freedom House 'political rights and civil liberties', Heritage 'developed economic institutions', the 'peg' dummy and different sets of control variables in the entire sample (second row: p-values of two-sided significance tests; number of asterisks: significance levels of 10%*, 5%** and 1%***).

Appendix 67 – '$GDP_{10\text{-}12}$' against different political openness indices, 'open access economic institutions' indices and different control variables in developed countries

	Dependent Variable: 'GDP10-12'; Sample: Developed Countries							
	(1)	(2)	(3)	(4)	(5)	(6)	(7)	(8)
Constant	-1.54	-26.93	-4.13	-4.46	-23.45	-22.85	-6.07	-20.61
	0.72	0.02**	0.12	0.27	0.01**	0.03**	0.04**	0.03**
WGI Voice & Accountability	-3.60	-3.74	-0.78	-3.02	-1.17	-3.37	-0.58	-0.97
	0.27	0.06*	0.69	0.28	0.45	0.08*	0.74	0.50
Fras. Open Access Econ. Institutions		3.68			2.84	2.84		2.26
		0.01***			0.01**	0.02**		0.04**
Financial Vulnerabilities			-3.91		-3.52		-3.61	-3.43
			0.00**		0.00**		0.00***	0.00***
Float				5.58		3.34	4.10	2.40
				0.02**		0.09*	0.01**	0.10
N	32	32	32	32	32	32	32	32
R^{2*}	0.01	0.19	0.41	0.13	0.52	0.21	0.47	0.52

Appendix 67a: Multivariate regressions of '$GDP_{10\text{-}12}$' against WGI 'voice and accountability', Fraser 'open access economic institutions', the 'float' dummy and different sets of control variables in the sub-sample of developed countries (second row: p-values of two-sided significance tests; number of asterisks: significance levels of 10%*, 5%** and 1%***).

	Dependent Variable: 'GDP10-12'; Sample: Developed Countries							
	(1)	(2)	(3)	(4)	(5)	(6)	(7)	(8)
Constant	-1.54	-25.02	-4.13	-4.46	-20.50	-22.89	-6.07	-18.73
	0.72	0.01***	0.12	0.27	0.01**	0.01***	0.04**	0.02**
WGI Voice &	-3.60	-5.45	-0.78	-3.02	-2.62	-4.92	-0.58	-2.20
Accountability	0.27	0.00***	0.69	0.28	0.06*	0.00***	0.74	0.08*
Her. Open Access		0.34			0.24	0.29		0.20
Econ. Institutions		0.00***			0.01**	0.01***		0.04**
Financial			-3.91		-3.20		-3.61	-3.16
Vulnerabilities			0.00**		0.00***		0.00***	0.00***
Float				5.58		2.49	4.10	2.13
				0.02**		0.22	0.01**	0.12
N	32	32	32	32	32	32	32	32
R^{2*}	0.01	0.29	0.33	0.12	0.54	0.29	0.41	0.47

Appendix 67b: Multivariate regressions of '$GDP_{10\text{-}12}$' against WGI 'voice and accountability', Heritage 'open access economic institutions', the 'float' dummy and 'financial vulnerabilities' in the sub-sample of developed democracies without Singapore and Hong Kong (second row: p-values of two-sided significance tests; number of asterisks: significance levels of 10%*, 5%** and 1%***).

	Dependent Variable: 'GDP10-12'; Sample: Developed Countries							
	(1)	(2)	(3)	(4)	(5)	(6)	(7)	(8)
Constant	15.80	-9.45	1.78	11.08	-16.33	-7.11	-0.79	-14.30
	0.00***	0.46	0.72	0.04**	0.15	0.57	0.88	0.22
FH Political Rights	-0.27	-0.22	-0.09	-0.24	-0.07	-0.21	-0.08	-0.06
& Civil Liberties	0.00***	0.00***	0.13	0.00***	0.23	0.00***	0.17	0.25
Her. Open Access		0.27			0.21	0.22		0.17
Econ. Institutions		0.02**			0.03**	0.05*		0.09*
Financial			-3.71		-3.27		-3.42	-3.19
Vulnerabilities			0.00***		0.00***		0.00***	0.00***
Float				5.25		3.05	4.06	2.41
				0.02**		0.13	0.01**	0.09*
N	32	32	32	32	32	32	32	32
R^{2*}	0.10	0.28	0.42	0.21	0.53	0.30	0.48	0.53

Appendix 67c: Multivariate regressions of '$GDP_{10\text{-}12}$' against Freedom House 'political rights and civil liberties', Heritage 'open access economic institutions', the 'float' dummy and 'financial vulnerabilities' in the sub-sample of developed countries (second row: p-values of two-sided significance tests; number of asterisks: significance levels of 10%*, 5%** and 1%***).

	Dependent Variable: 'GDP10-12'; Sample: Developed Countries							
	(1)	(2)	(3)	(4)	(5)	(6)	(7)	(8)
Constant	15.80 0.00***	-12.03 0.47	1.78 0.72	11.08 0.04**	-22.80 0.11	-6.82 0.67	-0.79 0.88	-18.85 0.19
FH Political Rights & Civil Liberties	-0.27 0.00***	-0.19 0.02**	-0.09 0.13	-0.24 0.00***	-0.02 0.80	-0.19 0.02**	-0.08 0.17	-0.03 0.71
Fras. Open Access Econ. Institutions		3.06 0.05**			2.76 0.03**	2.12 0.14		2.14 0.10
Financial Vulnerabilities			-3.71 0.00***		-3.57 0.00***		-3.42 0.00***	3.43 0.00***
Float				5.25 0.02**		3.69 0.06*	4.06 0.01**	2.49 0.09*
N	32	32	32	32	32	32	32	32
R^{2*}	0.10	0.21	0.42	0.21	0.51	0.24	0.48	0.52

Appendix 67d: Multivariate regressions of 'GDP_{10-12}' against Freedom House 'political rights and civil liberties', Fraser 'open access economic institutions', the 'float' dummy and 'financial vulnerabilities' in the sub-sample of developed countries (second row: p-values of two-sided significance tests; number of asterisks: significance levels of 10%*, 5%** and 1%***).

Appendix 68 – 'GDP$_{10-12}$' against different political openness indices, 'open access economic institutions' indices and different control variables in developed democracies

	Dependent Variable: 'GDP$_{10-12}$'; Sample: Developed Democracies							
	(1)	(2)	(3)	(4)	(5)	(6)	(7)	(8)
Constant	-11.17 0.10*	-25.71 0.03**	-8.56 0.11	-12.95 0.03**	-25.41 0.01***	-17.68 0.10	-10.16 0.04**	-21.74 0.03**
WGI Voice & Accountability	4.03 0.41	-1.57 0.76	2.67 0.49	3.72 0.37	-3.94 0.20	1.84 0.69	2.53 0.45	-2.25 0.45
Fras Open Access Econ. Institutions		3.11 0.07*			3.63 0.01***	1.07 0.52		2.67 0.07*
Financial Vulnerabilities			-3.55 0.00***		-3.71 0.00***		-3.25 0.00***	-3.52 0.00***
Float				5.39 0.02**		4.60 0.05**	4.19 0.01**	2.11 0.23
N	30	30	30	30	30	30	30	30
R^{2*}	-0.00	0.05	0.33	0.12	0.44	0.10	0.41	0.43

Appendix 68a: Multivariate regressions of 'GDP$_{10-12}$' against WGI 'voice and accountability', Fraser 'open access economic institutions', the 'float' dummy and different sets of control variables in the sub-sample of developed democracies (second row: p-values of two-sided significance tests; number of asterisks: significance levels of 10%*, 5%** and 1%***).

	Dependent Variable: 'GDP$_{10-12}$'; Sample: Developed Democracies							
	(1)	(2)	(3)	(4)	(5)	(6)	(7)	(8)
Constant	-11.17 0.10*	-25.53 0.01***	-8.56 0.11	-12.95 0.03**	-21.61 0.01***	-22.45 0.01**	-10.16 0.04**	-20.08 0.02**
WGI Voice & Accountability	4.03 0.41	-7.40 0.14	2.67 0.49	3.72 0.37	-7.54 0.02**	-4.37 0.38	2.53 0.45	-5.95 0.06*
Her. Open Access Econ. Institutions		0.37 0.01***			0.34 0.01***	0.27 0.07*		0.28 0.04**
Financial Vulnerabilities			-3.55 0.00***		-3.36 0.00***		-3.25 0.00***	-3.29 0.00***
Float				5.39 0.02**		2.81 0.24	4.19 0.01**	1.48 0.35
N	30	30	30	30	30	30	30	30
R^{2*}	-0.00	0.16	0.33	0.12	0.48	0.16	0.41	0.47

Appendix 68b: Multivariate regressions of 'GDP$_{10-12}$' against WGI 'voice and accountability', Heritage 'open access economic institutions', the 'float' dummy and 'financial vulnerabilities' in the sub-sample of developed democracies without Singapore and Hong Kong (second row: p-values of two-sided significance tests; number of asterisks: significance levels of 10%*, 5%** and 1%***).

	Dependent Variable: 'GDP$_{10-12}$'; Sample: Developed Democracies							
	(1)	(2)	(3)	(4)	(5)	(6)	(7)	(8)
Constant	-14.50	-5.93	-20.80	-19.72	-12.53	-13.98	-24.33	-17.01
	0.72	0.87	0.52	0.58	0.66	0.70	0.40	0.54
FH Political Rights	0.10	-0.29	0.19	0.14	-0.18	-0.07	0.21	-0.06
& Civil Liberties	0.84	0.52	0.62	0.75	0.56	0.87	0.54	0.86
Fras. Open Access		3.32			3.17	1.71		2.22
Econ. Institutions		0.01**			0.00***	0.17		0.04**
Financial			-3.64		-3.59		-3.34	-3.43
Vulnerabilities			0.00***		0.00***		0.00***	0.00***
Float				5.50		4.11	4.26	2.43
				0.02**		0.09*	0.02**	0.19
N	30	30	30	30	30	30	30	30
R^{2*}	-0.03	0.06	0.33	0.10	0.43	0.09	0.41	0.43

Appendix 68c: Multivariate regressions of 'GDP$_{10-12}$' against Freedom House 'political rights and civil liberties', Fraser 'open access economic institutions', the 'float' dummy and 'financial vulnerabilities' in the sub-sample of developed democracies without Singapore and Hong Kong (second row: p-values of two-sided significance tests; number of asterisks: significance levels of 10%*, 5%** and 1%***).

	Dependent Variable: 'GDP$_{10-12}$'; Sample: Developed Democracies							
	(1)	(2)	(3)	(4)	(5)	(6)	(7)	(8)
Constant	-14.50	10.01	-20.80	-19.72	-0.86	1.13	-24.33	-7.58
	0.72	0.75	0.52	0.58	0.97	0.97	0.40	0.76
FH Political Rights	0.10	-0.51	0.19	0.14	-0.29	-0.33	0.21	-0.16
& Civil Liberties	0.84	0.18	0.62	0.75	0.28	0.39	0.54	0.55
Her. Open Access		0.32			0.25	0.24		0.19
Econ. Institutions		0.00***			0.00***	0.02**		0.03**
Financial			-3.64		-3.24		-3.34	-3.18
Vulnerabilities			0.00***		0.00***		0.00***	0.00***
Float				5.50		2.93	4.26	2.29
				0.02**		0.22	0.02**	0.17
N	30	30	30	30	30	30	30	30
R^{2*}	-0.03	0.16	0.33	0.10	0.45	0.16	0.41	0.45

Appendix 68d: Multivariate regressions of 'GDP$_{10-12}$' against Freedom House 'political rights and civil liberties', Heritage 'open access economic institutions', the 'float' dummy and 'financial vulnerabilities' in the sub-sample of developed democracies without Singapore and Hong Kong (second row: p-values of two-sided significance tests; number of asterisks: significance levels of 10%*, 5%** and 1%***).

Appendix 69 – '$GDP_{08\text{-}09}$' against different political openness indices, different government size indices, different financial openness indices and different control variables in less developed countries

	Dependent Variable: '$GDP_{08\text{-}09}$'; Sample: Emerging and Developing Countries							
	(1)	(2)	(3)	(4)	(5)	(6)	(7)	(8)
Constant	1.77	-6.26	20.21	11.50	1.51	-5.07	12.93	5.30
	0.40	0.11	0.00***	0.05*	0.46	0.17	0.01***	0.40
FH Political Rights	-0.09	-0.08	-0.07	-0.06	-0.10	-0.09	-0.08	-0.08
& Civil Liberties	0.02**	0.04**	0.09*	0.10*	0.01***	0.02**	0.04**	0.05*
Fraser Government		1.08		0.88		0.88		0.78
Consumption		0.01**		0.02**		0.02**		0.03**
Fraser Credit			-2.34	-2.07			-1.46	-1.21
Market Regulation			0.00***	0.00***			0.02**	0.05**
Financial					-2.21	-2.06	-1.44	-1.61
Vulnerabilities					0.02**	0.00***	0.10*	0.03**
Industrial					-2.01	-1.79	-1.90	-1.67
Orientation					0.00***	0.02**	0.00***	0.01**
N	52	50	50	50	52	50	50	50
R^{2*}	0.06	0.15	0.20	0.25	0.29	0.37	0.35	0.39

Appendix 69a: Multivariate regressions of '$GDP_{08\text{-}09}$' against Freedom House 'political rights and civil liberties', Fraser 'credit market regulation', Fraser 'government consumption' and different sets of control variables in emerging and developing countries (second row: p-values of two-sided significance tests; number of asterisks: significance levels of 10%*, 5%** and 1%***; residuals in regressions 1 and 3, 4, 7 and 8 are not normally-distributed).

	Dependent Variable: '$GDP_{08\text{-}09}$'; Sample: Emerging and Developing Countries							
	(1)	(2)	(3)	(4)	(5)	(6)	(7)	(8)
Constant	-3.36	-10.36	-0.95	-7.89	-4.01	-6.17	-0.46	-2.67
	0.00***	0.01***	0.80	0.09*	0.00***	0.13	0.89	0.55
WGI Voice &	-2.65	-1.88	-2.28	-1.48	-2.73	-2.50	-2.20	-1.94
Accountability	0.02**	0.11	0.12	0.35	0.01***	0.03**	0.08*	0.19
Heritage Govern-		0.09		0.10		0.03		0.03
ment Spending		0.06*		0.06*		0.55		0.54
Heritage Finan-			-0.05	-0.05			-0.07	-0.07
cial Freedom			0.52	0.50			0.30	0.30
Financial					-2.15	-2.01	-1.98	-1.81
Vulnerabilities					0.02**	0.04**	0.02**	0.05**
Industrial					-1.94	-1.90	-2.22	-2.14
Orientation					0.00***	0.00***	0.00***	0.00***
N	52	52	52	52	52	52	52	52
R^{2*}	0.07	0.11	0.06	0.10	0.29	0.27	0.29	0.28

Appendix 69b: Multivariate regressions of '$GDP_{08\text{-}09}$' against WGI 'voice and accountability', Heritage 'financial freedom', Heritage 'government spending' and different sets of control variables in emerging and developing countries (second row: p-values of two-sided significance tests; number of asterisks: significance levels of 10%*, 5%** and 1%***; residuals in regressions 1 to 8 are not normally-distributed).

	Dependent Variable: 'GDP08–09'; Sample: Emerging and Developing Countries							
	(1)	(2)	(3)	(4)	(5)	(6)	(7)	(8)
Constant	1.77 0.40	-6.88 0.14	3.60 0.20	-5.06 0.27	1.51 0.46	-1.55 0.74	4.08 0.12	1.07 0.82
FH Political Rights & Civil Liberties	-0.09 0.02**	-0.07 0.09*	-0.08 0.12	-0.05 0.30	-0.10 0.01***	-0.09 0.02**	-0.08 0.08*	-0.07 0.15
Heritage Govern-ment Spending		0.10 0.03**		0.10 0.04**		0.04 0.45		0.03 0.46
Heritage Financial Freedom			-0.05 0.48	-0.05 0.49			-0.07 0.28	-0.07 0.29
Financial Vulnerabilities					-2.21 0.02**	-2.02 0.04**	-2.01 0.02**	-1.85 0.05**
Industrial Orientation					-2.01 0.00***	-1.91 0.00***	-2.25 0.00***	-2.16 0.00***
N	52	52	52	52	52	52	52	52
R^{2*}	0.06	0.11	0.06	0.11	0.29	0.28	0.30	0.29

Appendix 69c: Multivariate regressions of '$GDP_{08\text{-}09}$' against Freedom House 'political rights and civil liberties', Heritage 'financial freedom', Heritage 'government spending' and different sets of control variables in emerging and developing countries (second row: p-values of two-sided significance tests; number of asterisks: significance levels of 10%*, 5%** and 1%***; residuals are non-normally-distributed in regressions 1 to 4 and 6 to 8).

Appendix 70 – Scatterplot of Heritage 'developed economic institutions' against the measure for interest group activity in the entire sample

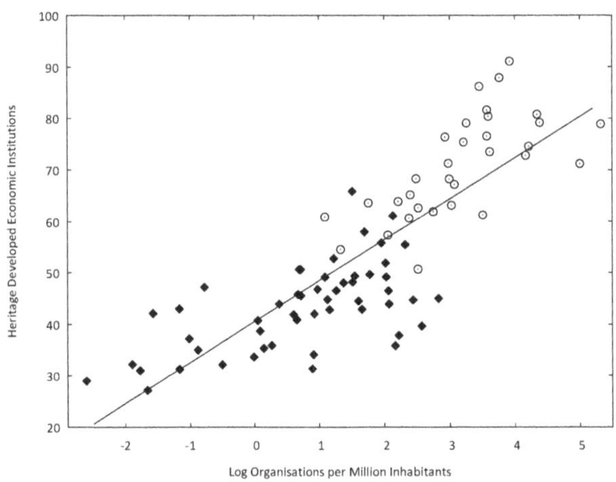

Appendix 70: Scatterplot of Heritage 'developed economic institutions' against log 'organizations per million inhabitants' (black dots: less developed countries; white circles: developed countries; upward-sloping line: fitted values for the entire sample).

Appendix 71 – Heritage 'developed economic institutions' against the measure for interest group activity in the entire sample

	Dependent Variable: Heritage 'Developed Economic Institutions'; Sample: All Countries									
	(1)	(2)	(3)	(4)	(5)	(6)	(7)	(8)	(9)	(10)
Constant	40.53 0.00***	39.89 0.00***	44.37 0.00***	38.95 0.00***	45.39 0.00***	43.80 0.00***	41.41 0.00***	35.69 0.00***	59.15 0.00***	39.36 0.00***
Log Org. per Mio. Inhabitants	7.96 0.00***	7.95 0.00***	7.61 0.00***	7.28 0.00***	7.89 0.00***	7.55 0.00***	7.86 0.00***	8.09 0.00***	7.44 0.00***	3.28 0.00***
British Legal Origin		2.33 0.23								
French Legal Origin			-7.03 0.00***							
Percentage Protestants				17.19 0.00***						
Percentage Catholics & Muslims					-9.92 0.00***					
Ethnic Fractionalization						-6.85 0.08*				
Linguistic Fractionalization							-1.66 0.65			
Religious Fractionalization								10.78 0.01***		
WB Inequality									-0.46 0.00***	
GDP per Capita										0.53 0.00***
N	84	84	84	83	83	84	82	83	84	84
R^{2*}	0.68	0.68	0.73	0.72	0.72	0.69	0.68	0.71	0.75	0.83

Appendix 71: Multivariate regressions of Heritage 'developed economic institutions' against log 'organizations per million inhabitants' and one additional control variable in the entire sample (second row: p-values of two-sided significance tests; number of asterisks: significance levels of 10%*, 5%** and 1%***).

Appendix 72 – Scatterplot of Heritage 'open access economic institutions' against the measure for interest group activity

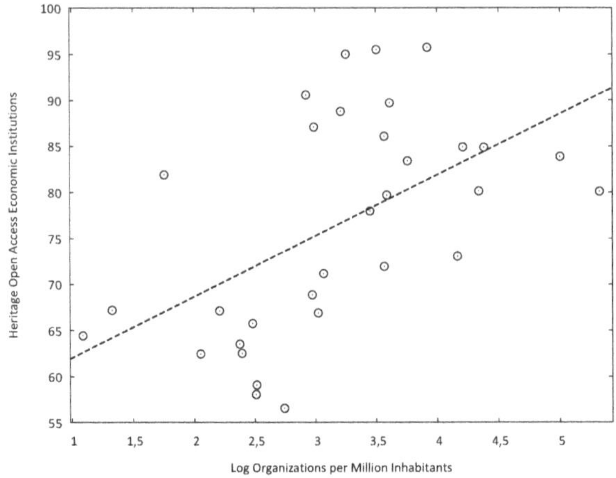

Appendix 72: Scatterplot of Heritage 'open access economic institutions' against log 'organizations per million inhabitants' in the sub-group of developed countries (upward-sloping line: fitted values for the sub-group of 32 developed countries).

Appendix 73 – Heritage 'open access economic institutions' against the measure for interest group activity in developed countries

	Dependent Variable: Heritage 'Open Access Economic Institutions'; Sample: Developed Countries									
	(1)	(2)	(3)	(4)	(5)	(6)	(7)	(8)	(9)	(10)
Constant	55.42 0.00***	53.88 0.00***	59.23 0.00***	56.63 0.00***	58.77 0.00***	55.71 0.00***	56.44 0.00***	44.13 0.00***	37.77 0.00***	55.74 0.00***
Log Org. per Mio. Inhabitants	6.62 0.00***	5.93 0.00***	6.09 0.00***	4.97 0.00***	6.83 0.00***	6.64 0.00***	6.71 0.00***	7.15 0.00***	6.65 0.00***	0.22 0.90
British Legal Origin		11.90 0.00***								
French Legal Origin			-8.48 0.00***							
Percentage Protestants				16.13 0.01***						
Percentage Catholics & Muslims					-11.72 0.02***					
Ethnic Fractionalization						-1.52 0.87				
Linguistic Fractionalization							-5.09 0.55			
Religious Fractionalization								20.51 0.01***		
WB Inequality									0.53 0.05**	
GDP per Capita										0.53 0.00***
N	32	32	32	31	31	32	32	32	32	32
R^{2*}	0.27	0.48	0.35	0.39	0.36	0.25	0.26	0.39	0.33	0.55

Appendix 73: Multivariate regressions of Heritage 'open access economic institutions' against log 'organizations per million inhabitants' and one additional control variable in the sub-sample of developed countries (second row: p-values of two-sided significance tests; number of asterisks: significance levels of 10%*, 5%** and 1%***).

Appendix 74 – Two indices for 'government spending' and 'financial freedom' against the measure for interest group activity in emerging and developing countries

	Dependent Variable: Heritage 'government spending'; Sample: Emerging and Developing Countries									
	(1)	(2)	(3)	(4)	(5)	(6)	(7)	(8)	(9)	(10)
Constant	77.29 0.00***	76.28 0.00***	71.20 0.00***	75.66 0.00***	72.26 0.00***	73.65 0.00***	70.11 0.00***	84.77 0.00***	39.90 0.00***	87.25 0.00***
Log Org. per Mio. Inhabitants	-3.31 0.04**	-3.13 0.06*	-4.19 0.03**	-3.36 0.04**	-4.07 0.01***	-3.00 0.08*	-1.54 0.40	-3.72 0.02**	-5.19 0.00***	0.82 0.60
British Legal Origin		3.52 0.38								
French Legal Origin			11.34 0.03**							
Percentage Protestants				15.04 0.32						
Percentage Catholics & Muslims					10.24 0.11					
Ethnic Fractionalization						7.37 0.41				
Linguistic Fractionalization							15.19 0.04**			
Religious Fractionalization								-16.04 0.06*		
WB Inequality									0.92 0.00***	
GDP per Capita										-3.05 0.00***
N	52	52	52	52	52	52	50	51	52	52
R^{2*}	0.05	0.04	0.14	0.04	0.07	0.04	0.09	0.07	0.27	0.31

Appendix 74a: Multivariate regressions of Heritage 'government spending' against log 'organizations per million inhabitants' and one additional control variable in the sub-sample of emerging and developing countries (second row: p-values of two-sided significance tests; number of asterisks: significance levels of 10%*, 5%** and 1%***).

	Dependent Variable: Heritage 'fin. freedom'; Sample: Emerging and Developing Countries									
	(1)	(2)	(3)	(4)	(5)	(6)	(7)	(8)	(9)	(10)
Constant	47.64 0.00***	48.01 0.00***	47.21 0.00***	45.00 0.00***	47.02 0.00***	39.87 0.00***	43.53 0.00***	40.06 0.00***	35.51 0.00***	48.13 0.00***
Log Org. per Mio. Inhabitants	4.43 0.01**	4.36 0.02**	4.37 0.01**	4.35 0.01**	4.33 0.02**	5.09 0.00***	5.25 0.00***	5.34 0.00***	3.82 0.04**	4.63 0.03**
British Legal Origin		-1.29 0.77								
French Legal Origin			0.80 0.83							
Percentage Protestants				24.22 0.04**						
Percentage Catholics & Muslims					1.26 0.83					
Ethnic Fractionalization						15.73 0.06*				
Linguistic Fractionalization							8.32 0.14			
Religious Fractionalization								16.85 0.01**		
WB Inequality									0.30 0.13	
GDP per Capita										-0.15 0.78
N	52	52	52	52	52	52	50	51	52	52
R^{2*}	0.13	0.12	0.12	0.17	0.12	0.18	0.14	0.19	0.15	0.32

Appendix 74b: Multivariate regressions of Heritage 'financial freedom' against log 'organizations per million inhabitants' and one additional control variable in the sub-sample of emerging and developing countries (second row: p-values of two-sided significance tests; number of asterisks: significance levels of 10%*, 5%** and 1%***).

Appendix 75 – 'GDP_{08-12}' against the measure for interest group activity, Heritage 'developed economic institutions' and different control variables in the entire sample

	Dependent Variable: 'GDP_{08-12}'; Sample: All Countries								
	(1)	(2)	(3)	(4)	(5)	(6)	(7)	(8)	(9)
Constant	-2.89 0.13	-3.95 0.04**	-3.50 0.02**	13.70 0.02**	-2.34 0.21	12.19 0.03**	2.21 0.62	-3.18 0.04**	2.09 0.63
Log Org. per Mio. Inhabitants	-2.77 0.00***	-2.14 0.02**	-2.41 0.00***	0.48 0.74	-1.72 0.04**	1.02 0.47	-1.32 0.26	-1.92 0.00***	-0.93 0.41
Her. Developed Econ. Institutions				-0.41 0.00***		-0.36 0.01***	-0.13 0.18		-0.13 0.23
Peg					-9.73 0.00***	-8.62 0.01***		-4.76 0.06*	-4.61 0.08*
Financial Vulnerabilities		-7.45 0.00***	-7.43 0.00***				-7.15 0.00***	-7.14 0.00***	-6.88 0.00***
Industrial Orientation		-4.06 0.00***	-4.01 0.00***				-3.73 0.00***	-3.60 0.00***	-3.35 0.00***
Economic Development		-0.45 0.73							
International Linkages		-0.81 0.29							
N	84	84	84	84	84	84	82	84	82
R^{2*}	0.12	0.55	0.56	0.20	0.20	0.26	0.56	0.57	0.58

Appendix 75: Multivariate regressions of 'GDP_{08-12}' against log 'organizations per million inhabitants', Heritage 'developed economic institutions', the 'peg' dummy and different sets of control variables in the entire sample (second row: p-values of two-sided significance tests; number of asterisks: significance levels of 10%*, 5%** and 1%***; misspecification in regression 4; residuals in regressions 2, 4, 8 and 9 are not normally-distributed).

Appendix 76 – 'GDP₀₈₋₀₉' against the measure for interest group activity, different measures for 'developed economic institutions' and different control variables in the entire sample

	Dependent Variable: 'GDP08-09'; Sample: All Countries								
	(1)	(2)	(3)	(4)	(5)	(6)	(7)	(8)	(9)
Constant	-3.21 0.01***	-3.85 0.00***	-3.69 0.00***	12.59 0.00***	-2.97 0.01***	12.47 0.00***	3.71 0.29	-3.58 0.00***	4.18 0.24
Log Org. per Mio. Inhabitants	-1.62 0.00***	-1.23 0.05*	-1.33 0.00***	-0.33 0.58	-1.17 0.01**	0.03 0.96	-0.75 0.17	-1.20 0.01***	-0.59 0.29
Fras. Developed Econ. Institutions				-2.88 0.00***		-2.82 0.00***	-1.36 0.03**		-1.42 0.03**
Peg					-4.14 0.02**	-3.62 0.03**		-1.41 0.35	-1.39 0.35
Financial Vulnerabilities		-3.20 0.00***	-3.19 0.00***				-2.87 0.00***	-3.11 0.00***	-2.78 0.00***
Industrial Orientation		-2.22 0.00***	-2.20 0.00***				-1.85 0.00***	-2.08 0.00***	-1.71 0.00***
Economic Development		-0.23 0.79							
International Linkages		-0.95 0.05*	-0.92 0.05*				-0.81 0.06*	-0.84 0.10*	-0.72 0.11
N	84	84	84	82	84	82	82	84	82
R^{2*}	0.13	0.40	0.41	0.24	0.17	0.27	0.43	0.41	0.58

Appendix 76a: Multivariate regressions of 'GDP₀₈₋₀₉' against log 'organizations per million inhabitants', Fraser 'developed economic institutions', the 'peg' dummy and different sets of control variables in the entire sample (second row: p-values of two-sided significance tests; number of asterisks: significance levels of 10%*, 5%** and 1%***; residuals in regressions 1 to 9 are not normally-distributed).

	Dependent Variable: 'GDP_{08-09}'; Sample: All Countries								
	(1)	(2)	(3)	(4)	(5)	(6)	(7)	(8)	(9)
Constant	-3.21	-3.85	-3.69	7.01	-2.97	6.42	2.02	-3.58	1.98
	0.01***	0.00***	0.00***	0.02**	0.01***	0.02**	0.43	0.00***	0.43
Log Org. per Mio.	-1.62	-1.23	-1.33	0.39	-1.17	0.61	-0.23	-1.20	-0.13
Inhabitants	0.00***	0.05*	0.00***	0.64	0.01**	0.48	0.76	0.01***	0.86
Her. Developed				-0.25		-0.23	-0.14		-0.14
Econ. Institutions				0.00***		0.00***	0.03**		0.04**
Peg					-4.14	-3.42		-1.41	-1.21
					0.02**	0.04***		0.35	0.42
Financial		-3.20	-3.19				-2.91	-3.11	-2.84
Vulnerabilities		0.00***	0.00***				0.00***	0.00***	0.00***
Industrial		-2.22	-2.20				-1.92	-2.08	-1.82
Orientation		0.00***	0.00***				0.00***	0.00***	0.00***
Economic		-0.23							
Development		0.79							
International		-0.95	-0.92				-0.99	-0.84	-0.93
Linkages		0.05*	0.05*				0.05**	0.10*	0.08*
N	84	84	84	84	84	84	84	84	84
R^{2*}	0.13	0.40	0.41	0.22	0.17	0.24	0.43	0.41	0.58

Appendix 76b: Multivariate regressions of 'GDP_{08-09}' against log 'organizations per million inhabitants', Heritage 'developed economic institutions', the 'peg' dummy and different sets of control variables in the entire sample (second row: p-values of two-sided significance tests; number of asterisks: significance levels of 10%*, 5%** and 1%***; residuals in regressions 1 to 9 are not normally-distributed).

Appendix 77 –'GDP_{10-12}' against the measure for interest group activity, different measures for 'developed economic institutions' and different control variables in the entire sample

	Dependent Variable: 'GDP_{10-12}'; Sample: All Countries								
	(1)	(2)	(3)	(4)	(5)	(6)	(7)	(8)	(9)
Constant	0.03 0.98	-0.47 0.63	-0.29 0.75	9.49 0.10*	0.38 0.70	9.29 0.09*	-1.34 0.77	-0.05 0.96	-0.39 0.93
Log Org. per Mio. Inhabitants	-1.24 0.00***	-0.94 0.05**	-1.05 0.00***	-0.56 0.37	-0.56 0.23	0.05 0.93	-1.20 0.02**	-0.69 0.07*	-0.78 0.13
Fras. Developed Econ. Institutions				-1.68 0.09*		-1.57 0.09*	0.21 0.78		0.09 0.90
Peg					-6.24 0.01***	-6.09 0.01**		-3.55 0.09*	-3.54 0.09*
Financial Vulnerabilities		-4.72 0.00***	-4.72 0.00***				-4.72 0.00***	-4.50 0.00***	-4.48 0.00***
Industrial Orientation		-1.83 0.00***	-1.81 0.00***				-1.87 0.00***	-1.50 0.00***	-1.53 0.00***
Economic Development		-0.27 0.73							
N	84	84	84	82	84	82	82	84	82
R^{2*}	0.06	0.46	0.46	0.08	0.14	0.17	0.46	0.41	0.48

Appendix 77a: Multivariate regressions of 'GDP_{10-12}' against log 'organizations per million inhabitants', Fraser 'developed economic institutions', the 'peg' dummy and different sets of control variables in the entire sample (second row: p-values of two-sided significance tests; number of asterisks: significance levels of 10%*, 5%** and 1%***; misspecification in regression 2; residuals in regressions 2, 3, 7, 8 and 9 are not normally-distributed).

Dependent Variable: 'GDP10-12'; Sample: All Countries									
	(1)	(2)	(3)	(4)	(5)	(6)	(7)	(8)	(9)
Constant	0.03 0.98	-0.47 0.63	-0.29 0.75	6.79 0.08*	0.38 0.70	5.77 0.14	-0.06 0.98	-0.05 0.96	-0.16 0.96
Log Org. per Mio. Inhabitants	-1.24 0.00***	-0.94 0.05**	-1.05 0.00***	0.09 0.92	-0.56 0.23	0.45 0.60	-1.01 0.21	-0.69 0.07*	-0.71 0.34
Her. Developed Econ. Institutions				-0.17 0.06*		-0.13 0.14	-0.01 0.95		0.00 0.97
Peg					-6.24 0.01***	-5.83 0.02**		-3.55 0.09*	-3.55 0.09*
Financial Vulnerabilities		-4.72 0.00***	-4.72 0.00***				-4.71 0.00***	-4.50 0.00***	-4.51 0.00***
Industrial Orientation		-1.83 0.00***	-1.81 0.00***				-1.80 0.00***	-1.50 0.00***	-1.51 0.00***
Economic Development		-0.27 0.73							
N	84	84	84	84	84	84	84	84	84
R^{2*}	0.06	0.46	0.46	0.08	0.14	0.16	0.43	0.41	0.48

Appendix 77b: Multivariate regressions of '$GDP_{10\text{-}12}$' against log 'organizations per million inhabitants', Heritage 'developed economic institutions', the 'peg' dummy and different sets of control variables in the entire sample (second row: p-values of two-sided significance tests; number of asterisks: significance levels of 10%*, 5%** and 1%***; misspecification in regressions 2, 6 and 9; heteroscedasticity in regression 4; residuals in regressions 2, 3, 4, 7, 8 and 9 are not normally-distributed).

Appendix 78 – Correlations between the measure for interest group activity and different political openness indices in different samples

	Log Organizations per Million Inhabitants			
	All 84 Countries	32 Developed Countries	30 Developed Democracies	52 Emerging & Developing Countries
WGI Voice & Accountability	**0.76**	**0.46**	**0.75**	**0.55**
FH Political Rights & Civil Liberties	**0.67**	0.19	**0.68**	**0.50**

Appendix 78: Correlations between log 'organizations per million inhabitants' and two measures for political openness in different samples (significant correlations at 5% level are bold).

Appendix 79 – Scatterplots of the measure for interest group activity against different political openness indices

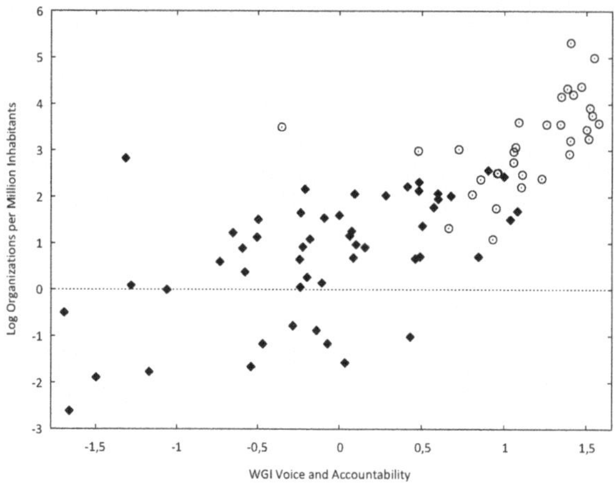

Appendix 79a: Scatterplot of log 'organizations per million inhabitants' against WGI 'voice and accountability' (black dots: less developed countries; white circles: developed countries; upward-sloping line: fitted values for the entire sample).

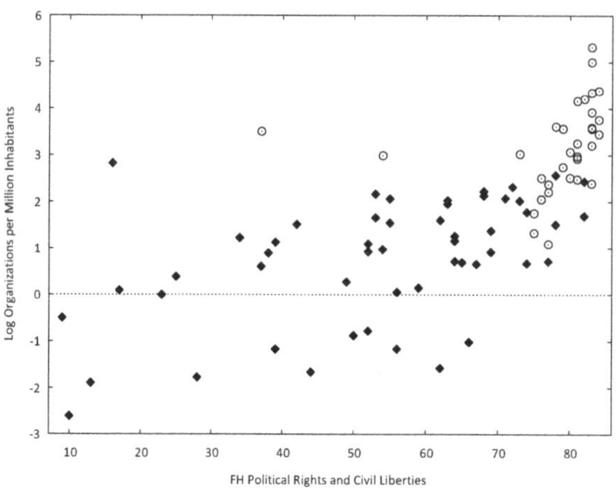

Appendix 79b: Scatterplot of log 'organizations per million inhabitants' against Freedom House 'political rights and civil liberties' (black dots: less developed countries; white circles: developed countries; upward-sloping line: fitted values for the entire sample).

References

Abiad, A. (2003). *Early-Warning Systems: A Survey and a Regime Switching Approach*. IMF Working Paper, No. 03/32.

Abiad, A., Balakrishnan, R., Koeva Brooks, P., Leigh, D. and Tytell, I. (2009). *What's the Damage? Medium-term Output Dynamics After Banking Crises*. IMF Working Paper, No. 09/245.

Abbritti, M. and Weber, S. (2010). *Labor Market Institutions and the Business Cycle – Unemployment Rigidities vs. Real Wage Rigidities*. ECB Working Paper, No. 1183.

Acemoglu, D. (2008). Oligarchic versus democratic societies. *Journal of the European Economic Association*, Vol. 6, No. 1, pp. 1-44.

Acemoglu, D., Johnson, S. and Robinson, J. (2001). The colonial origins of comparative development: An empirical investigation. *American economic review*, Vol. 91, No. 5, 1369-1401.

Acemoglu, D., Johnson, S. and Robinson, J. (2005). Institutions as a Fundamental Cause of Long-Run Growth. In: Aghion, P. and Durlauf, S., eds. *Handbook of economic growth: Volume 1, part A*. Amsterdam: Elsevier, pp. 385 – 472.

Acemoglu, D., Johnson, S., Robinson, J. and Thaicharoen, Y. (2003). Institutional causes, macroeconomic symptoms: volatility, crisis and growth. *Journal of Monetary Economics*, Vol. 50, No. 1, pp. 49 – 123.

Acemoglu, D., Naidu, S., Restrepo, P. and Robinson, J. (2014). *Democracy does cause growth*. NBER Research Papers, No. 20004.

Acemoglu, D. and Robinson, J. (2012). *Why nations fail: the origins of power, prosperity, and poverty*, 1st ed., New York, NY: Crown Publications.

Aixalá Pastó, J. and Fabro Esteban, G. (2008). Determinantes de la calidad institutional de los países. *Revista Economía Aplicada*, Vol. 16, No. 46, pp. 119-144.

Aleksynska, M. and Schindler, M. (2011). *Labor Market Regulations in Low-, Middle- and High-Income Countries: A New Panel Database*. IMF Working Paper, No. 11/154.

Alesina, A., Ardagna, S. and Trebbi, F. (2006). Who adjusts and when? *IMF Staff Papers*, Vol. 53, No. 1, pp. 1-29.

Alesina, A., Campante, F. and Tabellini, G. (2008). Why is fiscal policy often procyclical? *Journal of the European economic association*, Vol. 6, No. 5, pp. 1006-1036.

Alesina, A., Devleeschauwer, A., Easterly, W., Kurlat, S. and Wacziarg, R. (2003). Fractionalization. *Journal of Economic Growth*, Vol. 8, No. 2, pp. 155-194.

Alesina, A. and Drazen, A. (1991). Why Are Stabilizations Delayed? *The American Economic Review*, Vol. 81, No. 5, pp. 1170-1188.

R. Fritzsch, *Adaptive Efficiency During the Great Recession*,
Wirtschaft und Politik, https://doi.org/10.1007/978-3-658-27409-2

Allansson, M., Melander, E. and Themnér, L. (2017). Organized violence, 1989-2016. *Journal of Peace Research*, Vol. 54, No. 4, pp. 523-532.

Almeida, H. and Ferreira, D. (2002). Democracy and the variability of economic performance. *Economics and Politics*, Vol. 14, No. 3, pp. 225-257.

Alonso, J. and Garcimartín, C. (2013). The determinants of institutional quality. More on the debate. *Journal of International Development*, Vol. 25, No. 2, pp. 206-226.

Angkinand, A. and Willet, T. (2006). Moral Hazard, Financial Crises, and Choice of Exchange Rate Regimes. Unpublished Manuscript. Available at: https://research.cgu.edu/economic-policy-studies/wp-content/uploads/sites/25/2016/11/2006-07.pdf [Accessed: 16.02.2018].

Aron, J. (2000). Growth and institutions: a review of the evidence. *The World Bank Research Observer*, Vol. 15, No. 1, pp. 99 – 135.

Aşıcı, A. (2011). Exchange rate regime choice and currency crisis. *Economic Systems*, Vol. 35, pp. 419-436.

Asongu, S. and Kodila-Tedika, O. (2016). *Determinants of Property Rights Protection in Sub-Saharan Africa*. AGDI Working Paper, No. 16/041.

Babecky, J., Havranek, T., Meteju, J., Rusnak, M., Smidkova, K. and Vasicek, B. (2013). *Early warning indicators of economic crises: evidence from a panel of 40 developed countries.* Czech National Bank Working Paper, No. 8.

Babecky, J., Havranek, T., Meteju, J., Rusnak, M., Smidkova, K. and Vasicek, B. (2013). Leading Indicators of crisis incidence: Evidence from developed countries. *Journal of International Money and Finance,* Vol 35, pp. 1-19.

Backhaus, K., Erichson, B., Plinke, W. and Weiber, R. (2011). *Multivariate Analysemethode: Eine anwendungsorientierte Einführung*, 13th ed. Heidelberg: Springer.

Baker, S., Bloom, N. and Davis, S. (2016). Measuring economic policy uncertainty. *The quarterly journal of economics*, Vol. 131, No. 4, pp. 1593-1636.

Barnebeck Andersen, T. and Malchow-Moller, N. (2014). *Denmark's fixed exchange rate regime and the delayed recovery from the Global Financial Crisis: A comparative macroeconomic analysis*. University of Southern Denmark Discussion Paper on Business and Economics, No. 10/2014.

Barro, R. (1991). Economic growth in a cross section of countries. *The quarterly journal of economics, Vol.* 106, No. 2, pp. 407-443.

Barro, R. (1996). Democracy and Growth. *Journal of Economic Growth*, Vol. 1, No. 1, pp. 1-27.

Barth, J., Caprio, G. and Levine, R. (2004). Bank regulation and supervision: what works best? *Journal of Financial Intermediation*, Vol. 13, No. 2, pp. 205-248.

Barth, J., Caprio, G. and Levine, R. (2013). *Bank Regulation and Supervision in 180 Countries from 1999 to 2011*. NBER Working Paper, No. 18733.

Beach, W. and Kane, T. (2008). Methodology: Measuring the 10 Economic Freedoms. In: Heritage Foundation. *2008 Index of Economic Freedom*. Available at: https://www.heritage.org/index/download [Accessed: 23.01.2018].

Belke, A. and Dreger, C. (2013). Current account imbalances in the euro area: does catching up explain the development? *Review of International Economics*, Vol. 21, No. 1, pp. 6-17.

Berggren, N. and Jordahl, H. (2005). Does free trade really reduce growth? Further testing using the economic freedom index. *Public Choice*, Vol. 122, No. 1, pp. 99-114.

Berglöf, E., Korniyenko, Y., Plekhanov, A. and Zettelmeyer, J. (2010). Understanding the Crisis in Emerging Europe. *Public Policy Review*, Vol. 6, No. 6, pp. 985 – 1008.

Berger, H. and Nitsch, V. (2010). *The Euro's Effect on Trade Imbalances*. IMF Working Paper, No. 10/226.

Berkman, P., Gelos, G., Rennhack, R. and Walsh, J. (2012). The global financial crisis: Explaining cross-country differences in the output impact. *Journal of International Money and Finance*, Vol 31, No. 1, pp. 42 – 59.

Bernal-Verdugo, L., Furceri, D. and Guillaume, D. (2012). *Crisis, Labor Market Policy, and Unemployment*. IMF Working Paper, No. 12/65.

Betcherman (2013). *Labor Market Institutions – A Review of the Literature*. World Bank Policy Research Working Paper, No. 6276.

Bischoff, I. (2000). *Interessenverbände in der Demokratie – Verursacher rückläufiger Wachstumsraten?: eine Analyse entlang des Argumentationsstranges von Mancur Olson*. Hamburg: Kovač.

Bischoff, I. (2007). Model Uncertainty, Political Learning, and Institutions: A Broader View on Mancur Olson's Theory of Institutional Sclerosis. *Southern Economic Journal*, Vol. 74, No. 1, pp. 34 – 49.

Bjornskov, C. (2016). Economic freedom and economic crisis. *European Journal of Political Economy*, Vol. 45, Supplement, pp. 11 – 23.

Blanchard, O. (2005). *Macroeconomics*, 4th ed., Upper Saddle River, NJ: Pearson Prentice Hall.

Blanchard, O., Das, M. and Faruqee, H. (2010). The Initial Impact of the Crisis on Emerging Market Countries. *Brookings Papers on Economic Activity*, No. 2010.1, pp. 263 – 307.

Blanchard, O., Jaumotte, F. and Loungani, P. (2014). Labor market policies and IMF advice in advanced economies during the Great Recession. *IZA Journal of Labor Policy*, Vol 3, No. 1.

Blanchard, O. and Portugal, P. (2001). What hides behind an unemployment rate: comparing Portuguese and US labor markets. *American Economic Review*, Vol. 91, No. 1, pp. 187-207.

Blanchard, O. and Summers, L. (1986). *Hysteresis and the European Unemployment Problem*. NBER Macroeconomics Annual, Vol. 1, pp. 15-78.

Blum, J. (1999). Do capital adequacy requirements reduce risks in banking? *Journal of Banking and Finance*, Vol. 23, No. 5, pp. 755-771.

Bordo, M., Eichengreen, B., Klingebiel, D. and Soledad Martinzes-Perie (2001). Is the crisis problem growing more severe? *Economic Policy*, Vol. 16, No. 32, pp. 52-82.

Borner, S., Bodmer, F. and Kobler, M. (2004). *Institutional Efficiency and its Determinants: The Role of Political Factors in Economic Growth*. Paris: OECD Publications.

Boyd, J., Kwak, S. and Smith B. (2005). The Real Output Losses Associated with Modern Banking Crises. *Journal of Money, Credit and Banking*, Vol. 37, No. 6, pp. 977-999.

Brennan, G. and Buchanan, J. (2000 [1985]). *The reason of rules: constitutional political economy*. Indianapolis: Liberty Fund.

Bricongne, J., Lapègue, V. and Monso, O. (2009). *Subprimes: from the financial crisis to the economic crisis*. INSEE Publication. Available at: https://www.insee.fr/en /statistiques/1407770?sommaire=1407772 [Accessed 14.01.2018].

Brock, W. (1983). Contestable Markets and Theory of Industry Structure: A Review Article. *Journal of Political Economy*, Vol 91, No. 6, pp. 1055-1066.

Brunnermeier, M. (2009). Deciphering the Liquidity and Credit Crunch 2007-2008. *Journal of Economic Perspectives*, Vol. 23, No. 1, pp. 77-100.

Burda, M. (2013). *The European Debt Crisis: How did we get into this mess? How can we get out of it?* SFB 649 Discussion Paper 2013-019.

Calmfors, L. and Driffill, J. (1988). Bargaining structure, corporatism and macroeconomic performance. Economic Policy, Vol. 3, No. 6, pp. 13-61.

Campbell, N. and Snyder, T. (2012). Economic Freedom and Economic Volatility. *Journal of International and Global Economic Studies*, Vol. 5, No. 2, pp. 60-76.

Carlsson, F., Lundström, S. (2002). Economic freedom and growth: Decomposing the effects. *Public Choice*, Vol. 112, No. 3, pp. 335-344.

Caprio, G., Klingebiel, D. (2002). Episodes of Systematic and Borderline Banking Crises. In: Klingebiel, D. and Laeven, L., eds. *Managing the Real and Fiscal Effects of Banking Crises*. World Bank Publication.

Caprio, G., D'Apice, V., Ferri, G. and Puoplo, G. (2010). *Macro Financial Determinants of the Great Financial Crisis: Implications for Financial Regulation*. MPRA Paper No. 26088.

Cavallo, A. and Cavallo, E. (2010). Are crises good for long-term growth? The role of political institutions. *Journal of Macroeconomics*, Vol. 32, No. 3, pp. 838-357.

Cazes, S., Khatiwada, S. and Malo, M. (2012). *Employment Protection and Collective Bargaining: Beyond the deregulation agenda*. ILO Employment Working Paper No. 133.

Cecchetti, S., Kohler, M. and Upper, C. (2009). *Financial crises and economic activity*. NBER Working Paper, No. 15379.

Chan, S. (1987). Growth with equity: A test of Olson's theory for Asian Pacific Rim countries. *Journal of Peace Research*, Vol. 24, No. 2, pp. 135-150.

Chang, H. (1995). Explaining 'flexible rigidities' in East Asia. In: Killick, T., ed. *The flexible economy: Causes and consequences of the adaptability of national economies*. London: Routledge, pp. 199 - 224.

Chinn, M. and Wei, S. (2013). A faith-based initiative meets the evidence: does a flexible exchange rate regime really facilitate current account adjustment? *The Review of Economics and Statistics*, Vol. 95, No. 1, pp. 168-184.

Choi, K. (1983). A statistical test of Olson's model. In: Mueller, D., ed. *The political economy of growth*. New Haven: Yale University Press, pp. 57-78.

Cihak, M., Demirgüc-Kunt, A., Feyen, E. and Levine, R. (2012). *Benchmarking financial systems around the world*. World Bank Policy Research Working Paper, No. 6175.

Claessens, S. and Klingebiel, D. (2001). Competition and scope of activities in financial services. *The World Bank Research Observer*, Vol. 16, No. 1, pp. 19-40.

Claessens, S., Dell'Ariccia, G., Igan, D. and Laeven, L. (2010). Cross-country experiences and policy implications from the global financial crisis. *Economic Policy*, Vol. 25, No. 62, pp. 267 – 293.

Claessens, S., Tong, H. and Wei, S. (2012). From the financial crisis to the real economy: Using firm-level data to identify transmission channels. *Journal of International Economics*, Vol. 88, No. 2, pp. 375-387.

Crotty, J. (2009). Structural causes of the global financial crisis: a critical assessment of the 'new financial architecture. *Cambridge Journal of Economics*, Vol. 33, No. 4, pp. 563-580.

Coase, R. (1937). The Nature of the Firm. *Economica*, Vol. 4, No. 16, pp. 386-405.

Coates, D. and Heckelman, J. (2003). Absolute and relative effects of interest groups on the economy. In: Coates, D. and Heckelman, J., eds. *Collective choice*. Berlin: Springer Verlag, pp. 129-142.

Combes, J., Minea, A. and Sow, M. (2016). Crises and Exchange Rate Regimes: Time to break down the bipolar view? *Applied Economics*, Vol 48, No. 46, pp. 4393-4409.

Cox, G. and McCubbins, M. (2001). The Institutional Determinants of Economic Policy Outcomes. In: Haggard, S. and McCubbins, M., eds. *Presidents, Parliaments, and Policy*. Cambridge: Cambridge University Press, pp. 21-63.

Cwik, T. and Wieland, V. (2011). Keynesian government spending multipliers and spillovers in the euro area. *Economic Policy*, Vol. 26, No. 67, pp. 493-549.

Dahl, R. (1971). *Polyarchy: participation and opposition*, New Haven, Conn: Yale University Press.

Dahlman, C. (1979). The problem of externality. *The journal of law and economics*, Vol 22, No 1, pp. 141-162.

Dawson, J. (2006). Regulation, investment, and growth across countries. *Cato Journal*, Vol. 26, No. 3, pp. 489-509.

Dawson, J. (2010). Macroeconomic Volatility and Economic Freedom – a Preliminary Analysis. In: Gwartney, J., Hall, J. and Lawson, R., eds. *Economic Freedom of the World - 2010 Annual Report*. Vancouver, B.C.: Fraser Institute, pp. 175-186.

De Haan, J., Lundström, S. and Sturm, J. (2006). Market-oriented institutions and policies and economic growth: A critical survey. *Journal of Economic Surveys*, Vol. 20, No. 2, pp. 157 – 191.

Debrun, X., Pisani-Ferry, J. and Sapir, A. (2008). *Government Size and Output Volatility: Should We Forsake Automatic Stabilization?* IMF Working Paper, No. 08/122.

Deutsche Bundesbank (2014). Realwirtschaftliche Anpassungsprozesse und Reformmaßnahmen. *Deutsche Bundesbank Monatsbericht Januar 2014*, Vol. 66, No. 1, pp. 21-40.

Diaz-Alejandro, C. (1985). Good-bye financial repression, hello financial crash. *Journal of Development Economics*, Vol. 19, No. 1-2, pp. 1-24.

Dolls, M., Fuest, C. and Peichl, A. (2012). Automatic stabilizers and economic crisis: US vs. Europe. *Journal of Public Economics*, Vol. 96, No. 3, pp. 279-294.

Domac, I. and Martinez Peria, M. (2003). Banking crises and exchange rate regimes: is there a link? *Journal of International Economics*, Vol. 61, No. 1, pp. 41-72.

Doménech, R. and Andrés, J. (2008). The stabilizing role of government size. *Journal of Economic Dynamics and Control*, Vol. 32, No. 2, pp. 571-593.

Doucouliagos, H. and Ulubaşoğlu, M. (2008). Democracy and Economic Growth: A Meta-Analysis. *American Journal of Political Science*, Vol. 52, No. 1, pp. 61-83.

Eichengreen, B. (2010). *Imbalances in the Euro Area*. Unpublished Manuscript, University of California. Available at: https://eml.berkeley.edu/~eichengr /Imbalances_Euro_Area_5-23-11.pdf [Accessed 08.06.2018].

Eichengreen, B., Rose, A. and Wyplosz, C. (1994). *Speculative attacks on pegged exchange rates: An empirical exploration with special reference to the European Monetary System.* NBER Working Paper, No. 4898.

Eichhorst, W., Escudero, V., Marx, P. and Tobin, S. (2010). *The Impact of the Crisis on Employment and the Role of Labour Market Institutions.* IZA Discussion Paper, No. 5320.

Eichhorst, W., Marx, P. and Tobsch, V. (2009). *Institutional Arrangements, Employment Performance and the Quality of Work.* IZA Discussion Paper No. 4595.

Esser, H. (1993). *Soziologie: Spezielle Grundlagen - Band 5: Institutionen.* 3rd ed. Frankfurt a. M.: Campus Verlag.

Essers, D. (2012). *Democracy and external shock resilience in developing countries: evidence from the Great Recession*. IOB Working Paper, No. 2012.02.

Everts, M. (2006). *Duration of Business Cycles*. MRPA Working Paper, No. 1219.

Fatás, A. and Mihov, I. (2001). Government size and automatic stabilizers: international and intranational evidence. *Journal of International Economics*, Vol. 55, No. 1, pp. 3-28.

Fisher, I. (1933). The Debt-Deflation Theory of Great Depressions. *Econometrica*, Vol. 1, No. 4, pp. 337-357.

Frankel, J. (2003). *Experience of and lessons from exchange rate regimes in emerging economies*. NBER Working Paper, No. 10032.

Frankel, J. and Rose, A. (1996). Currency crashes in emerging markets: An empirical treatment. *Journal of International Economics*, Vol. 41, No. 3-4.

Frankel, J. and Rose, A. (2002). An estimate of the effect of common currencies on trade and income. *The Quarterly Journal of Economics*, Vol. 117, No. 2, pp. 437-466.

Frankel, J. and Saravelos, G. (2012). Can leading indicators assess country vulnerability? Evidence from the 2008-09 global financial crisis. *Journal of International Economics*, Vol. 87, No 2, pp. 216 – 231.

Freedom House (2008). *Freedom in the World Report 2008 - Methodology*. Available at: https://freedomhouse.org/report/freedom-world-2008/methodology [Accessed 27.04.2018].

Friedman, M. (1953). The case for flexible exchange rates. In: Friedman, M., ed. *Essays in Positive Economics*. Chicago: Chicago University Press, pp. 157-204.

Furlong, F. and Keeley, M. (1989). Capital Regulation and Bank Risk-Taking: A Note. *Journal of Banking and Finance*, Vol. 13, No. 6, pp. 883-891.

Galbraith, K. (1952). *American Capitalism: The Concept of Countervailing Power*. Cambridge, MA: The Riverside Press.

Galí, J. (1994). Government size and macroeconomic stability. European Economic Review, Vol. 38, No. 1, pp. 117-132.

Gastil, R. (1980). *Freedom in the world: political rights and civil liberties, 1980*. New York: Freedom House.

Gaulier, G. and Vicard, V. (2012). Current account imbalances in the euro area: competitiveness or demand shock. *Banque de France Quarterly selection of articles*, Vol. 27, pp. 5-26.

Gavin, M. and Perotti, R. (1997). Fiscal Policy in Latin America. In: Bernanke, B. and Rotemberg, J., eds., *NBER Marcoeconomics Annunal 1997*, pp. 11-61.

Gerring, J., Bond, P., Barndt, W. and Moreno, C. (2005). Democracy and Economic Growth: A Historical Perspective. *World Politics*, Vol. 57, No. 3, pp. 323-364.

Giannone, D., Lenza, M. and Reichlin, L. (2011). Market Freedom and the Global Recession. *IMF Economic Review*, Vol. 59, No. 1, pp. 111 - 135.

Gleditsch, N., Wallensteen, P., Eriksson, M., Sollenberg, M. and Strand, H. (2002). Armed Conflict 1946-2001: A New Dataset. *Journal of Peace Research*, Vol. 39, No. 5, pp. 615-637.

Gnocchi, S., Lagerborg, A. and Pappa, E. (2015). Do labor market institutions matter for business cycles? *Journal of Economic Dynamics and Control*, Vol. 51, pp. 299-317.

Gosh, A., Qureshi, M. and Tsangarides, C. (2014). *Friedman Redux: external adjustment and exchange rate flexibility*. IMF Working Paper, No. 14/146.

Gray, V. and Lowery, D. (1988). Interest Group Politics and Economic Growth in the U.S. States. *American Political Science Review*, Vol. 82, No. 1, pp. 109-131.

Gray, G., Joshi, B., Kehayova, P., Llaudes, R., Presciuttini, G. and Saenz, M. (2010). *How Did Emerging Markets Cope in the Crisis?* Washington DC: IMF Publication.

Groot, S., Möhlmann, J., Garretsen, J. and de Groot, H. (2011). The crisis sensitivity of European countries and regions: stylized facts and spatial heterogeneity. *Cambridge Journal of Regions, Economy and Society*, Vol. 4, No. 3, pp. 437 – 456.

Grusky, D., Western, B. and Wimer, C. (2011). The Consequences of the Great Recession. In: Grusky, D., Western, B. and Wimer, C., eds., *The Great Recession*, New York: Russell Sage Foundation, pp. 3 – 20.

Gwartney, J. and Lawson, R. (2009). Economic Freedom of the World – 2009 Annual Report. Vancouver, B.C.: Fraser Institute.

Hall, R. and Jones, C. (1999). Why do some countries produce so much more output per worker than others? *The quarterly journal of economics*, Vol. 114, No. 3, pp. 83-116.

Hall, P. and Soskice (2001). An Introduction to Varieties of Capitalism. In: Hall, P. and Soskice, eds., *Varieties of Capitalism – The Institutional Foundations of Comparative Advantage*, reprint. Oxford: Oxford University Press, pp. 1-68.

Hayek, F. (1945). The Use of Knowledge in Society. *The American Economic Review*, Vol. 35, No. 4, pp. 519-530.

Hayek, F. (2011 [1960]). *The Constitution of Liberty: The Definitive Edition*. London: Routledge.

Hayek, F. (1980). *Recht, Gesetzgebung und Freiheit Band 1: Regeln und Ordnung*. München: Verlag Moderne Industrie.

Hayek, F. (1981). *Recht, Gesetzgebung und Freiheit Band 3: Die Verfassung einer Gesellschaft freier Menschen*. München: Verlag Moderne Industrie.

Heckelman, J. (2000). Consistent estimates of the impact of special interest groups on economic growth. *Public Choice*, Vol. 104, No. 3, pp. 319-327.

Heckelman, J. (2007). Explaining the Rain: "Rise and Decline of Nations" after 25 Years. *Southern Economic Journal*, Vol. 74, No. 1, pp. 18 – 33.

Higgs, R. (1997). Regime Uncertainty: Why the Great Depression Lasted So Long and Why Prosperity Resumed after the War. *The Independent Review*, Vol. 1, No. 4, pp. 561-590.

Hill, C., Griffiths, W. and Lim, G. (2008). *Principles of Econometrics*, 3rd ed. Hoboken, NJ: John Wiley & Sons, Inc.

Hoggarth, G., Reis, R. and Saporta V. (2002). Costs of banking system instability: some empirical evidence. *Journal of Banking & Finance*, Vol. 26, No. 5, pp. 825-855.

Horgos, D. and Zimmermann, K. (2009). Interest Groups and Economic Performance: Some New Evidence. *Public Choice*, Vol. 138, No. 3-4, pp. 301-315.

Imbs, J. (2010). The First Global Recession in Decades. *IMF Economic Review*, Vol. 58, No. 2, pp. 327 – 354.

International Monetary Fund (1998). *World Economic Outlook, Mai 1998 – Financial Crises: Causes and Indicators*. Washington DC: IMF Publications.

International Monetary Fund (2009). *World Economic Outlook, April 2009 – Crisis and Recovery*. Washington DC: IMF Publication.

International Monetary Fund (2016). *World Economic Outlook, October 2016 – Subdued Demand, Symptoms and Remedies*. Washington DC: IMF Publication.

Irvin, R. and Stansbury, J. (2004). Citizen participation in decision making: Is it worth the effort? *Public administration review*, Vol. 64, No. 1, pp. 55-65.

Islam, N. (2003). What have we learnt from the convergence debate? *Journal of economic surveys*, Vol. 17, No. 3. pp. 309-362.

Islam, R. and Montenegro, C. (2002). *What Determines the Quality of Institutions?* World Bank Policy Research Working Paper, No. 2764.

Jarque, C. and Bera, A. (1980). Efficient tests for normality, homoscedasticity and serial independence of regression residuals. *Economic Letter*, Vol. 6, No. 3, pp. 255-259.

Jenkins, S., Brandolini, A., Micklewright, J. and Nolan, B. (2013). Scope, review of approaches, and evidence from the past. In: Jenkins, S., Brandolini, A., Micklewright, J. and Nolan, B., eds.: *The Great Recession and the Distribution of Household Income*, Oxford: Oxford University Press, pp. 1 - 32.

John, K., John, T. and Saunders, A. (1994). Universal banking and firm risk-taking. *Journal of Banking & Finance*, Vol. 18, No, 2, pp. 307-323.

Jovanovic, B. (2012). *How Policy Actions Affect Short-term Post-crisis Recovery?* Centre for Economic and International Studies Research Paper, No. 253.

Kaminsky, G., Lizondo, S. and Reinhart, C. (1998). Leading Indicators of currency crises. *IMF Staff Paper*, Vol. 45, No. 1.

Kaminsky, G., Reinhart, C. and Végh, C. (2004). *When it rains, it pours: procyclical capital flows and macroeconomic policies.* NBER Working Paper, No. 10780.

Kaufmann, D., Kraay, A. and Mastruzzi, M. (2010). *The Worldwide Governance Indicators Methodology and Analytical Issues*. World Bank Policy Research Working Paper, No. 5430.

Keefer, P. and Knack, S. (1997). Why don't poor countries catch up? A cross-national test of an institutional explanation. *Economic Inquiry*, Vol. 35, No. 3, pp. 590-602.

Killick, T. (1995). Relevance, meaning and the determinants of flexibility. In: Killick, T., ed. *The flexible economy: Causes and consequences of the adaptability of national economies*. London: Routledge, pp. 1 - 33.

Knack, S. (2003). Groups, growth and trust: Cross-country evidence on the Olson and Putnam hypotheses. *Public Choice*, Vol. 117, No. 3-4, pp. 341-355.

Knack, S. and Keefer, P. (1995). Institutions and economic performance: cross-country tests using alternative institutional measures. *Economics and Politics*, Vol. 7, No. 3, pp. 207-227.

Knack, S. and Keefer, P. (1997). Does social capital have an economic payoff? A cross-country investigation. *Quarterly Journal of Economics*, Vol. 112, No. 4, pp. 1251-1288.

Kohler, M. (2010). Exchange rate during financial crises. *BIS Quarterly Review*, March, pp. 39-50.

Kormendi, R. and Meguire, P. (1985). Macroeconomic determinants of growth: cross-country evidence. *Journal of Monetary Economics*, Vol. 16, pp. 141-163.

Krueger, A. (1974). The Political Economy of the Rent-Seeking Society. *The American Economic Review*, Vol. 64, No. 3, pp. 291-303.

Krugman, P. (2009). *Die neue Weltwirtschaftskrise.* Frankfurt a. M.: Campus Verlag.

La Porta, R., Lopez-de-Silanes, F., Shleifer, A. and Vishny. R. (1997). Legal Determinants of External Finance. *The Journal of Finance*, Vol. 52, No. 3, pp. 1131-1150.

La Porta, R., Lopez-de-Silanes, F., Shleifer, A. and Vishny, R. (1999). The quality of government. *The Journal of Law, Economics, and Organization*, Vol. 15, No. 1, pp. 222-279.

La Porta, R., Lopez-de-Silanes, F. and Shleifer, A. (2008). The Economic Consequences of Legal Origins. *Journal of Economic Literature*, Vol. 46, No. 2, pp. 285-332.

Laeven, L. and Valencia, F. (2008). *Systematic Banking Crises: A New Database*. IMF Working Paper, No. 08/224.

Lane, P. and Milesi-Ferretti G. (2006): *The external wealth of nations mark II: Revised and extended estimates of foreign assets and liabilities, 1970-2004.* IMF Working Paper, No. 06/69.

Lane, P. and Milesi-Ferretti G. (2011): The Cross-Country Incidence of the Global Crisis. *IMF Economic Review*, Vol. 59, No. 1, pp. 77 – 110.

Leschke, J. and Watt, A. (2010). *How do institutions affect the labor market adjustment to the economic crisis in different EU countries?* ETUI Working Paper, No. 2010.04.

Lindblom, C. and Woodhouse, E. (1993): *The Policy-Making Processs*, 3rd ed., Upper Saddle River: Prentice-Hall Inc.

Lipford, J. (2007). Short Run Macroeconomic Performance and Economic Freedom: Can Economic Growth Rates be Higher and More Stable? *Journal of Private Enterprise*, Vol. 23, No. 1, pp. 3-29.

Lipset, S. (1959): Some Social Requisites of Democracy: Economic Development and Political Legitimacy. *The American Political Science Review*, Vol. 53, No. 1, pp. 69-105.

Luhmann, N. (1990). *Ökologische Kommunikation: Kann die moderne Gesellschaft sich auf ökologische Gefährdungen einstellen?* 3rd ed. Opladen: Westdeutscher Verlag.

Mankiw, G., Romer, D. and Weil, D. (1992). A contribution to the empirics of economic growth. *The quarterly journal of economics*, Vol. 107, No. 2, pp. 407-437.

Maoz, Z. and Henderson, E. (2013). The World Religion Dataset, 1945-2010: Logic, Estimates, and Trends. *International Interactions*, Vol. 39, No. 3, pp. 265-291.

Martin, R. (2011). Regional economic resilience, hysteresis and recessionary shocks. *Journal of economic geography*, Vol. 12, No. 1, pp. 1-32.

Martin, J. and Scarpetta, S. (2012). Setting it right: Employment protections, labour reallocation and productivity. *De Economist*, Vol. 160, No. 2, pp. 89-116.

Mauro, P. (1995). Corruption and growth. *The quarterly journal of economics*, Vol. 110, No. 3, pp. 681-712.

McCallum, B. and Blais, A. (1987). Government, special interest groups, and growth. *Public Choice*, Vol. 54, No. 1, pp. 3-18.

Meltzer, A. and Richard, S. (1981). A Rational Theory of the Size of Government. *Journal of Political Economy*, Vol. 89, No. 5, pp. 914-927.

Merkl, C. and Schmitz, T. (2011). Macroeconomic volatilities and the labor market: First results from the euro experiment. *European Journal of Political Economy*, Vol. 27, No. 1, pp. 44-60.

Mian, A. and Sufi, A. (2014). What explains the 2007-2009 drop in employment? *Econometrica*, Vol. 92, No. 6, pp. 2197-2223.

Nielsen, L. (2011). *Classification of Countries Based on Their Level of Development: How it is Done and How it Could be Done*. IMF Working Paper, No. 11/31.

North, D. (1990). *Institutions, Institutional Change and Economic Performance*. Cambridge UK: Cambridge University Press.

North, D. and Thomas (1973). *The Rise of the Western World: A New Economic History*. Cambridge, UK: Cambridge University Press.

North, D., Wallis, J. and Weingast, B. (2009). *Violence and Social Orders: A Conceptual Framework of Interpreting Recorded Human History*, 1st paperback edition, New York, NY: Cambridge University Press.

Olson, M. (1963). Rapid Growth as a Destabilizing Force. *The Journal of Economic History*, Vol 23, No. 4, pp. 529-552.

Olson, M. (1975 [1965]). *The logic of collective action: public goods and the theory of groups*, 5th print. Cambridge, Mass.: Harvard University Press.

Olson, M. (1982). *The Rise and Decline of Nations: Economic Growth, Stagflation, and Social Rigidities*. New Heaven: Yale University Press.

Olson, M. (2000). *Power and Prosperity: Outgrowing Communist and Capitalist Dictatorships*. New York: Basic Books.

Pană, M. (2013). A review of the economic crisis: solutions and failures in the European Union. *Theoretical and Applied Economics*, Vol. 20, No. 2, pp. 69-80.

Patzelt, W. (2013). *Einführung in die Politikwissenschaft: Grundriss des Faches und studiumbegleitende Orientierung*, 7th ed. Passau: Wissenschaftsverlag Richard Rothe.

Pelikan, P. (1986). *Institutions, Self-Organizations and Adaptive Efficiency: A Dynamic assessment of Private Enterprise*. IUI Working Paper, No. 158.

Persson, T. and Tabellini, G. (2007): *The Growth Effect of Democracy: Is it Heterogenous and How Can It Be Estimated?* NBER Working Paper, No. 13150.

Posner, R. (1975). The Social Costs of Monopoly and Regulation. *The Journal of Political Economy*, Vol. 83, No. 4, pp. 808-828.

Putnam, R., Leonardi, R. and Nanetti, R. (1994). *Making democracy work: civic traditions in modern Italy*, 5th print. Princeton, NJ: Princeton University Press.

Przeworski, A. and Limongi, F. (1993). Political Regimes and Economic Growth. *Journal of Economic Perspectives*, Vol. 7, No. 3, pp. 51-69.

Ramsey, J. (1969). Tests for specification errors in classical linear least-squares regression analysis. *Journal of the Royal Statistical Society. Series B (Methodological)*, Vol. 31, No. 2, pp. 350-371.

Reinhart, C. and Rogoff, K. (2009). *This time is different – eight centuries of financial folly*. Princeton NJ: Princeton University Press.

Rode, M. and Coll, S. (2012). Economic freedom and growth. Which policies matter most? *Constitutional Political Economy*, Vol. 23, No. 2, pp. 95-133.

Rodrik, D. (1998). Why do More Open Economies Have Bigger Governments? *Journal of Political Economy*, Vol. 106, No. 5, pp. 997-1032.

Rodrik, D. (1999). Where Did All the Growth Go? External Shocks, Social Conflict, and Growth Collapses. *Journal of Economic Growth*, Vol. 4, No. 4, pp. 385 – 412.

Rodrik, D. (2000). *Institutions for high-quality growth: what they are and how to acquire them*. NBER Working Paper. No. 7540.

Rodrik, D. and Subramanian, A. (2003). The Primacy of Institutions: and what this does and does not mean. *Finance and Development*, Vol. 40, No. 2, pp. 31 - 34.

Rodrik, D. and Wacziarg, R. (2005). Do Democratic Transitions Produce Bad Economic Outcomes. *The American Economic Review*, Vol. 95, No. 2, pp. 50-55.

Rose, A. (2000). One money, one market: the effect of common currencies on trade. *Economic Policy*, Vol. 13, No. 30, pp. 8-45.

Rose, A. and Spiegel, M. (2010). Cross-country causes and consequences of the 2008 crisis: International linkages and American exposure. *Pacific Economic Review*, Vol. 15, No. 3, pp. 340 – 363.

Rose, A. and Spiegel, M. (2011). Cross-country causes and consequences of the 2008 crisis: An update. *European Economic Review*, Vol. 55, No. 3, pp. 309 - 324.

Rose, A. and Spiegel, M. (2012). Cross-country causes and consequences of the 2008 crisis: Early warning. *Japan and the World Economy*, Vol. 24, No. 1, pp. 1 – 16.

Rosser, B. (2007). The Rise and Decline of Mancur Olson's View of "the Rise and Decline of Nations". *Southern Economic Journal*, Vol. 74, No. 1, pp. 4-17.

Rothstein, J. (2011). *Unemployment Insurance and Job Search in the Great Recession.* NBER Working Paper No. 17534.

Rumler, F. and Scharler, J. (2011). Labor Market Institutions and Macroeconomic Volatility in a Panel of OECD Countries. *Scottish Journal of Political Economy*, Vol. 58, No. 3, pp. 396-413.

Sah, R. (1991). Fallibility in Human Organizations and Political Systems. *Journal of Economic Perspectives*, Vol. 5, No. 2, pp. 67-88.

Sala-i-Martin, X. (1997). I just ran two million regressions. *The American Economic Review*, Vol. 87, No. 2, pp. 178-183.

Santos, J. (2001). Bank capital regulation in contemporary banking theory: A review of the literature. *Financial Markets, Institutions & Instruments*, Vol. 10, No. 2, pp. 41-84.

Schmidt, M. (2008). *Demokratietheorien: Eine Einführung*, 4th ed. Wiesbaden: Verlag für Sozialwissenschaften.

Schumpeter, J. (1936 [1934]). *The Theory of Economic Development: An Inquiry into Profits, Capital, Credit, Interest, and the Business Cycle*, 2nd printing. Cambridge, MA: Harvard University Press.

Schumpeter, J. (1996 [1943]). *Capitalism, Socialism, and Democracy*. London: Routledge.

Schwab, K. and Porter, M. (2008). *The Global Competitiveness Report 2008-2009*. Geneva: World Economic Forum.

Scully, G. (1988). The institutional framework and economic development. *Journal of Political Economy*, Vol. 96, No. 3, pp. 652-662.

Smith, A. (1776 [1960]. *An inquiry into the nature and causes of the wealth of nations*. New York: Collier.

Solow, R. (1956). A contribution to the theory of economic growth. *The quarterly journal of economics*, Vol. 70. No. 1, pp. 65-94.

Spilimbergo, A., Symansky, S., Blanchard, O. and Cottarelli, C. (2009): Fiscal Policy for The Crisis. *CESifo Forum*, Vol. 10. No. 2, pp. 26-32.

Stiglitz, J. (2009). The anatomy of a murder: Who killed America's economy? *Critical Review*, Vol. 21, No. 2-3. pp. 329-339.

Stiglitz, J. and Rosengard, J. (2015). *Economics of the Public Sector*, 4th edt. New York: W. W. Norten & Company, Inc.

Straub, S. (2000). *Empirical Determinants of Good Institutions: Do We Know Anything?* Inter-American Development Bank Working Paper, No. 4215.

Streeck, W. (2011). The Crisis of Democratic Capitalism. *New Left Review*, Vol. 71, pp. 5 – 29.

Stock, J. and Watson, M. (2007). *Introduction to Econometrics*, 2nd ed. Boston, MA: Pearson.

Sunde U. (1996). Wirtschaftliche Entwicklung und Demokratie – Ist Demokratie ein Wohlstandsmotor oder ein Wohlstandsprodukt? *Perspektiven der Wirtschaftspolitik*, Vol. 7, No. 4, pp. 471-499.

Talvi, E. and Végh, C. (2005). Tax base variability and procyclical fiscal policy in developing countries. *Journal of Development Economics*, Vol. 78, No. 1, pp. 156-190.

Tang, E. and Hedley, A. (1998). Distributional Coalitions, State Strength, and Economic Growth: Toward a Comprehensive Theory of Economic Development. *Public Choice*, Vol. 96, No. 3-4, pp. 295-323.

Tavares, J., Wacziarg, R. (2001). How democracy affects growth. *European Economic Review*, Vol. 45, No. 8, pp. 1341-1378.

Tavlas, G., Dellas, H. and Stockman, A. (2008). The classification and performance of alternative exchange-rate systems. *European Economic Review*, Vol. 52, No. 6, pp. 941-963.

Tocqueville, A. (1990). *Democracy in America*, New York, NY: Vintage Books.

Tridico, P. (2013). The impact of the economic crisis on EU labour markets: A comparative perspective. *International Labour Review*, Vol. 152, No. 2, pp. 175-190.

Ugur, M. (2010). *Institutions and economic performance: a review of the theory and evidence*. MPRA Paper, No. 25909.

Uxó, J., Jusús, P. and Febrero, E. (2011). Current account imbalances in the Monetary Union and the Great Recession: causes and policies. *Panoeconomicus*, Vol. 58, No. 5, pp. 571-592.

Verick, S. and Islam, I. (2010). *The Great Recession of 2008-2009: Causes, Consequences and Policy Responses.* IZA Discussion Paper, No. 4934.

Wagner, A. (1958) [1883]. Three extracts on public finance. In: Musgrave, R. and Peacock, A., ed. *Classics in the Theory of Public Finance*. London: Macmillan Press Ltd, pp. 1-15.

Wagner, H. (2000). Which exchange rate regimes in an era of high capital mobility? *The North American Journal of Economics and Finance*, Vol. 11, No. 2, pp. 191-203.

Weber, M. (2016 [1920]). *Die protestantisch Ethik und der "Geist" des Kapitalismus: Neuausgabe der ersten Fassung von 1904-05 mit einem Verzeichnis der wichtigsten Zusätze und Veränderungen aus der zweiten Fassung von 1920*. Wiesbaden: Springer, 2016.

Weede, E. (1984). Democracy, creeping socialism, and ideological socialism in rent-seeking societies. *Public Choice*, Vol. 44, No. 02, pp. 349-366.

Weingast, B. (1995). The Economic Role of Political Institutions: Market-Preserving Federalism and Economic Development. *Journal of Law, Economics & Organization*, Vol. 11, No. 1, pp. 1-31.

White, H. (1980). A heteroscedasticity-consistent covariance matrix estimator and a direct test for heteroscedasticity. *Econometrica: Journal of the Econometric Society*, Vol. 48, No. 4, pp. 817-338.

Wooldridge, J. (2006). *Introductory Econometrics: A Modern Approach*, 3rd ed. Mason, OH: Thomson Higher Education.

World Bank (2016). *Doing Business 2016 – Measuring Regulatory Quality and Efficiency*, 13th ed. Washington D.C.

Wu, W. and Davis, O. (1999). The two freedoms, economic growth and development: An empirical study. *Public Choice*, Vol. 100, No. 1-2, pp. 39-64.

Zanetti, F. (2007). *Labour market institutions and aggregate fluctuations in a search and matching model.* Bank of England Working Paper, No. 333.

Zemanek, H., Belke, A. and Schnabl, G. (2009). *Current Account Imbalances and Structural Adjustment in the Euro Area: How to Rebalance Competitiveness.* CESifo Working Paper, No. 2639.

Zils, M. (2002). *World guide to trade associations.* München: Saur Verlag.

The manufacturer's authorised representative in the EU is Springer Nature Customer Service Centre GmbH, Europaplatz 3, 69115 Heidelberg, Germany. If you have any concerns regarding our products, please contact ProductSafety@springernature.com

Printed and bound by CPI Group (UK) Ltd, Croydon, CR0 4YY
25/09/2026
02222848-0001